53

Introduction to
ACCOUNTING AND FINANCE

Visit the *Introduction to Accounting and Finance, second edition* Companion Website at:

www.pearsoned.co.uk/black

to find valuable **student** learning material including **multiple choice questions** to help test your learning.

Introduction to
ACCOUNTING
AND FINANCE

Geoff Black

Prentice Hall
FINANCIAL TIMES

An imprint of **Pearson Education**

Harlow, England • London • New York • Boston • San Francisco • Toronto • Sydney • Singapore • Hong Kong
Tokyo • Seoul • Taipei • New Delhi • Cape Town • Madrid • Mexico City • Amsterdam • Munich • Paris • Milan

Pearson Education Limited

Edinburgh Gate
Harlow
Essex CM20 2JE
England

and Associated Companies around the world

Visit us on the World Wide Web at:
www.pearsoned.co.uk

_____

First published 2005

ISBN 0 273 68870 7

British Library Cataloguing-in-Publication Data
A catalogue record for this book is available from the British Library

Library of Congress Cataloging-in-Publication Data
Black, Geoff.
    Introduction to accounting / Geoff Black.
        p. cm.
    Includes bibliographical references and index.
    ISBN 0-273-68870-7
        1. Accounting. I. Title.

    HF5635.B6623 2005
    657--dc22
                                                    2004065352

10 9 8 7 6 5 4 3 2 1
08 07 06 05 04

Typeset in 9.5/12.5pt Stone by 30.
Printed and bound by Mateu-Cromo, Artes Graficas, Spain.

The publisher's policy is to use paper manufactured from sustainable forests.

Contents

Chapter 15   Break-even and cost–volume–profit analysis   258

Chapter 16   Budgeting   271

Chapter 17   Investment appraisal   283

Chapter 18   Revision chapter (3)   **299**

Supporting resources

Visit **www.pearsoned.co.uk/black** to find valuable online resources

Companion Website for students
- Multiple choice questions to help test your learning

For instructors
- PowerPoint slides that can be downloaded and used as OHTs

Also: The Companion Website provides the following features:
- Search tool to help locate specific items of content
- E-mail results and profile tools to send results of quizzes to instructors
- Online help and support to assist with website usage and troubleshooting

For more information please contact your local Pearson Education sales representative or visit **www.pearsoned.co.uk/black**

Preface

The typical ... accountant is a man past middle age, spare, wrinkled, intelligent, cold, passive, noncommittal, with eyes like a codfish, polite in contact, but at the same time unresponsive, cool, calm, and as damnably composed as a concrete post or plaster of Paris cast; a human petrification with a heart of feldspar, and without charm or the friendly germ, minus passions and a sense of humour. Happily, though, they seldom reproduce – and all of them finally go to Hell.

(H. L. Mencken, as quoted in *Accounting for Life* by Henry Benson[1])

My aim in writing this book is to make your initial study of accounting interesting and enjoyable and to help you complete your studies with a much more positive image of accountants than that quoted above. Who knows, you might even become an accountant one day! This is said in the knowledge that most students think that accountancy requires:

- advanced mathematical skills
- an IQ of 200+
- a high boredom threshold.

In the 18 chapters of this book, I have borne in mind that most students reading it will be coming to the subject for the first time, with or without these preconceptions. Many will be on modular courses lasting one semester, with limited access to tutorial help and higher demand than supply in terms of library and other support. To make the learning process as smooth as possible, there is a logical progression in the subject matter from chapter to chapter. I have chosen the pattern of topics to reflect most closely the majority of introductory courses within universities and colleges.

Each chapter commences with a statement of objectives, indicating what you should be able to do after completing that chapter. There are three revision chapters – Chapters 6, 11 and 18 – which will help you to consolidate your knowledge. Within each chapter you will find a number of further features in addition to the textual explanation of the subject matter:

- **Pause for thought.** Either a thought-provoking or a humorous diversion to get you looking at the topic in a different way, or an added explanation of a difficult topic.
- **Did you know?** A factual item of information to back up the subject text.
- **Activities.** Practical exercises for you to tackle to ensure that you have understood the subject matter. Answers to these follow directly, so to get the maximum benefit you should conceal the answers whilst attempting each activity.
- **Glossary.** A glossary of terms (those highlighted in **red**) found within the chapter.
- **Self-check questions.** Multiple-choice questions with answers in Appendix 1 at the back of the book.

---

[1] Benson, Lord (1989) *Accounting for Life*. London: Kogan Page.

- **Self-study questions**. Longer questions with answers in Appendix 2.
- **Case study**. To provide a synoptic link between chapters, each chapter has a case study based on a business which starts in Chapter 1 and then develops and expands throughout subsequent chapters, to form a 'book within a book'. Each case study is self-standing but builds on the knowledge gained in the previous chapters.
- **References**. Most of the references given are to pages on the World Wide Web. These are to enhance research into particular areas, or else to provide further practical activities. Website references have a habit of changing over time, but with perseverance and the use of search engines such as Google, most sites can be accessed.

The chart on p. xvi shows how the book is structured.

There are also significant resources to help both students and lecturers on the dedicated website which accompanies this book. See the end of each chapter for details of specific help available.

I am always interested in getting feedback from students and lecturers using this book, whether they like it, dislike it, find errors in it or simply want to give suggestions for improving it. Feedback can be sent directly to me at **IntroAcctg@hotmail.com**, or by contacting the publishers. I sincerely hope that you do enjoy studying accounting and that by the time you get to the final page you will take a kinder view of accountants than the one quoted at the start.

Geoff Black

A note for lecturers

Double-entry bookkeeping

Authors of introductory accounting texts are faced with a decision regarding what to do with double-entry bookkeeping. Should they integrate the topic within the text or relegate it to an appendix?

The BBC's chief economic correspondent Peter Jay nailed his colours to the mast by making the following reference to bookkeeping in a television documentary charting the most significant milestones in man's economic progress:

> *It seems crazy to praise accountants; but dry as it sounds, double-entry book-keeping really was a stunning breakthrough. For the first time accurate accounts gave businessmen a true picture of what profits they were making and how they were making them. Without double-entry bookkeeping capitalism itself can hardly be imagined.*
>
> Peter Jay, *The Road to Riches*, BBC TV documentary series, 2000

As one of the basic functions of accounting will always be the day-to-day recording of financial transactions, it seems reasonable to this author that the 'stunning breakthrough' should have some relevance to an introductory accounting course. Giving students at least a rudimentary understanding of double-entry bookkeeping (omitting anything that might be regarded as 'specialised') could be both useful and practical (dare we use such words when considering accounting as an *academic* subject?) for the students' future careers. However, due to time and other constraints, many lecturers may wish to exclude a detailed appraisal of double-entry bookkeeping in order to concentrate on the products of the system, the summarised financial statements. In such cases, lecturers could choose to omit the following parts of the book:

- Chapter 2 (other than pages 16–18, which can be used for a simple introduction to the topic).
- In Chapter 3, 'Control accounts' (though the T accounts used to explain stock, accruals, prepayments and depreciation help to explain how the figures appearing in the financial summaries are calculated).
- In Chapter 5, the double-entry accounts within Activities 5.1 and 5.7–5.10.

Finance

Regarding the question of *finance*, the author has integrated such topics as sources of short- and long-term financing, types of share capital and risk implications within relevant chapters, rather than artificially extricating them into a separate section. For convenience, key finance topics can be found in the following sections:

- Sources of sole trader financing   7.2
- Sources of partnership financing   7.3
- Limited company financing   7.4
    types of share capital   7.4.1
    long-term loans   7.4.1
    rights issues   7.4.2
- Short- and long-term sources of financing   7.5
    share sales   7.5.1
    loans   7.5.2
    finance leases   7.5.3
    bank overdrafts   7.5.4
    debt factoring   7.5.5
    internal sources of financing   7.5.6
- Short- and long-term solvency and liquidity   10.5

International Accounting and Financial Reporting Standards

From 1 January 2005, all listed companies within the EU must prepare their consolidated financial statements in accordance with International Accounting and Financial Reporting Standards (IFRSs and IASs). Although extremely important to major companies, in practice it will be several years before the impact of the international standards will filter down to smaller enterprises. In the UK at the time of writing, there are 11,136 plcs (of which only 1,400 will be immediately affected by the introduction of international standards), 1,809,131 private limited companies (unaffected) and 4.5 million self-employed businesses (unaffected). In the context of an introductory accounting and finance text, references to international standards have only been made where directly relevant – specifically within Chapter 7, Section 7.4 (accounting requirements of limited companies) and in various pages where 'Did you know?' boxes give additional information.

The term 'fixed assets' has been retained rather than 'non-current assets', and also 'long-term liabilities' rather than 'non-current liabilities', even though balance sheets drawn up under IASs will use the 'non-current' descriptions.

The structure of the book

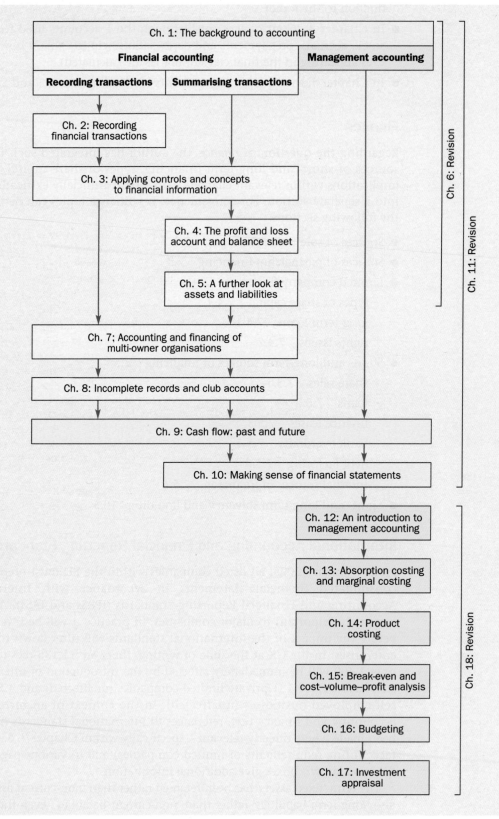

Acknowledgements

I would like to thank Paula Harris of Pearson Education for her encouragement, and my wife Linda for her love and support. This book is dedicated to my son Michael: *Citius, altius, fortius*.

The publishers are grateful to the following for permission to reproduce copyright material:

Figure 7.1 Halfords Group Plc share offer notice reprinted courtesy of Halfords Group Plc; Chapter 9 Tesco Plc cash flow statement for the year ended 27 February abridged from *Tesco Plc Annual Report and Financial Statements 2002* reprinted by permission of Tesco Stores Limited; Chapter 10 cartoon on page 186 reprinted by permission of Alex Cartoon; Figure 10.1 reprinted by permission of Hyde Mahon Bridges Solicitors.

Accounting Standards Board for extracts from Statement of Standard Accounting Practice (SSAP) 9, *Stocks and Long-Term Contracts* (ASB 1990), *Statement of Principles for Financial Reporting* (ASB 1999) and Financial Reporting Standard (FRS) 15, *Tangible Fixed Assets* (ASB 1999). Material from Accounting Standards Board documents is reproduced by kind permission of The Accounting Standards Board Ltd.; American Accounting Association for an extract from *A Statement of Accounting Theory*, Copyright American Accounting Association (AAA 1966); BBC for a quotation by Peter Jay from *The Road to Riches*, BBC television documentary series, 2000; Elsevier for extracts reprinted from *Official Terminology 2000 Edition*, CIMA, Copyright 2000, with permission from Elsevier; Guardian Newspapers Limited for an extract from 'Getting on a cunning wheeze: Worm's eye' by Dan Atkinson in *The Guardian*, 1 September 1997, Copyright Guardian Newspapers Limited 1997.

Photo on page 75, Ian Britton, Freefoto.com; photo on page 128, Bettmann/Corbis; photo on page 148, Bruce Ayres/Getty Images; photo on page 168, Ian Britton, Freefoto.com; photo on page 234, Ted Horowitz/Corbis; photo on page 262, Royalty-Free/Corbis; photo on page 296, Mauro Fermariello/Science Photo Library.

In some instances we have been unable to trace the owners of copyright material, and we would appreciate any information that would enable us to do so.

Chapter 1

The background to accounting

Objectives

When you have read this chapter you will be able to:

➤ Explain what is meant by 'accounting'

➤ Distinguish between financial accounting and management accounting

➤ Identify the main users of accounting information

➤ Understand the fundamental concepts on which accounting is based

➤ Distinguish between assets, liabilities, capital, income and expenses

➤ Understand the 'accounting equation'

1.1 Introduction

This chapter introduces you to the whole area of accounting – what it is, who it is for, and who makes the rules and regulations that govern it. Accounting has a number of divisions, the main two being financial accounting and management accounting. The two areas are explained in this chapter, as well as the fundamental concepts that underpin accounting. The chapter also introduces some key terms: assets, liabilities, capital, income and expenses, and how they are linked within an 'accounting equation'. This equation helps us to understand the logical basis of accounting and see how the financial affairs of even the most complex organisation can be summarised and analysed.

1.2   What is accounting?

You may think that you know nothing at all about accounting, but consider this snippet of conversation:

*'Rita wrote her car off yesterday. She'd gone **into the red** to pay for it, but – would you credit it – the car wasn't insured. There's no accounting for some people. The bottom line is – you need to protect your assets!'*

You may be surprised that this contains six separate accounting references! Most of the terms are so familiar that they are used without thinking where they came from. The origins of accounting can in fact be traced back to ancient times, with the need for accurate records of trading transactions. A logical system of recording financial information, known as **double-entry bookkeeping**, was in use in medieval Italy, and the first published accounting work, *Summa de Arithmetica, Geometria, Proportioni et Proportionalità*, was written in 1494 by a Venetian monk, Luca Pacioli. The principles of double-entry bookkeeping are still in use today, even where all financial data is processed by computers.

Accounting can be defined simply as the recording, summarising and interpretation of financial information. A more detailed definition is that offered by the American Accounting Association (1966), as follows:

The process of identifying, measuring and communicating economic information about an organisation or other entity, in order to permit informed judgements by users of the information.

The key aspects of accounting are therefore identifying, measuring and communicating:

- *Identifying* the key financial components of an organisation, such as assets, liabilities, capital, income, expenses and cash flow.

- *Measuring* the monetary values of the key financial components in a way which represents a true and fair view of the organisation.

- *Communicating* the financial information in a way which is useful to the users of that information.

1.3   Who needs accounting?

Did you know?

There is also an *International* Accounting Standards Board, whose 'Framework' also identifies the seven user groups.

In the United Kingdom, the Accounting Standards Board (ASB) was set up in 1990 with the aim of improving standards of financial accounting and reporting. In 1999 the ASB produced a *Statement of Principles*[1] which set out certain fundamental principles for the preparation and presentation of financial statements. The Statement of Principles identifies the following seven groups of users of financial information, together with the information which they need from the financial statements:

---

[1] Accounting Standards Board (1999) *Statement of Principles for Financial Reporting*. London: ASB.

User group	Information needs
Investors	Investors need to assess the financial performance of the organisation they have invested in to consider the risk inherent in, and return provided by, their investments
Lenders	Lenders need to be aware of the ability of the organisation to repay loans and interest. Potential lenders need to decide whether to lend, and on what terms
Suppliers and other trade creditors	Should suppliers sell to the organisation? Will they be paid?
Employees	People will be interested in their employer's stability and profitability, in particular of that part of the organisation (such as a branch) in which they work. They will also be interested in the ability of their employer to pay their wages and pensions
Customers	Customers who are dependent on a particular supplier or are considering placing a long-term contract will need to know if the organisation will continue to exist
Governments and their agencies	Reliable financial data helps governments to assemble national economic statistics which are used for a variety of purposes in controlling the economy. Specific financial information from an organisation also enables tax to be assessed
The public	Financial statements often include information relevant to local communities and pressure groups such as attitudes towards environmental matters, plans to expand or shut down factories, policies on employment of disabled persons, etc.

Did you know?

In medieval times, a steward was a trusted person who managed the affairs of a household or an estate for the owner.

We could also add an eighth group – *the management of the organisation* – as they are the **stewards** of the organisation and need to have reliable financial information on which to base their decisions.

1.4 Financial accounting and management accounting

Accounting information can be classified broadly between financial accounting and management accounting.

Financial accounting is the day-to-day recording of an organisation's financial transactions and the summarising of those transactions to satisfy the information needs of the user groups listed above. It is sometimes referred to as meeting the *external* accounting needs of the organisation, and as such is subject to many rules and regulations (a **regulatory framework**) imposed by company legislation and the UK and International Accounting Standards Boards.

Did you know?

The UK's Chartered Institute of Management Accountants, founded in 1919, has over 62,000 members.

Management accounting is sometimes referred to as meeting the *internal* accounting needs of the organisation, as it is designed to help managers with decision making and planning. As such it often involves estimates and forecasts, and is not subject to the same regulatory framework as financial accounting. Chapters 12–17 explore some of the management accounting areas such as marginal costing and break-even analysis.

1.5 Key accounting concepts

Accounting procedures and practices have evolved over many centuries and are now known by the acronym GAAP (Generally Accepted Accounting Principles). There are many accounting concepts which underpin GAAP, and the following four **key concepts** are referred to in UK legislation:[2]

Going concern concept

It is assumed that the organisation will continue to operate indefinitely.

This just means that when we draw up financial summaries, we do not assume that the organisation is in severe financial difficulties.

Accruals concept

When calculating the profit or loss of an organisation, all income and related expenditure for a specified period should be included, not simply money paid or received. This is also known as the 'matching' concept.

This means that, for example, if a summary of income and expenditure for a year is drawn up under financial accounting principles, *all* relevant revenues and costs must be included, not just the money paid or received. Consider a company which always summarises its finances according to calendar years. If, by the end of 2004, electricity bills had been received for the period up to 31 October only, the summary must include an estimate of electricity used in November and December. Conversely, if in January 2004 rent had been paid in advance for the 18 months to 30 June 2005, the summary would include only the rent for the 12 months to 31 December 2004.

Consistency concept

Accounting procedures used should be the same as those applied previously for similar items. This allows comparability of financial summaries over time.

Accountants must not be consistently wrong, so they are allowed to change procedures if there are good reasons for doing so, provided an explanation of the change is given.

Prudence concept

Accountants should be cautious in the valuation of assets or the measurement of profit. The *lowest* reasonable estimate of an asset's value should be taken, whilst a forecast loss would be included but not a forecast profit. This is also known as the 'conservatism' concept.

The prudence concept is of great importance to users of the accounting information, as it ensures that the accounting summaries have not been drawn up on the basis of over-optimistic or speculative forecasts, and that foreseeable losses and expenses have been included.

---

[2] Companies Act 1985, Schedule 4, paras 10–13.

There is another principle to be considered which is so important that it overrides the requirements of all other concepts. This is the need for the financial summaries to show a **true and fair view**. Consequently, if a misleading result is disclosed by following one of the four fundamental concepts, that concept must be abandoned.

An example is a company which bought a machine costing £5m. When it was bought, the company's directors forecast that it would last 5 years, and quite correctly showed a loss of value (depreciation) of £1m in its first year of ownership. By the end of the second year of ownership, it became clear that, due to greater than expected use, the machine had come to the end of its working life. Although *consistency* is a fundamental concept, it would not show a true and fair view to again show a loss in value of just £1m in the second year. The true and fair view overriding concept would require the full remaining £4m to be shown as a loss in value in the second year.

1.6 Assets, liabilities and capital

Much of the work of financial accountants consists in summarising financial information in accordance with generally accepted accounting principles. This information is derived from the double-entry bookkeeping system, which will be explained in detail in Chapters 2 and 3. The system is based on the relationship between the three key components of assets, liabilities and capital.

Assets

Did you know?

Large companies which are subject to International Accounting Standards (see Chapter 7) will refer to 'fixed assets' as 'non-current assets'.

An 'official' definition of **assets**, as contained in the Statement of Principles, is 'rights or other access to future economic benefits controlled by an entity as a result of past transactions or events'. Typical business assets are divided between **fixed assets**, which are expected to be retained by the business for at least a year and are of significant value, and **current assets**, which are constantly changing during the course of the business's activities.

Typical examples of fixed assets are:

- Land
- Buildings
- Motor vehicles
- Machinery
- Computers.

Nearly all fixed assets will be subject to depreciation, a topic dealt with in Chapter 3. Another term used to describe the acquisition of fixed assets is **capital expenditure**, i.e. expenditure on assets contributing to the long-term capital accumulation of the organisation.

Typical examples of current assets are:

- Stock of unsold goods (also called inventories)
- Debtors (the amounts owed to the business by customers)
- Prepayments (amounts paid in advance for items such as rent)
- Bank balances (cash in the bank)
- Cash balances (cash held by the business, but not in the bank).

Activity 1.1

Make a list of any assets you own, with a rough estimate of their value. You could start by considering what you are wearing!

Answer

Your answer might include fixed assets, such as a car, motorbike or bicycle, clothes, watch, jewellery, etc., and current assets, such as cash and bank balances. Make a total of their estimated value.

Liabilities

The 'official' definition of **liabilities** contained within the Statement of Principles is 'obligations of an entity to transfer economic benefits as a result of past transactions or events'. Typical business liabilities are divided between **current liabilities**, which are expected to be paid within one year, and **long-term liabilities**, which are expected to be paid after more than one year.

Typical examples of current liabilities are:

- Trade creditors (the amounts owed by the business to suppliers of goods)
- Accruals (amounts owing for expenses such as electricity, where the bills have not yet been received)
- Bank overdrafts.

A typical example of a long-term liability is:

- A loan due for repayment in more than one year's time.

Activity 1.2

Make a list of any liabilities you have, with a rough estimate of their value. Do you have a bank overdraft or a student loan?

Answer

Apart from an overdraft or a student loan, you might owe a credit card balance, rent, telephone bills and so on.

Capital

Capital is also sometimes referred to as 'ownership interest', that is, the value which the owner or owners have invested in their business. The Statement of Principles defines it as 'the residual amount found by deducting all of the entity's liabilities from all of the entity's assets'.

Activity 1.3

Deduct the total of your liabilities which you found in Activity 1.2 from the total assets found in Activity 1.1.

Answer

If your assets exceed your liabilities, you have *positive* capital. If your liabilities exceed your assets, you have *negative* capital.

1.7 The accounting equation

As we have seen, we find the value of the owner's interest (capital) by deducting liabilities from assets. This equation can be represented in a number of different ways (for simplicity, we shall ignore long-term liabilities, and assume that assets exceed liabilities):

> **Assets – Liabilities = Capital**

or

> **(Fixed Assets + Current Assets) – (Current Liabilities) = Capital**

or

> **Fixed Assets + (Current Assets – Current Liabilities) = Capital**

This final version of the **accounting equation** is followed by accountants in the UK when preparing the financial summary of assets, liabilities and capital, which is known as a **balance sheet**. We shall be looking at balance sheets in detail in Chapter 4.

Did you know?

In most mainland European countries, the version of the formula followed when producing the balance sheet is:

Fixed Assets
+
Current Assets
=
Liabilities + Capital

Activity 1.4

For each of the following transactions, show the effect (as pluses and minuses) on assets, liabilities and capital.

	Assets £	Liabilities £	Capital £
1 Owner starts business with £3,000 paid into a business bank account on 1 April			
2 Business buys machinery with a cheque for £800 on 2 April			
3 Business buys office computer for £800 on credit from Lupin plc on 4 April			
4 On 5 April, business borrows £10,000 on loan from a bank. Money is paid into business's bank account			
5 Business pays Lupin plc £800 by cheque on 6 April			
6 Owner takes £100 from bank for personal spending money			
Summary (overall change)			

	Assets £	Liabilities £	Capital £
1 Owner starts business with £3,000 paid into a business bank account on 1 April	+3,000 (bank)		+3,000 (capital)
2 Business buys machinery with a cheque for £800 on 2 April	+800 (machinery) −800 (bank)		
3 Business buys office computer for £800 on credit from Lupin plc on 4 April	+800 (computer)	+800 (creditor: Lupin plc)	
4 On 5 April, business borrows £10,000 on loan from a bank. Money is paid into business's bank account	+10,000 (bank)	+10,000 (loan)	
5 Business pays Lupin plc £800 by cheque on 6 April	−800 (bank)	−800 (creditor: Lupin plc)	
6 Owner takes £100 from bank for personal spending money	−100 (bank)		−100 (capital)
Summary (overall change)	+12,900	+10,000	+2,900

Pause for thought

Applying the accounting equation, A − L = C, we see that the overall change in assets (£12,900) less the change in liabilities (£10,000) is matched by the change in capital (£2,900).

1.7.1 How does the value of capital change?

The owner's value will change for a number of reasons, most obvious of which is if more capital is contributed by the owner, or capital is withdrawn by the owner. However, the other main reason is the business making either a profit or a loss. We calculate profit or loss by comparing a business's **revenue income** with its **revenue expenses**.

● If revenue income exceeds revenue expenses, the business makes a profit, and the owner's capital increases.

● If revenue expenses exceed revenue income, the business makes a loss, and the owner's capital decreases.

Revenue income and expenses are defined as follows:

● **Revenue income:** The revenue generated by the business by selling its goods or services, plus any sundry income such as bank interest received.

● **Revenue expenses**: The expenditure made by a business related to the revenue generated within the same financial period. The cost of fixed assets is not considered as a revenue expense, as the assets last for *several* financial periods. Confusingly, the cost of fixed assets is known as capital expenditure. However, an estimate is made, known as **depreciation**, of the proportion of the fixed asset's value used up in the *specific* financial period. This loss in value is then treated as a *revenue* expense when calculating the profit or loss and is also deducted from the fixed assets value in the balance sheet.

The distinction between capital expenditure and revenue expenditure is shown diagramatically in Figure 1.1.

Figure 1.1
Capital expenditure and revenue expenditure

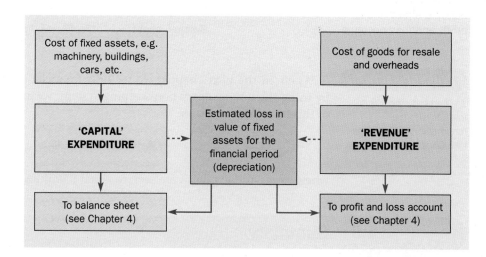

Remember that the accruals concept tells us to include *all* the revenue income and revenue expenses for a period, not just cash received or paid in that period.

From now on within this book, assume that 'Income' and 'Expenses' refer to *revenue* income and *revenue* expenses, unless told otherwise.

The comparison of income and expenses leads us to another set of equations, the first of which is:

$$\text{Income} - \text{Expenses} = \text{Profit}$$

(assuming that income exceeds expenses).

This formula is represented in another main financial summary, the *profit and loss account*, which we shall be looking at in detail in Chapter 4.

If we combine the accounting equations for capital and profit, we see that the capital figure grows over a specific period (known, in algebraic terms, as from time zero to time one) as follows:

$$A_0 - L_0 = C_0$$

that is, total assets minus total liabilities equal capital at time zero.

If a profit is made during time one:

$$A_1 - L_1 = C_0 + (I_1 - E_1)$$

i.e. total assets at the end of time one minus total liabilities at the end of time one equal capital at the start (time zero) plus the profit (income less expenses) earned during time one.

The two financial summaries which have been referred to – the balance sheet and the profit and loss account – reflect this formula, as shown in Figure 1.2.

Figure 1.2
How the accounting equation relates to the balance sheet and profit and loss account

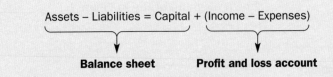

Assets – Liabilities = Capital + (Income – Expenses)

Balance sheet   **Profit and loss account**

Did you know?

You can remember this formula with the mnemonic 'All Elephants Like Choc Ices'.

When, in the next chapter, we see how financial transactions are recorded by using the double-entry bookkeeping system, we are using a rearrangement of this formula, as follows:

$$A + E = L + C + I$$

where assets and expenses are seen to equal liabilities, capital and income.

1.8   Summary

We have seen four basic equations in this chapter:

1 **Balance sheet equation**	Assets – Liabilities = Capital
2 **Profit equation**	Income – Expenses = Profit
3 **1 and 2 combined**	Assets – Liabilities = Capital + (Income – Expenses)
4 **Double-entry equation** (same as 3 but in a different order)	Assets + Expenses = Liabilities + Capital + Income

1.9   Glossary

Accounting   The process of identifying, measuring and communicating economic information about an organisation or other entity, in order to permit informed judgements by users of the information.

Accounting equation   The formula representing the relationship between a business's assets, liabilities and capital, usually expressed as A – L = C or, when extended to include income and expenses, A + E = L + C + I.

Assets	Rights or other access to future economic benefits controlled by an entity as a result of past transactions or events.
Balance sheet	A financial summary showing the assets, liabilities and capital at a specific date.
Bookkeeping	The process of recording financial transactions.
Capital	The value of the investment of the owner or owners in the business, found by deducting all of the organisation's liabilities from all of the organisation's assets.
Capital expenditure	Another term for fixed assets.
Current asset	An asset whose value constantly changes during the course of a business's activities.
Current liability	A liability expected to be paid within one year of the date of the balance sheet.
Depreciation	An estimate of the loss in value of a fixed asset.
Double-entry bookkeeping	The system, first described by Luca Pacioli in 1494, which allows a logical record to be made of all the components of the accounting equation.
Financial accounting	The day-to-day recording of an organisation's financial transactions and the summarising of those transactions to satisfy the information needs of various user groups in accordance with the regulatory framework.
Fixed assets	Assets which are expected to be retained by the business for at least a year from the date of the balance sheet and are of a significant value. Most are subject to depreciation. Also referred to as capital expenditure or 'non-current' assets.
'In the red'	In the days before computers, banks used to use red ink to show overdrawn balances, hence you were 'in the red' if you had an overdraft.
Key concepts	Important principles underlying the preparation of financial summaries.
Liabilities	Obligations of an entity to transfer economic benefits as a result of past transactions or events.
Long-term liability	A liability expected to be paid more than one year after the balance sheet date.
Management accounting	The internal accounting needs of an organisation, involving planning, forecasting and budgeting for decision-making purposes.
Regulatory framework	The rules and regulations followed by financial accountants, imposed (in the UK) mainly by company legislation and the Accounting Standards Board.
Revenue expenditure	Literally 'expenditure to gain revenue'. It includes goods bought for resale, and overheads such as light and heat, wages and salaries.
Revenue expense	The expenditure made by a business related to the revenue generated within the same financial period.
Revenue income	The revenue generated by the business by selling its goods or services, plus sundry income such as interest received.
Stewardship	The trust placed in the managers of an organisation, who are acting on behalf of the owners.
True and fair view	An overriding accounting concept, requiring financial summaries to reflect truth and fairness in their representation of the organisation's affairs.

? Self-check questions

1 Financial accounting is:
   a Mainly concerned with forecasting the future
   b Used only by the management of the business
   c Used only by people outside the business
   d Used by people both inside and outside the business

2 The key aspects of accounting are:
   a Identifying, measuring and communicating economic information
   b Processing, recording and publishing financial information
   c Summarising, analysing and interpreting business information
   d Conveying inside information about the company to the owners

3 A steward is:
   a The accountant of the organisation
   b The owner of the organisation
   c A trusted person who manages an organisation for others
   d A security guard who patrols the organisation's premises

4 Which of the following is not a key accounting concept?
   a Going concern
   b Conservatory
   c Prudence
   d Accruals

5 Fixed assets are assets which are:
   a Likely to last at least a year and are valuable
   b Not going to be depreciated
   c Unlikely to last a year
   d The unsold goods of the business

6 Current assets are assets which:
   a Keep their value over at least a year
   b Constantly change their value
   c Are depreciated
   d Sometimes change their value

7 Liabilities are usually divided between:
   a Urgent and non-urgent
   b Fixed and current
   c Current and long-term
   d Medium-term and long-term

8 A bank overdraft is usually classified as:
   a A current asset
   b A long-term liability
   c A current liability
   d Capital

9 The accounting equation can be shown as:
   a Capital – Liabilities = Assets
   b Capital + Assets = Liabilities
   c Assets + Liabilities = Capital
   d Assets – Liabilities = Capital

10 Which of the following will not result in a change in capital?
   a A fixed asset bought by the business for £10,000
   b A profit made by the organisation
   c A loss made by the organisation
   d The owner withdrawing £5,000 from the organisation

(Answers in Appendix 1)

? Self-study questions

(Answers in Appendix 2)

Question 1.1 Using your knowledge of the accounting equation, fill in the white boxes in the following table (all figures in £):

	Assets £	Liabilities £	Capital £
1	25,630	14,256	
2		23,658	15,498
3	619,557	352,491	
4	69,810		14,863
5		21,596	35,462
6	36,520		24,510
7		65,342	86,290
8	114,785	17,853	
9	212,589		146,820
10		63,527	201,581
Totals			

Question 1.2 The annual report of a major public limited company included the following statement:

Going concern
The directors consider that the group and the company have adequate resources to remain in operation for the foreseeable future and have therefore continued to adopt the going concern basis in preparing the financial statements. As with all business forecasts the directors' statement cannot guarantee that the going concern basis will remain appropriate given the inherent uncertainty about future events.

(Tesco plc Annual Report 2004)

a Explain why the going concern concept is of importance to a user of an annual report.
b The Companies Act 1985 includes the 'going concern' concept as one of four key accounting concepts. State and explain the other three concepts.
c Which concept can override other concepts, and why?

Question 1.3 Tesco plc and J. Sainsbury plc are the UK's largest retail supermarket groups. View (and print if possible) the latest available annual reports from the websites of the two companies (**www.tesco.com** and **www.sainsburys.co.uk**). Find the (group) balance sheets and profit and loss accounts of the two companies, and then complete the boxes in this table:

(£m)	Tesco		J. Sainsbury	
	Latest year	*Previous year*	*Latest year*	*Previous year*
(from the balance sheets)				
Total net assets (i.e. fixed and current assets, less liabilities)				
(from the profit and loss accounts)				
Total sales ('turnover') for the year				
Operating profit before taxation				

Compare the two companies in terms of:

a their relative overall value as shown in the balance sheets for the latest year,

b their relative dominance of the UK supermarket sector as revealed by their sales figures in the latest year,

c their profitability as disclosed in the latest year's figures,

d what the trends between the latest and previous years reveal about the progress of the two companies.

► Case study

Marvin makes a career choice

Marvin always had an ambition to be a magician. As a child he took great delight in making his younger brothers and sisters disappear and he was often in demand to perform conjuring tricks at birthday parties. It was a natural career choice for him when, at the age of 21, he decided to leave college on 1 July 2000 and make his fortune in the world, setting up in business as a magician. He made the following payments in his first week out of college.

On 1 July he paid £3,000 for a glittering costume with a top hat and cloak; on 2 July he paid £2,000 for a special edition of a book, 'The ancient secrets of magic'; and on 3 July he bought four packs of magicians' playing cards from Kazam Limited for £100 each. Marvin expected to use these items for many years. He paid cash from his own savings for the costume and the book, but he agreed that he would pay for the playing cards in a few weeks' time from the business bank account.

His first appearance as a magician was on 7 July at the Skittleborough Annual Conjuring Show, for which he was paid a fee of £750 by cheque, with which he opened a business bank account on the same day. He incurred £20 travel expenses which he again paid from his own savings.

Required:

a Prepare a summary of Marvin's income and expenses for the week ended 7 July. Ignore any depreciation on Marvin's assets.

b Draw up a list as at 7 July of Marvin's fixed assets and current assets, then deduct any current liabilities from the assets. What is Marvin's capital at that date? Show how you can prove that the capital figure is correct.

(Answers in Appendix 3)

References

Tesco plc: **www.tesco.com/corporateinfo/**

J. Sainsbury plc: **www.j-sainsbury.co.uk/investors/**

A list of the websites of most, if not all, of the top 100 companies in the UK:
www.bl.uk/collections/business/annrpsuk.html

Professional accountancy bodies

Institute of Chartered Accountants in England and Wales: **www.icaew.co.uk**

Chartered Institute of Management Accountants: **www.cimaglobal.com**

Association of Chartered Certified Accountants: **www.acca.org.uk**

> **Now look at this book's dedicated website at www.pearsoned.co.uk/black and work through the various additional exercises for this chapter.**

Chapter 2

Recording financial transactions

Objectives

When you have read this chapter you will be able to:

➤ Understand the concept of double-entry bookkeeping

➤ Apply the concept of double-entry bookkeeping to the recording of financial transactions

➤ Prepare a simple trial balance whilst appreciating its limitations

➤ Understand the role of the books of prime entry and ledgers which comprise the double-entry bookkeeping system

2.1 Introduction

In the previous chapter, the accounting equation showed us that

Assets + Expenses = Liabilities + Capital + Income

Records of financial transactions of the vast majority of commercial organisations are made according to the *double-entry bookkeeping system*, which is based on this equation. The system is highly structured and logical and enables even the largest organisation to keep track of its financial position over time.

2.2 The principles of double-entry bookkeeping

As the name implies, double-entry bookkeeping requires each financial transaction to be recorded in two locations within the accounting records of the organisation. This is due to the recognition that there is a *dual aspect* to each transaction: that the organisation both receives and gives value when the transaction is made. For example, a business buying a machine with a cheque for £10,000 not only *receives* a machine costing £10,000 but also *gives* a cheque for £10,000. In terms of the accounting equation we can see that the increase in one asset (machine + £10,000) is matched by the decrease in another asset (bank balance – £10,000). If the business sells goods for £4,000 to a customer paying by cheque, the business both *gives* goods valued at £4,000 and *receives* a cheque for the same amount. The accounting equation stays in balance as the asset of the bank balance increases (+ £4,000) whilst income in the form of sales increases by the same amount.

Activity 2.1

Look at the following transactions of Michael Shelton. How will they affect the accounting equation? Enter the changes to each component of the equation (as pluses and minuses) in the table below, and then show the overall effect on the accounting equation. The changes relating to the first two transactions have been entered as an example. (Note that all amounts are, for convenience, shown as whole pounds. In practice, of course, pence would be shown as well.)

1	1 January	Starts a business by opening a bank account with £4,000
2	2 January	Buys goods for resale with a cheque for £2,000
3	3 January	Sells goods for cash, £700
4	4 January	Pays wages £300 by cash
5	5 January	Buys stationery from Ink Stores valued at £700. Michael expects to pay for the stationery in a month's time
6	6 January	Buys a computer with a cheque, £1,000
7	7 January	Sells goods to Anna Butler for £820. Anna hopes to pay in two months' time
8	8 January	Michael pays a lottery win of £1,000 into the business bank account
9	9 January	Michael draws out £100 from the business bank account for his own use
10	10 January	Michael buys goods for resale costing £1,500 from Bettabuys, and intends to pay for them in a month's time

	Assets £	Expenses £	Liabilities £	Capital £	Income £
1	+4,000 (Bank)			+4,000	
2	–2,000 (Bank)	+2,000 (Purchases)			
3					
4					
5					
6					
7					
8					
9					
10					

Overall effect:

Answer

	Assets £	Expenses £	Liabilities £	Capital £	Income £
1	+4,000 (Bank)			+4,000	
2	−2,000 (Bank)	+2,000 (Purchases)			
3	+700 (Cash)				+700 (Sales)
4	−300 (Cash)	+300 (Wages)			
5		+700 (Stationery)	+700 (Creditors)		
6	+1,000 (Computer) − 1,000 (Bank)				
7	+ 820 (Debtor)				+820 (Sales)
8	+1,000 (Bank)			+1,000	
9	−100 (Bank)			−100	
10		+1,500 (Purchases)	+1,500 (Creditors)		

The overall effect of the ten transactions is:

Assets £	Expenses £	Liabilities £	Capital £	Income £
+4,120	+4,500	+2,200	+4,900	+1,520
	=+8,620		= +8,620	

Pause for thought

In transactions 1 and 8, Michael is increasing the value of his capital, but transaction 9 reduces this value. When an owner takes out money or goods from the organisation, it is classed as 'drawings'.

In transactions 2 and 10, because the goods are for resale, they are referred to as 'purchases'. Expenses such as stationery, petrol, and so on, which are used up in running the business, are not classed as purchases, but might be entered as 'office expenses', 'motor expenses', and so forth.

In transaction 5, the stationery company is a **creditor** (a liability) until Michael pays the amount owing.

In transaction 6, the computer is a fixed asset, not an expense (see Chapter 1), as it is expected to last for several accounting periods and is of substantial value.

In transaction 7, Anna Butler is Michael's **debtor** (an asset of Michael) until she pays the amount she owes.

2.3 The double-entry bookkeeping system

Did you know?

Readers whose course does not cover detailed bookkeeping can omit the rest of this chapter.

The dual aspect of the accounting equation, as we have seen, applies to every financial transaction of the organisation, and this should be recorded by the business in the double-entry bookkeeping system.

The entries are made in a **ledger**, which is a collection of individual records known as **accounts**. There is no limit to the number of accounts which a business can open, but for convenience they tend to be grouped as follows:

Accounts grouped within:			
('Personal' ledgers)		('Impersonal' ledger)	
Sales (or debtors) ledger	**Purchases (or creditors) ledger**	**General (or nominal) ledger**	**Cash book (and petty cash book)**
Contains the individual personal accounts of customers who buy on credit	Contains the individual personal accounts of suppliers from whom we buy on credit	Contains all other accounts, except bank, cash and **petty cash**	Contains the bank account, cash account and petty cash account

Each account is split into two sides, a **debit** side and a **credit** side. The debit side is always on the left. The words 'debit' and 'credit' are often abbreviated to Dr and Cr. The accounting equation reflects these two sides, as follows:

Assets + Expenses = Liabilities + Capital + Income	
Accounts with more debit entries than credit entries	Accounts with more credit entries than debit entries

An account, in its simplest form, can be represented by two lines, forming a letter 'T'. Such accounts are often known as **T accounts**. Looking back at Activity 2.1, the first transaction, where Michael Shelton starts a business by opening a bank account with £4,000, would be shown in T accounts as follows:

Bank account (part of the Cash Book)

(Debit side)	£	(Credit side)	£
1 Jan M. Shelton's capital	4,000		

M. Shelton's capital account (part of the General Ledger)

(Debit side)	£	(Credit side)	£
		1 Jan Bank	4,000

Pause for thought

The asset of the bank balance has increased. Therefore, based on the accounting equation, the account is debited. The owner's capital has also increased, so the capital account is credited. It is vital that you understand how the entries in the bank account (and cash account) are shown. The golden rule is:

**Money paid IN to the bank appears on the DEBIT side
Money paid OUT of the bank appears on the CREDIT side.**

This is a mirror image of how you would see the details of the bank account shown on a bank statement, because the statement shows the state of the business's bank account in the *bank*'s ledger, not the business's. So every additional amount the business pays in increases the *bank*'s liabilities, which are credits in the bank's ledger according to the accounting equation (i.e. the bank's creditors have increased). This is often confusing to accounting students, as if we have money in the bank, it is normal English usage to say we have a 'credit balance', even though the bank is our debtor!

The T account entries for the next four of Michael Shelton's transactions are as follows. Note that, from now on, the words 'debit side' and 'credit side' will be omitted from the accounts, as will the word 'account' itself. Where several entries affect the same account they are shown within that one account rather than separate accounts being opened for each entry.

2 January	Buys goods for resale with a cheque for £2,000
3 January	Sells goods for cash, £700
4 January	Pays wages £300 by cash
5 January	Buys stationery from Ink Stores valued at £700. Michael expects to pay for the stationery in a month's time

Michael Shelton's business

Cash Book

Bank

		£			£
1 Jan	M. Shelton's capital	4,000	2 Jan	Purchases	2,000

Cash

		£			£
3 Jan	Sales	700	4 Jan	Wages	300

General Ledger

M. Shelton's capital

	£			£
	£	1 Jan	Bank	4,000

Sales

	£			£
	£	3 Jan	Cash	700

Purchases

		£	£
2 Jan	Bank	2,000	

Wages

		£	£
4 Jan	Cash	300	

Stationery

		£	£
5 Jan	Ink Stores	700	

Purchases Ledger

Ink Stores

	£			£
		5 Jan	Stationery	700

Pause for thought

Notice that the Ink Stores transaction affects neither the bank nor cash accounts as it is on credit terms, with no payment yet being made.

Activity 2.2

Complete the following ledger accounts with the remaining entries (from Activity 2.1) required for the transactions up to January 10. The transactions are:

6 January Buys a computer with a cheque, £1,000
7 January Sells goods to Anna Butler for £820. Anna hopes to pay in two months' time
8 January Michael pays a lottery win of £1,000 into the business bank account
9 January Michael draws out £100 from the business bank account for his own use
10 January Michael buys goods for resale costing £1,500 from Bettabuys, and intends to pay for them in a month's time

Michael Shelton's business

Cash Book

Bank

		£			£
1 Jan	M. Shelton's capital	4,000	2 Jan	Purchases	2,000

General Ledger

M. Shelton's capital

	£			£
		1 Jan	Bank	4,000

Computer

	£		£

Activity 2.2
continued

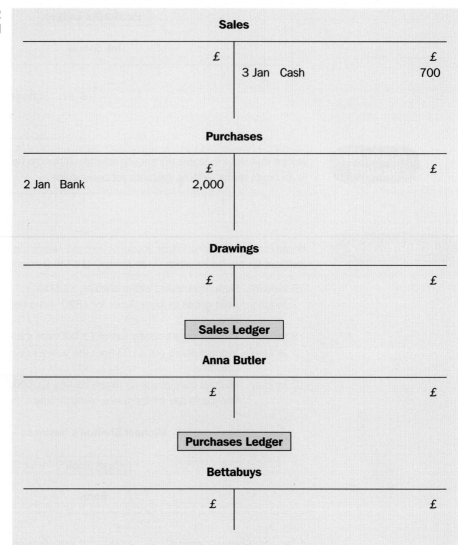

Sales

	£			£
		3 Jan	Cash	700

Purchases

	£			£
2 Jan Bank	2,000			

Drawings

	£		£

Sales Ledger

Anna Butler

	£		£

Purchases Ledger

Bettabuys

	£		£

Answer

The following shows the ledger accounts and entries needed to record all transactions from 1 January, including those for 6–10 January.

Cash Book

Bank

		£			£
1 Jan	M. Shelton's capital	4,000	2 Jan	Purchases	2,000
8 Jan	M. Shelton's capital	1,000	6 Jan	Computer	1,000
			9 Jan	Drawings	100

Cash

		£			£
3 Jan	Sales	700	4 Jan	Wages	300

General Ledger

M. Shelton's capital

		£			£
			1 Jan	Bank	4,000
			8 Jan	Bank	1,000

Computer

		£		£
6 Jan	Bank	1,000		

Sales

		£			£
			3 Jan	Cash	700
			7 Jan	Anna Butler	820

Purchases

		£		£
2 Jan	Bank	2,000		
10 Jan	Bettabuys	1,500		

Wages

		£		£
4 Jan	Cash	300		

Stationery

		£		£
5 Jan	Ink Stores	700		

Drawings

		£		£
9 Jan	Bank	100		

Sales Ledger

Anna Butler

		£		£
7 Jan	Sales	820		

Answer continued

Purchases Ledger

Ink Stores

	£			£
		5 Jan	Stationery	700

Bettabuys

	£			£
		10 Jan	Purchases	1,500

Pause for thought

Each entry has the date, a brief description (a cross-reference to the account with the other side of the double-entry) and the amount. Try to record the information as neatly as possible, using a ruler where necessary.

2.4 Balancing accounts

After entering numerous transactions, the ledger accounts may need to be **balanced** to show the net value contained within them. At the end of a financial period this is referred to as **closing off** the accounts. The procedure to balance an account is shown below.

Account with more debit entries than credit entries:

Motor expenses

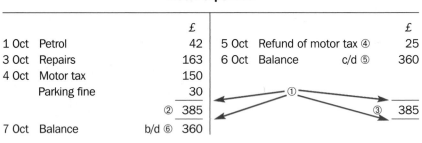

		£				£
1 Oct	Petrol	42	5 Oct	Refund of motor tax ④		25
3 Oct	Repairs	163	6 Oct	Balance	c/d ⑤	360
4 Oct	Motor tax	150				
	Parking fine	30				
		② 385				③ 385
7 Oct	Balance	b/d ⑥ 360				

Account with more credit entries than debit entries:

Clifford Supplies

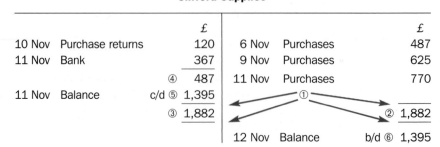

		£			£
10 Nov	Purchase returns	120	6 Nov	Purchases	487
11 Nov	Bank	367	9 Nov	Purchases	625
		④ 487	11 Nov	Purchases	770
11 Nov	Balance	c/d ⑤ 1,395			
		③ 1,882			② 1,882
			12 Nov	Balance	b/d ⑥ 1,395

Notes:

1 Draw in 'total lines' on both sides of the account, making sure there is enough room to write in two further lines of information underneath the last entry on the side with the lower overall value of entries.

2 The side with the greater value should then be totalled, with the amount shown within the total lines.

3 This value is repeated on the other side, on the same line.

4 The side with the smaller value is subtotalled (not needed if there is only one entry recorded).

5 On the line below the subtotal (or the one entry), write the date of the balance and 'Balance c/d' (note that 'c/d' stands for 'carried down'), and the amount needed to increase the subtotal to equal the grand total.

6 On the opposite side to the 'Balance c/d' entry, write in below the total lines the entry date, 'Balance b/d' and the same amount as shown against 'Balance c/d' (note that 'b/d' stands for 'brought down'). It is usual to date this one day later than the balance c/d, as one period has closed and another one has started.

Activity 2.3

Balance off the bank account of Michael Shelton at 10 January.

Bank

		£			£
1 Jan	M. Shelton's capital	4,000	2 Jan	Purchases	2,000
8 Jan	M. Shelton's capital	1,000	6 Jan	Computer	1,000
			9 Jan	Drawings	100

Answer

Bank

		£			£
1 Jan	M. Shelton's capital	4,000	2 Jan	Purchases	2,000
8 Jan	M. Shelton's capital	1,000	6 Jan	Computer	1,000
		5,000	9 Jan	Drawings	100
					3,100
			10 Jan	Balance c/d	1,900
		5,000			5,000
11 Jan	Balance b/d	1,900			

Pause for thought

Note that the b/d balance is not underlined, as it is the starting point for the following period's entries. Sometimes an opening balance might be described as 'b/f' (brought forward) if its corresponding closing balance from the previous period is not shown on the same page. Similarly, a closing balance c/f (carried forward) does not have its corresponding opening balance for the following period shown on the same page.

2.5   A simple trial balance

Now that we know how to balance each account, we can perform a simple but essential check on the arithmetical accuracy of the entries we have made. This is known as a **trial balance**, and shows, at a specific date, every balance in every ledger account, listed under the headings 'debit' and 'credit'.

Activity 2.4

Prepare a trial balance for Michael Shelton as at 10 January, by entering every balance from the T accounts shown on pages 22–24 in the appropriate column. The first two balances have been entered.

	Debit £	Credit £
Bank	1,900	
Cash	400	

Answer

	Debit £	Credit £
Bank	1,900	
Cash	400	
M. Shelton's capital		5,000
Computer	1,000	
Sales		1,520
Purchases	3,500	
Wages	300	
Stationery	700	
Drawings	100	
Anna Butler (a debtor)	820	
Ink Stores (a creditor)		700
Bettabuys (a creditor)		1,500
	8,720	8,720

Pause for thought

This proves that all the debit entries equal the total of all the credit entries, as they should under the accounting equation. It is not telling us that all the entries are accurate, as we may have omitted an entry completely, reversed entries, entered the wrong amount in the correct accounts or the correct amounts in the wrong accounts! However, the trial balance is an essential check to be made before proceeding to summarise the financial information as explained in Chapter 4.

2.6   Books of prime entry

The double-entry bookkeeping system, as we have seen, requires entries to be made within ledger accounts. Because of the mass of information generated by businesses, it is helpful to management to keep certain parts of the system within a number of self-contained areas, as follows:

● Bank and cash transactions within a cash book

● Small cash transactions within a petty cash book

● Invoices received or issued within day books

● Returns of goods within day books

● Specialised adjustments within a journal.

These are known as **books of prime entry** (or primary accounting records) as they show the first stage of the bookkeeping process prior to the **posting** of the information into the ledger accounts.

2.6.1   The cash book

The cash book is used to record the transactions affecting both the business's bank account and also its unbanked cash (notes and coins), shown within a cash account. Often, the two accounts are shown in what is known as a 'columnar' form, with two debit columns and two credit columns. Michael Shelton's cash book could be shown as follows:

Cash Book

		Cash £	Bank £			Cash £	Bank £
1 Jan	Capital		4,000	2 Jan	Purchases		2,000
3 Jan	Sales	700		4 Jan	Wages	300	
8 Jan	Capital		1,000	6 Jan	Computer		1,000
				9 Jan	Drawings		100

The advantage of this layout is that details of all the cash and bank transactions are within the same part of the ledger.

2.6.2   The petty cash book

Most organisations spend cash on low value items such as tea and coffee, postage stamps, window cleaning, and so forth. These items are considered too immaterial (that is, insignificant) to be left within the main cash book, so they are given their own book within the system, known as the petty cash book, which contains the petty cash account.

This is usually operated under an **imprest system**, where the petty cash has a 'float' of a predetermined amount, which is topped up at regular intervals. For example, assume that in Michael Shelton's business a cash float of £80 was decided upon on 8 January as a typical amount to cover a week's petty cash expenditure. Firstly, £80 would be transferred from the 'main' cash account within the cash book (though it may, alternatively, have been drawn out from the bank account):

Cash Book ('cash' columns only)

		£			£
3 Jan	Sales	700	4 Jan	Wages	300
			8 Jan	Transfer to Petty Cash	80

The petty cash book is then opened. This book looks different from the cash book seen earlier as it has only one account within it (petty cash) whereas the cash book has two (cash and bank). Also, because the vast majority of the items are expenses and therefore credit entries, there is usually no separate column on the debit side for the date or details of amounts received. Using a 'typical' week's petty cash expenditure for illustration and assuming that the cash float is topped up at the start of the following week, the petty cash book for Michael Shelton is as follows:

Petty Cash Book

£/p				£/p
80.00	8 Jan	Transfer from Cash Book		
	9 Jan	Window cleaning		9.50
	10 Jan	Refreshments		2.35
	11 Jan	Bus fares		2.55
	12 Jan	Parcel tape		3.65
	13 Jan	Postage stamps		21.20
	14 Jan	Advertising – local newspaper		32.55
		Total expenditure for the week		71.80
		Balance c/d		8.20
80.00				80.00
8.20	15 Jan	Balance b/d		
71.80		Transfer from Cash Book		
80.00				

During the week, £71.80 has been spent from the opening cash float of £80. At the start of the following week, the float must be 'topped up' by drawing the total of the previous week's expenditure from the main cash account, and transferring it to the petty cash to again make up the £80. The imprest system is a useful control against fraud, as the person responsible for the petty cash would normally have to present evidence of the expenditure (vouchers, receipts, and so on) to the person controlling the main cash book when requesting the top-up for the petty cash float.

Activity 2.5

From the following details, write up the petty cash book of Maggie Pepper:

1 October	Petty cash book opened with a float of £100
2 October	Repair to office chair £13.50
3 October	Bought milk for office £4.80
4 October	Bought raffle tickets from local charity £5
5 October	Paid £35.90 for a train ticket
6 October	Paid a car parking charge of £4.50
7 October	Paid a laundry bill of £7.80. Petty cash balance to be shown at the end of this day
8 October	Petty cash float topped up

Answer

Maggie Pepper: Petty Cash Book

£/p			£/p
100.00	1 Oct	Transfer from Cash Book	
	2 Oct	Repair to office chair	13.50
	3 Oct	Milk	4.80
	4 Oct	Raffle tickets	5.00
	5 Oct	Train ticket	35.90
	6 Oct	Car parking	4.50
	7 Oct	Laundry	7.80
		Total expenditure for the week	71.50
		Balance c/d	28.50
100.00			100.00
28.50	8 Oct	Balance b/d	
71.50		Transfer from Cash Book	
100.00			

2.6.3 Day books

In Activity 2.1, only three of the transactions were on *credit terms*, where there was a delay between the date on which goods were bought or sold and the date of paying or receiving the amounts due. It is vital to keep the individual personal accounts of debtors and creditors (as seen with the ledger accounts for Anna Butler – a debtor, and Ink Stores and Bettabuys – both creditors), so that the business knows at any time to whom it owes money and who owes it money. However, it is often unnecessary to show every individual purchase and sale in the relevant account in the general ledger. Even a moderately sized business may generate many hundreds or thousands of invoices over a financial period, so it makes sense to show them in separate books known as day books.

There will be four day books:

● Purchases
● Sales
● Purchase returns (or 'Returns out')
● Sales returns (or 'Returns in').

At intervals, totals are transferred from the day books to the relevant accounts within the general ledger, thus reducing the number of entries within the ledger accounts.

The day books are also useful for resolving queries, as they provide a chronological list of all invoices issued or received and goods returned to or by the business. They also have a role to play in the creation of control accounts (see Chapter 3).

Activity 2.6

Wayne Allan's business recorded the following transactions during the period 7–14 July. Show how they would appear in the day books, the personal ledgers (sales ledger and purchases ledger) and the general ledger.

7 Jul   Invoices received from T. Rogers £300, P. Cox £800, J. Wall £450
10 Jul   Invoices sent to L. Kenwood £790, A. Gardiner £980, L. Kerr £340
11 Jul   Invoice received from P. Cox £100, and invoice sent to L. Kerr, £490
12 Jul   Wayne Allan returned goods worth £125 to P. Cox
13 Jul   A. Gardiner returned goods to Wayne Allan which cost £50
14 Jul   Wayne Allan paid the amount owing to P. Cox, and L. Kerr paid in full

Answer

Wayne Allan's Business

Purchases Day Book

		£
7 Jul	T. Rogers	300
	P. Cox	800
	J. Wall	450
11 Jul	P. Cox	100
		1,650

Sales Day Book

		£
10 Jul	L. Kenwood	790
	A. Gardiner	980
	L. Kerr	340
11 Jul	L. Kerr	490
		2,600

Purchase Returns Day Book

		£
12 Jul	P. Cox	125
		125

Sales Returns Day Book

		£
13 Jul	A. Gardiner	50
		50

Purchases Ledger

T. Rogers

					£
			7 Jul	Invoice	300

P. Cox

		£			£
12 Jul	Purchases Returns	125	7 Jul	Invoice	800
14 Jul	Bank	775	11 Jul	Invoice	100
		900			900

J. Wall

	£			£
		7 Jul	Invoice	450

Sales Ledger

L. Kenwood

		£	£
10 Jul	Invoice	790	

A. Gardiner

		£			£
10 Jul	Invoice	980	13 Jul	Sales Returns	50

L. Kerr

		£			£
10 Jul	Invoice	340	14 Jul	Bank	830
11 Jul	Invoice	490			
		830			830

General Ledger

Sales

	£			£
		14 Jul	Sales Day Book	2,600

Purchases

		£	£
14 Jul	Purchases Day Book	1,650	

Purchase returns

	£			£
		14 Jul	Purchase Returns Day Book	125

Sales returns

		£	£
14 Jul	Sales Returns Day Book	50	

Answers continued

Cash Book

Bank account

	£			£
14 Jul L. Kerr	830	14 Jul P. Cox		775

Pause for thought

The day books take the detail out of the general ledger accounts, as only the totals of the invoices or returns are shown. It is vital that full records are still maintained within the personal ledgers. Note that the day book totals are transferred into the general ledger at the last day of the period, 14 July.

2.6.4 The journal

Occasionally there may be adjustments or corrections to the financial information recorded within the ledger system. **Journal** entries show which accounts are to be debited and which to be credited (always in that order), with a simple explanation for the entries, known as a 'narrative'.

Activity 2.7

Assume that the following errors were made when entering the transactions of Wayne Allan in Activity 2.6:

- The invoice (£300) from T. Rogers was credited to P. Bodger's account.
- The invoice from J. Wall was entered in the Purchases day book and J. Wall's ledger account as £540 instead of £450.

Answer

The Journal

	Dr £	Cr £
1. Debit P. Bodger	300	
Credit T. Rogers		300
– Correction of misposting to P. Bodger's account		
2. Debit J. Wall	90	
Credit Purchases		90
– Error in amount posted to J. Wall's account and Purchases day book		

Pause for thought

The journal is not used very often, but is useful for explaining the reasons for making essential changes to ledger accounts.

2.7 Computerised accounts

As would be expected, most businesses use computers for some or all of their accounting needs. The bookkeeping system described in this chapter forms the basis of accounting software programs. These programs give the following advantages:

- Speed
- Accuracy of calculation
- Integration of functions, avoiding duplication of effort
- Reduction in costs of professional accountancy services
- Provision of detailed financial reports for management
- Provision of summarised financial information complying with the regulatory framework.

References are given at the end of this chapter to the websites of a number of leading accounting software suppliers. Some might let you download 'demo' accounting programs for evaluation with no obligation to purchase them. Alternatively, try searching the Internet for freeware or shareware accounting software. If possible, download one of these programs, respecting any copyright, and see how they work by entering Michael Shelton's transactions from Activity 2.1. There are many more features available on these programs than can be utilised by this simple example, but it should give you the confidence to explore these further.

2.8 Summary

The ledger (all the accounts of the business) is divided into:		
Personal ledgers		Impersonal ledgers
Sales ledger (also known as debtors ledger)	Purchases ledger (also known as creditors ledger)	General ledger (also known as nominal ledger)
Accounts for each of the customers who buy on credit terms	Accounts for each supplier of goods and services who allows a period of credit	All other accounts, but note that the bank and cash accounts are usually shown in a separate cash book, with 'petty cash' shown in a 'petty cash book'

2.9 Glossary

Account The individual record contained within the ledger.

Balancing The process of inserting a closing balance into the ledger account to show the net value of the account at a specific date.

Books of prime entry The location of the first stage of the bookkeeping process: the cash book, petty cash book, day books and journal.

Cash book The book containing the bank account and cash account. Part of the general (impersonal) ledger.

Closing off Balancing accounts at the end of a financial period.

Credit The right-hand side of a ledger account. Liability, capital and income accounts have credit balances. Abbreviated to Cr.

Creditor A supplier of goods or services who is owed money by the business.

Debit The left-hand side of a ledger account. Asset and expenses accounts have debit balances. Abbreviated to Dr.

Debtor A customer or client who owes an amount to the business.

General ledger The impersonal ledger containing accounts for capital and types of assets, expenses, liabilities and income.

Impersonal ledger The general (or nominal) ledger.

Imprest system A method of controlling petty cash by keeping a 'float' which is topped up at intervals.

Journal A book of prime entry used to record the correction of errors and other adjustments between ledger accounts.

Ledger A collection of individual records known as accounts.

Nominal ledger Another name for the general ledger.

Personal The Sales (Debtors) and Purchases (Creditors) ledgers, containing the individual accounts of customers and suppliers who trade on credit terms.

Petty cash Small items of expenditure, usually shown in a separate book.

Posting A word used to describe the entering of information in the double-entry system.

Purchases The name of an account in the general ledger which records goods bought for resale.

T account Simple representation of the layout of a ledger account.

Trial balance A list of all the account balances, divided between debit and credit balances at a specific time. If the total debit balances equal the total credit balances, the trial balance is said to 'agree' and shows that the arithmetic of all the entries is correct. It is not a perfect check of overall accuracy.

? Self-check questions

1 A business sells goods for £1,000 paid into its bank account. The entries to be made are:
   a Debit Sales   Credit Bank
   b Debit Stock   Credit Bank
   c Debit Bank   Credit Sales
   d Debit Bank   Credit Purchases

2 Goods bought for resale will be debited to the:
   a Stock account
   b Office expenses account
   c Sales account
   d Purchases account

3 When the owner takes out cash from the business for personal use it is referred to as:
   a Drawings
   b Wages
   c Capital
   d Salary

4 Creditors are:
   a Customers who pay cash
   b Customers who owe money to the business
   c Suppliers who are owed money by the business
   d Suppliers who have been paid by the business

5 Which of the following is a personal ledger?
   a General ledger
   b Purchases ledger
   c Cash book
   d Balance sheet

6 The cash book contains which of the following accounts?
   a Petty cash and Bank
   b Drawings and Bank
   c Bank and Cash
   d Capital and Cash

7 A T account is:
   a The account of all debtors whose names begin with the letter T
   b The account which shows the cost of office refreshments
   c The account of a golfer
   d A simple representation of the layout of an account

8 C/d and b/d are abbreviations for:
   a Carried down and Brought down
   b Carried down and Balance down
   c Correctly drawn and Badly drawn
   d Cash deposit and Bank deposit

9 A trial balance is:
   a A perfect check on the bookkeeping system
   b A check on the accuracy of the bookkeeping entries
   c A check on the arithmetical accuracy of the bookkeeping entries
   d A way of proving that the business has made a profit

10 A business operates an imprest system with a cash float of £150 topped up at the start of every week. During a week it spends £90 on petty cash items. How much will be transferred from the main cash account at the start of the following week?

a £150

b £90

c £240

d £60

(Answers in Appendix 1)

? Self-study questions

(Answers in Appendix 2)

Question 2.1 Balance the following accounts at 31 December, bringing down balances on 1 January.

Sales account

		£			£
12 Dec	Cash repaid to customer	65	17 Dec	Cash received	84,000
			22 Dec	Sales day book	125,600

Bank charges account

		£			£
12 Oct	Charges	112	13 Dec	Refund due to bank error	26
12 Nov	Charges	145			

Question 2.2 For each of the following transactions, show the effect (as pluses and minuses) on assets, expenses, liabilities, capital and income.

	Assets £	Expenses £	Liabilities £	Capital £	Income £
1 The business pays a cheque of £100 for phone charges					
2 The business pays a creditor £250					
3 The owner takes out £100 in cash from the business					
4 Goods are sold to a debtor for £900					
5 Petrol is bought on credit for £60					
Summary (overall change)					

Question 2.3 For each of the following transactions, show the effect (as pluses and minuses) on assets, expenses, liabilities, capital and income.

	Assets £	Expenses £	Liabilities £	Capital £	Income £
1 The owner pays in £6,000 to start the business's bank account					
2 The business pays wages of £250 by cheque					
3 Goods are bought for £400 on credit from Goff Limited					
4 Goods are sold on credit to Plod plc for £510					
5 A computer is bought for £600 with a cheque					
6 Stationery is bought for £50 with a cheque					
Summary (overall change)					

Question 2.4 From the following transactions of Rachel Roberts, write up a cash book showing cash and bank transactions and T accounts for all other transactions. Balance off the bank and cash accounts only, then extract a trial balance at 7 October.

1 Oct   Started the business by paying £9,000 into the business bank account and also providing £100 as an opening cash balance
1 Oct   Bought goods for resale with a cheque for £4,000 and paid £60 in cash for stationery
2 Oct   Sold goods for £600 cheque and £280 cash
3 Oct   Paid a cheque for £30 for advertising and a cheque for £45 for printing
4 Oct   Paid rent by cheque, £100
5 Oct   Sold goods for £700 cheque and £130 cash
6 Oct   Paid wages £260 cash. Owner withdrew £400 from the bank for personal use
7 Oct   A customer was given a refund by cheque £40 for faulty goods returned to the business

Question 2.5 Casper Peabody's business recorded the following transactions during the week ended 7 May. Show how they would appear in the day books, the personal ledgers (sales ledger and purchases ledger) and the general ledger.

1 May   Invoices received from C. Moss £630, J. Carter £419 and A. McKeane £330
2 May   Invoices sent to K. Palfreyman £199 and L. Patel £870
3 May   Invoice received from A. Iqbal £560 and A. McKeane £210
4 May   Casper Peabody returned goods worth £80 to J. Carter
5 May   L. Patel returned goods to Casper Peabody which cost £62
6 May   Casper Peabody paid the amount owing to J. Carter, and L. Patel paid in full
7 May   Casper Peabody returned goods worth £40 to A. Iqbal

Question 2.6 Lara Kelly recorded the following petty cash transactions during the week ended 20 October.

14 Oct   Started the week with the normal cash float of £200.00. Paid £25.56 travel expenses
15 Oct   Paid £14.29 for window cleaning
16 Oct   Paid £18.45 for train fares
17 Oct   Paid £40 for new kennel for guard dog, and £19 for dog food
18 Oct   Paid postage £2.65
19 Oct   Made a loan of £10 to Hiram Decker, a member of staff
20 Oct   Paid £23.85 for window cleaning

The cash float was topped up at the start of the following week.

Show the petty cash book for the week, balance the book at the end of the week, carry down the balance and show the cash float being topped up at the start of the following week.

Question 2.7 Show how the following errors would be corrected by means of journal entries in the books of Paul Pascoe:

a £400 received from Andrew Cheung which should have been posted to his account in the sales ledger but was entered in Andrew Young's account.

b A cheque for £40 paid for stationery which was entered on the debit side of the bank account in the cash book and the credit side of the stationery account.

c An invoice for £200 for goods for resale received from a supplier, Dingle Dynamics, was omitted entirely from the books.

> ## Case study

Marvin buys rabbits!

Marvin the magician (see Chapter 1's case study) entered his second week of business and was offered fees to appear as an entertainer at three parties during the week. Realising that he had no rabbits to pull out of his top hat, he contacted the United Rabbit Corporation, which agreed, on 8 July, to supply six white rabbits at a cost of £40 each on the condition that Marvin treated them kindly and fed them well. On the same day, Amalgamated Carrots plc supplied several sacks of rabbit food at a total cost of £250. Both companies sent Marvin invoices. Marvin built a rabbit hutch from scrap materials at no cost.

On 10 July, Marvin travelled to William Green's party, which was a success, and he was paid £100 in cash. Travel expenses cost £15 cash. On 11 July he paid a cheque for £18 for cleaning his costume, which became soiled after handling the rabbits. On 12 July he paid £9 for a train ticket in cash, and travelled to Violet Cartwright's party, which was also successful, and he received a cheque for £120. On 13 July he performed at Jasper Peter's party which was only partly successful, since a child felt sorry for the rabbits and let them all escape. They were never seen again. Marvin gave an invoice to Mr and Mrs Peter for £250 for his magic act at the party.

On 14 July, he returned the unused rabbit feed to Amalgamated Carrots plc, which gave him a credit of £60. He paid the United Rabbit Corporation invoice by cheque and also paid Kazam Limited's account for the playing cards bought in the first week.

Required:

a Enter the first week's transactions in a cash book and T accounts. Day books and a petty cash book are not required. The transactions (as shown in Chapter 1's case study) were:

1 July	Bought costume £3,000, using own capital
2 July	Bought ancient book £2,000, using own capital
3 July	Bought playing cards £400, by invoice from Kazam Limited
7 July	Received £750 for magic show and opened a bank account. Paid £20 travel expenses, using own savings

b Enter the second week's transactions into the cash book and T accounts.

c Balance all the accounts at 14 July, and carry the balances down at 15 July.

d Prepare a trial balance as at 14 July.

(Answers in Appendix 3)

References

Accounting software developers

Dosh: **www.dosh.co.uk**

MYOB (Mind Your Own Business): **www.myob.com**

Pegasus: **www.pegasus.co.uk**

Sage: **www.sage.com**

Tas Books: **www.tassoftware.com**

Business and Accounting Software Developers Association: **www.basda.org**

Now look at this book's dedicated website at **www.pearsoned.co.uk/black** and work through the various additional exercises for this chapter.

Chapter 3

Applying controls and concepts to financial information

Objectives

When you have read this chapter you will be able to:

➤ Understand that financial information needs to be more than just cash flow analysis

➤ Understand and prepare simple bank reconciliation statements and personal ledger control accounts

➤ Understand the accounting adjustments for opening and closing stock, and the normal basis of valuation of stock

➤ Appreciate the need for accruals and prepayments and make the related book-keeping entries

➤ Understand what is meant by 'depreciation' and make the related bookkeeping entries

➤ Understand the layout of a simple profit and loss account and balance sheet

3.1 Introduction

In Chapter 1, four key accounting concepts were identified: *going concern, accruals, consistency* and *prudence*, plus the overriding concept of the *true and fair view*. Every business needs to prepare periodic summaries of their finances, and this chapter looks at how the concepts affect the way in which these summaries are prepared. We also look at accounting control over accuracy and completeness of data. In the previous chapter we have already seen two types of control: the trial balance and the imprest system of petty cash. This chapter looks at two further aspects of control over the accuracy and completeness of data within the bookkeeping system prior to preparing the financial summaries: bank reconciliation statements and control accounts. The way in which accounting concepts affect what appears within financial summaries is also explained.

3.2   Cash flow statements and beyond

The double-entry bookkeeping system described in Chapter 2 records the business's assets, expenses, liabilities, capital and income. From time to time, a business needs to summarise its financial position by comparing its income with its expenditure over a specific period, in a statement known as a **profit and loss account**, and by summarising its assets and its liabilities (and therefore its capital) at the end of that period, in a statement known as a **balance sheet**.

What must be understood at the outset is that these two key financial summaries are *accounting* summaries – and must therefore comply with the key concepts. It could be argued that all a business needs to understand its financial position is a summary of its cash and bank accounts – a **cash flow statement**. Many individuals, after all, look at their bank balance and the amount of cash in their purses or wallets as a guide to how affluent they are. However, for a business to understand fully its financial position it is also vital to know:

- how much is owed to or by the business by customers, suppliers and lenders
- the values of unsold stocks of goods
- whether all the expenses for the period have been included
- whether some of the expenses paid in the period relate to a future period
- whether fixed assets have lost value during the period
- how much profit or loss has been made
- what overall assets and liabilities the business has accumulated, not just those bought in the current period.

None of this information would be disclosed by a cash flow statement.

3.3   Bank reconciliation statements

Another factor which should be considered by a business before relying on the information contained within bank statements is whether the statements reconcile with the business's own record of the bank account as shown in the cash book. Usually there are items in the bank statements which have not yet been recorded in the cash book, such as bank charges, standing orders and direct debits, and items in the cash book which are not yet shown in the bank statement, such as **unpresented cheques** (i.e. cheques not yet banked by the recipients). A **reconciliation** should be made to agree the two versions of the account.

Activity 3.1

Julia Ronson is trying to reconcile her business's bank statements with the bank account details as shown in the business's cash book. She had previously reconciled the opening balance at 1 November, and has subsequently received the following bank statement for the month of November:

Activity 3.1
continued

Grimley's Bank plc Higglethorpe Branch
Julia Ronson Current Account No. 563428974

		Debits £	Credits £	Balance £
1 Nov	Opening balance			563.21 Cr
3 Nov	Cheque 563121	48.23		514.98 Cr
5 Nov	Standing order: Water company	20.00		494.98 Cr
9 Nov	Cheque 563123	145.23		349.75 Cr
15 Nov	Bank credit		600.52	950.27 Cr
19 Nov	Bank charges	8.62		941.65 Cr
24 Nov	Cheque 563124	621.56		320.09 Cr
27 Nov	Cheque 563125	453.62		133.53 Dr
30 Nov	Bank credit		704.26	570.73 Cr
30 Nov	Direct debit: HP Finance	30.00		540.73 Cr

The details of the bank account as contained in her cash book are as follows:

Cash Book

Bank

		£			£
1 Nov	Opening balance b/f	563.21	1 Nov Lotty Miller Fashions		48.23
12 Nov	Cash to bank	600.52	6 Nov Garry Hill Ltd		263.25
29 Nov	Netta Muskett Ltd	704.26	7 Nov Lilly Trotter		145.23
		1,867.99	23 Nov UK Gas plc		621.56
			24 Nov Modaphone plc		453.62
			26 Nov Kibbley Limited		65.32
					1,597.21
			30 Nov Closing balance c/d		270.78
		1,867.99			1,867.99
1 Dec	Opening balance b/d	270.78			

Reconcile the bank statement details with the cash book as at 30 November.

Answer

First, we compare items shown in the bank statement with those shown in the cash book, by placing a tick against each one in each record. This leaves the standing order, the bank charges and the direct debit unticked in the statement, and the entries on 6 and 26 November unticked in the cash book.

We must then update the cash book for the three items unticked in the statement, as follows:

Bank

		£			£
1 Nov	Opening balance b/f	563.21	1 Nov Lotty Miller Fashions		48.23
12 Nov	Cash to bank	600.52	6 Nov Garry Hill Ltd		263.25
29 Nov	Netta Muskett Ltd	704.26	7 Nov Lilly Trotter		145.23
		1,867.99	23 Nov UK Gas plc		621.56
			24 Nov Modaphone plc		453.62
			26 Nov Kibbley Limited		65.32
					1,597.21
			30 Nov Closing balance c/d		270.78
		1,867.99			1,867.99
1 Dec	Opening balance b/d	270.78	5 Nov Water company		20.00
			19 Nov Bank charges		8.62
			30 Nov HP Finance		30.00
					58.62
			1 Dec Revised balance c/d		212.16
		270.78			270.78
1 Dec	Revised balance b/d	212.16			

Pause for thought

As we are adjusting the 1 December balance for the omitted entries, that date is used for both the c/d and b/d revised balances.

Then we reconcile the revised balance with the statement balance:

	£	£	
Balance as per bank statement		540.73	In hand
Less Unpresented cheques:			
Garry Hill Ltd	263.25		
Kibbley Limited	65.32		
		(328.57)	
Balance as per cash book		212.16	In hand

Pause for thought

Because debits and credits in the bank statement are reversed when shown in the cash book, it is better to avoid referring to bank balances as 'debit' or 'credit' balances. Use **in hand** or **overdrawn** to avoid confusion. Note also that brackets have been placed around the £328.57 figure. This is common practice to show an amount which is deducted from the figure immediately above it.

3.4 Control accounts

In the previous chapter, we saw how the two 'personal' ledgers, the sales ledger and the purchases ledger, contain the individual accounts of all the debtors and creditors of the business. Even a relatively small business may have hundreds of such accounts, whilst large companies may have many thousands, most of them within the sales ledger. With computer packages, the information can be processed speedily and efficiently. Information entered in, for example, a customer's invoice will automatically adjust the balance on that customer's sales ledger account. Where the system is non-computerised, it is possible to confirm the overall accuracy of the personal ledger entries by producing **control** (or 'total') **accounts**. These work on the simple principle that if you can produce one account which summarises the totals of all the thousands of individual entries which appear in a personal ledger, then the closing balance on that one account should be the same as the total of all the individual account balances within the personal ledger (see Figure 3.1). If they do not agree, one or more errors are present and must be rectified.

The 'control' operates due to the fact that the 'summarised totals' do not come from the personal ledger itself but from the appropriate book of prime entry. As these totals are used within the bookkeeping system to complete the

**Figure 3.1
Control accounts**

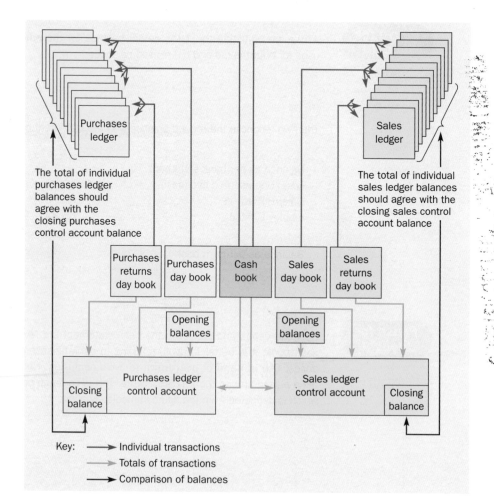

double-entry recording (e.g. by the total of the purchases day book being posted to the debit of the purchases account in the general ledger), the successful reconciliation of the control account with the total of the individual personal ledger accounts proves the arithmetical accuracy of that part of the system.

The main entries, and their source, which would be found in a typical sales ledger control account are shown below.

Sales ledger control account

Debit entries	(Source)	Credit entries	(Source)
Opening debtors[a]	Previous closing balance	Sales returns (Returns inwards)	Sales returns day book
Total credit sales	Sales day book	Cash and cheques received from debtors[b]	Cash book
		Closing debtors	(Balancing figure to be compared with total of individual balances in sales ledger)

[a] There may also be some credit balances within the sales ledger brought forward, resulting from overpayments, duplicated payments or customers returning goods after having paid for them.
[b] Any discounts allowed to customers would be shown separately (see Chapter 4), as would bad debts written off (see Chapter 5).

A typical purchases ledger control account would contain the following main entries:

Purchases ledger control account

Debit entries	(Source)	Credit entries	(Source)
Purchases returns (Returns outwards)	Purchases returns day book	Opening creditors[a]	Previous closing balance
Cash and cheques paid to creditors[b]	Cash book	Total credit purchases	Purchases day book
Closing creditors	(Balancing figure to be compared with total of individual balances in purchases ledger)		

[a] There may also be some debit balances within the purchases ledger brought forward, resulting from overpayments, duplicated payments or the company returning goods to suppliers after having paid for them.
[b] Any discounts received from suppliers would be shown separately (see Chapter 4).

Control accounts have a number of advantages for management:

● Total debtors and creditors figures can be produced at any time by balancing the control accounts. This avoids the need to calculate every individual balance within the personal ledgers.

● Fraud can be prevented if the person responsible for compiling and checking the control accounts is a supervisor unconnected with the day-to-day bookkeeping procedures. This also provides an independent check on the quality and accuracy of the accounting records.

● Errors within a double-entry bookkeeping system can be located to a specific ledger, which avoids unnecessary effort when finding mistakes.

● The control accounts themselves can be brought within the double-entry bookkeeping system as part of the general ledger, with the debtors' and creditors' individual accounts in the personal ledgers then being treated as detailed, 'subsidiary' records outside the system. This has the great advantage of summarising all the sales ledger and purchases ledger information within just two ledger accounts, with the balances on these accounts providing the debtors and creditors figures for the trial balance.

Activity 3.2

The following totals were extracted from the books of prime entry of Davinia Draycott for November:

	£
Cheques received from debtors	297,640
Cheques paid to creditors	216,900
Goods returned by customers	130
Goods returned to suppliers	650
Invoices issued to customers	316,595
Invoices received from suppliers	284,100

At 1 November, opening debtors were £47,210 and opening creditors were £14,600. At 30 November, the individual balances within the sales ledger totalled £66,035 and the individual balances within the purchases ledger totalled £82,750.

When Davinia extracted a trial balance as at 30 November, there was a difference of £1,600. Assuming that the entries in the general ledger and cash book were correct, which personal ledger contained the error? Draw up control accounts for each personal ledger to find out.

Answer

Sales ledger control account

	£		£
Opening debtors	47,210	Sales returns	130
Total sales invoices	316,595	Cheques received	297,640
		Closing debtors	66,035
		(balancing figure)	
	363,805		363,805

This ledger appears to be arithmetically correct, as the closing balance on the control account is the same as the total of the individual ledger balances.

Purchase ledger control account			
	£		£
Purchases returns	650	Opening creditors	14,600
Cheques paid	216,900	Total purchase invoices	284,100
Closing creditors (balancing figure)	81,150		
	298,700		298,700

As the total of the individual purchases ledger balances is £82,750 and the control account balance is £81,150, the error of £1,600 must be within this ledger.

3.5 Accounting adjustments

Once the bank reconciliation is completed and the control accounts agree with the personal ledgers, we can progress to consider the various accounting adjustments which are needed to comply with accounting concepts prior to preparation of the financial summaries of the business.

These summaries are prepared in relation to a **financial period**, which can be as short or as long as suits the business. However, it is usual for *annual* summaries to be prepared for taxation purposes or to comply with legislation. These are referred to as being for the *financial year*. The financial year need not be a calendar year, but usually ends on the last day of a month, for example 31 March.

Did you know?

Businesses set up as limited companies in the UK (see Chapter 7) have to comply with Acts of Parliament known as the Companies Acts, which set out detailed accounting requirements.

Pause for thought

Seasonal businesses traditionally choose a 'quiet' month to end their financial year so that their busiest trading time is not disrupted by the need to obtain accounting information. Many retail fashion stores choose February or March to end their financial year (i.e. the time between the January sales and the new spring collections appearing).

3.5.1 Unsold stock

This is **stock** which the business has bought during the period which is unsold at the end of the period and carried forward to the next period. In the general ledger, we show the information in a 'stock account'. This records *only* information relating to opening and closing stock, not goods bought during the period (which are shown in the purchases account in the general ledger). Due to the *prudence concept*, stock is valued at the *lower of cost and net realisable value*,[1] which in simple terms means either what the stock cost the business or the value it might fetch if for some reason (damage, changing fashions, etc.) it is anticipated that it could only be sold at a price less than cost (see Chapter 5 for further explanation of this). Stock is never valued at normal selling price, as that would anticipate a profit, which is unacceptable under the prudence concept.

---

[1] Accounting Standards Board (1990) Statement of Standard Accounting Practice (SSAP) 9 *Stocks and Long-term Contracts*. London: ASB.

Example 3.1

Bulk Buys, which has a financial year ending on 28 February, had opening unsold stock of £90,000 on 1 March 2004 and £70,000 unsold stock a year later on 28 February 2005. Show the entries in the Stock account.

General Ledger				

Stock

		£			£
1/3/04	Opening stock b/f	90,000	28/2/05	P & L account	90,000
28/2/05	P & L account	70,000	28/2/05	Closing stock c/d	70,000
		160,000			160,000
1/3/05	Opening stock b/d	70,000			

Pause for thought

'P & L account' stands for 'profit and loss account', the financial summary of income and expenditure (see section 3.6.1 of this chapter).

Note that we use the abbreviation **b/f** for 'brought forward' where we do not see the other side of the double entry on the same page. Similarly, we would use **c/f** (carried forward) instead of c/d for a closing balance where the balance is transferred to a different page.

In a trial balance prepared at the end of a financial period, it is usual to see the opening stock (i.e. the balance brought forward) as a debit entry representing the opening asset of unsold stock. The value of closing stock then appears as a note (usually the first) appended to the trial balance. The way in which stock values are shown in the financial summaries is explained later in this chapter. The accruals concept is relevant here, as by transferring values of unsold goods into the financial summaries, we are ensuring that the income from the sale of goods is matched only by the cost of those goods, and excludes the value of any *unsold* stock at the end of the period.

3.5.2 Accruals and prepayments

At the end of the financial period there are likely to be some expenses which are owing, other than normal 'trade creditors'. Often the bills have not been received, so an estimate must be made. Conversely, some expenses may have been paid in advance for a future period, in which case we extract the **prepayment** from the current period.

We have to make sure that the expenses shown in the financial summary cover only the stated period, neither more nor less than that. This is due to the application of the accruals concept, which states that *all* income and related expenditure for a specified period should be included, not simply money paid or received.

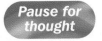

Example 3.2 **Adjustment for accruals**

Bulk Buys paid £4,000 for electricity during the year to 28 February 2005. The last bill paid was for the quarter ended 31 December 2004. Average bills for the winter quarter are £1,500.

Electricity

		£			£
(to 31/12/04)	Bank	4,000	28/2/05	P & L account	5,000
28/2/05	Accrual c/d	1,000			
		5,000			5,000
			1/3/05	Accrual b/d	1,000

Pause for thought

A quarter of a year is three months, but we need only an extra two months (January and February) to complete the information for Bulk Buys' financial year. We therefore estimate how much electricity would be used ($\frac{2}{3} \times$ £1,500) and insert this into the account as an accrual. The accrual is then brought down as a liability (credit balance) at the start of the new accounting period. £5,000 will be shown as the electricity expense for the year, whilst a liability of £1,000 is shown in the balance sheet.

Remember: **Add A**ccruals to expenses!

Example 3.3 **Adjustment for prepayments**

Bulk Buys paid £9,000 on 1 March 2004 for rent for the nine months to 30 November 2004 and £6,000 on 30 November 2004 for the half-year to 31 May 2005.

Rent

		£			£
1/3/04	Bank (9 months)	9,000	28/2/05	P & L account	12,000
30/11/04	Bank (6 months)	6,000	28/2/05	Prepayment c/d	3,000
		15,000			15,000
1/3/05	Prepayment b/d	3,000			

Pause for thought

If a financial summary is drawn up for a year, then it must show 12 months' information, not 9 or 15! The £15,000 paid during the year ended 28 February 2005 is for 15 months' rent, so we must take out the 'extra' three months, which is shown as a prepayment to be carried down as an asset (debit) balance at the start of the new accounting period. £12,000 is shown as the expense for rent in the profit and loss account, whilst £3,000 will be shown as an asset in the balance sheet.

Remember: **RE**duce expenses by the p**RE**payment!

Activity 3.3

Claudia Grimaldi completed her first year of business on 31 December 2004. During the year she paid an insurance premium of £2,400 by cheque on 1 October to insure a building for a twelve-month period from that date.

During the year 2004, she also paid three quarterly telephone bills on 1 April, 1 July and 1 October of £120, £180 and £240 respectively. Future bills are expected to keep increasing at the same rate as previously.

Show the insurance account and telephone account in the general ledger for the year ended 31 December 2004, showing the balances to be transferred to the profit and loss account and the balances brought down at the start of the following year.

Answer

Insurance

		£			£
1/10/04	Bank	2,400	31/12/04	P & L account	600
			31/12/04	Prepayment c/d	1,800
		2,400			2,400
1/1/05	Prepayment b/d	1,800			

Telephone

		£			£
1/4/04	Bank	120	31/12/04	P & L account	840
1/7/04	Bank	180			
1/10/04	Bank	240			
		540			
31/12/04	Accrual c/d	300			
		840			840
			1/1/05	Accrual b/d	300

Pause for thought

The profit and loss account will show insurance and telephone expenses for the year of £600 and £840 respectively, whilst the balance sheet at 31 December 2004 will record an asset of £1,800 (the insurance prepayment) and a liability of £300 (the telephone accrual).

3.5.3 Depreciation

Did you know?

'Tangible' means 'capable of being touched', i.e. 'physical' assets such as cars, machinery, buildings etc.

'Effluxion of time' means 'the passage of time'.

'Obsolescence' means becoming obsolete.

All fixed assets, with the exception of most freehold land, are subject to depreciation. **Depreciation** is defined as

The measure of the cost or revalued amount of the economic benefits of the tangible fixed asset that have been consumed during the period. Consumption includes the wearing out, using up or other reduction in the useful economic life of a **tangible fixed asset** *whether arising from use, effluxion of time or obsolescence through either changes in technology or demand for the goods and services produced by the asset.*[2]

_____

[2] Accounting Standards Board (1999) Financial Reporting Standard (FRS) 15 *Tangible Fixed Assets*. London: ASB.

Due to the accruals and prudence concepts, accountants have to make an estimate of the amount of depreciation which has been suffered by fixed assets during the financial period. This is then included within the profit and loss account as an expense. This estimate is based on three components, the last two of which are 'best guesses':

- The cost of the fixed asset, which is easily determined if purchased from an outside supplier. However, any installation costs incurred to bring the asset into a working condition should also be included as part of the cost. For example, if a factory wall had to be dismantled and rebuilt to allow the installation of a large machine, the building costs would be included as part of the cost of the fixed asset. If the fixed asset is built by the business itself, then labour costs and other directly attributable costs would be included as part of the cost of the asset.
- The **useful economic life** of the asset, which is the estimate of how long the fixed asset will continue to provide economic benefits to the organisation.
- The **residual value**, which is the estimate, based on prices prevailing at the date of acquiring the asset, of the value which the asset may have at the end of its useful economic life. In many cases, it is assumed that the asset will have no residual value.

For example, a welding robot is bought by a car manufacturer for £200,000 on 1 January 2004. It costs £40,000 to install the robot and it is expected to be used for a period of 10 years, after which it is expected to be sold to an industrial museum for £4,000.

- The cost is £240,000 (£200,000 + £40,000).
- The useful economic life is 10 years.
- The estimated residual value is £4,000.

A variety of methods can be used to calculate the amount of depreciation to be allocated to a specific financial period. The two most common methods are the straight line method and the reducing balance method.

The straight line method

This assumes that depreciation occurs evenly over the life of the asset, so the asset is written off in equal instalments over its useful economic life. In fact, the **straight line method** is sometimes called the equal instalment method. Straight line depreciation is used by most businesses for the vast majority of fixed assets. The formula for calculating depreciation under this method is:

$$\frac{\text{Cost} - \text{Estimated residual value}}{\text{Useful economic life in years}}$$

Did you know?

The depreciation rate under the straight line method can also be expressed as a percentage. For example, 20% p.a. straight line depreciation means equal instalments over 5 years, 25% p.a. straight line is over 4 years, and so on.

The welding robot (see above) would be depreciated over 10 years at:

$$\frac{(£240,000 - £4,000)}{10} = £23,600 \text{ p.a.}$$

Bulk Buys bought a forklift truck for £30,000 on 1 March 2004. It was estimated to last for 5 years, when it would be worth about £4,000. What is the annual depreciation under the straight line method?

Answer

$$\text{Annual depreciation} = \frac{(\text{Cost} - \text{Residual value})}{\text{Useful economic life in years}}$$

$$= \frac{(30,000 - 4,000)}{5} = £5,200 \text{ p.a.}$$

The reducing balance method

The **reducing balance method** assumes higher depreciation in earlier years than in later years and is used where it is clear that greater economic benefits are provided by assets when new than when they become older – perhaps as a result of general wear causing them to become more prone to breakdown or less capable of producing a high-quality product. The method (sometimes called the 'diminishing balance' method) works by applying a given (or calculated) percentage to the net book value (i.e. cost less accumulated depreciation up to the date of the calculation).

Pause for thought

It is rare for students to be asked to calculate the percentage used for the reducing balance method! However, the formula is:

$$r = 1 - \sqrt[n]{\frac{s}{c}}$$

where r = percentage, n = useful life, s = residual value and c = original cost.

Bulk Buys paid £12,000 for a car for a sales manager on 1 March 2003. The depreciation rate is 40% p.a. Show the depreciation on a reducing balance basis.

Answer

Cost	12,000
Depreciation: Year to 29 February 2004 (40% × £12,000)	4,800
	7,200
Depreciation: Year to 28 February 2005 (40% × £7,200)	2,880
	4,320
Depreciation: Year to 28 February 2006 (40% × £4,320)	1,728
	2,592

and so on until sold or scrapped

Bookkeeping for depreciation

Depreciation is an expense – a loss – to the business, so the depreciation for the financial period will be included within the profit and loss account. The value of the fixed asset, as adjusted for depreciation, will be included on the balance sheet. Fixed assets are not shown individually, but grouped into classes of assets, for example 'land and buildings', 'machinery', 'motor vehicles', 'fixtures and fittings'. The process of charging depreciation is known as 'making a provision', or **providing** for depreciation, and the bookkeeping requires separate provision accounts to be opened for each class of asset.

Pause for thought

If a company has leasehold premises (buildings which it does not own, but for which it has paid an amount to the owner for the right to use them over a defined period), the term **amortisation** is used rather than 'depreciation'. Amortisation is derived from two French words, *à mortir*, meaning 'to the death', as the cost of the lease is being reduced to zero over its life, usually by the straight line method. For example, if a business paid £50,000 for the right to use a building over 20 years, it would be amortised at the rate of £2,500 p.a. over that time.

Activity 3.6

Show the ledger accounts required to record the bookkeeping entries for Bulk Buys in Activities 3.4 and 3.5 above, for the first three years of the assets' lives.

Answer

Forklift truck

		£			£
1/3/04	Cost	30,000	28/2/05	Balance c/d	30,000
1/3/05	Balance b/d	30,000	28/2/06	Balance c/d	30,000
1/3/06	Balance b/d	30,000	28/2/07	Balance c/d	30,000
1/3/07	Balance b/d	30,000			

Car

		£			£
1/3/03	Cost	12,000	29/2/04	Balance c/d	12,000
1/3/04	Balance b/d	12,000	28/2/05	Balance c/d	12,000
1/3/05	Balance b/d	12,000	28/2/06	Balance c/d	12,000
1/3/06	Balance b/d	12,000			

Provision for depreciation on forklift truck

		£			£
28/2/05	Balance c/d	5,200	28/2/05	P & L account	5,200
28/2/06	Balance c/d	10,400	1/3/05	Balance b/d	5,200
			28/2/06	P & L account	5,200
		10,400			10,400
			1/3/06	Balance b/d	10,400
28/2/07	Balance c/d	15,600	28/2/07	P & L account	5,200
		15,600			15,600
			1/3/07	Balance b/d	15,600

Answer
continued

Provision for depreciation on car

		£			£
29/2/04	Balance c/d	4,800	29/2/04	P & L account	4,800
28/2/05	Balance c/d	7,680	1/3/04	Balance b/d	4,800
			28/2/05	P & L account	2,880
		7,680			7,680
28/2/06	Balance c/d	9,408	1/3/05	Balance b/d	7,680
			28/2/06	P & L account	1,728
		9,408			9,408
			1/3/06	Balance b/d	9,408

Pause for thought

Every balance carried down at the end of each financial period will appear in the balance sheet at that date. For example, the car will be shown in the balance sheet at 28 February 2006 at cost £12,000, less depreciation £9,408, leaving a 'net book value' of £2,592. Each of the items marked 'P & L account' will be shown as an expense (loss) in the profit and loss account for that financial period, for example £1,728 will be shown in the profit and loss account for the year ended 28 February 2006 as 'depreciation on car'.

3.6 The financial summaries?

We can now consider the way in which the two key financial summaries, the profit and loss account and balance sheet, are presented. Let's recall the various stages we have passed through to reach this point.

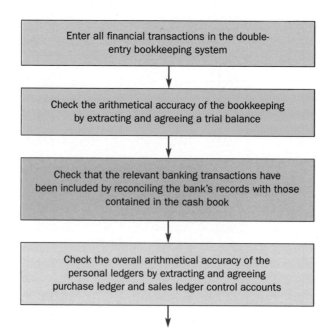

Enter all financial transactions in the double-entry bookkeeping system

Check the arithmetical accuracy of the bookkeeping by extracting and agreeing a trial balance

Check that the relevant banking transactions have been included by reconciling the bank's records with those contained in the cash book

Check the overall arithmetical accuracy of the personal ledgers by extracting and agreeing purchase ledger and sales ledger control accounts

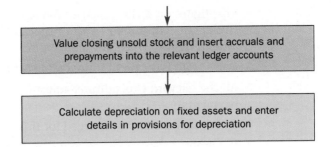

Value closing unsold stock and insert accruals and prepayments into the relevant ledger accounts

Calculate depreciation on fixed assets and enter details in provisions for depreciation

3.6.1 The profit and loss account

Also known as the income, or revenue, statement, this summary of all the income and expenditure for the financial period is part of the double-entry bookkeeping system but, unlike all other accounts, is not usually split into debit and credit sides but is shown in a 'vertical' or 'columnar' format. In many mainland European countries, however, it is normal practice to show expenses on the debit side and income on the credit side. In the UK, the normal layout for a trading business's profit and loss account is shown below, using invented data for illustration.

ABC & Co.
Profit and loss account for the year ended 30 June 2005[1]

	£	£
Sales[2]		500,000
Less Cost of goods sold		
Opening stock at 1 July 2004	15,000	
Add Purchases[3]	230,000	
	245,000	
Less Closing stock at 30 June 2005	(45,000)	
		(200,000)[4]
Gross profit[5]		300,000
Less Expenses[6]		
Wages	45,000	
Rent and rates	23,000	
Depreciation[7]	32,000	
(other expenses listed . . .)	80,000	
		(180,000)
Net profit[8]		120,000

Notes:

1 Sometimes this statement is referred to as the 'trading and profit and loss account', as the first section leading to the gross profit is known as the **trading account**. However, the modern style of heading usually omits the reference to 'trading'.

2 All the sales for the period, whether paid for or not.

3 All the goods bought for resale in the period, whether paid for or not.

4 This figure (and the expenses figure of £180,000 below it) is derived from the details contained in the inner column. Brackets are usually placed around figures which are deducted from the figure immediately above.

5 **Gross profit** is the profit from trading before overhead expenditure is deducted.

6 All the relevant expenditure, adjusted where necessary for accruals and pre-payments.

7 Only the depreciation charged for this financial period.

8 **Net profit** is sometimes referred to as **operating profit**. It is the profit after all expenses have been deducted.

3.6.2 The balance sheet

This summary of all the assets, liabilities and capital balances at the end of the financial period is not part of the double-entry bookkeeping system but is, like the trial balance, a list of balances remaining within the accounts at a specific time. As with the profit and loss account, many countries show the balance sheet in a two-sided 'account' format but, in the UK, the normal layout for a balance sheet is as follows, again using invented data for illustration.

ABC & Co.
Balance sheet as at 30 June 2005[1]

	Cost	Depreciation[2]	Net book value[3]
	£	£	£
Fixed assets[4]			
Land and buildings	153,600	42,500	111,100
Motor vehicles	65,000	17,500	47,500
Fixtures	15,100	8,300	6,800
	233,700	68,300	165,400
Current assets[5]			
Stock		45,000	
Debtors		23,000	
Prepayments		4,000	
Bank		2,000	
Cash		600	
		74,600	
Less Current liabilities			
Creditors	33,000		
Accruals	5,200		
		(38,200)	
Net current assets[6]			36,400[7]
Total net assets			201,800
Capital			
Opening balance, 1 July 2004		146,700	
Add Net profit[8]		120,000	
		266,700	
Less Drawings		(64,900)	
Closing balance, 30 June 2005			201,800

Notes:

1 The balance sheet is always dated as the last day of the financial period, never for the year ended . . . .

2 All the depreciation on each class of assets, not just the depreciation for that financial period.

3 These three headings refer only to the fixed assets section.

4 There are other acceptable ways of showing this information, e.g.:

Land and buildings at cost	153,600
Less Accumulated depreciation	42,500
	111,100

and so on.

5 Shown in increasing order of liquidity, so the most liquid asset, cash, is shown at the end. 'Liquidity' simply means the ability to be converted into cash.

6 Also known as working capital.

7 As with the profit and loss account, figures in the right-hand columns are derived from the details contained in the inner columns.

8 The net profit for the year, as shown in the profit and loss account (see page 55).

3.7 Summary

A trial balance extracted from the ledger at the end of a financial period will show:

- Information derived from opening balances at the start of the year
- Invoiced transactions during the year
- Cash paid and received during the year

All entered in accordance with the double-entry bookkeeping system.

A trial balance extracted from the ledger at the end of a financial period will *not* show the following, which must therefore be adjusted before preparing the profit and loss account and balance sheet:

Closing stock	*Closing accruals*	*Closing prepayments*	*Depreciation for the current period*
Unsold goods at the end of the financial period, valued at the lower of 'cost and net realisable value'	Overheads incurred in the period but not yet invoiced	Overheads paid for in the period but relating in whole or in part to the following period	The estimated loss in value of a fixed asset caused by factors such as wear and tear and obsolescence

3.8 Glossary

Accrual	An expense owing at the end of a financial period where the bill has not yet been received.
Amortisation	The equivalent of depreciation, as applied to leasehold premises.
B/f	Abbreviation for 'brought forward', used where we do not see the other side of the double-entry of an opening account balance on the same page.
Balance sheet	The financial summary which records assets, liabilities and capital at the end of a financial period.
Bank reconciliation statement	A statement prepared to reconcile the information appearing in the bank account in the business's cash book with the bank statements showing the bank's records of the account.
C/f	Abbreviation for 'carried forward', used where we do not see the other side of the double-entry of a closing account balance on the same page.
Cash flow statement	A summary of all the inflows and outflows of cash and bank transactions during a period.
Control accounts	Total accounts summarising all the individual transactions in the purchases ledger and sales ledger to check on accuracy and completeness.
Depreciation	The loss in value of a fixed asset over time.
Financial period	The period, often a year, used as the time interval for summarising financial information.
Gross profit	The difference between income from sales and the cost of the goods sold, before overhead expenditure has been deducted.
In hand	A bank balance with a positive balance (a debit balance in the business's books, but a credit balance in the bank's ledger).
Net profit	Also called *operating profit*, this is the gross profit plus any sundry income, less overhead expenditure.
Operating profit	Another term for *net profit*, usually seen in the profit and loss account of a limited company (see Chapter 7).
Overdraft	A bank balance with a negative balance (a credit balance in the business's books, but a debit balance in the bank's ledger).
Prepayment	An expense paid in one financial period where the benefits are not received until some future period.
Profit and loss account	The financial summary which records the income and expenditure for a financial period.
Provision	An amount set aside out of profits where the amount cannot be determined with accuracy, for example, a provision for depreciation.
Reducing balance method	A method of calculating depreciation using the assumption that the loss in value is greater in the early years than in the later years of the asset's life.
Residual value	The estimate of value at the end of a fixed asset's useful economic life.
Stock	The value of unsold goods, also known as an inventory.
Straight line method	A method of calculating depreciation using the assumption that the loss in value occurs evenly over the life of the asset.
Tangible fixed asset	A fixed asset with physical properties, such as land, machinery, cars, etc.
Trading account	The first section of the profit and loss account, where the gross profit is calculated. Sometimes included as part of the description of that statement, that is, *Trading and profit and loss account*.
Unpresented cheque	A cheque sent to a creditor by the business but not yet banked by that creditor.
Useful economic life	The estimate of how long a fixed asset will be of use to the business.
Working capital	Another term for net current assets, the difference between current assets and current liabilities on the balance sheet.

1 A cash flow statement shows:
   a The profit of a business
   b The money coming into and going out of a business
   c The income and expenditure of a business
   d The assets and liabilities of a business

2 On checking a bank statement against the bank account details in the cash book, you find that a direct debit for rates has not been entered in the cash book. Do you:
   a Debit the bank account and credit the rates account
   b Debit the rates account and credit the bank account
   c Debit the rates account and credit the bank statement
   d Not enter the direct debit as it affects only the bank statement

3 A credit balance may appear on a sales ledger account because:
   a A supplier has overpaid
   b A sales invoice has been duplicated
   c A customer may have returned goods after paying for them
   d The business has repaid an overpayment by a customer

4 Which of the following represent advantages of control accounts?
   a They can make it harder to find total debtors and creditors figures
   b They can help in finding spelling mistakes
   c They can help in locating errors to a specific ledger
   d They can help to find if a payment for rent has been posted to the rates account

5 Relating to the opening and closing stock for a financial period, which of the following is true?
   a Both figures are shown in the profit and loss account but only the opening stock is shown in the balance sheet
   b Only the opening stock is shown in the profit and loss account, but both figures are shown in the balance sheet
   c Both figures are shown in the profit and loss account but only the closing stock is shown in the balance sheet
   d Only the closing stock is shown in the profit and loss account, but both figures are shown in the balance sheet

6 If a business has paid gas bills totalling £34,000 during a financial period but owes £3,000 for gas by the end of the period, what will be the opening balance in the gas account at the start of the following period?
   a £37,000 credit
   b £3,000 debit
   c £31,000 debit
   d £3,000 credit

7 A business paid a £720 subscription to a trade magazine on 30 June 2004, for the two years to 1 July 2006. The business's financial year ends on 30 November 2004. What relevant figures for subscriptions will be shown in the financial summaries for that period?
   a £150 in the profit and loss account, £570 prepayment in the balance sheet
   b £720 in the profit and loss account, nil in the balance sheet
   c £360 in the profit and loss account, £360 prepayment in the balance sheet
   d £1,440 in the profit and loss account, £720 prepayment in the balance sheet

8   A business buys a car which costs £15,000. This price includes £500 for insurance and £60 for road tax. The business's name was painted on the side of the car at an additional cost of £160. The car is expected to be in use for 5 years, after which time it will have an estimated value of £4,600. What is the annual depreciation if the straight line method is used?

   a £2,000

   b £2,112

   c £1,968

   d £2,080

9   A machine is bought for £18,000, plus £3,000 installation costs. It is to be depreciated on a reducing balance basis using a rate of 60% p.a. What is the depreciation to be charged in the second year of the asset's ownership?

   a £12,600

   b £4,320

   c £5,040

   d £8,400

10 Cost of goods sold equals:

   a Opening stock plus purchases plus closing stock

   b Opening stock less purchases plus closing stock

   c Closing stock plus purchases less opening stock

   d Opening stock plus purchases less closing stock

(Answers in Appendix 1)

 ## Self-study questions

(Answers in Appendix 2)

Question 3.1
   a Explain the need for, and give examples of, *controls* within a bookkeeping system.

   b From the following information, produce sales ledger and purchase ledger control accounts, showing the closing debtors and creditors in the relevant accounts.

	£
Opening creditors	92,100
Opening debtors	86,250
Opening credit balances on the sales ledger	370
Cheques paid to suppliers	472,450
Cheques received from debtors	577,800
Goods returned by 'credit' customers	3,200
Goods returned to suppliers	770
Sales invoices issued	610,200
Purchase invoices received	463,750

Question 3.2
   a Explain how the *accruals concept* affects the information to be disclosed within a profit and loss account.

   b Write up the relevant general ledger accounts of Polly Harris for the year ended 30 April 2005 for the following information:

     (i)   She had opening unsold stock of £50,000 and £60,000 unsold stock a year later.

     (ii) She paid £4,000 for telephone charges during the year for 10 months' usage, but the final two months are owing. The next quarter's bill is expected to be £1,350.

     (iii) She paid £15,000 at the very start of the year for rent for the first six months and then paid £22,500 on 1 November 2004. The monthly rent did not change during the period.

Question 3.3 **a** Define *depreciation* and explain its relevance to key accounting concepts.

b Show the relevant fixed asset accounts and provision for depreciation accounts for the following information for each of the three financial years ending 31 December 2006.

	£
Machinery at cost, 1 January 2004	65,000
Computers at cost, 1 January 2004	20,000
Motor cars at cost, 1 January 2005	45,000
Estimated residual value of machinery after 5 years' useful economic life	5,000
Estimated residual value of computers after 4 years' useful economic life	nil

Basis of depreciation: machinery and computers – straight line
Basis of depreciation: motor cars – 40% on reducing balance

c Show how the information relating to fixed assets and depreciation would appear in the profit and loss account for the year ended 31 December 2006 and the balance sheet as at that date.

Question 3.4 From the following information relating to Louise Jones, prepare the profit and loss account for the year ended 30 November 2005 and a balance sheet as at that date. Assume that relevant expense totals have been adjusted for accruals and prepayments.

	£
Accountancy	350
Accruals at 30 November 2005	130
Advertising	285
Bank balance (asset)	3,600
Bank charges (an expense)	74
Cash balance	120
Closing stock	12,400
Creditors at end of period	8,140
Debtors at end of period	7,384
Depreciation for the year on fixtures and fittings	800
Depreciation for the year on motor van	1,600
Drawings	7,500
Fixtures and fittings at cost	11,400
Light and heat	1,030
Motor van at cost	8,900
Motor expenses	518
Net profit for the year	?
Opening stock	7,224
Opening capital balance at 1 December 2004	23,652
Postage and printing	390
Prepayments at 30 November 2005	200
Purchases	49,600
Rent and rates	2,900
Repairs	810
Sales	75,972
Telephone and insurance	619
Total depreciation on fixtures and fittings at 30 November 2005	4,200
Total depreciation on motor van at 30 November 2005	4,800
Wages	11,590

> Case study

Esmeralda appears, then disappears

The busiest time for any children's entertainer is Christmas, and Marvin (see previous case studies) was finding that as the year progressed he was in great demand. He felt he needed an assistant so decided to employ Esmeralda, who had previously been chief inventor at Kaboosh Limited, a company manufacturing equipment for magic tricks and novelties. As a leaving present, that company had given Esmeralda a 'disappearing lady' apparatus. Being unsentimental about such things, she promptly sold it to Marvin on 1 December 2000 for £2,000. Esmeralda started to appear (and disappear) as part of Marvin's magic act.

After two months in her new job, Esmeralda persuaded Marvin to diversify by buying in items made by her former employers and selling them at the children's parties to the parents and guests.

During January 2001, Marvin received a letter from his bank, asking for financial summaries for his first six months in business. January is a quiet month for him, so he spent some time producing the following information:

Cash and cheques received

	£
Sales of novelties bought from Kaboosh Ltd	2,500
Appearance fees as entertainer	18,320

Cash and cheques paid

Kaboosh Ltd for novelties to be sold	1,500
Wages	1,200
Kazam Limited for playing cards	400
Travel expenses	2,600
Rabbits and rabbit food, less returns (expenses)	430
Cleaning	140
Esmeralda for 'disappearing lady' apparatus	2,000
Marvin's drawings	11,890

Other information

Cash balance at 31 December 2000	560
Bank balance at 31 December 2000	120
Total invoices received from Kaboosh Ltd up to 31 December 2000	1,700
Stock of unsold novelties at cost price at 31 December 2000 (NB: no 'opening stock')	80
Amounts owing from customers for novelties	350
Other fixed assets still owned at 31 December 2000:	
Costume at cost	3,000
Magic book at cost	2,000
Opening capital (see case study in Chapter 2)	5,020

Notes:

1 The costume, the magic book and the playing cards are to be grouped as 'Magician's equipment' and depreciated at 20% p.a. (that is, over 5 years), straight line method, with no residual value. Note that the period here is only six months.

2 The 'disappearing lady' apparatus is to be depreciated at 40% p.a. on the reducing balance method. The full six months' depreciation is to be deducted, even though it was owned for only part of that time.

3 Marvin owed £100 wages to Esmeralda at 31 December, and had paid £50 in December for a train ticket which was going to be used in January.

Required:
Prepare, as neatly as possible, Marvin's profit and loss account for the six months to 31 December 2000, and a balance sheet as at that date. Note that in the profit and loss account, gross profit on novelties should be calculated first and the fees added to that before deducting the expenses.

(Answers in Appendix 3)

References

A discussion on cash flow can be found on the Biz/ed site:
www.bized.ac.uk/stafsup/options/cashflow5.htm

> Now look at this book's dedicated website at **www.pearsoned.co.uk/black** and work through the various additional exercises for this chapter.

Chapter 4

The profit and loss account and balance sheet

Objectives	When you have read this chapter you will be able to:

- ➤ Appreciate that accounting is not an exact science
- ➤ Understand and apply the profit and loss account layouts for manufacturing, trading and service businesses
- ➤ Be aware of the use of the appropriation account by partnerships and limited companies
- ➤ Understand the place of the profit and loss account and balance sheet within the bookkeeping system and be aware that they can be shown in an 'account' format as well as in vertical or columnar style
- ➤ Be aware that limited companies publish financial summaries which must follow prescribed formats
- ➤ Draw up a detailed profit and loss account and balance sheet from a trial balance, adjusting for such items as accruals, prepayments and depreciation

4.1   Introduction

In the previous chapter we saw how the financial summaries reflect the application of accounting concepts to financial information. The two key summaries we have already encountered are the *profit and loss account*, showing income and expenses for a financial period, and the *balance sheet* showing assets, liabilities and capital at the end of the financial period. In this chapter we look in more detail at these, showing how the statements can be made more meaningful for different types of business organisations and also how they link with the double-entry bookkeeping system. We also address some specific problem areas.

4.2 What is 'profit'?

Profit (or, indeed, **loss**) is ascertained by comparing income with expenses which, according to the accruals (matching) concept, must reflect all the relevant transactions for the financial period, not just those which represent cash and cheques received or paid. Although this appears quite straightforward, jokes are sometimes made about accountants who, when asked by a business owner what profit their business has made, would reply, 'How much would you like it to be?', implying that by skilful accounting surgery the final figures could be as high or low as suited the needs of the business. Indeed, one author went so far as to suggest that 'Every company in the country is fiddling its profits. Every set of published accounts is based on books which have been gently cooked or completely roasted.'[1] Because some of the information (such as depreciation) found in the financial summaries relies on estimates, it is true to say that accounting is not an exact science. However, in the past 30 years, and particularly since the formation of the Accounting Standards Board in 1990, the UK regulatory framework has tightened in a concerted attempt to overcome the real anxieties expressed by users regarding the reliability of financial information. For many years, all limited companies had to appoint an independent **auditor** to report on whether the financial summaries reflected a *true and fair view* of the company's affairs. In recent times, however, this requirement for a compulsory audit has been removed from small companies, though they can opt to appoint an independent auditor if they wish.

4.3 The format of the profit and loss account

The format of the **profit and loss account** will vary depending upon whether the organisation is

- a manufacturing business (i.e. making the goods they sell),
- a trading business (i.e. buying goods for resale), or
- a service business (i.e. selling a service for a fee).

There will be further differences depending upon whether the organisation has been structured as

- a sole trader (i.e. a one-person business),
- a partnership (two or more owners of the business), or
- a limited company (a business with shareholders).

Figure 4.1 shows the various components within the profit and loss account for each type of business.

Note that the statement as a whole is referred to as the *profit and loss account* despite the fact that it might contain three, or even four, separate accounts. It is permissible to include the names of each of the accounts within the title, so for a manufacturing business you could call the statement the 'manufacturing, trading and profit and loss accounts' rather than simply the 'profit and loss account'. However, nearly all UK limited companies use the simplified heading in their published financial information.

---

[1] Griffiths, I. (1986) *Creative Accounting*. London: Waterstone & Co.

Figure 4.1
Components of the profit and loss account

	Type of organisation					
	Manufacturing	Trading	Service	Sole trader	Partnership	Limited company
Component of P & L account						
Manufacturing account	✓	✗	✗		✓ (if manufacturing)	
Trading account		✓	✗		✓ (if trading)	
Profit and loss account		✓			✓	

Key: ✓ = Relevant   ✗ = Not relevant

4.3.1 Manufacturing businesses

Companies which manufacture the products which they sell will have specific costs relating to the manufacturing process, which are summarised in a separate account before being transferred into the trading account. The expenses are allocated as follows:

- **Direct costs**, which can be readily identified with the items being produced. For example, in a ship-building company, the cost of metal and the other fittings used to construct the ship, plus the wages paid to the metalworkers and fitters, are direct costs. In a sweet factory, direct costs would be the cost of sugar, colourings and other ingredients. Another name for direct costs is **prime costs**.

- **Indirect costs** are all other manufacturing expenses which cannot be directly associated with the items being produced. These could include the rent of a shipyard or factory, the wages paid to supervisors, the cost of running the staff canteen, etc.

More information regarding the classification of costs is given in Chapter 12.

Activity 4.1

During the year to 31 December 2005, Bert Bodlington incurs the following costs in his factory, which produces cakes for sale to hotels and restaurants:

	£
Flour	63,250
Sugar	23,580
Chocolate	12,560
Cream	3,562
Wages to factory workers	74,120
Wages owed to factory workers	6,300
Factory rent and rates	12,500

	£
Factory light and heat	8,543
Wages to supervisors	26,100
Depreciation of factory machinery	3,910
Stock of raw materials on 1 January 2005	12,400
Stock of raw materials on 31 December 2005	11,500
Partly completed stock (work-in-progress) on 1 January 2005	1,540
Partly completed stock (work-in-progress) on 31 December 2005	640

Prepare the manufacturing account for the year ended 31 December 2005.

Answer

Bert Bodlington
Manufacturing account for the year ended 31 December 2005

	£	£
Raw materials		
Opening stock at 1 January 2005	12,400	
Add Purchases of raw materials	102,952	
	115,352	
Less Closing stock at 31 December 2005	(11,500)	
Cost of raw materials		103,852
Other direct costs:		
Production labour		80,420
Prime cost of production		184,272
Indirect factory costs:		
Rent and rates	12,500	
Light and heat	8,543	
Wages to supervisors	26,100	
Depreciation of factory machinery	3,910	
		51,053
		235,325
Add Opening work-in-progress	1,540	
Less Closing work-in-progress	(640)	
		900
Total factory production cost c/d		236,225

Pause for thought

The **manufacturing account** summarises all the factory costs for the period (including those not yet paid for, such as the accrued wages), dividing them between direct and indirect and adjusting for opening and closing stocks of raw materials and **work-in-progress**. The 'c/d' on the last line indicates that this figure is taken into the next section, the trading account, to form part of the 'cost of sales' to be compared with the sales revenue (see p. 68).

4.3.2 The trading account

The **trading account** calculates the *gross profit* of the organisation for the financial period by comparing the total sales revenue with the cost of the goods sold. In a business which does not make the products it sells, the layout of the trading account (using invented figures) would be as follows:

(Name of trader)
Trading account for the year ended 30 June 2005

	£	£
Sales		600,000
Less Cost of goods sold		
Opening stock at 1 July 2004	35,000	
Add Purchases	460,000	
	495,000	
Less Closing stock at 30 June 2005	(52,000)	
		(443,000)
Gross profit		157,000

In a manufacturing business, the **total factory production cost** is 'brought down' as part of the cost of goods sold.

Activity 4.2

Bert Bodlington (see Activity 4.1), in addition to his own manufactured cakes, buys in speciality wedding cakes from another manufacturer. He provides the following further information for the year ended 31 December 2005:

	£
Sales to hotels and restaurants for the year (all products)	488,060
Purchases from Gretna Cake plc during the year	25,670
Stock of cakes on 1 January 2005	36,709
Stock of cakes on 31 December 2005	29,670

Prepare the trading account for the year ended 31 December 2005.

Answer

Bert Bodlington
Trading account for the year ended 31 December 2005

	£	£
Sales		488,060
Less Cost of goods sold		
Opening stock at 1 January 2005	36,709	
Add Purchases	25,670	
Total factory production cost b/d	236,225	
	298,604	
Less Closing stock at 31 December 2005	(29,670)	
		(268,934)
Gross profit		219,126

Pause for thought

Total factory production cost is 'b/d' from the manufacturing account (see Activity 4.1).

In a manufacturing business, there are likely to be three different types of stock at the start and end of the financial period: raw materials, work-in-progress (partly completed goods) and finished goods. The first two stock types appear in the manufacturing account, the last in the trading account, but all three closing stock figures would appear in the balance sheet.

4.3.3 Service businesses

An organisation which does not buy or make goods for resale is known as a 'service' business. Neither a manufacturing nor a trading account would be appropriate in this case. Instead, the financial summary starts with the fees earned from the services provided, any sundry income is added to this and then overhead expenses are deducted to calculate net profit, as in the example of an architect (using invented figures) which follows.

Len Corbusier, Architect
Profit and loss account for the year ended 30 April 2005

	£	£
Fees – professional services		192,410
Add Bank interest received		120
		192,530
Less Expenses		
Assistants' wages	65,310	
Secretarial wages	19,640	
Stationery	7,296	
Travel and accommodation	17,630	
Telephone charges	3,260	
Office rent and rates	14,633	
Depreciation of motor car	4,000	
Depreciation of office fittings	2,500	
Sundry expenses	3,400	
		(137,669)
Net profit		54,861

Did you know?

Net profit is also known as operating profit, and all limited companies would describe it as such in their published profit and loss accounts (see Chapter 7).

Trading and manufacturing companies also have to calculate their net profit, in which case the format of the profit and loss account would follow that of the architect given above, with 'gross profit' being substituted for 'fees for professional services'.

Activity 4.3

Show the combined manufacturing, trading and profit and loss accounts of Bert Bodlington (see Activities 4.1 and 4.2) for the year ended 31 December 2005, assuming that the office expenses totalled £110,320 and other administration expenses (including depreciation) totalled £68,471.

Bert Bodlington
Profit and loss account for the year ended 31 December 2005

	£	£
Raw materials		
Opening stock at 1 January 2005	12,400	
Add Purchases of raw materials	102,952	
	115,352	
Less Closing stock at 31 December 2005	(11,500)	
Cost of raw materials		103,852
Other direct costs:		
Production labour		80,420
Prime cost of production		184,272
Indirect factory costs:		
Rent and rates	12,500	
Light and heat	8,543	
Wages to supervisors	26,100	
Depreciation of factory machinery	3,910	
		51,053
		235,325
Add Opening work-in-progress	1,540	
Less Closing work-in-progress	(640)	
		900
Total factory production cost c/d		236,225
Sales		488,060
Less **Cost of goods sold**		
Opening stock at 1 January 2005	36,709	
Add Purchases	25,670	
Total factory production cost b/d	236,225	
	298,604	
Less Closing stock at 31 December 2005	(29,670)	
		(268,934)
Gross profit		219,126
Less **expenses**		
Office expenses	110,320	
Administration expenses (including depreciation)	68,471	
		(178,791)
Net profit		40,335

If Bert did not manufacture products, the statement would start with the 'sales' figure, and then 'cost of goods sold' (excluding the factory production cost) would be deducted to arrive at the gross profit.

Pause for thought

Many students have difficulties in knowing which numbers are entered in which columns. In Bert's profit and loss account above, there are two columns. The right-hand column has the summarised totals, which are derived from the detail placed in the inner column. Sometimes you see a third column (for example, see the answer to Activity 4.4 on page 76), where further detail is given to analyse the information in the second column. So the information flows like this:

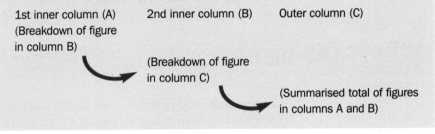

1st inner column (A)
(Breakdown of figure in column B)

2nd inner column (B)

Outer column (C)

(Breakdown of figure in column C)

(Summarised total of figures in columns A and B)

4.3.4 The appropriation account

Some types of businesses also show an **appropriation account,** which follows on immediately after the net profit or loss shown on the last line of the profit and loss account. Whilst it is not relevant where the business has a *sole* owner, for a partnership its function is to reflect the financial implications of the partnership agreement by allocating profits or losses between partners. For a limited company it shows deductions for taxation liabilities, dividends and transfers to reserves. Example 4.1 shows the basic layout, but these topics are covered in detail in Chapter 7.

Example 4.1

Appropriation accounts

a Assume that Bert Bodlington (see Activity 4.3) has a partner, Betty Worthingdene, and that they have agreed to share profits in the ratio 3:2. The appropriation account follows on directly after the net profit as shown in the profit and loss account:

(Bodlington and Worthingdene)

	£	£
Net profit (as in profit and loss account)		40,335
Divided as follows:		
Bert Bodlington ($^3/_5$)	24,201	
Betty Worthingdene ($^2/_5$)	16,134	
		40,335

If the partnership agreement includes other financial implications such as salaries to partners, etc., these would also be shown.

b Assume that Bert Bodlington set up his business as a limited company (i.e. a separate legal entity with shareholders). The company would be subject to taxation on its profits, might declare a dividend to transfer profit to shareholders, and will keep any surplus profit as a reserve within the company. As with the partnership example shown above, a limited company appropriation account follows on directly after the net profit, as shown below (using estimated figures for taxation and dividends):

(Bodlington Limited)

	£
Net profit (as in profit and loss account)	40,335
Less Taxation	(10,230)
Net profit after taxation	30,105
Less Dividends	(14,000)
Retained profit for the year, added to reserves	16,105

4.4 The balance sheet

This is the summary of a business's assets, liabilities and capital, reflecting the accounting equation Assets – Liabilities = Capital (A – L = C). It shows all the balances carried down within ledger accounts at the end of the financial period, though 'interim' balance sheets could be produced at any time. The basic contents of the balance sheet are similar, whether the business is in the manufacturing, trading or service sectors. However, if the business is structured as either a partnership or a limited company, additional items of information will be given, as shown in Figure 4.2. This is covered in more detail in Chapter 7.

Figure 4.2
Balance sheets for different forms of business organisations

	Business type		
	Sole trader	Partnership	Limited company
Balance sheet heading			
Fixed assets	✓	✓	✓
Current assets	✓	✓	✓
Current liabilities (Creditors due for payment within one year)	✓	✓	✓ (with taxation included in this heading)
Long-term liabilities (Creditors due for payment after more than one year)	✓ (if any)	✓ (if any)	✓ (if any)
Capital account	✓	✓ (one for each partner)	✗
Partners' current accounts[a]	✗	✓ (one for each partner if maintained)	✗
Share capital[a]	✗	✗	✓
Reserves[a]	✗	✗	✓

Key: ✓ = Relevant   ✗ = Not relevant
[a] explained in Chapter 7.

4.5 Alternative formats: 'horizontal' layout

The financial statements presented within this chapter have all been produced following the **vertical** or **columnar layout**, which is followed by the vast majority of UK organisations. Remember that the profit and loss account (though not the balance sheet) is part of the double-entry bookkeeping system, so even though that account might not be shown as being split between debit and credit sides, each entry within it will have been transferred from the debit or credit side of a general ledger account. Figure 4.3 shows how this works in a typical general ledger 'expense' account.

Figure 4.3
Typical general ledger 'expense' account showing how profit and loss account and balance sheet figures are derived

Electricity			
	£		£
(1st quarter) Cheques paid for 4th quarter in previous year and current quarter	1,200	Opening accrual b/f (4th quarter of previous year owing at start of this year)	600
(2nd quarter) Cheque	900	Profit and loss account	3,050
(3rd quarter) Cheque	800		
Accrual (4th quarter owing) c/d	750		
	3,650		3,650
		Accrual b/d	750

Credit balance listed in balance sheet within the current liabilities heading as 'Accrual'

Total expense for the year debited to the profit and loss account to complete the double-entry

In many countries, the position of the profit and loss account within the double-entry system is reinforced by presenting the information in a **horizontal layout**, divided into a conventional debit and credit side. For example, the architect's profit and loss account seen earlier (page 69) could be rearranged on a horizontal basis, as follows:

Len Corbusier, Architect
Profit and loss account for the year ended 30 April 2005

	£		£
Assistants' wages	65,310	Fees – professional services	192,410
Secretarial wages	19,640	Bank interest received	120
Stationery	7,296		
Travel and accommodation	17,630		
Telephone charges	3,260		
Office rent and rates	14,633		
Depreciation of motor car	4,000		
Depreciation of office fittings	2,500		
Sundry expenses	3,400		
	137,669		
Net profit for the year	54,861		
	192,530		192,530

It is clear that there is neither more nor less information than in the vertical style, but advocates of the vertical style argue that the data flows more logically as 'Income less Expenses equals Profit', which accords with the accounting equation seen in Chapter 1.

Similarly, the balance sheet could be shown in a horizontal format (usually with assets on the left and liabilities and capital on the right), but it is *not* part of the double-entry system. Like the trial balance it is merely a list of balances as at a specific date.

4.6 Published profit and loss accounts and balance sheets

Businesses operating with sole owners or as partnerships do not have to publish their financial summaries – in fact, the only people likely to see them are the owners themselves, their accountants, the tax authorities and possibly their bankers. Members of the public have no right of access to the information. Limited companies, however, must make their summarised financial information available to the public by way of **published accounts**. Although there are some restrictions on the amount of information which small and medium-sized companies have to divulge, larger companies (including all plc's – public limited companies) must publish an annual report including their profit and loss account and balance sheet. Bearing in mind that many plc's are extremely complicated multinational conglomerates conducting millions of transactions each year, how can this mass of information be made informative and readable?

The answer is that the data is summarised into main headings via the double-entry bookkeeping system and is also presented according to Generally Accepted Accounting Principles (GAAP) as specified by national or international accounting standards and legislation. This ensures a degree of uniformity when presenting financial information so that an increasing number of businesses within Europe and beyond follow the same procedures when presenting their profit and loss account and balance sheet. We shall be looking in more detail at limited companies in Chapter 7.

BP plc is one of the world's largest petroleum companies, with sales in 2003 totalling $236,045,000,000 ($236 bn). The company's published profit and loss account contained only 26 lines of information on half a page!

4.7 Odds and ends

There is a handful of minor points which need to be covered when considering the presentation of a fully detailed profit and loss account. These are:

- Sales returns and purchase returns (also known as 'returns inwards and outwards')
- Carriage inwards and outwards, which is the cost of transporting goods into or out of the business
- Discounts allowed and received, which represent amounts deducted from debtors' and creditors' accounts for prompt payment of amounts owing.

Work carefully through Activity 4.4 to see how these items are shown within the profit and loss account.

Errol Lewis sells fruit and vegetables from a market stall and also has a home delivery service, selling on credit but offering a 2% discount for prompt payment. Sometimes he pays an extra carriage charge for fresh strawberries to be flown in during winter months. During the year ended 30 November 2005 he records the following income and expenses:

	£
Sales	75,968
Sales returns (poor quality goods returned by customers)	405
Purchase of produce	32,710
Purchase returns (over-ripe bananas returned to supplier)	620
Carriage inwards (air freight of strawberries)	2,150
Carriage outwards (home delivery costs)	3,752
Assistants' wages	6,530
Rent and rates	3,520
Advertising	265
Depreciation of weighing scales	50
Accountant's fees	350
Bank interest and charges	600
Sundry expenses	3,600
Discount received from suppliers for prompt payment	240
Discount allowed to customers for prompt payment	320
Note: Opening stock of produce at 1 December 2004	3,680
Note: Closing stock of produce at 30 November 2005	3,420

Prepare Errol Lewis's profit and loss account for the year ended 30 November 2005.

▶

Errol Lewis
Profit and loss account for the year ended 30 November 2005

	£	£	£
Sales		75,968	
Less Sales returns		(405)	
			75,563
Less Cost of goods sold			
Opening stock at 1 December 2004		3,680	
Add Purchases	32,710		
Carriage inwards	2,150		
	34,860		
Less Purchase returns	(620)		
		34,240	
		37,920	
Less Closing stock at 30 November 2005		(3,420)	
			(34,500)
Gross profit			41,063
Add Discount received			240
			41,303
Less expenses			
Assistants' wages		6,530	
Carriage outwards		3,752	
Rent and rates		3,520	
Advertising		265	
Depreciation of weighing scales		50	
Accountant's fees		350	
Bank interest and charges		600	
Discount allowed		320	
Sundry expenses		3,600	
			(18,987)
Net profit			22,316

Pause for thought

To accommodate the extra detail, a third column has been added. The right-hand column provides the summarised information, with the detail being shown in the inner columns as required (see page 71).

4.8 From the trial balance to the profit and loss account and balance sheet

We are now ready to see how a detailed profit and loss account and balance sheet can be prepared from the trial balance. Remember that the trial balance is the summary of all the balances within the double-entry bookkeeping system at a specific date and therefore includes the 'ingredients' needed to produce the two financial summaries. Figure 4.4 shows how they fit in to the overall structure of the double-entry bookkeeping system.

Activities 4.5 and 4.6 explain in detail the procedures to be followed when preparing the profit and loss account and balance sheet from a trial balance.

Figure 4.4
The production of the profit and loss account and balance sheet from the double-entry bookkeeping system

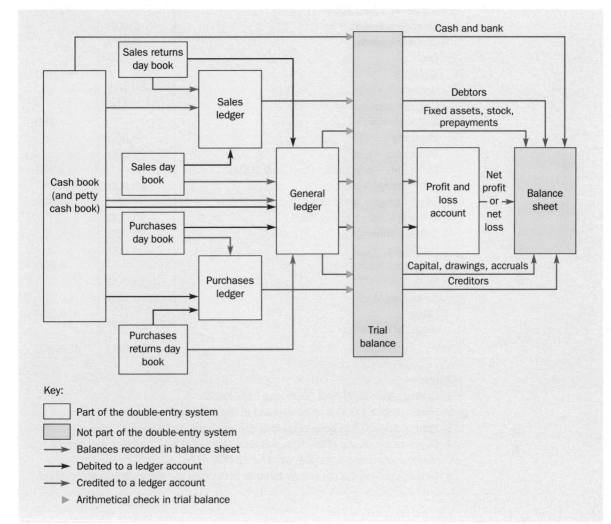

Activity 4.5

From the following trial balance, prepare the profit and loss account of Charlie Owen for the year ended 30 April 2005:

	Dr £	Cr £
Bank	3,800	
Capital at 1 May 2004		22,154
Carriage outwards	2,400	
Carriage inwards	6,850	
Cash	250	
Creditors		27,600
Debtors	35,200	
Discount allowed	420	
Discount received		386
Electricity	4,000	
Motor cars – cost	22,000	
Motor cars – depreciation to 1 May 2004		13,200
Office fittings – cost	20,000	
Office fittings – depreciation to 1 May 2004		10,800
Opening stock at 1 May 2004	90,000	
Owner's drawings	25,000	
Purchases	204,000	
Purchases returns		4,500
Rent	15,000	
Sales returns	3,920	
Sales		416,200
Wages and salaries	62,000	
	494,840	494,840

Notes:

1 Closing stock at 30 April 2005 was £110,000.
2 Electricity of £1,000 is to be accrued at the year-end.
3 Rent of £3,000 has been prepaid at the year-end.
4 Depreciation on the office fittings is calculated over 5 years using the straight line method, assuming a residual value of £2,000.
5 Depreciation on the car is calculated at 60% using the reducing balance method.

Answer

Before constructing the profit and loss account we need to follow a series of steps.

Step 1
Read through the trial balance items, making a mental note of possible problem areas – these could include the treatment of the carriage in and out, the discount allowed, etc.

Step 2
Read through the notes, and write in the adjustments needed for accruals and pre-payments against the relevant trial balance items. These appear as follows:

Electricity (+1000)	4,000	
Rent (−3000)	15,000	

Step 3

Using the information in Notes 4 and 5, calculate the year's depreciation charge. The workings (which should be shown as a note to the answer) would be as follows:

Motor cars

Cost	22,000
Less Depreciation to 1 May 2004	(13,200)
Net book value at 1 May 2004	8,800
Depreciation @ 60% × 8,800	(5,280)

Office fittings

(Cost − Residual value)/5
= (£20,000 − £2,000)/5
= £18,000/5 = £3,600

We can then write this into the trial balance as follows:

Motor cars: depreciation to 1 May 2004 (+5,280)		13,200
Office fittings: depreciation to 1 May 2004 (+3,600)		10,800

Note that only the bracketed figures appear in the year's profit and loss account, but the total depreciation of £18,480 and £14,400 will be shown in the balance sheet.

Step 4

Start the profit and loss account by writing the heading at the top of a new page, drawing three columns about 3 cm wide on the right-hand side. The 'trading account' is the first part of the summary, ending with the gross profit. Remember the sequence **'Sales − Cost of goods sold = Gross profit'**. Tick items in the trial balance as you enter them.

Step 5

Complete the summary by entering the remaining items of income and expenses, adjusting for the accrual and prepayment. Don't forget to include only the current year's depreciation. The completed profit and loss account is shown below.

Charlie Owen
Profit and loss account for the year ended 30 April 2005

	£	£	£
Sales		416,200	
Less Sales returns		(3,920)	
			412,280
Less Cost of goods sold			
Opening stock at 1 May 2004		90,000	
Add Purchases	204,000		
Carriage inwards	6,850		
	210,850		
Less Purchases returns	(4,500)		
		206,350	
		296,350	
Less Closing stock at 30 April 2005		(110,000)	
			(186,350)
Gross profit			225,930
Add Discount received			386
		c/f	226,316

Answer continued

Less expenses		b/f
Carriage outwards	2,400	226,316
Discount allowed	420	
Electricity	5,000	
Depreciation: motor cars	5,280	
Depreciation: office fittings	3,600	
Rent	12,000	
Wages and salaries	62,000	
		(90,700)
Net profit		135,616

Pause for thought

The trial balance items not used above represent the assets, liabilities and capital (including 'drawings', which are deducted from the owner's capital) at the end of the period, which are all entered into the balance sheet (see Activity 4.6).

Activity 4.6

Construct the balance sheet for Charlie Owen (see Activity 4.5). Use the layout shown on page 56.

Answer

Charlie Owen
Balance sheet as at 30 April 2005

	Cost	Depreciation	Net book value
	£	£	£
Fixed assets			
Office fittings	20,000	14,400	5,600
Motor cars	22,000	18,480	3,520
	42,000	32,880	9,120
Current assets			
Stock		110,000	
Debtors		35,200	
Prepayments		3,000	
Bank		3,800	
Cash		250	
		152,250	
Less **Current liabilities**			
Creditors	27,600		
Accruals	1,000		
		(28,600)	
Net current assets			123,650
Total net assets			132,770
Capital			
Opening balance, 1 May 2004		22,154	
Add Net profit		135,616	
		157,770	
Less Drawings		(25,000)	
Closing balance, 30 April 2005			132,770

4.9 Summary

The key components of the financial summaries for manufacturers, traders and service providers are shown below.

	Manufacturer	*Trader*	*Service provider*
Manufacturing account	Yes, showing direct and indirect costs of manufacturer, as adjusted for any work-in-progress	Not applicable	Not applicable
Trading account	Yes, bringing down the total factory production cost into the 'cost of goods sold' calculation	Yes, sales less cost of goods sold = gross profit	Not applicable
Profit and loss account	Yes, showing gross profit *less* expenses = net profit (or loss)	Yes, showing gross profit *less* expenses = net profit (or loss)	Yes, showing fees receivable *less* expenses = net profit (or loss)
Balance sheet	Yes (note that current assets will include closing stock of raw materials, work-in-progress and finished goods)	Yes (note that the only stock figure included as a current asset is closing stock of unsold goods)	Yes (note that service providers do not usually have a stock figure)

4.10 Glossary

Appropriation account An additional part of the profit and loss account, inserted after the net profit or loss, showing, for a partnership, the financial implications of the partnership agreement or, for a limited company, tax and dividend deductions and reserve transfers.

Auditor An independent accountant who reports on whether the financial summaries reflect a true and fair view of a business's affairs.

Columnar layout *See* Vertical layout.

Direct costs Costs which can be readily identified with the items being produced, for example sugar in a biscuit factory.

Final accounts A name given to the profit and loss account and balance sheet when prepared at the end of a financial period.

Horizontal layout A traditional account format used for the profit and loss account and balance sheet by many mainland European and other countries. Nowadays, it is very unusual in the UK.

Indirect costs All manufacturing costs other than direct costs, e.g. the rent of a biscuit factory.

Loss An excess of expenses over income.

Manufacturing account	The first part of a manufacturing company's profit and loss account, showing total factory production cost.
Prime costs	Another name for direct costs.
Profit	An excess of income over expenses.
Profit and loss account	The part of the financial summary which shows the net profit or loss of the organisation. It can be used to describe the whole summary, including manufacturing and trading accounts.
Published accounts	Condensed versions of a limited company's final accounts following Generally Accepted Accounting Principles (GAAP).
Total factory production cost	All the costs, direct and indirect, of producing the goods manufactured in the period.
Trading account	The first part of the profit and loss account for a business which buys in goods for resale. It shows the gross profit.
Vertical layout	The presentation of the financial summaries in columns, where the information is read from top to bottom in logical sequence, irrespective of whether it represents debit or credit balances.
Work-in-progress	Partly completed stock.

? Self-check questions

1 Profit is calculated by:
   a Comparing assets with liabilities
   b Comparing assets with expenses
   c Comparing income and expenses
   d Comparing income with liabilities

2 An independent auditor is:
   a An independent accountant who prepares the financial summaries
   b An independent accountant who reports on whether financial summaries show a true and fair view
   c An accountant employed by a business to check if the financial summaries of that business show a true and fair view
   d An independent accountant who reports on whether the financial summaries are totally accurate

3 The profit and loss account of a partnership which manufactures the goods it sells will include:
   a Manufacturing, trading, profit and loss, and appropriation accounts
   b As (a) but without the appropriation account
   c As (a) but with a partnership account
   d Only the trading account

4 For a soft drinks factory, direct costs could include:
   a The cost of machinery used to liquidise oranges
   b Depreciation of a bottle washing machine
   c Factory rent
   d Flavourings

5 Which of the following headings does not appear in a manufacturing account?
   a Prime cost of trading
   b Total factory production cost
   c Raw materials
   d Indirect factory costs

6 A company has opening stock £3,900, closing stock £2,800, purchases £18,650, carriage inwards £850 and purchases returns £1,600. What is its cost of goods sold?
   a £22,200
   b £12,200
   c £19,000
   d £17,300

7 In a manufacturing company which also buys completed goods for resale, 'cost of goods sold' is found by the formula:
   a Opening stock of raw materials + Purchases + Factory production cost – Closing stock of raw materials
   b Opening stock of finished goods + Purchases + Factory production cost – Closing stock of finished goods
   c Opening stock of finished goods + Purchases – Factory production cost – Closing stock of finished goods
   d Opening stock of finished goods + Purchases + Factory production cost + Closing stock of finished goods

8 A horizontal layout for a profit and loss account is:
   a The same as a columnar format
   b Where the information is read from top to bottom
   c Where the account has debit and credit sides
   d A special format which is easier to use by drunken accountants

9 Which of these is not an expense?
   a Carriage inwards
   b Carriage outwards
   c Discount allowed
   d Discount received

10 Which type of business organisation has to publish its profit and loss account?
   a Public limited company
   b Partnership
   c Architect
   d Sole trader

(Answers in Appendix 1)

? Self-study questions

(Answers in Appendix 2)

Question 4.1 From the following information, prepare suitable profit and loss accounts for each organisation.

Name:	Amber	Blue	Cerise
Type of business:	Manufacturer	Trader	Service provider
Year ended:	30 April 2005	31 May 2005	30 June 2005
	£	£	£
Sales	253,620	184,162	–
Closing stock:			
Finished goods	13,671	10,700	–
Raw materials	9,641	–	–
Work-in-progress	32,040	–	–
Purchases (finished goods)	–	65,210	–
Carriage inwards	–	360	–
Sales returns	–	580	–
Discount allowed	840	320	160
Carriage outwards	–	240	–
Purchases returns	–	2,600	–
Raw materials purchased	52,450	–	–
Opening stock:			
Finished goods	12,634	12,700	–
Raw materials	8,320	–	–
Work-in-progress	35,620	–	–
Fees from clients	–	–	85,400
Factory indirect expenses	89,322	–	–
General office expenses	34,600	54,923	21,500
Depreciation: factory	6,000	–	–
Depreciation: office	3,600	2,300	1,600
Discount received	114	120	–
Production labour	47,653	–	–

Question 4.2 From the following information, produce the profit and loss account of Wesley Timpson for the year ended 30 November 2005.

	£
Bank interest received	140
Carriage inwards	6,200
Carriage outwards	900
Closing stock, 30 November 2005	16,822
Depreciation on office furniture for the year	2,500
Depreciation on computers for the year	900
Depreciation on motor cars for the year	4,500
Discount allowed	533
Discount received	640
Light and heat	5,230
Opening stock, 1 December 2004	15,684
Postage and stationery	2,710
Purchase returns	2,910
Purchases	124,100
Sales returns	2,350
Sales	245,610
Sundry office expenses	3,571
Telephone	1,499
Wages and salaries	47,231

Question 4.3 From the following trial balance and notes relating to Betta Buys, prepare a profit and loss account for the year to 28 February 2006, and a balance sheet as at that date.

	Dr £	Cr £
Bank	960	
Cash	250	
Shop fittings – cost	30,000	
Shop fittings – depreciation to 1 March 2005		10,400
Motor car – cost	12,000	
Motor car – depreciation to 1 March 2005		4,800
Sales		425,000
Purchases	204,000	
Opening stock at 1 March 2005	90,000	
Rent	15,000	
Electricity	4,000	
Debtors	35,200	
Creditors		27,600
Wages and salaries	62,000	
Owner's drawings	25,000	
Capital		10,610
	478,410	478,410

Notes:
1 Closing stock is £70,000.
2 Electricity of £1,000 is to be accrued at the year-end.
3 Rent of £3,000 has been prepaid at the year-end.
4 Depreciation on the shop fittings is calculated over 5 years on the straight line method, assuming a residual value of £4,000.
5 Depreciation on the car is calculated at 40% using the reducing balance method.

Question 4.4 Helen Thorne, a retail jeweller, extracted the following trial balance for her business as at 31 May 2005.

	Dr £	Cr £
Sales of jewellery		324,650
Sales returns	1,250	
Opening stock, 1 June 2004	34,500	
Purchases	168,220	
Discount received		690
Discount allowed	1,520	
Insurance	5,900	
Assistants' wages	33,100	
Telephone and e-mail	5,200	
Light and heat	6,230	
Security guards' wages	12,400	
Repairs to premises	3,970	
Amortisation of leasehold premises to 1 June 2004		18,000
Depreciation of safe to 1 June 2004		4,800
Depreciation of shop fittings to 1 June 2004		10,200
Rent and rates	17,000	
Sundry expenses	3,940	
Leasehold premises, at cost	60,000	

	Dr £	Cr £
Safe, at cost	12,000	
Shop fittings, at cost	34,000	
Debtors	3,400	
Creditors		19,670
Bank overdraft		2,380
Cash in hand	520	
Website maintenance expenses	1,430	
Publicity and advertising	9,740	
Opening capital, 1 June 2004		58,630
Owner's drawings	24,700	
	439,020	439,020

Notes:

1 Closing stock at 31 May 2005, £27,880.

2 Security guards were owed £400 wages at 31 May 2005 and £200 was owing for telephone and e-mail.

3 £900 of the charge for maintaining the company website was paid on 1 January 2005 to cover a year from that date.

4 Depreciation is to be calculated as follows:

  (i) leasehold premises are amortised in equal instalments over a 20-year period,

  (ii) the safe is depreciated at 40% p.a. by the reducing balance method,

  (iii) the shop fittings are depreciated at 10% p.a. by the straight line method, assuming no residual values.

Prepare Helen Thorne's profit and loss account for the year ended 31 May 2005 and a balance sheet as at that date.

▶ Case study

Marvin makes magic

During the second half of his first year in business, Marvin (see previous case studies) decided to supplement his income by manufacturing and selling magic sets. This was in addition to his fees as an entertainer and any profit made by selling bought-in novelties from Kaboosh Limited. He rented a workshop on 1 March 2001 and employed his assistant Esmeralda's seven brothers and sisters as production workers. At the end of his first year of business, 30 June 2001, he produced the following trial balance:

	Dr £	Cr £
Appearance fees as entertainer		34,300
Cleaning	280	
Cost of machinery used in workshop	3,600	
Cost of magician's equipment	5,400	
Cost of disappearing lady apparatus	2,000	
Light and heat of workshop	2,400	
Other workshop expenses	4,100	
Production wages paid to Esmeralda's brothers and sisters	5,620	

	Dr £	Cr £
Purchase of materials used to manufacture magic sets	15,621	
Purchases of novelties bought-in from Kaboosh Limited	3,400	
Rabbit expenses	430	
Sales of novelties and magic sets		45,821
Marvin's drawings	19,720	
Opening capital		5,020
Creditor – Kaboosh Limited		240
Travel to performance venues	5,510	
Bank balance	660	
Cash in hand	40	
Wages to assistant (Esmeralda)	12,400	
Workshop costs: rent and rates	4,200	
	85,381	85,381

At the end of the year, the following further information was provided:

1 Closing stock of materials used to manufacture magic sets was valued at £6,320 and closing stock of bought-in novelties was valued at £2,400. All the manufactured magic sets were sold in the year. There was no work-in-progress at the year-end.

2 £200 was owed to Grimstock, one of the workers on the production line, whilst £100 was owed for light and heat.

3 One-seventh of the rent and rates had been prepaid for the following financial period. Marvin was owed £200 at the year-end by Mrs Featherskew for a party fee. This had not been shown in Marvin's accounting records.

4 Depreciation for the year on the magician's equipment totalled £1,080, and depreciation for the year on the disappearing lady apparatus was £800. Depreciation on the workshop machinery was to be calculated on the straight line method over 6 years, assuming a residual value of £600. A full year's depreciation was to be charged, even though the machinery had been owned for less than a year.

Required:
Prepare Marvin's manufacturing, trading and profit and loss account for the year ended 30 June 2001, and a balance sheet as at that date.

(Answers in Appendix 3)

References

BP plc financial report: www.bp.com then click on 'Investors'

Leading audit firms

Deloitte: www.deloitte.com

Ernst and Young: ey.com

KPMG: www.kpmg.co.uk

PricewaterhouseCoopers: www.pricewaterhousecoopers.co.uk

> Now look at this book's dedicated website at www.pearsoned.co.uk/black and work through the various additional exercises for this chapter.

Chapter 5

A further look at assets and liabilities

Objectives

When you have read this chapter you will be able to:

➤ Make adjustments when fixed assets are sold

➤ Understand and apply the key methods of stock valuation

➤ Understand why provisions for doubtful debts are needed and make adjustments for bad and doubtful debts

➤ Distinguish between current and long-term liabilities

5.1 Introduction

In this chapter we look at some further aspects of key components found within the balance sheet, answering such questions as 'what happens if fixed assets are sold?', 'how is stock valued?' and 'what if customers don't pay their debts?' We look at these in the order in which the relevant items would be found on the balance sheet: fixed assets, current assets, current liabilities, long-term liabilities.

5.2 Sales of fixed assets

In Chapter 3 we saw how all fixed assets, with the exception of most freehold land, are subject to depreciation ('amortisation' in the case of leasehold land and buildings). Depreciation recognises the loss in value of a fixed asset due to various factors, including wearing out, usage or becoming obsolete due to changes in technology. When an asset reaches the end of its useful life, the business has the following choices:

- Scrap the asset, in which case it may have a scrap value, for example an old machine may contain recyclable metal and components. Alternatively the item may be simply thrown away (also known as 'writing it off').

- Part-exchange the asset, where any value given for the old asset is used partly to pay for a replacement asset.

- Sell the asset at the market value.

Whatever happens to the asset, it will have a 'book' value in the business's ledger, which is usually the cost of the asset less all the depreciation charged to the date of sale. Often companies do not depreciate assets in the year of sale, but policy varies from business to business. Whatever the eventual fate of the asset being disposed of, a calculation must be made of the profit or loss, by comparing the book value with the disposal proceeds. This is done by creating a disposal of fixed assets account and transferring to it the following three amounts:

- The asset's cost from the relevant fixed asset account.

- The total depreciation from the relevant depreciation account.

- The proceeds (or part exchange value) of disposal.

The balance is either a profit (proceeds are greater than net book value), which is added to gross profit in the profit and loss account, or a loss (net book value is less than proceeds), which is shown as an expense in the profit and loss account.

Pause for thought

Strictly speaking, a **profit or loss on the sale of a fixed asset** should be described as an over- or under-provision for depreciation over the asset's life. This is because depreciation is an estimate and it is only when the asset is disposed of that the exact amount of depreciation can be known.

Activity 5.1

Amy has been in business as a commercial photographer for several years. At 1 January 2004 her fixed assets and accumulated depreciation balances were as follows:

	Cost £	Accumulated depreciation £
Pintax camera	650	450
Tripod	125	100
Darkroom equipment	1,600	1,300
Hunda car	5,000	3,600

During the year to 31 December 2004, the following transactions occurred:

- The Pintax camera was exchanged for a Fujitsu 200XL costing £800. A £100 part-exchange allowance was given, and the balance was paid by cheque.
- The tripod was thrown away and not replaced.
- The darkroom equipment was sold for £200 and not replaced.
- The Hunda car was sold in March for £1,600. A Kamari estate car was bought in May for £7,000.

**Activity 5.1
continued**

Cameras are depreciated at 10% p.a. straight line method and cars at 25% straight line method. It is Amy's policy not to depreciate assets in the year of sale, but to charge a full year's depreciation in the year of purchase, even if bought part way through the year.

Show the entries required to record the above in Amy's general ledger and profit and loss account for the year ended 31 December 2004 and her balance sheet as at that date.

Answer

Even without knowing anything about bookkeeping, we can use common sense to work out if a profit or loss was made, as follows:

- The Pintax camera had a net book value of £200 (£650 – £450) but fetched only £100 in part exchange, therefore a loss of £100.
- The tripod had a net book value of £25 (£125 – £100) but had no value when it was scrapped, therefore a loss of £25.
- The darkroom equipment had a net book value of £300 (£1,600 – £1,300) when it was sold for £200, therefore a loss of £100.
- The Hunda car had a net book value of £1,400 (£5,000 – £3,600) but was sold for £1,600, a profit of £200.

The entries in the general ledger as shown below take the cost and depreciation on the 'disposed' assets out of the relevant fixed asset and depreciation accounts into a 'disposal of assets' account (one account can be used for all disposals). The new fixed assets are added into the relevant asset accounts, with depreciation calculated in the usual way.

General Ledger

Cameras account

		£			£
1 Jan	Balance b/f (cost) (Pintax)	650	31 Dec	Disposal of fixed assets account	650
31 Dec	Cost – Fujitsu 200XL:			Balance c/f	800
	Bank	700			
	Part exchange (disposal of assets account)	100			
		1,450			1,450

Tripod account

		£			£
1 Jan	Balance b/f (cost)	125	31 Dec	Disposal of fixed assets account	125
		125			125

Darkroom equipment account

		£			£
1 Jan	Balance b/f (cost)	1,600	31 Dec	Disposal of fixed assets account	1,600
		1,600			1,600

Cars account

		£			£
1 Jan	Balance b/f (cost) (Hunda)	5,000	31 Dec	Disposal of fixed assets account	5,000
1 May	Bank (Kamari)	7,000		Balance c/f	7,000
		12,000			12,000

Provision for depreciation on cameras account

		£			£
31 Dec	Disposal of fixed assets account	450	1 Jan	Balance b/f	450
	Balance c/f	80		P & L account[a]	80
		530			530

[a] The depreciation on the new camera (10% × £800).

Provision for depreciation on tripod account

		£			£
31 Dec	Disposal of fixed assets account	100	1 Jan	Balance b/f	100

Provision for depreciation on darkroom equipment account

		£			£
31 Dec	Disposal of fixed assets account	1,300	1 Jan	Balance b/f	1,300

Provision for depreciation on cars account

		£			£
31 Dec	Disposal of fixed assets account	3,600	1 Jan	Balance b/f	3,600
	Balance c/f	1,750		P & L account[b]	1,750
		5,350			5,350

[b] The depreciation on the new car (25% × £7,000).

Answer continued

Disposal of fixed assets account

		£			£
31 Dec	Transfer cost of disposed assets:		31 Dec	Transfer depreciation on disposed assets:	
	Cameras	650		Dep'n on cameras	450
	Tripod	125		Dep'n on tripod	100
	Darkroom			Dep'n on darkroom	
	equipment	1,600		equipment	1,300
	Cars	5,000		Dep'n on car	3,600
		7,375	31 Dec	Proceeds of disposals:	
				Cameras account	100
				Bank (re darkroom)	200
				Bank (re car)	1,600
					7,350
				Profit and loss account:	
				Overall loss on disposal[c]	25
		7,375			7,375

[c] This is the balancing figure on the account. If there had been a balance on the opposite side it would have indicated an overall profit.

Profit and loss account for the year ended 31 December 2004 (extracts)

	£	£
Gross profit		
Less Expenses (including):		
Loss on disposal of fixed assets	25	
Depreciation on camera	80	
Depreciation on car	1,750	

Balance sheet as at 31 December 2004

Fixed assets	*Cost*	*Depreciation*	*Net book value*
	£	£	£
Camera	800	80	720
Car	7,000	1,750	5,250
	7,800	1,830	5,970

The balance sheet shows only the fixed assets owned at the end of the year (the new camera and car), all other assets having been disposed of. If fully detailed final accounts are required, then a summary of the changes of each category of fixed asset would be given as a note. This would be shown as follows:

	Cameras	Tripod	Darkroom equipment	Cars	Total
	£	£	£	£	£
Cost, 1 January 2004	650	125	1,600	5,000	7,375
Additions in the year	800	–	–	7,000	7,800
	1,450	125	1,600	12,000	15,175
Less Disposals	(650)	(125)	(1,600)	(5,000)	(7,375)
Cost, 31 December 2004	800	–	–	7,000	7,800
Depreciation, 1 January 2004	450	100	1,300	3,600	5,450
Provision for the year	80	–	–	1,750	1,830
	530	100	1,300	5,350	7,280
Less Depreciation on disposed assets	(450)	(100)	(1,300)	(3,600)	(5,450)
Depreciation, 31 December 2004	80	–	–	1,750	1,830
Net book value, 31 December 2004	720	–	–	5,250	5,970
Net book value, 1 January 2004	200	25	300	1,400	1,925

5.3 Stock valuation

5.3.1 The importance of the valuation

From a financial accounting viewpoint, the key date for valuing stock is the end of the financial year, as the valuation affects the cost of goods sold calculation in the 'trading account' part of the profit and loss account and also the current assets total in the balance sheet. If stock is overvalued it will increase this year's profit but reduce next year's, as the closing stock of one period is the opening stock of the next. Balance sheet values will also be distorted. How, then, should stock be valued? The relevant accounting standard, SSAP 9,[1] states that 'stock is to be stated at the total of the lower of cost and net realisable value of the separable items of stock or of groups of similar items'. It also contains these definitions:

There is also an International Accounting Standard (IAS 2) that refers to stock as 'inventories'. The valuation basis is identical with SSAP 9.

- **Cost (of stock)**: 'that expenditure which has been incurred in the normal course of business in bringing the product to its present location and condition'.
- **Net realisable value**: 'the estimated proceeds from the sale of items of stock less all further costs to completion and less all costs to be incurred in marketing, selling and distributing directly related to the items in question'.

The prudence concept requires us to be cautious in valuing assets and we would never anticipate a profit by valuing stock at its selling price. The only

---

[1] Accounting Standards Board (1990) Statement of Standard Accounting Practice (SSAP) 9 *Stocks and Long-term Contracts*. London: ASB.

exception is where the likely selling price (after deducting relevant costs to enable the stock to be sold) is less than the cost price, in which case the SSAP 9 definition is applied. This may happen in cases such as where stock has deteriorated in some way or is unfashionable.

Another problem is deciding what can be included as 'cost'. It might be as simple as looking up an invoice and reading off the price paid: for example, the owner of a bicycle shop with four Speedwing Racers in stock is probably able to find their purchase price quite easily; but in many cases the price paid cannot be matched to actual goods, perhaps due to the physical nature of the stock.

Activity 5.2

A retailer of pet fish looks in the fish tank at the end of his first financial year, 31 December, and counts 500 goldfish. All the fish are bought from the same supplier, but prices change frequently. Details of stock purchases and sales are as follows:

		Number (fish)	Cost of each fish (£)	Sales at end of month (fish)
1 Jan	Purchases	350	2	–
1 Mar	Purchases	600	3	300
1 Jul	Purchases	800	4	550
1 Oct	Purchases	700	5	1,000
1 Dec	Purchases	650	6	750
31 Dec	(Closing stock)	500	?	

What value should be placed on the closing stock?

Answer

We cannot tell by looking at them! Goldfish do not swim around with price labels on them, and it would be very difficult to look at one goldfish and say with certainty when it was bought. What has to be done is to apply a **theoretical valuation method** such as FIFO, LIFO or AVCO.

5.3.2 FIFO, LIFO and AVCO

FIFO stands for first in, first out, **LIFO** for last in, first out, and **AVCO** for average cost. Each of these methods of stock valuation is theoretical and does not necessarily reflect the way in which stock physically moves through the business, so a cake shop could use FIFO without getting into trouble with the health and hygiene regulations! AVCO can be either *periodic or perpetual*: periodic means that the average is calculated at intervals (for example, once a year or quarterly); perpetual requires recalculation every time a price change is recorded. Refer to the website listed under 'References' at the end of the chapter for further details on stock valuation.

In times of rising prices, using FIFO will result in a higher stock value than the other methods (the latest prices being applied to closing stock). LIFO would result in the earliest and lowest prices being used. This would result in a low stock value and also a lower profit figure as stock values are part of the 'cost of sales' calculation. Low profits would result in low tax payments, which is why the UK tax authorities do not allow LIFO to be used for the calculation of taxable profits.

Did you know?

LIFO is also not allowed under international accounting standards.

Activity 5.3

Use the FIFO method to value the goldfish at 31 December (see Activity 5.2).

Answer

Use a 'price grid' to establish which fish are, in theory, sold at which prices.

Purchase price	£2	£3	£4	£5	£6
January Purchases	350				
March Purchases		600			
Subtotal	350	600			
March Sales (FIFO)	(300)				
July Purchases			800		
Subtotal	50	600	800		
July Sales (FIFO)	(50)	(500)			
October Purchases				700	
Subtotal	–	100	–	700	
October Sales (FIFO)		(100)	(800)	(100)	
December Purchases					650
Subtotal	–	–	–	600	650
December Sales (FIFO)				(600)	(150)
December Closing Stock	–	–	–	–	500

Closing stock = 500 × £6 = £3,000

Activity 5.4

Use the LIFO method to value the goldfish at 31 December.

Answer

Use another 'price grid' to establish which fish are, in theory, sold at which prices.

Purchase price	£2	£3	£4	£5	£6
January Purchases	350				
March Purchases		600			
Subtotal	350	600			
March Sales (LIFO)		(300)			
July Purchases			800		
Subtotal	350	300	800		
July Sales (LIFO)			(550)		
October Purchases				700	
Subtotal	350	300	250	700	
October Sales (LIFO)		(50)	(250)	(700)	
December Purchases					650
Subtotal	350	250	–	–	650
December Sales (LIFO)		(100)			(650)
December Closing Stock	350	150	–	–	–

Closing stock = (350 × £2 = £700) + (150 × £3 = £450), total £1,150

Activity 5.5

Use the AVCO method (perpetual inventory) to value the goldfish at 31 December.

Answer

Use a third 'price grid' to establish which fish are, in theory, sold at which prices.

	Fish in stock	Price £	Value £	Average £
January Purchases	350	2	700	
March Purchases	600	3	1,800	
Subtotal	950		2,500	
Average (£2,500/950 fish)				2.632
March Sales	(300)	2.632	(790)	
July Purchases	800	4	3,200	
Subtotal	1,450		4,910	
Average (£4,910/1,450 fish)				3.386
July Sales	(550)	3.386	(1,862)	
October Purchases	700	5	3,500	
Subtotal	1,600		6,548	
Average (£6,548/1,600 fish)				4.093
October Sales	(1,000)	4.093	(4,093)	
December Purchases	650	6	3,900	
Subtotal	1,250		6,355	
Average (£6,355/1,250 fish)				5.084
December Sales	(750)	5.084	(3,813)	
December Closing stock	**500**	**5.084**	**2,542**	

Pause for thought

Closing stock using each of the three methods is:

FIFO   £3,000
LIFO   £1,150
AVCO   £2,542

Activity 5.6

Calculate the gross profit for the year, using each of the three stock valuation methods. Assume that each goldfish is sold for £10 and that no goldfish died during the year.

Answer

	FIFO		LIFO		AVCO	
	£	£	£	£	£	£
Sales (2,600 × £10)		26,000		26,000		26,000
Less Cost of sales						
Opening stock	–		–		–	
Purchases[a]	13,100		13,100		13,100	
	13,100		13,100		13,100	
Less Closing stock	(3,000)		(1,150)		(2,542)	
		(10,100)		(11,950)		(10,558)
Gross profit		15,900		14,050		15,442

[a] (350 × £2) + (600 × £3) + (800 × £4) + (700 × £5) + (650 × £6).

5.4   Bad and doubtful debts

The next current asset listed after 'stock' in the balance sheet is 'debtors', which is the total of all the individual customers' account balances within the sales ledger at the balance sheet date. Because accountants need to be prudent (cautious, conservative, realistic, and so on), they must be reasonably sure that the total shown in the balance sheet represents **good debts** (that is, debts that will be paid), as there can also be:

- **Bad debts** – where there is no possibility of the customer paying, and
- **Doubtful debts** – where there is uncertainty whether the debt can be paid.

5.4.1 Bad debts

Bad debts are the nightmare of any business – the customer has been sold goods or services and does not pay for them. It is an extreme step to consider a debt as bad, and is usually the culmination of a long-drawn-out process involving reminders, threats of legal action, solicitors' letters, and so on. The bad debts are 'written off' to the profit and loss account, that is, they are shown as a loss to the business, and the customer's sales ledger account is closed. Sometimes, miracles happen and a debt previously written off is paid.

Activity 5.7

Tarquin Micawber owed £650 to the Crisp 'n' Tasty Pizza Company. Despite many reminders and phone calls, Tarquin refused to pay. The company has now received a letter from Peru saying, 'Having a lovely time – not coming back! Tarquin'. The company has reluctantly decided to write off the debt at 31 December 2004. Total debts at that date, including Tarquin's, amounted to £6,950.

Show the entries required in the pizza company's ledger and the relevant extracts from the financial summaries.

In that case, the amount is added to profit as a 'bad debt recovered'.

Answer

Sales Ledger

Tarquin Micawber's account

2004		£	2004		£
1 Jan	Opening debtor	650	31 Dec	Bad debts account	650

General Ledger

Bad debts account

2004		£	2004		£
31 Dec	Bad debts account	650	31 Dec	Profit and loss account	650

Profit and loss account for the year ended 31 December 2004 (extract)

	£
Expenses include:	
Bad debt written off	650

Balance sheet as at 31 December 2004 (extract)

	£
Current assets include:	
Debtors	6,300

(Notice that there is no reference to the bad debt on the balance sheet. The amount is no longer a balance within the sales ledger so cannot be included as a debtor.)

Activity 5.8

Two years later, on 1 December 2006, the managing director of the Crisp 'n' Tasty Pizza Company gets another letter from Peru. It states: 'Made a fortune selling Peruvian marmalade. Cheque enclosed. Sorry! Tarquin'.

What entries would be made in the company's books?

Cash Book

Bank account

2006		£		£
1 Dec	Tarquin Micawber:			
	Bad debt recovered	650		

General Ledger

Bad debt recovered account

2006		£	2006		£
31 Dec	Profit and loss account	650	1 Dec	Cash book	650

Profit and loss account for the year ended 31 December 2006 (extract)

	£
Added to the gross profit as sundry income:	
Bad debt recovered	650

(No relevant entries in the balance sheet)

Pause for thought

Once the bad debt was written off, Tarquin's sales ledger account was closed. Two years later, there is no reason to reopen it as there is no indication that Tarquin will be sold any more goods by the pizza company.

5.4.2 Doubtful debts

Some debts are neither good nor bad – instead there is an element of doubt as to whether or not they will be paid. Reasons for this include:

- Disputes over quality of goods or services
- Unresolved queries such as duplicated invoices
- Temporary financial difficulties of a customer
- Customers whose debts have been outstanding for a long period.

The major difference between doubtful debts and bad debts is that if a debt is considered doubtful there is still some hope that the customer will pay, so the sales ledger account is kept 'alive'. However, due to the prudence concept, an amount of profit is transferred to a **provision** to recognise the potential loss if the debt eventually turns bad. This provision is adjusted up or down in subsequent years, depending upon whether there are more or fewer doubtful debts to be provided for by the end of the financial period.

The provision can be either:

- Specific (relating to actual amounts owing by named customers), or
- General (a percentage of total debts is provided for, after bad debts have been written off).

Did you know?

A **provision for doubtful debts** is also known as either a **provision for bad debts** or a **provision for bad and doubtful debts**. They all mean the same thing: a provision against the future possibility of a debt becoming bad. They must never be confused with 'bad debts', which are written off as a loss.

Activity 5.9

Assume that the Texas Tea company's doubtful debts were as follows:

2003 (no doubtful debts)
2004 Total doubtful debts = £6,900
2005 Total doubtful debts = £8,200
2006 Total doubtful debts = £7,800

What provision would be needed in each year?

Answer

- In 2003 there is no provision.
- In 2004 a provision of £6,900 is created (show £6,900 as an expense in the profit and loss account and deduct £6,900 from total debtors in the balance sheet).
- In 2005 the provision needs to be increased by £1,300 (show £1,300 as an expense in the profit and loss account and deduct £8,200 from total debtors in the balance sheet).
- In 2006 the provision needs to be decreased by £400 (show £400 as income in the profit and loss account and deduct £7,800 from total debtors in the balance sheet).

Note that there are no entries needed in the debtors' accounts in the sales ledger. The 'Provision for doubtful debts' account in the general ledger for the years 2004–2006 would be as follows:

General Ledger

Provision for doubtful debts account

		£			£
31/12/04	Balance c/d	6,900	31/12/04	P & L account	6,900
31/12/05	Balance c/d	8,200	1/1/05	Balance b/d	6,900
			31/12/05	P & L account	1,300
		8,200			8,200
31/12/06	P & L account	400	1/1/06	Balance b/d	8,200
	Balance c/d	7,800			
		8,200			8,200
			1/1/07	Balance b/d	7,800

Pause for thought

Ninety per cent of all accountancy students have difficulty understanding how provisions work. Look very carefully at the amounts either coming out of the profit and loss account (2003: £6,900, 2004: £1,300) or going back into the profit and loss account (2005: £400). What do you notice? Apart from the first year, you do not need to take out all the provision in each year – you are just 'fine tuning' it to make sure that the closing balance on the provision equals the total of doubtful debts at the balance sheet date. Re-read this activity and then see if you can apply its principles to the next one.

Activity 5.10

Barker & Co., a company which started on 1 January 2003, had identified the following balances on its sales ledger:

As at 31 December:	2003 £	2004 £	2005 £
Total debtors	49,310	39,551	37,690
including:			
Bad debts:			
Carl Fraudmeister	2,500		
Lola Noepay	560		
Frank Leebroke		630	
Owen Millions			1,700
Doubtful debts:			
Luke Ivenocash	300		
Linda Safiver	2,600	1,600	1,200
Adam Disgrace		1,700	
Robin Cash			1,800

Show the entries required in Barker & Co.'s sales and general ledgers, and relevant extracts from the financial summaries for each of the three years.

Answer

Sales Ledger

Carl Fraudmeister

	£			£
31/12/03 Balance b/f	2,500	31/12/03 Bad debts account		2,500

Lola Noepay

	£			£
31/12/03 Balance b/f	560	31/12/03 Bad debts account		560

Frank Leebroke

	£			£
31/12/04 Balance b/f	630	31/12/04 Bad debts account		630

Owen Millions

	£			£
31/12/05 Balance b/f	1,700	31/12/05 Bad debts account		1,700

Answer continued

General Ledger

Bad debts account

		£			£
31/12/03	Carl Fraudmeister	2,500	31/12/03	P & L account	3,060
	Lola Noepay	560			
		3,060			3,060
31/12/04	Frank Leebroke	630	31/12/04	P & L account	630
31/12/05	Owen Millions	1,700	31/12/05	P & L account	1,700

Provision for doubtful debts account

		£			£
31/12/03	Balance c/d	2,900	31/12/03	P & L account	2,900
31/12/04	Balance c/d	3,300	1/1/04	Balance b/d	2,900
			31/12/04	P & L account	400
		3,300			3,300
31/12/05	P & L account	300	1/1/05	Balance b/d	3,300
31/12/05	Balance c/d	3,000			
		3,300			3,300
			1/1/06	Balance b/d	3,000

Profit and loss account for the year ended 31 December 2003

	£	£
Expenses include:		
Bad debts written off		3,060
Increase in provision for doubtful debts		2,900

Balance sheet as at 31 December 2003

	£	£
Current assets include:		
Debtors (49,310 – 3,060)[a]	46,250	
Less Provision for doubtful debts	(2,900)	
		43,350

[a] This calculation would not be shown on the balance sheet.

Profit and loss account for the year ended 31 December 2004

	£	£
Expenses include:		
Bad debts written off		630
Increase in provision for doubtful debts		400

Balance sheet as at 31 December 2004

	£	£
Current assets include:		
Debtors (39,551 – 630)	38,921	
Less Provision for doubtful debts	(3,300)	
		35,621

Profit and loss account for the year ended 31 December 2005

	£	£
Added to gross profit:		
Decrease in provision for doubtful debts		300
Expenses include:		
Bad debts written off		1,700

Balance sheet as at 31 December 2005

	£	£
Current assets include:		
Debtors (37,690 – 1,700)	35,990	
Less Provision for doubtful debts	(3,000)	
		32,990

5.5 Current and long-term liabilities

Current liabilities can also be called 'creditors due for payment within one year', and this description is usually given if the balance sheet has been prepared for a limited company. The main creditors found within this section are:

- Trade creditors, being amounts owed for goods or services
- Accruals, which are expenses owing at the end of a financial period where the bills have not yet been received
- Bank overdrafts.

In addition, for a limited company, there may be:

- Taxation due on the profits on the year (this is not relevant to a sole trader or partnership as the individual owners are responsible for meeting the tax on profits)
- Proposed dividends, which is the amount expected to be paid to shareholders as a return on the capital invested by them (see Chapter 7).

Did you know?

Under International Accounting Standards, 'long-term liabilities' are referred to as 'non-current liabilities'.

Long-term liabilities are also referred to as 'creditors due for payment after more than one year', and again, this term might be used if a limited company's balance sheet is being prepared. This heading refers mainly to loans due for repayment after more than 12 months from the balance sheet date. The term **debenture** is often used to describe such a loan in the case of limited companies.

5.6 Summary

Sales of fixed assets	Open 'disposal of asset account' to record proceeds, and transfer cost and total depreciation from relevant accounts. Balance on the disposal account represents either profit or loss on disposal, taken to P & L account
Stock valuation	LIFO gives lowest value and lowest profits when prices are rising, but is not allowed by accounting standards. FIFO and AVCO are acceptable
Bad and doubtful debts	Bad debts are irrecoverable and are written off to the P & L account. Doubtful debts – there is still hope, so do not write off, just make a provision against the possibility of a loss in the future

5.7 Glossary

AVCO	*Average cost*, a method of stock valuation which applies average prices to value closing stock. 'Perpetual valuation' requires constant updating of the average when prices change; 'periodic valuation' changes only at intervals, for example annually.
Bad debts	Debts where there is no hope of collecting the amount due.
Cost of stock	Expenditure incurred on stock to bring it to its present location and condition.
Current liability	A creditor due for payment within one year of the balance sheet date.
Debenture	A name often given to a loan repayable by a limited company.
Doubtful debts	Debts where there is uncertainty as to whether the amount due will be paid, but the business has not given up hope of payment.
FIFO	*First in, first out*, a method of stock valuation which assumes that the earliest stock acquired is the first to be used, resulting in closing stock being valued at most recent prices.
Good debts	Debts which are expected to be paid in the normal course of business.
LIFO	*Last in, first out*, a method of stock valuation which assumes that the most recently acquired stock is the first to be used, resulting in closing stock being valued at earliest prices. Not allowed by the UK tax authorities and accounting standards.
Long-term liability	A creditor due for payment after more than one year of the balance sheet date.
Net realisable value	Selling price of stock, after deducting all relevant costs to enable it to be sold.
Profit or loss on sale of fixed asset	Another way of describing an over- or under-provision for depreciation over the life of a fixed asset.
Provision	An amount set aside out of profits to reduce the value of an asset, due to factors such as wear and tear (provision for depreciation) or uncertainty of value (provision for doubtful debts).
Provision for bad debts	Another term for a provision for doubtful debts.
Provision for bad and doubtful debts	Another term for a provision for doubtful debts.
Provision for doubtful debts	An amount of profit set aside to cover the possibility of some debts becoming bad in the future.
Theoretical valuation methods	Stock valuation methods such as FIFO and LIFO which assume that stock moves through the business in a particular way.

? Self-check questions

1   A business sells an asset on 1 January for £8,000. The asset was bought exactly three years previously for £24,000 and depreciation was charged at 30% p.a. on the reducing balance method. What is the profit or loss on disposal?
    a   £5,600 profit
    b   £232 profit
    c   £232 loss
    d   £16,000 loss

2   A profit on the disposal of a fixed asset can also be described as:
    a   An over-provision for depreciation on the asset
    b   An increase in fixed assets on the balance sheet
    c   An increase in the bank balance
    d   An under-provision for depreciation on the asset

3   What is the effect of overvaluing closing stock on the current year's profit?
    a   Decreases the gross profit and net profit
    b   Increases the gross profit but decreases net profit
    c   Decreases the gross profit but increases net profit
    d   Increases the gross profit and net profit

4   Applying the FIFO method of stock valuation in a period of rapidly rising prices will result in:
    a   Stock valued at low prices
    b   Stock valued at high prices
    c   Stock valued at average prices
    d   Stock valued at selling prices

5   Why can LIFO not be used to compute profits for tax purposes in the UK?
    a   It results in low profits which would mean low tax payments to the government
    b   It would result in high profits and tax payments, and the government does not want to be greedy
    c   It would mean that businesses would always have old stock and the government wants to discourage this
    d   It is a theoretical method, unrelated to actual prices

6   A company bought 50 dresses at £40 each. Normal selling price is £60 each but the dresses are now thought to be old-fashioned and have to be shortened at a cost of £5 each. What should be their total value as part of closing stock?
    a   £2,750
    b   £3,000
    c   £2,000
    d   £1,750

7   What is a bad debt?
    a   A debt where there is some hope of getting paid
    b   A debt where there is no hope of getting paid
    c   A debt which is doubtful
    d   A debt where the customer has gone abroad

8   Graham Pickle is owed £400 by Harvey Willow. Graham now regards Harvey as a bad debtor. What will be the effect of writing off the debt as bad?
    a   No effect on profit, but debtors decrease
    b   The bank balance goes down and the profits decrease
    c   Profit decreases, as do current assets
    d   Profit decreases, but no effect on the balance sheet

9   A business starts its year with £800 in a provision for doubtful debts. At the end of the year, debtors total £12,000 of which £600 are considered doubtful. What is the effect on the P & L account and balance sheet?

a   £200 is added to profit and the balance sheet shows Debtors less provision as £11,400

b   £600 is deducted from profit and the balance sheet shows Debtors less provision as £11,400

c   £1,400 is deducted from profit and the balance sheet shows Debtors less provision as £10,600

d   £800 is added to profit and the balance sheet shows Debtors less provision as £11,400

10 A long-term liability is:

a   A creditor due for payment within 12 months

b   A liability where it is not known when it is to be repaid

c   A creditor due for payment after more than 12 months

d   The same as an accrual

(Answers in Appendix 1)

 Self-study questions

(Answers in Appendix 2)

Question 5.1 Straits Liners is a shipping company which at 1 January 2005 owned the following vessels:

- SS Invisible, bought for £450,000 on 1 July 2000
- SS Submersible, bought for £600,000 on 1 August 2001
- SS Outrageous, bought for £900,000 on 1 March 2002

All the ships are depreciated over 5 years on the straight line basis, assuming a residual value of 25% of cost price, with a full year's depreciation in the year of purchase but no depreciation in the year of sale. During the year ended 31 December 2005, the following events occurred:

- SS Invisible disappeared in the Bermuda Triangle and was considered lost.
- SS Submersible was part-exchanged for a new ship, SS Implausible, on 3 October. The cost of the new ship was £700,000. £200,000 was given in part exchange, with the balance paid by cheque.
- SS Outrageous was still owned at 31 December 2005.

Show all the relevant entries in the profit and loss account for the year ended 31 December 2005 and in the balance sheet as at that date. Show all workings.

Question 5.2 Martha started business on 1 October 2000 buying and selling computer mouse mats. Each year in October she placed an order for mats with the North Caledonian Mouse Mat Company. During her first four years of trading, Martha's purchases and sales of mouse mats were as follows:

Year ended 30 September	Purchases	Sales
2001	120,000 @ 70p	100,000
2002	120,000 @ 90p	100,000
2003	120,000 @ £1.10	140,000
2004	120,000 @ £1.30	100,000

a Calculate the value of stock on 30 September 2004, using each of the following stock valuation methods:
   (i) FIFO (first in, first out)
   (ii) LIFO (last in, first out)
   (iii) AVCO (average cost).
b Explain why, under accounting standards, FIFO is used in preference to LIFO.

Question 5.3   Trimmings plc manufactures textiles which are sold to fashion designers to be made into garments.

Although the majority of patterns in stock at 31 May 2005 were likely to be sold at prices significantly above the manufacturing cost, the company accountant is concerned about the following product lines:

1 Orange Lace. Manufacturing cost £9,000. This stock has been on a shelf since 1990. The accountant believes that the only way of selling it would be to shred and bundle it (at a cost of £500) and sell it as industrial cleaning wipes for an anticipated price of £2,000.
2 Injured Turtles. Originally printed to meet a high demand for garments linked to a popular television series, there is no further demand for the textile in this country. Stocks cost £16,000, and the only possible source of revenue would be to export the material at a cost of £2,750 for use as dusters in Guatemala. Administration costs to handle the sale are estimated at £2,650, and the sale price is estimated at £4,000.

a Explain what is meant by the term 'stock is valued at the lower of cost and net realisable value'.
b Explain, with reasons, how each of the above product lines should be accounted for in the annual accounts of the company for the year ended 31 May 2005.

Question 5.4   Bickley Brothers sell luxury picnic hampers from their prestigious shop in London. When the firm's accountant drew up the list of sales ledger balances at the business's year-end, 31 May 2003, the following information was revealed:

	£
Total balances	13,525
This total includes the following customer who is considered a bad debt:	
Lord Fitztightly	2,400
and a further number of doubtful debtors, amounting to	3,500

Bickley Brothers had an opening balance of £3,000 on its provision for doubtful debts at 1 June 2002.

On 31 May 2004, the business had total sales ledger balances of £17,630. Of that total, one customer, Lady Agapanthus, owes £600 which is considered to be irrecoverable. £3,200 of debts is considered doubtful at that date.

a Explain the difference between bad and doubtful debts.
b Show the relevant extracts from the profit and loss accounts for each of the years ended 31 May 2003 and 31 May 2004 and the balance sheets ended on those dates.
c What would be the effect on the profit and loss account for the year ended 31 May 2005 and the balance sheet as at that date if Lord Fitztightly pays the amount he owed on 4 December 2004?

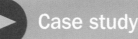

Case study

Esmeralda doesn't disappear, so Chiquita appears

As Marvin (see previous case studies) entered the second year of his business things appeared to be going well. His fame was spreading and he was invited to appear on 1 July 2001 at a special royal command performance. As the highlight of his act was the 'disappearing lady' trick, he was highly embarrassed when, after saying the 'magic words' and tapping the correct number of times with his wand, the curtains drew back to reveal Esmeralda in a close embrace with a stagehand. Marvin was so furious that as soon as the show was over he not only sacked Esmeralda but also closed his magic set factory (thereby putting Esmeralda's seven brothers and sisters, the factory's only employees, out of work). Immediately, all the factory's stock was sold at cost and the factory machinery was sold at its net book value.

During the following six months, the following events occurred:

1 The disappearing lady apparatus was sold on 1 August 2001 for £1,000. Its net book value at 30 June 2001 was £1,200 (cost £2,000 less 40% p.a. reducing balance depreciation). One month's depreciation is to be charged prior to calculating the profit or loss on disposal.

2 Marvin took on a new assistant, Chiquita, who was previously employed as a sales ledger clerk at Kaboosh Limited. She was to perform in a new 'saw the lady in half' routine (for which a new prop costing £3,000 was bought on 1 September 2001) as well as supervising the collection of Marvin's debtors. She immediately prepared a report on the sales ledger, showing that at 31 August he was owed £900, including £200 from a Mrs Featherskew who was a 'bad' debtor, and £150 from Crispin Fairbright whose cheque had been returned three times marked 'no funds available – refer to drawer' and was to be considered doubtful.

Required:

a Calculate the profit or loss on disposal of the 'disappearing lady' apparatus.

b Explain the effect on Marvin's profit and assets of classifying debts as 'bad' or 'doubtful'.

(Answers in Appendix 3)

References

For further details on accounting standards, including SSAP 9 *Stocks and Long-term Contracts*: Black, Geoff (2003) *Students' Guide to Accounting and Financial Reporting Standards*, 9th edition. Harlow: Financial Times Prentice Hall.

For an interesting slide show on stock valuation, US-style:

nersp.nerdc.ufl.edu/~acadian/legacct/class4/slide1.htm (and subsequent slides). Note that the term 'inventory' is used in the USA for stock.

> Now look at this book's dedicated website at **www.pearsoned.co.uk/black** and work through the various additional exercises for this chapter.

Chapter 6

Revision chapter (1)

Objectives   **When you have read this chapter you will be able to:**

➤ Consolidate your knowledge gained in previous chapters

➤ Prepare a detailed profit and loss account and balance sheet from a trial balance with appropriate adjustments

➤ Understand how extended trial balances can help the process of preparing financial summaries

6.1   Introduction

Having got this far, you may be feeling rather overwhelmed by the amount of information and explanations you have had to absorb. This chapter, whilst hardly light relief, is included to give you a chance to consolidate your knowledge. The only new topic introduced is the idea of an 'extended' trial balance which can speed up the process of producing the profit and loss account and balance sheet.

The following section requires you to prepare the financial summaries from a detailed trial balance with several adjustments. Work through the question before checking the answer.

6.2 Revision question

Abigail Harvey's trial balance at 31 May 2005 was as follows:

	Dr £	Cr £
Advertising	18,563	
Bad debts	5,835	
Bank overdraft		14,852
Bank interest paid	5,231	
Capital at 1 June 2004		100,000
Cash in hand	650	
Creditors		24,510
Debtors	16,540	
Delivery expenses to customers	4,230	
Depreciation on fixtures and fittings, at 1 June 2004		6,503
Depreciation on motor cars, at 1 June 2004		26,800
Drawings	67,500	
Electricity	6,420	
Fixtures and fittings (cost)	24,210	
Insurance	2,640	
Loan interest (half-year)	2,400	
Long-term 6% loan (repayable in 2009)		80,000
Motor cars (cost)	65,920	
Provision for doubtful debts at 1 June 2004		2,000
Purchases	478,000	
Rent and rates	5,900	
Sales		626,220
Stock at 1 June 2004	87,355	
Sundry expenses	13,700	
Telephone	11,240	
Wages and salaries	64,551	
	880,885	880,885

Notes:

1 Stock at 31 May 2005 was valued at £84,800.

2 Depreciation is to be provided as follows:
Motor cars at 40% p.a. on reducing balance
Fixtures and fittings at 10% on cost

3 Sales includes a receipt of £2,000 from Wem Garage for the sale of a car which was bought two years previously at a cost of £6,000. No entries relating to the disposal of the car have been made, and the car has been fully depreciated for the two years prior to sale.

4 At 31 May 2005 £1,300 was owed for electricity, and £200 of the insurance was pre-paid. The second half-year's loan interest is owing.

5 The provision for doubtful debts is to be increased by £500.

Prepare Abigail Harvey's profit and loss account for the year ended 31 May 2005 and her balance sheet as at that date. Show all relevant workings.

6.3 Answer to revision question

Methodology

Before constructing the profit and loss account and balance sheet we need to follow a series of steps.

Step 1

Read through the trial balance items, making a mental note of possible problem areas – these could include the treatment of the delivery expenses, the loan interest and the provision for doubtful debts. This enables you to get an overall 'feel' of the problem. You could also write in 'T' for trading account, 'P & L' for profit and loss account and 'B/S' for balance sheet against relevant items, though this is not essential.

Step 2

Read through the notes, and write in the adjustments needed for notes 3, 4 and 5 against the relevant trial balance items. These will appear as follows:

	£	£
Sales (−£2,000)		626,220
Depreciation on motor cars, at 1 June 2004 (− £3,840)[a]		26,800
Electricity (+£1,300)	6,420	
Insurance (−£200)	2,640	
Loan interest (half-year) (+£2,400)	2,400	
Motor cars (cost) (−£6,000)	65,920	
Provision for doubtful debts at 1 June 2004 (+£500)		2,000

[a] The depreciation on the car that was sold: first year £2,400, second year £1,440.

Step 3

Using the information in notes 2 and 3, calculate the year's depreciation charge and the loss on disposal of the car. Ledger accounts are not required, unless specifically asked for. The workings would be as follows:

Motor cars:

	£	£
At cost per trial balance		65,920
Less Cost of car sold		(6,000)
		59,920
Depreciation at 1 June 2004	26,800	
Less depreciation on car sold	(3,840)	
		22,960
'Reduced' value to be depreciated at 40%		36,960
Depreciation for the year (40% × 36,960)		14,784
Accumulated depreciation (for balance sheet) (22,960 + 14,784)		37,744

Profit or loss on disposal of car

	£
Cost of car sold	6,000
Less Depreciation to date of sale	(3,840)
Net book value at date of sale	2,160
Proceeds of sale	(2,000)
Loss on disposal	160

Fixtures and fittings:
Depreciation for the year 10% × £24,210 = £2,421
Accumulated depreciation (for balance sheet) £6,503 + £2,421 = £8,924

Did you know?

After drawing the three lines on your two pages, you should insert the heading of the profit and loss account. Headings should contain the 'Three W's': Who, What and When. Who – the business name; What – the name of the statement (e.g. profit and loss account); When – its date (e.g. year ended 31 May 2005). So the first things you should do when drawing up financial summaries are '3 lines, 3W's'.

Step 4

Draw three columns each about 3 cm wide on the right-hand side of two sheets of A4 paper. Sometimes it is not necessary to have a third column in the profit and loss account, but it is useful to draw it, just in case it is needed. Write in the heading and then start compiling the 'trading account' part of the profit and loss account, leading to the gross profit (no manufacturing account is required in this question). Continue with the rest of the profit and loss account, leading to the net profit or loss, making sure that all the adjustments previously noted have been made. Then complete the balance sheet.

The answer

Abigail Harvey
Profit and loss account for the year ended 31 May 2005

	£	£
Sales		624,220
Less **Cost of goods sold**		
Opening stock at 1 June 2004	87,355	
Add Purchases	478,000	
	565,355	
Less Closing stock at 31 May 2005	(84,800)	
		(480,555)
Gross profit		143,665
Less **Expenses**		
Wages and salaries	64,551	
Advertising	18,563	
Bad debts written off	5,835	
Bank interest paid	5,231	
Delivery expenses to customers	4,230	
Depreciation on fixtures and fittings	2,421	
Depreciation on motor cars	14,784	
Electricity	7,720	
Increase in provision for doubtful debts	500	
Insurance	2,440	
Loan interest	4,800	
Loss on disposal of motor car	160	
Rent and rates	5,900	
Telephone	11,240	
Sundry expenses	13,700	
		(162,075)
Net loss		(18,410)

Note that we did not need to use the 'third column' in this example.

Abigail Harvey
Balance sheet as at 31 May 2005

	Cost	Depreciation	Net book value
	£	£	£
Fixed assets			
Motor vehicles	59,920	37,744	22,176
Fixtures	24,210	8,924	15,286
	84,130	46,668	37,462
Current assets			
Stock		84,800	
Debtors	16,540		
Less Provision for doubtful debts	(2,500)		
		14,040	
Prepayments		200	
Cash		650	
		99,690	
Less Current liabilities			
Creditors	24,510		
Accruals	3,700		
Bank overdraft	14,852		
		(43,062)	
Net current assets			56,628
			94,090
Less Long-term liability			
6% loan (repayable 2009)			(80,000)
Total net assets			14,090
Capital			
Opening balance, 1 June 2004		100,000	
Less Net loss		(18,410)	
		81,590	
Less Drawings		(67,500)	
Closing balance, 31 May 2005			14,090

6.4 Extended trial balances

Many accountants use a technique known as an **extended trial balance** to summarise all the trial balance adjustments. Further columns show the profit and loss account entries (with the balance of profit or loss shown) and also the balance sheet figures. This format is useful where spreadsheets and computerised accounting methods are used. The extended trial balance for Abigail Harvey (see previous question) would be shown as in Figure 6.1. Look carefully at the format and see if you can trace back all the adjustments shown.

Figure 6.1
Abigail Harvey extended trial balance as at 31 May 2005

(All figures in £)	Trial balance Dr	Cr	Adjustments Dr	Cr	Profit and loss account Dr	Cr	Balance sheet Dr	Cr
Advertising	18,563				18,563			
Bad debts	5,835				5,835			
Bank overdraft		14,852						14,852
Bank interest paid	5,231				5,231			
Capital at 1 June 2004		100,000						100,000
Cash in hand	650						650	
Creditors		24,510						24,510
Debtors	16,540						16,540	
Delivery expenses to customers	4,230				4,230			
Depreciation on fixtures and fittings, at 1 June 2004		6,503		2,421				8,924
Depreciation on motor cars, at 1 June 2004		26,800	3,840	14,784				37,744
Drawings	67,500						67,500	
Electricity	6,420		1,300		7,720			
Fixtures and fittings (cost)	24,210						24,210	
Insurance	2,640			200	2,440			
Loan interest (half-year)	2,400		2,400		4,800			
Long-term 6% loan (repayable in 2009)		80,000						80,000
Motor cars (cost)	65,920			6,000			59,920	
Provision for doubtful debts at 1 June 2004		2,000		500				2,500
Purchases	478,000				478,000			
Rent and rates	5,900				5,900			
Sales		626,220	2,000			624,220		
Stock at 1 June 2004	87,355				87,355			
Sundry expenses	13,700				13,700			
Telephone	11,240				11,240			
Wages and salaries	64,551				64,551			
	880,885	880,885						
Closing stock (to profit and loss)			84,800			84,800		
Closing stock (to balance sheet)				84,800			84,800	
Accruals				3,700				3,700
Prepayments			200				200	
Increase in provision for doubtful debts			500		500			
Depreciation on cars for the year			14,784		14,784			
Loss on sale of car			160		160			
Depreciation on fixtures and fittings for the year			2,421		2,421			
			112,405	112,405				
Net loss for the year						18,410	18,410	
					727,430	727,430	272,230	272,230

6.5 Glossary

Extended trial balance   An adaptation of a conventional trial balance, with extra columns showing adjustments and profit and loss and balance sheet items.

? Self-check questions

(These can be used as a revision test of Chapters 1–5.)

1   Management accounting is:
  a   Used to make the business more cost-efficient
  b   Required by the Companies Act
  c   Used only by people outside the business
  d   Used to prepare a trial balance

2   Double-entry bookkeeping means:
  a   There are two doors leading into the accountant's office
  b   Every transaction is entered twice on the debit side and twice on the credit side
  c   Transactions are entered in two separate parts of the bookkeeping system
  d   All work is duplicated with no real benefit

3   GAAP stands for:
  a   Generally Available Accounting Practices
  b   Generally Accepted Accounting Principles
  c   Government Authorised Accounting Principles
  d   Give Accountants A Present

4   Which of the following is a fundamental accounting concept?
  a   Prepayments
  b   Prudish
  c   Gone Concern
  d   Consistency

5   Current assets include:
  a   Stock, debtors and prepayments
  b   Stock, debtors and accruals
  c   Stock, creditors and prepayments
  d   Stock, creditors and accruals

6   Depreciation is provided because:
  a   Most fixed assets tend to lose value over time
  b   Money must be set aside to replace the assets
  c   Every fixed asset loses value over time
  d   The owners know exactly how much fixed assets lose in value over time

7   Long-term liabilities are those which:
  a   Are due for repayment in less than one year
  b   Are never repaid
  c   Are due for repayment after more than one year
  d   Will be repaid in one year's time

8 'Drawings' is shown on the balance sheet as:
   a An addition to the capital account
   b A deduction from the capital account
   c Part of current liabilities
   d Part of current assets

9 The accounting equation can be written as:
   a Assets – Expenses = Liabilities + Capital + Income
   b Assets + Expenses = Liabilities – Capital + Income
   c Assets + Expenses = Liabilities + Capital – Income
   d Assets + Expenses = Liabilities + Capital + Income

10 Which of the following will result in a change in capital?
   a A fixed asset bought by the business for £10,000
   b A profit made by the organisation
   c A payment received from a debtor
   d A creditor paid by the business

11 A grocer buys a delivery van from Homer Motors for £9,000 by cheque. The entries to be made in the grocer's accounting system are:
   a Debit Delivery van, Credit Bank
   b Debit Purchases, Credit Bank
   c Debit Delivery van, Credit Homer Motors
   d Debit Bank, Credit Delivery van

12 Another name for the impersonal ledger is:
   a Purchase ledger
   b General ledger
   c Sales ledger
   d Cash ledger

13 In a business's bank account as shown in its cash book, a debit balance means:
   a The business has paid out too many cheques
   b The business owes the bank some money
   c The business has an overdraft
   d The business has money in the bank

14 Debtors are:
   a Customers who owe money to the business
   b Customers who buy goods for cash
   c Suppliers who are owed money by the business
   d Suppliers who have been paid by the business

15 A jam factory pays £3 for a stapler for use in its office. How would this be shown in the financial summaries?
   a As a fixed asset in the balance sheet
   b As purchases in the profit and loss account
   c As stationery in the profit and loss account
   d As a current asset in the balance sheet

16 The imprest system is used to control which of the following?
   a The design of the company's advertising campaigns
   b Petty cash expenditure
   c The rate of pay of employees
   d The amount of money the owner can take from the business

17 If a ledger account has debit entries totalling £450 and credit entries totalling £200, the balance on the account is:
   a Credit balance £250
   b Debit balance £250

c Debit balance £650

d Credit balance £650

18 During a month a business spends £195 on petty cash items and pays into petty cash a £5 note which the owner had borrowed previously. There was a cash float of £200 at the start of the month. Using the imprest system, how much will be paid into petty cash at the start of the next month?

a £200

b £10

c £190

d £390

19 An unpresented cheque is:

a A cheque which has not been processed by a bank

b A cheque which a customer forgot to pay to the business

c A cheque without all the necessary details filled in

d A duplicated cheque

20 A bank reconciliation:

a Checks the completeness of the information in the cash book and bank statements

b Is a statement of the maximum amount a bank is prepared to lend a business

c Tells the business that the cash book is 100% accurate

d Compares the bank balances of two separate businesses

21 A debit balance may appear on a purchases ledger account because:

a A supplier has overpaid

b A purchase invoice has been duplicated

c A business may have returned goods to a supplier after paying for them

d The business has paid the amount it owes a creditor

22 Relating to the closing stock for a financial period, which of the following is true?

a The figure is shown only in the profit and loss account

b The figure is shown only in the balance sheet

c The figure is shown in both the profit and loss account and the balance sheet

d The figure is shown as part of 'purchases' in the profit and loss account

23 A business started its year owing £4,000 for electricity. During the year it paid electricity bills totalling £24,000 but owed £5,000 by the end of the period. What will be the figure transferred to the profit and loss account for electricity?

a £33,000

b £15,000

c £23,000

d £25,000

24 A business installs a machine costing £40,000. The machine is expected to last for 5 years and have a residual value of £4,000. What is the machine's net book value at the end of 2 years' ownership?

a £25,600

b £7,200

c £14,400

d £21,600

25 A car is bought for £16,000. It is to be depreciated on a reducing balance basis using a rate of 40% p.a. What is the car's net book value at the end of 2 years' ownership?

a £9,600

b £5,760

c £12,800

d £3,200

26 For a pen factory, indirect costs could include:
  a The cost of gold to make the pens
  b The cost of heating the factory
  c The wages paid to the skilled workers making the pens
  d The cost of velvet-lined boxes in which each pen is packaged

27 Which of the following headings appears in a manufacturing account?
  a Cost of sales
  b Gross profit
  c Prime cost of production
  d Net profit

28 A company has opening stock £6,900, closing stock £7,800, purchases £33,650, carriage inwards £700 and purchases returns £400. What is its cost of goods sold?
  a £31,650
  b £33,850
  c £33,050
  d £48,650

29 An appropriation account is *not* part of the profit and loss account for which type of business organisation?
  a Sole trader
  b Partnership
  c Limited company
  d Plc (public limited company)

30 A business sells an asset on 1 January for £12,000. The asset was bought exactly 2 years previously for £24,000 and depreciation was charged over 5 years on the straight line method, assuming no residual value. What is the profit or loss on disposal?
  a £7,200 loss
  b £2,400 loss
  c £12,000 loss
  d £12,000 profit

31 A company starts business on 1 January. In that month it buys 300 grecks at £40 each, then 200 at £50 each. On the last day of the month it sells 400 grecks. If it uses FIFO to value stock, what is the stock value at 31 January?
  a £4,500
  b £4,000
  c £5,000
  d £5,500

32 A company selling designer watches bought 400 for £60 each. Normal selling price is £100 per watch, but a change in fashion has resulted in all the watches being saleable at only £30 each, after a different strap, costing £2 each, has been fitted to them. How should the stock of watches be valued?
  a £11,200
  b £24,000
  c £39,200
  d £12,000

33 What is a doubtful debt?
  a A debt where there is some hope of getting paid
  b A debt where there is no hope of getting paid
  c A debt which is bad
  d A debt where the customer has queried an invoice

34 At the start of a year, a business has £3,000 on its provision for doubtful debts account. By the end of the year, doubtful debts have increased to £4,200. What entries would be shown in the financial summaries?

a Expenses include £7,200 and debtors are reduced by £7,200

b Expenses include £4,200 and debtors are reduced by £4,200

c Profit is increased by £1,200 and debtors are reduced by £4,200

d Expenses include £1,200 and debtors are reduced by £4,200

35 If a bad debt is unexpectedly paid some years after it was written off, what would be the effect in the financial summaries for that year?

a Increase profit and decrease debtors' balances

b Increase profit and increase the bank account

c Increase the debtors' balances shown under current assets

d No effect

(Answers in Appendix 1)

 ## Self-study questions

(Answers in Appendix 2)

Question 6.1 From the following trial balance and attached notes, prepare a profit and loss account for the year ended 30 September 2005 and a balance sheet as at that date.

Felicity Frankton
Trial balance as at 30 September 2005

	Dr £	Cr £
Bad debts written off	500	
Bank balance	1,260	
Capital, 1 October 2004		15,940
Carriage inwards	320	
Carriage outwards	430	
Computers, at cost	3,610	
Creditors		13,600
Debtors	24,200	
Depreciation on computers, 1 October 2004		1,850
Depreciation on motor cars, 1 October 2004		7,600
Discount allowed	340	
Drawings	16,900	
Light and heat	2,200	
Motor cars, at cost	16,500	
Opening stock, 1 October 2004	16,520	
Proceeds of sale of motor car		1,500
Provision for doubtful debts, 1 October 2004		800
Purchases	32,410	
Rent and rates	3,200	
Sales		105,800
Sundry office expenses	10,200	
Wages and salaries	18,500	
	147,090	147,090

Notes:

1 Closing stock was valued at £14,560.

2 A car costing £7,900 on 1 October 2002 was sold during the year for £1,500. Depreciation to the date of sale was £6,000. No entries had been made relating to this sale, other than crediting the proceeds to a separate general ledger account.

3 £600 was owed for rent and rates at the end of the year, and £200 had been prepaid at the end of the year relating to sundry office expenses.

4 The provision for doubtful debts was to be adjusted to 5% of the closing debtors total.

5 Depreciation is charged as follows:

Computer equipment: over 5 years on the straight line basis, assuming no residual values

Motor cars: 60% p.a. on the reducing balance basis, with no depreciation being charged in the year of sale.

Question 6.2 From the following trial balance and attached notes, prepare a profit and loss account for the year ended 31 December 2004 and a balance sheet as at that date.

Patrick Cooper
Trial balance as at 31 December 2004

	Dr £	Cr £
Sales		289,512
Purchases	132,950	
Opening stock	5,620	
Discount allowed	200	
Bank interest	950	
Wages and salaries	39,540	
Drawings	22,000	
Administration expenses	55,500	
Capital at 1 January 2004		16,268
Debtors	6,300	
Creditors		5,210
Provision for doubtful debts		300
Bad debts written off	250	
Selling expenses	37,790	
Equipment at cost	14,000	
Depreciation on equipment at 1 January 2004		2,350
Bank overdraft		1,600
Cash in hand	140	
	315,240	315,240

Notes:

1 Closing stock was valued at £4,900.

2 There was an accrual of £300 for selling expenses and £150 of the administration expenses were prepaid.

3 An item of equipment bought for £600 on 1 January 2001 was sold for £100 on 1 January 2004. The proceeds are shown as part of 'Sales'. Equipment is depreciated at 20% p.a. on the straight line basis, with no residual values.

4 The provision for doubtful debts is to be increased to £550.

Case study

Marvin's second birthday

Marvin (see previous case studies) celebrated two years in business on 30 June 2002. At that date, his versatile assistant, Chiquita, produced the following trial balance:

	Dr £	Cr £
Appearance fees as entertainer		45,200
Cost of magician's equipment	7,700	
Cost of 'saw the lady in half' prop	3,000	
Bad debt	200	
Purchases of novelties for resale	15,600	
Sales of novelties		35,900
Marvin's drawings	32,000	
Wages to assistant (Chiquita)	24,600	
Travel to performance venues	6,220	
Cleaning	1,320	
Loss on disposal of 'disappearing lady' apparatus	160	
Opening stock of novelties	2,400	
Opening capital, 1 July 2001		18,300
Creditors		480
Debtors	2,600	
Bank balance	5,160	
Depreciation on magician's equipment, 1 July 2001		1,080
	100,960	100,960

Notes:

1 At the very start of the year he closed down the manufacturing section, selling stock of raw materials and machinery at their book values. There is no need to prepare a manufacturing account.

2 Closing stock of bought-in novelties at 30 June 2002 was £2,500.

3 Marvin owed £250 for dry-cleaning at 30 June 2002, but had paid £600 on 1 April 2002 for a rail season ticket lasting 12 months.

4 Depreciation for the year on the magician's equipment was £1,300. The 'saw the lady in half' prop is depreciated over 4 years, assuming a residual value of 20% of cost price.

5 A provision for doubtful debts is to be created of 5% of the closing debtors total.

Required:

Prepare Marvin's profit and loss account for the year ended 30 June 2002 and a balance sheet as at that date.

(Answers in Appendix 3)

References

Look in your college library for introductory financial accounting textbooks (Library section 657). They will all contain questions requiring the preparation of financial summaries from a trial balance. Practise as many as possible.

Chapter 7

Accounting and financing of multi-owner organisations

Objectives

When you have read this chapter you will be able to:

➤ Identify the accounting requirements of sole traders, partnerships and limited companies

➤ Appreciate the different financing possibilities for various types of business organisation

➤ Distinguish between rights issues and bonus issues

➤ Understand the meaning of 'published accounts'

➤ Give a simple definition of a 'group' of companies

7.1 Introduction

In the preceding chapters, the main emphasis has been on the preparation and summarising of a sole trader's accounting information. Many businesses, including the largest in terms of sales and profitability, are not sole traders but are formed as partnerships or limited companies. Limited companies themselves can be either 'private' limited companies (Ltd) or public limited companies (plc's). Many limited companies are *subsidiary* companies, owned by another company, in what is known as a 'group' of companies. All these have differing accounting requirements, some more complex than others. In this chapter we take an overview of these, with the emphasis on limited company accounts. We also look at the sources of finance available for the different forms of business enterprise.

7.2 Sole traders

Sole traders, by definition, are businesses owned by one person. The advantages of operating as a sole trader are as follows:

- The owner has absolute control over the business.
- The business can be established without any legal formalities.
- Personal supervision by the owner may result in a better service to customers and clients.
- The owner does not have to reveal the financial results of the business to the general public.

However, there are also disadvantages, including the following:

- The owner has personal liability for all the debts of the business, without limit.
- Total control and personal supervision usually require long hours and very hard work.
- There is no co-owner with whom to share the problems and anxieties associated with running the business.
- If the owner is absent from the business due to sickness or other reasons, this may have a serious effect on the state of the business.
- Future prospects for expansion are restricted, as they depend on the owner's ability to raise finance.

Did you know?

A UK Department of Trade and Industry survey showed that, at the start of 2003, there were approximately 3.8 million businesses in the UK, divided as follows:

	% of total businesses in UK	% of total employed in UK	% of total business turnover in UK
Small (0–49 employees)	99.1	43.7	37
Medium (50–249 employees)	0.7	11.9	15
Large (over 250 employees)	0.2	44.4	48
Total businesses/employees/ turnover	3.8m	22.7m	£2,200m

The main sources of finance for a sole trader are:

- Capital introduced by the owner
- Loans from friends and family
- Bank borrowings, through overdrafts or loans
- Profits ploughed back into the business.

Although many people prefer independence and quite happily continue as sole traders, it is extremely difficult to expand a business without also increasing the number of people who own it. The main choice for sole traders wishing to convert to or form multi-ownership enterprises is between a partnership and a limited liability company.

7.3 Partnerships

A **partnership** is defined in the Partnership Act of 1890 as:

The relation which subsists between persons carrying on a business in common with a view of profit.

Did you know?

The accounting firm PricewaterhouseCoopers has nearly 8,000 partners worldwide.

Often, partnerships are formed by professional people such as architects, accountants and solicitors. Whilst the minimum number of partners is two, there is no maximum number, so major professional partnerships of solicitors or accountants might have hundreds or even thousands of partners.

The advantages of partnership include the following:

- The problems and pleasures of running the business are shared.
- There is access to greater expertise and financial input.
- Losses as well as profits are shared.
- Few legal formalities are involved, though a partnership agreement should be drawn up to avoid misunderstandings.
- The financial results do not have to be made public.

Disadvantages include the following:

- Personality clashes may threaten the business and ultimately cause the break-up of the partnership.
- In the vast majority of partnerships, there is no restriction on the personal liability of partners for the debts of the business (occasionally a limited partnership may be formed, but at least one partner must have unlimited liability).
- Generally, a partnership has less access to funding for expansion than does a limited company.

The main sources of finance for a partnership are:

- Capital introduced by the partners
- Loans from friends and family of partners
- Bank borrowings, through overdrafts or loans, secured either on the partnership's assets or on the personal assets of individual partners
- Profits ploughed back into the business.

7.3.1 Accounting requirements of partnerships

In most respects, including the day-to-day bookkeeping aspects, partnership accounting is identical with that of a sole trader. The only difference is that accounts must be opened showing the financial implications of the partnership agreement. These include details of:

- Shares of profits and losses
- Capital introduced and withdrawn by each partner
- Drawings made by each partner
- Whether any partners are to receive a guaranteed salary (for example, if only one partner works full-time for the partnership)
- Interest charged on drawings (to discourage individual partners from drawing excessive amounts)
- Interest allowed on capital balances (to reward those partners who have invested more than others).

Occasionally, partners cannot agree over vital matters such as how to split profits and losses. In such cases the Partnership Act 1890 states that they should be shared equally.

7.3.2 Capital accounts and current accounts

Partnership capital accounts and **partnership current accounts** are the key accounts recording the details of each partner. Sometimes all relevant transactions are recorded in capital accounts, which work in a similar way to a sole trader's capital account. In many partnerships, capital accounts record only 'fixed' agreed capital balances, with all other transactions recorded in 'current' accounts (not to be confused with bank current accounts).

7.3.3 Partnership appropriation accounts

When preparing a partnership's financial summaries, the profit and loss account will be produced in exactly the same way as that for a sole trader. The only additional information, an appropriation account, comes in a separate section after the net profit or loss has been determined, as the profit or loss has to be 'appropriated' between the partners according to their partnership agreement. If partners have also agreed to pay themselves salaries or charge interest on drawings or capital, these items are also shown in this section.

Activity 7.1

Gilbert and Bufton are partners sharing profits and losses in the ratio 3:2. The net profit for the year ended 31 December 2004 was £60,000. As Gilbert worked full-time whilst Bufton worked part-time for the partnership, Gilbert was allowed a salary of £12,000 p.a. No interest was charged on drawings or credited on capital balances. Show the appropriation account section of the profit and loss account for the year.

Answer

	£	£
Net profit for the year		60,000
Appropriated as follows:		
Gilbert: salary		(12,000)
		48,000
Gilbert: share of profit (60% × £48,000)	28,800	
Bufton: share of profit (40% × £48,000)	19,200	
		48,000

Pause for thought

Gilbert's salary, unlike employees' salaries, is not shown as an 'expense' in arriving at the net profit figure. It is part of the way in which the partners have decided to share the profit. If interest on capital or drawings had been agreed, the amounts would be added (interest on drawings) or deducted (interest on capital) from the £48,000 subtotal prior to the calculation of the share of profits.

7.3.4 Partnership balance sheet

The top part of the balance sheet, showing fixed and current assets and liabilities, is identical with that of a sole trader. However, the sole trader's capital account is replaced by details of partners' capital accounts (and current accounts if they are maintained).

Activity 7.2

Gilbert and Bufton (see Activity 7.1) started the year with capital balances of £25,900 and £15,750 respectively. During the year, Gilbert had drawings of £35,000 whereas Bufton drew £17,000. No current accounts were maintained for the partnership.

Show the relevant extract from the partnership balance sheet as at 31 December 2004.

Answer

	£	£
(Assets less liabilities)		49,650
Gilbert's capital account		
Opening balance, 1 January 2004	25,900	
Add Salary	12,000	
Share of profit	28,800	
	66,700	
Less Drawings	(35,000)	
Closing balance, 31 December 2004		31,700
Bufton's capital account		
Opening balance, 1 January 2004	15,750	
Add Share of profit	19,200	
	34,950	
Less Drawings	(17,000)	
Closing balance, 31 December 2004		17,950
		49,650

Pause for thought

Any interest on capital or drawings would also have been adjusted within the capital accounts. Interest on capital is added, whereas interest on drawings is deducted.

7.4 Limited companies

Although there are many advantages in running a business as a sole trader or a partnership, these can be outweighed by the fact that the owner or partners have personal responsibility for meeting all the debts of their business. Whilst this may be of little concern to the proprietors of healthy, profitable businesses, it can have a devastating effect on the fortunes of owners of failing or loss-making enterprises, as they must meet the claims of creditors from their personal assets if the business's assets are insufficient.

Another major disadvantage for ambitious business owners is the restricted scope they have for raising funds for expansion. To overcome these, many businesses are organised as **limited companies**. Their main features are:

- They are separate legal entities, able to trade, own assets and owe liabilities (including tax on their profit) in their own right independently from their owners.

- Ownership is (with rare exceptions) divided into shares ('the share capital') which can be bought and sold.

- The owners (known as **shareholders** or **members**) have **limited liability** for the debts of the company, so even if the company fails with considerable debts, their loss is restricted to the value of their part of the share capital.

- Management is in the hands of **directors**, who might own only a small part of the share capital. They are elected by the shareholders.

- **Public limited companies (plc's)** are allowed to sell their shares to the general public, which enables them to have access to massive funds for expansion. Public limited companies are the largest businesses in the country. **Private limited companies (Ltd)** cannot sell their shares to the public.

- Limited companies can raise money by issuing **debentures** (also known as 'bonds'), meaning fixed interest loans usually secured on the company's assets, and by issuing **convertible loan stock**, meaning loans which can be converted into shares at a later date. *Neither debentures nor loan stocks are part of a company's share capital.*

Limited companies do have a number of disadvantages when compared with other forms of business organisations:

- Lack of secrecy, as companies have to publish financial information, though large companies have to disclose more than small ones.

- Extra costs of complying with legislation, which includes the Companies Act 1985. For large companies this requires the appointment of an **auditor** who is an independent qualified accountant responsible for reporting whether the published financial information shows a true and fair view.

- More formality – shareholders' meetings must be held, annual returns must be completed and sent to the government, etc.

7.4.1 Accounting requirements of limited companies

As with partnerships, the day-to-day bookkeeping will be identical with that of sole traders. Records are also needed of the following items which are specific to limited companies.

Expenses

- Payments to directors (also called remuneration or emoluments), which are classified as an expense of the company, and therefore included within the profit and loss account under that heading.

- Auditors' fees (though not all companies have auditors).

- Interest on debentures and interest on loan stock.

Appropriations of profit

As with partnerships, the profit or loss needs to be 'appropriated'.

- A limited company is responsible for taxation on its own profits, so the first appropriation is to the government in the form of the corporation tax provision for the year.

- Rewards to the owners are in the form of **dividends** on their shares. These are usually expressed as 'pence per share' and might be paid once a year (a 'final' dividend) or more frequently ('interim' dividends and a final dividend).

- The last appropriation is to the company itself, as it can hold profits in the form of **reserves**. The main reserve is known simply as the profit and loss account – it represents the profits retained in the company after all other appropriations have been made.

Balance sheet items

The total net assets section of a limited company's balance sheet looks very similar to any other balance sheet, though sometimes you might see an asset called 'goodwill', which occurs when one business has taken over another business and paid a price greater than the value of the individual net assets acquired. Under 'creditors due for payment within one year' (current liabilities), the following additional items are shown:

- Taxation, being the corporation tax due to the government at the balance sheet date.

- Proposed dividend, being the final dividend for the year which will be paid to shareholders once it has been approved at the company's annual general meeting (**AGM**). The AGM takes place some months after the date of the balance sheet.

Did you know?

International Accounting Standards (IASs) refer to long-term liabilities as 'non-current liabilities'.

'Creditors due for payment after more than one year' (long-term liabilities) may also include the following:

- Debentures, assuming that the loan has more than one year before it is due to be repaid. Otherwise it will be shown as a current liability.

It is the 'capital' side of a limited company's balance sheet which shows major differences compared with the balance sheets of sole traders or partnerships. It is divided into two main sections:

- Share capital, which is the total share capital issued to shareholders. The vast majority of these shares are known as **ordinary shares** or the **equity capital** of the company. Each share carries an equal right to vote at company meetings and to share in any dividends, so the more shares owned, the more votes and dividends a shareholder has. Shares have a **nominal value** (also called a **par value**), for example 25p or 5p. Sometimes dividends are expressed as a percentage of this nominal value. Each company has a maximum number of shares which it is allowed to issue (its **authorised share capital**), whilst the actual amount of share capital in the hands of shareholders is known as the **issued or called-up share capital**. Some companies, as well as having ordinary shares, issue **preference shares**, which carry a fixed rate of dividend and have priority over the ordinary shares in respect of the payment of their dividends and the repayment of capital in the event of the company's **liquidation**. These shares might be *redeemable*, which means that the company can refund the preference shareholders' capital (subject to certain rules to protect the overall capital of the company) after a specified time.

Did you know?

Tesco plc had issued 7.2 billion ordinary shares of 5p nominal value at its 2004 balance sheet date.

Did you know?

Tesco plc's profit and loss account stood at £4 billion at its 2004 balance sheet date.

- Reserves, which are classified as either **capital** (non-distributable) **reserves** or **revenue** (distributable) **reserves**. The main revenue reserve is the profit and loss account, which represents all the **retained** ('unappropriated') **profits** of the company, not just for the current year but since the company formed. Revenue reserves are known as 'distributable' because they can be used for paying company dividends.

The main capital reserve is the **share premium account**, which is the amount *above the nominal value* paid into the company by shareholders. For example, a company might sell its 25p nominal value shares for £2.75, in which case the 25p's go into the share capital section of the balance sheet, whilst the remaining £2.50's are shown under 'share premium account'.

Did you know?

Tesco plc's share premium account totalled £3.5 billion at its 2004 balance sheet date.

Another capital reserve would arise if a company decided to *revalue* some of its fixed assets (specifically land and buildings). For example, if a plot of land bought several years ago for £30,000 is now worth £90,000, the company might wish to show this increase by adding £60,000 to the fixed asset value and creating an **asset revaluation reserve** for the same amount. The £60,000 is known as an **unrealised gain** ('unrealised' meaning that the land has not been sold), and is not included in the profit and loss account. However, the overall result is that the asset value shown in the balance sheet is more realistic. It is important to note that capital reserves are 'non-distributable' because they cannot be used to pay a dividend.

Activity 7.3

Smithdown Ltd's trial balance as at 31 May 2005 was as follows:

	Dr £	Cr £
Advertising	3,400	
Bank overdraft		4,000
Carriage out	1,890	
Directors' remuneration	77,300	
Fixed assets (office equipment and showroom) – net book value as at 1 June 2004	248,720	
Interest	1,900	
Interim dividend, paid 10 January 2005	5,000	
Office expenses	10,930	
Office salaries	26,200	
Opening stock at 1 June 2004	23,500	
Profit and loss account as at 1 June 2004		245,000
Purchases	117,620	
Sales		345,000
Salesforce wages	36,640	
Share capital (25p nominal shares)		100,000
Share premium account		140,000
Trade creditors		86,200
Trade debtors	367,100	
	920,200	920,200

Notes:

1 Closing stock at 31 May 2005 was £27,900.
2 Depreciation for the year: office equipment £3,820, showroom £4,500.
3 There were neither accruals nor prepayments at the year-end.
4 Corporation tax amounting to £16,000 was to be provided for.
5 A final dividend of 2p per share was proposed and agreed by shareholders.

Prepare the company's profit and loss account for the year ended 31 May 2005 and its balance sheet as at that date.

Answer

Smithdown Ltd
Profit and loss account for the year ended 31 May 2005

	£	£
Sales		345,000
Less **Cost of goods sold**		
Opening stock at 1 June 2004	23,500	
Add Purchases	117,620	
	141,120	
Less Closing stock at 31 May 2005	(27,900)	
		(113,220)
Gross profit	c/f	231,780

Gross profit	b/f	231,780
Less **Expenses**		
Directors' remuneration	77,300	
Salesforce wages	36,640	
Office salaries	26,200	
Advertising	3,400	
Interest	1,900	
Carriage out	1,890	
Depreciation on office equipment	3,820	
Depreciation on showroom	4,500	
Office expenses	10,930	
		(166,580)
Net profit for the year, before taxation		65,200
Less Provision for taxation		(16,000)
Net profit for the year, after taxation		49,200
Less Dividends:		
Interim (paid)	5,000	
Final (proposed)	8,000	
		(13,000)
Retained profit for the year		36,200

Smithdown Ltd
Balance sheet as at 31 May 2005

	£	£	£
Fixed assets			
(details would be shown)			240,400
Current assets			
Stock		27,900	
Trade debtors		367,100	
		395,000	
Less **Creditors due for payment within one year**			
Trade creditors	86,200		
Taxation	16,000		
Proposed dividend	8,000		
Overdraft	4,000		
		(114,200)	
Net current assets			280,800
Total net assets			521,200
Capital and reserves			
Called-up share capital (25p shares)			100,000
Share premium account			140,000
Profit and loss account:			
Balance at 1 June 2004		245,000	
Retained profit for the year		36,200	
			281,200
			521,200

Did you know?

International Accounting Standards (IASs) refer to fixed assets as 'non-current assets'.

Of the £65,200 net profit, £16,000 goes to the government, £13,000 to shareholders (the final dividend is calculated as 400,000 shares @ 2p each) and the balance of £36,200 is left within the company and added to the retained profits at the start of the year. Note that the word 'reserve' is *not* the same as 'cash'. Reserves are represented by many different types of net assets, one of which might or might not be a cash balance.

7.4.2 Rights issues and bonus issues

A company's share capital might change for a number of reasons, including, for a plc, a new share issue to the general public or, for a private limited company, new shares issued to family and friends. Two other reasons for a change are as follows.

- A **rights issue**, which is a further share issue to existing shareholders, in proportion to existing holdings (for example, a '3 for 2' rights issue gives the holders of two existing shares the 'right' to buy a further three shares, so if you hold 6,000 shares you could buy a further 9,000 shares). A rights issue is often the easiest way for a company to raise more capital, and shares are usually offered at an attractive price to tempt investors. Obviously, an unsuccessful company may have difficulties in attracting more capital from their shareholders.

- A **bonus issue** is a *free* issue of shares to existing shareholders, again in proportion to their existing holdings, so a '1 for 4' bonus issue would mean that a shareholder with 1,200 shares would be *given* a further 300. Bonus share issues (also called scrip or capitalisation issues) are a way of transferring reserves (revenue or capital) back to the shareholders, without the need for any cash payments to be made by the company. It is, on the face of it, a cosmetic exercise to rearrange a balance sheet where reserves have grown disproportionately in relation to the company's share capital. However, if a company uses its revenue reserves to make a bonus issue, it is thereby reducing the reserves available for dividend payments in the future (remember that only revenue (distributable) reserves can be used for dividend payments). This may not be welcomed by all shareholders.

The 'share capital and reserves' section of Smithdown Ltd's balance sheet at 31 May 2005 (see Activity 7.3) was as follows:

	£	£
Capital and reserves		
Called-up share capital (25p shares)		100,000
Share premium account		140,000
Profit and loss account:		
Balance at 1 June 2004	245,000	
Retained profit for the year	36,200	
		281,200
		521,200

Assume that on 1 June 2005 a rights issue on a '3 for 5' basis was made at 80p per share. All the existing shareholders decided to take up their shares, and paid for them in full by 30 June 2005. Six months later, the company made a bonus issue on a '2 for 1' basis, the issue being paid up equally from the share premium account and the profit and loss account.

Show the revised 'share capital and reserves' section (a) after the rights issue and (b) after the bonus issue. Ignore any trading profit which may have been made in the period.

Answer

a Balance sheet after the rights issue:

	£	£
Capital and reserves		
Called-up share capital (25p shares)[1]		160,000
Share premium account[2]		272,000
Profit and loss account:		
Balance at 1 June 2005		281,200
		713,200

Note that the balance sheet totals will agree, as £192,000 will be added to the bank balance under 'current assets' (240,000 shares issued at 80p = £192,000).

Notes:

1 Original 400,000 shares, plus 240,000 issued as '3 for 5' = 640,000 @ 25p nominal value = £160,000.

2 Original £140,000, plus share premium on rights issue [240,000 × (80p − 25p)] = £272,000.

b Balance sheet after the rights issue and the bonus issue:

	£	£
Capital and reserves		
Called-up share capital (25p shares)[1]		480,000
Share premium account[2]		112,000
Profit and loss account[3]		
Balance at 1 June 2005		121,200
		713,200

Notes:

1 '2 for 1' trebles the previous share capital (an extra 1,280,000 shares @ 25p each = £320,000).

2 Half of the bonus comes out of the share premium account (£272,000 − £160,000 = £112,000).

3 Half of the bonus comes out of the profit and loss account (£281,200 − £160,000 = £121,200).

Pause for thought

Note that the bonus issue has no effect on the balance sheet total.

7.5 Short- and long-term sources of financing

When a business is considering how it can continue and develop, it will have to make many vital decisions regarding alternative ways in which finance can be raised. Profitable businesses may be able to thrive by ploughing back profits into the company (known as 'internal financing'), but to expand or cope with occasional trading difficulties additional external finance may be necessary. For short-term needs, bank overdrafts might be used, as they are the most flexible type of borrowing, but other possibilities exist, including debt factoring. For longer-term financing needs, ordinary or preference shares can be sold, or loans can be raised with fixed or variable interest rates which are repayable (or convertible into equity capital) at an agreed future date. As a way of avoiding large cash outlays, many businesses decide not to pay for fixed assets in one lump sum but instead enter finance leasing contracts, where smaller payments are made over a prolonged period. Efficient management of stock, debtors and creditors will also result in a more financially viable business. This section summarises various financing possibilities, both short- and long-term.

7.5.1 Long-term sources of finance: share sales

Private companies comprise the vast majority of limited liability enterprises, and are not allowed to offer their shares for sale to the general public. However, they *are* able to sell their shares, but the persons who buy are likely to be friends, relatives or business aquaintances of existing shareholders. A public limited company (plc) wanting to raise capital by means of a share issue will usually do so by an *offer for sale*, whereby the shares are sold first by the company to a financial institution (for example, a bank), which then offers the shares for sale to the general public by placing advertisements in national newspapers. When a company offers its shares to the public for the first time, this is known as an initial public offering (IPO).

It is unusual for public limited companies to sell their own shares directly to the public. Where relatively small amounts are involved, one or more financial institutions might buy all the available shares off the company and then sell the shares to their own customers. This is known as a 'placing'. Most large share sales will be *underwritten*, which means that if insufficient shares are taken up by the general public, 'underwriters' will buy the unsold shares at an agreed price, charging a comission to the company as their fee for taking the risks involved. The underwriters will then sell on their shares at the appropriate time through the stock market. The underwriting process guarantees that the company will sell all the shares.

Figure 7.1 shows details of Halfords Group plc's share offer in mid 2004, where it sold 102 million shares at £2.60 each.

Activity 7.5

Look at today's share prices for Halfords Group plc. Has the share price risen or fallen since the share issue?

Figure 7.1
Halfords Group plc's share offer

This notice is issued in compliance with the requirements of the UK Listing Authority and appears as a matter of record only. It does not constitute an offer or invitation to any person to subscribe for or purchase any securities in Halfords Group Plc (the **"Company"**). The ordinary shares of the Company (the **"Ordinary Shares"**) have not been and will not be registered under the US Securities Act of 1933, as amended (the **"Securities Act"**), under the applicable state securities laws of the United States or under the applicable securities laws of Australia, Canada or Japan and, subject to certain exceptions, the Ordinary Shares may not be offered or sold directly, or indirectly, in or into the United States, Australia, Canada or Japan, or to any person resident in Australia, Canada or Japan. This notice is not an offer of securities for sale in the United States. The securities discussed herein have not been and will not be registered under the Securities Act, and may not be offered or sold in the United States absent registration or an exemption from registration under the Securities Act. No public offering of the Ordinary Shares is being made in the United States. This notice does not constitute an offer of, or solicitation of an offer to subscribe for or buy, any of the Ordinary Shares offered hereby to any person in any jurisdiction as to whom it is unlawful to make such an offer or solicitation in such jurisdiction.

Application has been made to the UK Listing Authority for admission of all of the Ordinary Shares, issued and to be issued in connection with the Global Offer, to the Official List and to the London Stock Exchange for such Ordinary Shares to be admitted to trading on the London Stock Exchange's market for listed securities (together **"Admission"**). Conditional dealings in the Ordinary Shares commenced on 3 June 2004. It is expected that Admission will become effective, and that unconditional dealings in the Ordinary Shares will commence on the London Stock Exchange, at 8.00 a.m. (London time) on 8 June 2004. All dealings in the Ordinary Shares prior to the commencement of unconditional dealings will be on a "when issued" basis and will be of no effect if Admission does not take place. Such dealings will be at the sole risk of the parties concerned.

HALFORDS GROUP PLC
(Incorporated in England and Wales under the Companies Act 1985
with registered number 4457314)

Global Offer of 102,563,988 Ordinary Shares of 1p each
at a price of 260p per Ordinary Share
and admission to the Official List and to trading on
the London Stock Exchange

Global Coordinator and Sponsor
Merrill Lynch International

Joint Bookrunners

Citigroup   Merrill Lynch International

Co-Lead Managers

UBS Investment Bank   Cazenove

Share Capital immediately following Admission

Authorised			*Issued and fully paid*	
Number	*Amount(£)*		*Number*	*Amount(£)*
295,000,000	*2,950,000*	*Ordinary Shares of 1p each*	*227,919,993*	*2,279,200*

Listing Particulars dated 3 June 2004 relating to the Company and the Global Offer have been published in the United Kingdom and have been approved by the UK Listing Authority as required by the Listing Rules made under section 74 of the Financial Services and Markets Act 2000. Copies of the Listing Particulars are available for inspection at the Document Viewing Facility, The Financial Services Authority, 25 The North Colonnade, Canary Wharf, London E19 5HS, and may be obtained in printed form during normal business hours on any weekday (Saturdays, Sundays and public holidays excepted) during the period up to and including 18 June 2004 from:

Halfords Group Plc	Merrill Lynch International	Citigroup Global Markets
Icknield Street Drive	Merrill Lynch Financial Centre	U.K. Equity Limited
Washford	2 King Edward Street	Citigroup Centre
Redditch	London	Canada Square
Worcestershire	EC1A 1HQ	London
B98 0DE		E14 5LB

4 June 2004

Source: *Financial Times*, 4 June 2004. Courtesy of Halfords Group plc.

7.5.2 Long-term sources of finance: loans

The loan capital of a company might comprise several different elements, including the following:

- Bank loans, which carry either a fixed or floating interest rate, and will usually be secured against company assets to protect the bank in the event of default. Repayments of capital and interest might be made over the loan period with the capital amount being repaid at the end.

- Debentures, also known as bonds, are also likely to be secured against assets and usually carry a fixed rate of interest. Debentures can be bought and sold after issue, in the same way that shares are traded. Holders of debentures and bonds are *creditors* of the company, not shareholders. As with shares, the market price will depend on supply and demand, but debentures are seen as a less risky investment owing to their security. However, lower risk also brings a lower reward in the form of the fixed interest rate which remains unchanged regardless of how profitable the company becomes. Another aspect of lower risk is that the interest is payable to debenture owners before any shareholders' dividends can be declared. Some loans (convertible loan stock) might be convertible into ordinary shares at a date (or dates) stated in the debenture deed, which may make them more attractive to investors. Some loans might even be termed 'irredeemable', meaning that there is no set repayment date.

The relationship between a company's share and loan capital is referred to as its *gearing*, and this is explained in section 10.5.4 on pages 199–200.

7.5.3 Long-term sources of finance: finance leases

A **finance lease** is a means by which companies obtain the right to use assets over a period of time. The ownership of the asset never passes to the actual user of the asset. For example, a company (A) that needs a machine costing £5m may enter a finance arrangement with a finance company (B), where B buys the machine and then leases it to A, with A paying a lease amount to B over an agreed period (for example, £1m p.a. over 6 years). B retains ownership of the machine, and can sell it at the end of the lease contract. A has the advantage of avoiding a large cash outlay compared with an outright purchase of the machine, enabling it to replace ageing or outdated assets in a cost-efficient way.

7.5.4 Short-term sources of finance: bank overdrafts

A bank overdraft is a flexible form of borrowing, usually secured on company assets. It tends to be used for short-term financing, but may become long-term if needed. The company will usually negotiate overdraft facilities annually, so that it can draw funds up to an agreed limit. Temporary increases in the limit can often be arranged by a telephone call or letter to the bank manager. The main drawback is that the overdraft is repayable on demand, but this would only happen if the company was in extreme financial difficulties. Normally some repayment scheme can be worked out, whereby the overdraft is transferred into a long-term loan.

The overdrawn company pays interest on the actual balance, not the agreed limit, so that if it has used £400,000 of an agreed £500,000 limit, it is only charged interest on the £400,000. Most banks charge a flat percentage fee when an overdraft is arranged or renegotiated, so there is a financial disincentive in having a higher limit than is necessary.

7.5.5 Short-term sources of finance: debt factoring

Uncollected debts from customers can represent a significant headache for a company, and significant amounts might be spent in credit control procedures. With debt factoring, outstanding debts are in effect sold to a specialised financial institution (a **factor**), which then takes on the responsibility of debt collection, leaving the business's management to concentrate on more profitable activities. The factor will initially advance up to 80% of the debts, and then pay the remainder, less a commission, when the debts are recovered. This improves the cash flow of the business, both by bringing in cash very soon after a credit sale is made, and by reducing the expense of credit control. The downside is that the factor will charge a fee (around 3%) based on the company's turnover, and it may be seen by customers as a signal that the company is in financial difficulty.

7.5.6 Internal sources of finance

As well as the short- and long-term external finance sources listed above, there are several internal sources that can be used. Some are obvious – for example, retaining profit rather than paying it out to shareholders as dividends – but others relate to the efficient management of stock, debtors and creditors, as follows:

- Stock should be kept to a minimum, otherwise too much stock may be held, resulting in high costs for storage and security, plus interest on overdrafts and loans used to pay for the stock.
- Debtors should be encouraged to pay as soon as possible, otherwise inadequate control of debtors may result in uncollected debts (see section 7.5.5 on debt factoring, above).
- The time taken to pay creditors (the creditors' payment period) might be lengthened to take advantage of interest-free credit periods.

Look at section 10.5.2 on page 195 for ways of calculating efficiency ratios relating to these items.

7.5.7 Summary of finance sources

	Internal	External
Long-term	Retaining profits	Share issues
		Bank loans
		Debentures
		Finance leases
Short-term	Reducing stock	Bank overdrafts
	Collecting debts faster	Debt factoring
	Delaying payment to creditors	

7.6 Published accounts

Companies legislation requires that all companies must publish financial statements. For smaller companies, only a brief summary of their finances is required, but for the largest companies, including all plc's, an annual report must be prepared (often at great expense) which is sent to all shareholders and Companies House, which is the UK government's storehouse of company information. The public have a right of access to the information – see the website www.companies-house.gov.uk/ for details.

Many plc's regard their annual report as an opportunity to show off the best of their company, in effect treating it as a public relations exercise. The glossy photographs of the company's products and exotic locations of major contracts can give some reports the style of a travel brochure. In recent years, companies have been allowed to save costs by producing two versions of their annual report:

- A summarised version, sent to all shareholders
- A fully detailed version, sent to Companies House and only those shareholders specifically requesting it.

A key feature of published profit and loss accounts and balance sheets is that they have to follow specific formats of presentation according to Generally Accepted Accounting Principles (GAAP), devised to ensure a degree of uniformity between companies and across national boundaries. Although there is a small amount of flexibility allowed (for example, a company can produce statements in either a vertical or a horizontal format), virtually all UK companies follow the vertical format. Companies also have to follow a regulatory framework laid down by either the Accounting Standards Board or the International Accounting Standards Board, which issue financial reporting standards which set out best practice to be adopted in specific accounting situations.

In practice, the production of **published accounts** follows all the normal conventions, but the following should be noted:

- Profit and loss expenses are grouped into two main categories, 'selling and distribution' and 'administration expenses'.
- Interest charges are shown separately.
- The Companies Act requires that certain expenses, such as the audit fee and directors' remuneration, must be shown, usually as a note.

The detailed requirements of the Companies Act and accounting standards are outside the scope of this book, but Activity 7.6 shows how a simple set of published statements can be produced.

Activity 7.6

Prepare the published version of Smithdown Ltd's profit and loss account as shown in the answer to Activity 7.3.

Answer

Smithdown Ltd
Published profit and loss account for the year ended 31 May 2005

	£	£
Sales		345,000
Less Cost of goods sold		(113,220)
Gross profit		231,780
Less Expenses		
Selling and distribution expenses[1]	46,430	
Administration expenses[2]	118,250	
		(164,680)
Operating profit for the year, before interest		67,100
Interest		(1,900)
Operating profit for the year, before taxation		65,200
Less Provision for taxation		(16,000)
Operating profit for the year, after taxation		49,200
Less Dividends		(13,000)
Retained profit for the year		36,200

Notes:

1 Salesforce wages, carriage out, advertising, depreciation on showroom.

2 All other expenses except interest.

Various notes will be given, including a breakdown of the cost of sales figure, dividends and key items required to be disclosed under the Companies Act, such as directors' remuneration.

Note that the published balance sheet will be identical to that shown in the answer to Activity 7.3, but with notes giving a detailed breakdown of items such as fixed assets.

7.7 Groups of companies

Many companies are owned by other companies. This means that either all, or a majority, of the voting shares of the one company (the 'subsidiary' company) are held by the other company (the 'parent' company). This relationship is referred to as a **group of companies**, and special accounting requirements exist to reflect the finances of the entire group, as well as the individual companies comprising the group. Specifically, a **consolidated** (or group) profit and loss account and a consolidated (or group) balance sheet must be prepared. The procedures relating to group accounting are outside the scope of this book, but you may come across the word 'consolidated' or 'group' when you look at the annual reports of public limited companies.

7.8 Summary

	Sole trader	Partnership	Limited company
Income statement			
Manufacturing account	Yes, if a manufacturer	Yes, if a manufacturer	Yes, if a manufacturer[a]
Trading account	Yes, if trading in goods	Yes, if trading in goods	Yes, if trading in goods
Profit and loss account	Yes	Yes	Yes, including directors' salaries, audit fees (if any), debenture interest (if any)
Appropriation account	No	Yes, showing split of profits or losses between partners	Yes, showing taxation, dividends and retained profit brought forward and carried forward
Balance sheet			
Fixed (or 'non-current') assets	Yes	Yes	Yes
Current assets	Yes	Yes	Yes
Current liabilities	Yes	Yes	Yes, but may be called 'creditors due for payment within one year'. Includes the corporation tax liability and agreed final dividend
Long-term (or 'non-current') liabilities	Yes (if any)	Yes (if any)	Yes, but may be called 'creditors due for payment after more than one year'
Capital account	Yes	Yes, for each partner (and possibly current accounts for each partner)	No
Share capital	No	No	Yes
Reserves	No	No	Yes

[a] Not shown in the published version, and the expenses shown in the profit and loss account are summarised.

7.9 Glossary

AGM   Annual general meeting, which must be held by a limited company for various official purposes including the approval of the accounts and the appointment of directors.

Asset revaluation reserve   A capital reserve created when an asset (usually land or buildings) is revalued. It records an *unrealised* gain.

Auditor   An independent qualified accountant who reports on whether published accounts show a true and fair view.

Authorised share capital   The maximum share capital a limited company is allowed to issue.

Bonus issue   Free shares given to existing shareholders to transfer part of a company's reserves to them without any cash changing hands.

Called-up share capital	The actual value of shares issued by a limited company. Also known as issued share capital.
Capital (non-distributable) reserves	Reserves built up from shareholders' contributions (the share premium account) or through unrealised gains (asset revaluation reserve).
Consolidated accounts	The accounts of a group of companies.
Convertible loan stock	Loans raised by a limited company which may be converted into shares of that company at a future date.
Debentures	Loans raised by a limited company, usually secured on the company's assets.
Directors	The officers who manage a limited company.
Dividend	The reward on capital which shareholders receive from a limited company.
Equity capital	The ordinary shares of a limited company.
Factor	Financial institution that takes over the credit control function of a company in return for a percentage fee. Debts are in effect sold to the factor to improve cash flow.
Finance lease	A legal contract enabling a company to use an asset without paying large sums to buy the asset outright.
Group of companies	A situation where one company (the parent company) owns one or more other companies (subsidiaries).
Issued share capital	Another term for called-up share capital.
Limited company	A business organisation whose owners have limited liability for the debts of their business.
Limited liability	The restriction on liability of shareholders for the debts of their company to the amount of the capital which they have invested in the company.
Liquidation	The end of a company's existence, whereby all its assets are sold and its liabilities paid, any surplus capital being returned to shareholders.
Ltd	Abbreviation denoting a private limited company.
Members	Another word for shareholders.
Nominal value	The 'face value' of a share, for example £1 or 25p. Also called par value.
Ordinary shares	The most common form of shares issued by limited companies. Each share carries equal voting and dividend rights. Also known as the equity capital.
Par value	Another term meaning nominal value.
Partnership	The relation which subsists between persons carrying on a business with a view of profit.
Partnership appropriation account	Part of the profit and loss account of a partnership, showing how profits or losses are apportioned between partners according to their partnership agreement.
Partnership capital account	The record of the capital of individual partners.
Partnership current account	The record of individual partners' financial dealings with the partnership, other than their capital balances.
plc	Abbreviation denoting a public limited company.
Preference shares	A class of shares carrying a fixed rate of dividend and giving the holders preference over equity shareholders regarding payment of dividends and repayment of capital in the event of the company's liquidation.
Private limited company	A limited company which is prohibited from selling its shares to the public.

Public limited company	A company which is allowed to sell its shares to the general public.
Published accounts	The annual financial report of a limited company, produced in accordance with the Companies Act and other relevant rules and regulations laid down by the accounting profession or the Stock Exchange.
Reserves	Funds set aside within a limited company, created from profits or paid in by shareholders. They are not the same as 'cash'.
Retained profits	The profits left over after all appropriations (tax, dividends, and so on) have been made.
Revenue (distributable) reserves	Reserves built up from retained profits via the profit and loss account of a limited company. They can be used to pay dividends.
Rights issue	The right given to existing shareholders to buy more shares.
Share premium account	The capital reserve built up from amounts paid by shareholders for their shares, in excess of the nominal value of those shares.
Shareholders	The owners of a limited company.
Sole trader	A business owned by one person.
Unrealised gain	A surplus arising after the revaluation of an asset such as land, where the asset itself is not sold. It is treated as a non-distributable reserve.

? Self-check questions

1 plc stands for:
   a Private limited company
   b Public liability company
   c Public limited company
   d Public limited corporation

2 Which of the following is a disadvantage of trading as a partnership?
   a Access to other people's expertise and finance
   b Sharing of losses
   c Privacy of financial results
   d Partners usually have unlimited liability for partnership debts

3 Share capital is:
   a The way in which capital is divided at the end of each year
   b The way in which partners decide to divide profits and losses
   c Another name for London's stock exchange
   d The way in which the ownership of a limited company is divided

4 Payments to directors would be shown in the financial statements as:
   a An expense in the profit and loss account
   b An appropriation of profit
   c A current asset
   d Part of share capital

5 Another name for 'current liabilities' in a company balance sheet is:
   a Creditors due for payment within six months
   b Creditors due for payment within one year
   c Creditors who are overdue
   d Creditors due for payment after more than one year

6 A debenture is:

   a Another name for share capital

   b A loan usually secured on a company's assets

   c A loan convertible into shares at some future time

   d The person who manages a company on behalf of the shareholders

7 If a new company has issued 200,000 ordinary shares of 20p nominal value at a price of £2, what will be the entries in the share capital and share premium accounts?

   a Share capital £40,000, Share premium £360,000

   b Share capital £40,000, Share premium £400,000

   c Share capital £400,000, Share premium £360,000

   d Share capital £400,000, Share premium £40,000

8 What is a major difference between a distributable reserve and a non-distributable reserve?

   a Non-distributable reserves can be used to pay a dividend but distributable reserves cannot

   b Non-distributable reserves can be used to pay company bills, but distributable reserves cannot

   c Non-distributable reserves cannot be used to pay a dividend but distributable reserves can

   d Non-distributable reserves all come from the profit and loss account, distributable reserves all come from the shareholders

9 If a '5 for 3' rights issue is made at £1.90 per share, how much would a shareholder who owns 15,000 shares pay to the company to buy all the shares he is entitled to?

   a £28,500

   b £17,100

   c £47,500

   d £5,700

10 If a '3 for 2' bonus issue is made to a shareholder who originally paid £2 per share for 10,000 shares, how much would the shareholder pay for the bonus shares if the current market value is £4 per share?

   a £30,000

   b £60,000

   c £45,000

   d Nothing – the shares are free

(Answers in Appendix 1)

 ## Self-study questions

(Answers in Appendix 2)

Question 7.1 'A partnership is just a collection of sole traders.' Discuss this statement.

Question 7.2 Disraeli and Gladstone are partners, sharing profits and losses in the ratio 2:1. They have agreed that Disraeli should receive a salary of £9,000 and that interest on both partners' opening capital of 5% p.a. should be allowed. Disraeli's opening capital was £20,000, whereas Gladstone's was £15,000. During the year ended 31 December 2004, Disraeli had drawings of £18,000 and Gladstone drew £14,000. Net profit for the year was £40,000. No partnership current accounts were maintained, and no interest was charged on drawings.

    Show the relevant extracts from the partnership profit and loss account for the year (appropriation section) and its balance sheet at the year-end.

Question 7.3 'After the ruinous departure of Mr Lane my father had taken into partnership another man, who had been a member of Lane and Newby's since its inception. Unfortunately, although the new partner was morally blameless, he was far less competent than his predecessor and the business suffered even more. Eventually death had removed him too and my father was forced to turn the business into a Limited Company.'

'It seems probable that no one ever succeeded in explaining to my father what the formation of a Limited Liability Company entailed. I think he believed that it was a polite fiction that divested him of the onus of liability and at the same time allowed him to be a partnership without a partner.'

(from *Something Wholesale: My Life and Times in the Rag Trade* by Eric Newby)

a Using the information in the above extract, identify two problems associated with partnerships.

b To what extent is the author's father correct in asserting that a limited liability company is 'a polite fiction that divested him of the onus of liability and at the same time allowed him to be a partnership without a partner'?

c Write a brief report (200 words maximum) explaining to the author's father the main advantages and disadvantages of forming a limited liability company.

Question 7.4 'The biggest confidence trick of all time has nothing to do with social-security fraud, insider dealing or any of the exotic forms of computer-based racketeering beloved of magazine and television journalists short of a good story. Two little words sum up the swindle of the century – limited liability.

'This cunning wheeze, dreamed up more than a century ago, is a bigger rip-off than the enclosure movement, colonisation and industrialisation rolled into one. It allows all the benefits of so-called risk-taking to flow to the owners of capital whilst passing off on to the community at large all the costs.

'When a giant concern fails, a chain reaction can bankrupt smaller and smaller units down the economic ladder right to the individual worker. Worse, the liquidation of capital value inevitably pushes up insurance and borrowing costs for everybody else. The innocent pay, the guilty – sorry, the "entrepreneurs" – walk free. No such protection is available to the hapless ex-employee of the aforementioned failed giant concern.'

(Dan Atkinson, *The Guardian*, 1 September 1997)

The author has taken an extreme view on the nature of limited liability, yet what he describes as a 'confidence trick', society appears to accept. To what extent do you think he is justified in his comments?

Question 7.5 From the following trial balance of Morse Ltd, prepare a detailed profit and loss account for the year ended 31 December 2004 and a balance sheet at that date.

	Dr £	Cr £
Directors' remuneration	59,200	
Wages of salesforce	65,230	
Office salaries	34,900	
Advertising and website charges	15,300	
Interest	2,502	
Carriage out	632	
Office expenses	33,897	
Sales		462,600
Opening stock at 1 January 2004	14,900	
Purchases	140,800	
Share capital (50p nominal shares)		25,000
Share premium account		15,000
Bad debts written off	750	
Profit and loss account as at 1 January 2004		12,600
Delivery vehicles, cost as at 1 January 2004	143,600	
Depreciation of delivery vehicles at 1 January 2004		27,800
Trade debtors	64,100	
Totals c/f	575,811	543,000

Totals b/f	575,811	543,000
Trade creditors		32,711
Debenture (repayable in 2012)		10,000
Provision for doubtful debts		1,600
Bank balance	11,500	
	587,311	587,311

Notes:
1 Closing stock at 31 December 2004 was £17,650.
2 Depreciation on delivery vehicles is chargeable at 30% on the reducing balance basis.
3 £800 was owing for office expenses and £160 had been prepaid for website charges at 31 December 2004.
4 The provision for doubtful debts was to be decreased by £600.
5 Taxation amounting to £24,000 is to be provided for.
6 The company's shareholders have agreed a dividend of 10p per share.

Question 7.6 A limited company's share capital and reserves in its balance sheet were as follows:

	£	£
Capital and reserves		
Called-up share capital (£1 shares)		100,000
Share premium account	75,000	
Asset revaluation reserve	140,000	
Profit and loss account	330,000	
		545,000
		645,000

a To what extent is it true to say that reserves equal cash?
b Explain the difference between a revenue reserve and a capital reserve and give one example of each from the above balance sheet.
c What is a share premium? If the company had only ever made one issue of shares, what price was each share sold for?
d Explain why an asset revaluation reserve is created. What other balance sheet item, not listed above, would have been affected when this reserve was created?
e Explain a way in which the company could return reserves to shareholders without paying cash to them.
f If the company, immediately after extracting the above balance sheet, made a rights issue on a '3 for 2' basis at £2.40 per share, what effect would that have on the balance sheet, assuming that all shareholders took up their rights?

Case study

Marvin and Chiquita make Machiq, but Esmeralda makes trouble

Marvin and Chiquita (see previous case studies) have been working very successfully together, so on 1 July 2002, the start of Marvin's third year in business, they decided to form a partnership, to be called Machiq & Co., sharing profits or losses in the ratio Marvin 3/5 and Chiquita 2/5. All of Marvin's assets and liabilities are transferred to the partnership at their book values on 30 June 2002. This totals £17,570, which is credited to Marvin's capital account. Chiquita pays in a cheque for £10,000 as her capital. No payment was required for the goodwill built up by Marvin in the previous two years.

They agree that no interest should be charged on their drawings or credited on their capital balances. No salaries are to be paid to either partner. During a successful year together the partnership earned a net profit of £58,800. Marvin had drawings of £32,850 and Chiquita drew £18,520.

Required:

a Show the relevant extracts from the partnership profit and loss account for the year ended 30 June 2003 (appropriation section) and its balance sheet at that date. Assume that no partnership current accounts are opened.

On 30 June 2003, the partners received the following letter from Esmeralda, Marvin's former assistant:

> Dear Marvin
>
> My seven brothers and sisters and I have consulted legal advice and are going to sue you for £10 million as compensation for wrongful dismissal when you sacked us two years ago. We would have written sooner but it has taken us this long to recover from the shock of losing our jobs.
>> Hope you are keeping well.
>> Esmeralda

Marvin thinks (incorrectly) that the only protection from this claim is to immediately form a limited company, so Machiq & Co. became Machiq Limited with effect from 1 July 2003. The company took over all the assets and liabilities of Machiq & Co. at their book values, and had a share capital of 14,000 ordinary shares of £1 each. The shares, which were issued at a premium, were allocated to Marvin and Chiquita in the same proportions as their closing capital balances in the partnership. During the year ended 30 June 2004, Machiq Limited made a net profit before taxation of £92,000. Taxation was to be provided on this amount at 20%, and a dividend of £2.25 per share was agreed to be paid. Nothing further was heard from Esmeralda or her family during the year, although there were rumours that she had rejoined her former employer, Kaboosh Limited.

Required:

b Show Machiq Limited's profit and loss account (appropriation section only) for the year ended 30 June 2004, and the 'capital and reserves' section of the balance sheet as at that date.

(Answers in Appendix 3)

References

The official website for Companies House: **www.companies-house.gov.uk**

Statistics on small and medium-sized businesses can be found on the Small Business Service website: **www.sbs.gov.uk**

Take a complete break from accounting, and learn a few magic tricks at: **www.montysmagic.com**

> Now look at this book's dedicated website at **www.pearsoned.co.uk/black** and work through the various additional exercises for this chapter.

Chapter 8

Incomplete records and club accounts

When you have read this chapter you will be able to:

➤ Identify what is meant by 'incomplete records'

➤ Understand the consequences of not having a complete accounting system

➤ Prepare a statement of affairs

➤ Use control accounts to find missing information where records are incomplete

➤ Identify the specific accounting requirements of clubs and associations

➤ Prepare a receipts and payments account

➤ Prepare an income and expenditure account

8.1 Introduction

This chapter focuses on two separate area: incomplete records and club accounts

● The section on *incomplete records* shows how the reliability of an organisation's accounting statements is undermined because less than a double-entry system is in operation.

● The section on *club accounts* sets out the special accounting needs of societies and associations, whose main activities are neither trading nor profit-making, but the provision of, for example, social, sporting or cultural activities for their members. Many such organisations have excellent financial systems in place, but occasionally a lack of accounting expertise amongst members may result in only very basic financial statements being prepared.

8.2 What are 'incomplete records'?

An organisation which does not use a full double-entry system is described as having **incomplete records**. There are varying levels of incompleteness, ranging from a total absence of written records through to a practical invoice-based system which provides details of debtors, creditors and cash balances but little else.

There might be various reasons why a full accounting system is not maintained, including:

- A calamity has happened such as a fire, or a virus has wiped out computer records.
- A deliberate attempt has been made to evade taxation by keeping no written records. All transactions are made in cash.
- Lack of expertise has restricted the records kept to a list of invoices issued and received and bank statements. Some of the documents may be missing, and a professional accountant is employed to prepare annual financial summaries.

Activity 8.1

Rodney is a second-hand car dealer. The only record he keeps is a list of purchases and sales of cars, which is written in pencil on the wall above his telephone. On hearing of a visit by the tax authorities, he hastily arranges for his office to be repainted to conceal the information.

What problems may result from Rodney's actions?

Answer

Did you know?

If businesses have a turnover (total sales) which exceeds a set limit (approximately £60,000 p.a.) they have to register for value added tax (VAT) in the UK. This means that they have to keep accurate records of sales and purchases and may be subject to periodic inspection visits from HM Customs and Excise officials.

Your answer should include:

- The taxation authorities are likely to take a dim view of the events and make an estimated punitive assessment of taxation owing.
- Rodney has no control over expenses and is unable to compare one period with another.
- It is difficult to deal with queries from customers or suppliers relating to car values.
- No continual record is made of assets, liabilities and owner's capital.
- Rodney may not know how much profit or loss has been made.
- The cost of employing an accountant to unravel the financial puzzle may outweigh any perceived savings.

Note that limited companies (see Chapter 7) are required by legislation to keep proper accounting records and it is the duty of the company's directors to ensure that an adequate system is in place.

8.3 Statement of affairs

Where no written records have been maintained, the first step towards establishing the financial position is to create a **statement of affairs** at the start of the period. This is effectively an opening balance sheet showing all the assets and liabilities of the business, though some detective work may be necessary to establish with any accuracy what assets and liabilities the owner had at that date. Using the accounting equation (see Chapter 1), the net assets total equals the owner's capital balance. A similar statement is prepared at the close of the period, and the closing capital is compared with the opening. After adjusting for owner's drawings and any capital introduced or withdrawn during the period, the difference between the two capital figures equals the profit or loss for the period.

Activity 8.2

Rodney (see Activity 8.1) asks an accountant, Cuthbert, to calculate his profit or loss for the year ended 31 December 2004. Cuthbert interviews Rodney and establishes the following facts:

- The premises are rented.
- At the start of the year, Rodney owned cars for resale which had cost £15,000, a car which he kept for business use worth £8,000, an office desk and chair which were worth £300, and he had a cash balance of £4,000 which he kept in his back pocket. He owed £3,000 to a car auction company and £600 for newspaper advertisements.
- At the end of the year, Rodney had cars for resale which had cost £18,000, the car which he kept for business use was now worth £6,000, the office desk and chair were worth £200 and he had a cash balance of £1,000. He was owed £2,000 by a customer and had a creditor of £500 for one car.
- During the year he withdrew £12,000 for personal use. He won £5,000 on a lottery, which he paid in to the business.

By drawing up statements of affairs at the start and end of 2004, calculate Rodney's profit or loss for the year.

Answer

(A columnar presentation has been used to avoid the need to repeat information. It would be perfectly acceptable to draw up two separate statements at the start and end of the year.)

Rodney's statement of affairs at the start and end of 2004

	1 January 2004		31 December 2004	
	£	£	£	£
Fixed assets				
Motor vehicle	8,000		6,000	
Fixtures	300		200	
		8,300		6,200
Current assets				
Stock	15,000		18,000	
Debtors	–		2,000	
Cash	4,000		1,000	
	c/f 19,000		21,000	

Answer continued

		b/f 19,000	21,000
Less **Current liabilities**			
Creditors	(3,600)		(500)
Net current assets		15,400	20,500
Total net assets		23,700	26,700
Capital		23,700	26,700

Calculation of the trading result for the year ended 31 December 2000

	£
Opening capital (see opening statement of affairs)	23,700
Add Cash introduced	5,000
	28,700
Less Drawings	(12,000)
Adjusted capital balance	16,700
Closing capital (see closing statement of affairs)	26,700
Increase in net worth (i.e. profit)	10,000

Pause for thought

Did you wonder why you were told that Rodney's premises were rented?

We knew that Rodney had had his office repainted (Activity 8.1), so we needed to know whether or not he owned the premises. If he had owned them, a value would have been required for the statement of affairs.

8.4 Use of control accounts to deduce information

Statements of affairs will be used only when an organisation's records are minimal. If sufficient information is available there is no reason why full financial statements should not be prepared even if a full double-entry system is lacking. Minimum information required is:

● Debtors and creditors at the start and end of the period
● Accruals and prepayments at the start and end of the period
● Details of cash paid and received
● Fixed and current asset valuations and details of liabilities other than creditors (for example, loans).

Activity 8.3

For the trading account, the key is the preparation of **control accounts**, using **balancing figures** to give the total sales and purchases figures. On the advice of Cuthbert, Rodney (see Activities 8.1 and 8.2) turns over a new leaf in the year ended 31 December 2005, and keeps some written records of cash payments and receipts during the year. He also gives the following information:

● Opening balances, 1 January 2005 (from Activity 8.2's 31 December 2004 figures): Fixed assets £6,200 (Motor vehicle £6,000, Fixtures £200), Current assets £21,000 (Stock £18,000, Debtors £2,000, Cash £1,000), Trade creditors £500.

- Closing balances, 31 December 2005: Fixed assets £5,100 (Motor vehicle £5,000, Fixtures £100), Current assets £19,000 (Stock £14,000, Debtors £3,000, Cash £2,000), Trade creditors £4,000.
- Cash paid for cars for resale £45,020, for office expenses £7,000.
- Cash received from customers for car sales £84,000.
- Discount allowed for prompt payment by a customer £250.
- Discount received for prompt payment for a car £80.
- Bad debt written off £850.
- Drawings for the year £30,980.
- There were neither accruals nor prepayments at the start or end of the year.

Prepare financial statements for Rodney for the year ended 31 December 2005.

Answer

(The starting point is to create an opening statement of affairs. We did this in Activity 8.2.)
The next step is to produce control accounts (see Chapter 3), as follows:

Sales control account

	£		£
Opening debtors	2,000	Cash received	84,000
Sales (balancing figure)	86,100	Discounts allowed	250
		Bad debt written off	850
		Closing debtors	3,000
	88,100		88,100

Purchases control account

	£		£
Cash paid for cars for resale	45,020	Opening creditors	500
Discount received	80	Purchases (balancing figure)	48,600
Closing creditors	4,000		
	49,100		49,100

The profit and loss account and balance sheet can then be prepared:

Rodney's profit and loss account for the year ended 31 December 2005

	£	£
Sales		86,100
Less **Cost of goods sold**		
Opening stock	18,000	
Purchases	48,600	
	66,600	
Less Closing stock	(14,000)	
		(52,600)
Gross profit		33,500
Add Discounts received		80
	c/f	33,580

Answer continued

		b/f	33,580
Less Expenses			
Office expenses	7,000		
Bad debt written off	850		
Discounts allowed	250		
Depreciation (6,000 + 200) – (5,000 + 100)	1,100		
			(9,200)
Net profit			24,380

Balance sheet as at 31 December 2005

	£	£
Fixed assets		
Motor vehicle	5,000	
Fixtures	100	
		5,100
Current assets		
Stock	14,000	
Debtors	3,000	
Cash	2,000	
	19,000	
Less Current liabilities		
Creditors	(4,000)	
Net current assets		15,000
Total net assets		20,100
Capital		
Opening balance, 1 January 2005	26,700	
Add Net profit	24,380	
	51,080	
Less Drawings	(30,980)	
Closing balance, 31 December 2005		20,100

8.5 Club accounts

Groups of individuals often form clubs or associations to pursue common aims and interests. For example, you might be a member of a golf club, music society or students' union society. All of these are known as **not-for-profit organisations** as their principal aims relate to the provision of services or activities for members rather than the generation of a profit for owners. We shall use the word 'club' when referring to all of these not-for-profit organisations.

Although most clubs will have a member who acts as a treasurer, it often happens that the individual appointed will have few or no accounting skills. Often their main role is to act as a cashier, taking responsibility for collecting and banking money and paying bills as they fall due. The only record kept might be a basic cash book. Because of this, periodic financial statements may be in the form of a simple summary of the cash book, known as a **receipts and payments account**.

The author was once treasurer of a students' union and had to present a financial report at its annual general meeting. Knowing the level of interest that students traditionally have in accountancy matters, he produced overhead slides of the financial statements and deliberately projected them on to a screen so out of focus that they were illegible. He then asked if anyone wanted to ask any questions on the accounts. Nobody did!

8.5.1 Receipts and payments account

If only very simple club accounts can be prepared, then a receipts and payments account represents the bare minimum which is acceptable as a financial statement. It summarises cash and bank transactions for a period, but *fails* to show:

- The club's assets (other than any bought or sold during the period and the cash and bank balances)
- The club's liabilities
- How the club's income compared with its expenditure
- Depreciation
- The accumulated total of the club's wealth.

Activity 8.4

Rodney (see previous activities) is treasurer of the Used Car Dealers' Cultural Association (UCDCA), which organises social events for car dealers. During the year ended 31 December 2004, the club's bank statements showed the following information:

UCDCA in account with Grimley's Bank plc 2004		Dr £	Cr £	Bal £
1 Jan	Opening balance			800 Cr
31Jan	Subscriptions		1,200	2,000 Cr
1 Feb	Visit to Glyndebourne Opera:			
	Cheque for coach travel	400		1,600 Cr
1 Feb	Opera tickets bought	600		1,000 Cr
16 Feb	Sales of opera tickets to members		1,350	2,350 Cr
1 May	Byte plc: Computer to keep club records	2,000		350 Cr
9 May	Honorarium to club secretary	100		250 Cr
12 Oct	Visit to British Museum:			
	Cheque for coach travel	150		100 Cr
18 Oct	Tickets for British Museum coach			
	trip sold to members		280	380 Cr
20 Dec	Bar sales: Christmas party		900	1280 Cr
22 Dec	The Temperance Brewery plc	650		630 Cr

Prepare a receipts and payments account for the year ending 31 December 2004.

Did you know?

An **honorarium** is a 'gift' of cash given to a club official in recognition of the time he or she spends on club administration.

Answer

The Used Car Dealers' Cultural Association
Receipts and payments account
for the year ended 31 December 2004

	£	£
Opening bank balance, 1 January 2004		800
Add Receipts:		
Subscriptions	1,200	
Ticket sales: Glyndebourne Opera visit	1,350	
British Museum visit	280	
Bar sales (Christmas party)	900	
		3,730
		4,530
Less Payments:		
Coach travel: Glyndebourne Opera visit	400	
British Museum visit	150	
Opera tickets purchased	600	
Computer	2,000	
Honorarium to club secretary	100	
Drinks from brewery	650	
		(3,900)
Closing bank balance, 31 December 2004		630

8.5.2 Income and expenditure account

The receipts and payments account is an imperfect reporting tool, as although it gives members a summarised view of the cash and bank transactions for the period it does not follow the accruals concept nor any other accounting convention. As a result, the club's financial position cannot be ascertained, which may result in mismanagement of its affairs. Assets might be sold without members' knowledge or debts amassed without proper financial provision being made to meet them.

Although a receipts and payments account might be sufficient where there is only a handful of members and very few financial complications, more sophisticated control must be exercised in other circumstances. This is achieved by producing an **income and expenditure account** and balance sheet which conform to all normal accounting principles. Within these statements there are a number of features which tend to be unique to clubs:

- For not-for-profit organisations, the words 'profit' and 'loss' are often replaced by 'surplus' and 'deficit'.

- Income often comes from ad hoc activities such as social events, raffles, jumble sales and bar sales. Where possible, income from such activities is matched to the relevant expenditure. For example, a 'bar account' can be included (the equivalent of a trading account) to let members see the bar's surplus or deficit for the period.

- The accruals concept (see Chapter 1) must be applied to membership subscriptions.

● The balance sheet does not show a capital balance. The equivalent item is termed an **accumulated fund** which increases or decreases by the surpluses or deficits for the period. Any donations made to the club will also increase the fund. There is no equivalent to 'owner's drawings'.

Activity 8.5

Rodney (see Activity 8.4) has decided that he should produce an income and expenditure account for the UCDCA for the year ended 31 December 2004. He obtains the following further information:

● Assets at 1 January 2004 (in addition to the bank balance) were a photocopier valued at £500 and bar stock which had cost £600. Membership subscriptions owing for 2003 totalled £120.
● Liabilities at 1 January 2004 were: Creditors: Temperance Brewery plc £400 and Photocopier Repairs Limited £180. Prepaid membership subscriptions for 2004 paid in 2003 totalled £90.
● In January 2004, all the bar stock owned at the start of the year was sold at a club party. The cash takings of £1,050 were used to pay the two creditors, who each allowed 10% cash discount. The balance of cash was used to buy stationery for the club.
● At the end of the year, in addition to the bank balance, there was a stock of stationery valued at £100, and subscriptions owing for 2004 totalled £180. Advance membership subscriptions totalling £70 had been received for 2005. Closing bar stock was valued at £500 and it was estimated that both the photocopier and the computer had depreciated by 25%. An advertisement placed in a local newspaper at a cost of £120 to recruit new members was owing.

Prepare the income and expenditure account for the year ended 31 December 2004 and a balance sheet as at that date.

Answer

The Used Car Dealers' Cultural Association
Income and expenditure account for the year ended 31 December 2004

	£	£
Income		
Bar Account:		
Sales of drinks (1,050 + 900)		1,950
Less Cost of drinks sold		
Opening stock	600	
Purchases	650	
	1,250	
Less Closing stock	(500)	
		(750)
Surplus on bar		1,200
Other income:		
Membership subscriptions (see Working 1)		1,280
Surplus on visit to Glyndebourne Opera		
[1,350 − (400 + 600)]		350
Surplus on visit to British Museum (280 − 150)		130
Discount received [10% × (400 + 180)]		58
Total income	c/f	3,018

155

Answer continued

Total income		b/f	3,018
Less **Expenditure**			
Honorarium to club secretary	100		
Stationery (see Working 2)	428		
Advertisement	120		
Depreciation: computer (25% × £2,000)	500		
Depreciation: photocopier (25% × £500)	125		
			(1,273)
Surplus of income over expenditure			1,745

Balance sheet as at 31 December 2004

	£	£	£
Fixed assets			
Computer		2,000	
Less Depreciation		(500)	
			1,500
Photocopier		500	
Less Depreciation		(125)	
			375
			1,875
Current assets			
Bar stock		500	
Stationery stock		100	
Subscriptions owing		180	
Bank		630	
		1,410	
Less **Current liabilities**			
Creditors	120		
Subscriptions paid in advance	70		
		(190)	
Net current assets			1,220
Total net assets			3,095
Accumulated fund			
Opening balance, 1 January 2004 (see Working 3)		1,350	
Add Surplus of income over expenditure		1,745	
Closing balance, 31 December 2004			3,095

Pause for thought

All the usual accounting conventions have been followed in preparing the income and expenditure account and balance sheet. Only some of the terminology used may be unfamiliar to you. If you are a member of a club or association, obtain a copy of its last annual report and see the extent to which the financial statements follow 'best practice'.

Answer continued

Workings

1

Subscriptions (2004)

	£		£
Opening unpaid subscriptions re 2003	120	Opening subscriptions paid in advance re 2004	90
Income and expenditure account (balancing figure)	1,280	Subscriptions received, as per bank account	1,200
Closing subscriptions paid in advance re 2005	70	Closing unpaid subscriptions re 2004	180
	1,470		1,470

2 Stationery

	£	£
Bar stock sold for cash, January		1,050
Less Payments to creditors:		
Temperance Brewery plc	400	
Photocopier Repairs Limited	180	
	580	
Less 10% cash discount	(58)	
		(522)
Stationery bought		528
Less Closing stock of stationery		(100)
Expense for the year		428

This working is needed because we need to calculate how much cash was used from the bar's takings to buy stationery. Of the £528 paid for stationery, £100 was still in stock, leaving £428 as the stationery used in the year.

3 Accumulated fund at start of 2004

	£	£
Assets		
Photocopier		500
Bar stock		600
Subscriptions owing		120
Bank balance		800
		2,020
Less Liabilities		
Subscriptions paid in advance	90	
Creditors (400 + 180)	580	
		(670)
Net assets		1,350

8.6 Summary

Receipts and payments account	A summary of all the cash and bank transactions for a period
Income and expenditure account and statement of affairs	Equivalent to profit and loss account and balance sheet, respectively, following all usual accounting conventions

8.7 Glossary

Accumulated fund — Shown in the balance sheet of a not-for-profit organisation, it represents the net worth (assets less liabilities) of the organisation at the start or end of the financial period. It is broadly equivalent to capital.

Balancing figure — A figure inserted into an account to make each side have the same total.

Control accounts — Accounts which summarise information, particularly purchases and sales, to either confirm the accuracy of underlying ledger accounts or calculate required totals as 'balancing figures' where records are incomplete.

Honorarium — A gift given by a not-for-profit organisation to an office holder in that organisation in recognition of services rendered.

Income and expenditure account — The equivalent of a trading and profit and loss accounts produced for a not-for-profit organisation.

Incomplete records — Any method of recording the financial transactions of an organisation which does not use a full double-entry system.

Not-for-profit organisation — An organisation which does not exist for the creation of profit. It may be a club or association which exists to provide a service or activities for its members.

Receipts and payments account — A simple financial statement created by summarising cash and bank records for a period.

Statement of affairs — Where records are incomplete, this is in effect a balance sheet prepared to show all the assets and liabilities of the business at the start and/or end of a financial period.

? Self-check questions

1 Accounting records are referred to as 'incomplete' when:
   a A supplier has forgotten to send an invoice to a business
   b A business has paid only some of its creditors
   c Less than a full double-entry system is in operation
   d A trial balance fails to balance

2 If a trader keeps poor accounting records, a consequence might be:
   a Higher accountants' fees
   b Lower accountants' fees
   c Lower tax to pay
   d Easier to deal with customers' queries

3 A business has opening creditors £22,000, cheques paid to suppliers £39,000, discount received £400 and closing creditors £16,000. What is the 'purchases' figure for the period?
   a £33,400
   b £45,400
   c £32,600
   d £1,400

4 A not-for-profit organisation is:
   a A business that always makes a loss
   b A business that has a moral objection to profit-making
   c An organisation that provides services or activities for its members
   d An inefficient organisation

5 A receipts and payments account is:
   a A copy of an organisation's bank statements
   b Another name for a balance sheet
   c Another name for an income and expenditure account
   d A summary of cash and bank transactions

6 Limited companies should not have incomplete records because:
   a The law requires companies to keep proper accounting records
   b Directors must be qualified accountants
   c Limited companies are wealthy enough to employ accountants
   d All limited companies are registered for value added tax

7 An accumulated fund of an organisation is the same as:
   a The bank balance of the organisation
   b The profit of the organisation
   c The net worth of the organisation
   d The assets of the organisation

8 From the following information, what figure for 'subscriptions' would be shown in a club's income and expenditure account for the year 2004?
   ● Balances at 1 January 2003: Owing re 2003 £190, Prepaid re 2004 £170
   ● Balances at 31 December 2003: Owing re 2004 £220, Prepaid re 2005 £60
   ● Subscriptions received during 2004: £3,260
      a £3,440
      b £3,080
      c £3,120
      d £3,400

9 An honorarium is:

a A room in the clubhouse where sporting trophies are displayed

b A payment made to a club official in recognition of services to the club

c A payment made by a club member for a life membership

d A payment made to a club member on being made an honorary member of the club

10 A subscription paid in advance by a member for the following year would be shown in the club's financial summaries for the current year as:

a A current asset in the balance sheet

b A current liability in the balance sheet

c Subscriptions in the income and expenditure account

d A fixed asset in the balance sheet

(Answers in Appendix 1)

Self-study questions

(Answers in Appendix 2)

Question 8.1 Delia Trelawney runs a music shop, known as Soul Trading. She does not have a full book-keeping system, but has given you the following information relating to the year ended 31 May 2005:

1 Summarised bank account information:

	£		£
Cash banked	35,500	Opening balance b/f	1,740
		Rent and rates	1,500
		Sundry expenses	603
		Telephone and electricity	871
		Shop fittings	6,402
		Paid to suppliers	10,854
		Drawings	6,670
		Advertising	520
		Closing balance c/f	6,340
	35,500		35,500

2 All sales were for cash.

3 Trade creditors at 31 May 2004 were £2,105, and at 31 May 2005 were £6,320.

4 The gross profit for the year was 55% of sales.

5 Closing stock was valued at £3,045.

6 A van with a book value of £3,480 on 31 May 2004 was sold for £3,000 on 1 June 2004. This was paid into the business bank account. No replacement van was purchased.

7 All takings from customers were banked with the exception of £720 which was used by Delia to pay for a holiday, and 50 weeks' wages at £120 per week paid to a shop assistant.

8 £140 was owing to the telephone company at the start of the year, and £203 was owing to the telephone company at the end of the year.

9 Shop fittings owned at 31 May 2004 had cost £7,900 and had been depreciated for a full two years at 30% on the reducing balance basis. A full year's depreciation is charged in the year of purchase, regardless of the purchase date.

a Prepare a profit and loss account for the year ended 31 May 2005, and a balance sheet as at that date.

b Delia needs advice on how she can improve her system for keeping track of her creditors. Currently she keeps all invoices in a box, and pays bills only when she gets a phone call from suppliers demanding payment. Suggest two ways in which she can keep better control over her creditors' invoices.

Question 8.2 Tilly Snowdon has operated a shop selling specialist mountaineering equipment for several years, but has never maintained full bookkeeping records. An analysis of her bank records for the year ended 31 December 2004 was as follows:

	£		£
Opening balance	2,800	Purchase of goods	66,200
Cash banked	86,900	New shop fittings	3,000
Closing balance	6,670	Rent and rates	4,600
		Light and heat	3,900
		New van (balance of purchase price)	4,000
		Van running expenses	1,400
		Wages to shop assistants	9,070
		Advertising	840
		Insurance	560
		Sundry expenses	2,800
	96,370		96,370

Details of Tilly's assets and liabilities at the start and end of the year are:

	1 January 2004 £	31 December 2004 £
Debtors	600	850
Creditors	2,400	3,300
Insurance prepaid	80	120
Advertising accrued	140	120
Stocks at cost	16,800	23,700
Van (net book value)	2,400	?
Shop fittings (cost)	1,500	?
Depreciation on shop fittings	450	?

Notes:
1 Tilly had banked all takings, with the exception of personal drawings of £200 per week for 50 weeks, and £500 which she had used to pay for a holiday.
2 Closing debtors included an amount of £100 which had been outstanding for over six months. It has now been decided to write it off as a bad debt.
3 The van owned on 1 January 2004 was traded in for £2,000 on a part-exchange deal to purchase a new one.
4 Depreciation policy is to provide a full year's depreciation in the year of purchase but none in the year of sale. Depreciation rates are 25% p.a. straight line on vans and 30% p.a. reducing balance on shop fittings. No shop fittings had been sold during the year.

Prepare a profit and loss account for Tilly Snowdon for the year ended 31 December 2004 and a balance sheet as that date.

Question 8.3 The treasurer of the Razmatazz Sports and Social Club prepared the following Receipts and Payments Account for the year ended 31 December 2004:

	£	£
Opening bank balance, 1 January 2004		1,470
Add Receipts		
Subscriptions re 2003	620	
re 2004	14,080	
Competition fees	2,590	
Proceeds from sale of van (1 January 2004)	1,000	
Sales of dance tickets	1,778	
		20,068
		21,538
Less Payments		
Wages	8,450	
Printing and advertising	2,070	
Repairs to sports equipment	800	
Competition prizes	2,200	
Dance expenses	2,060	
Purchase of new van (1 January 2004)	6,300	
Motor expenses	1,200	
Sundry expenses	1,180	
		(24,260)
Bank overdraft at 31 December 2004		(2,722)

It was felt by many members that this information was inadequate to give a full picture of the club's financial situation, and the treasurer subsequently produced the following additional information:

1 The assets and liabilities at the start and end of 2004 were:

	1 January	31 December
	£	£
Subscriptions due from members	1,440	1,620
Subscriptions received in advance	–	720
Stock of competition prizes	850	450
Value of computer (cost £2,000)	1,600	1,400
Value of sports equipment (cost £8,000)	6,200	5,400
Van	(see below)	(see below)

2 The van sold during the year had originally cost £4,000 in 2002 and had been depreciated at 25% p.a. on the reducing balance method for exactly 2 years up to the date of sale. The new van is to be depreciated on the same basis as the previous one.

Prepare an income and expenditure account for the year ended 31 December 2004 and a balance sheet as at that date.

Question 8.4 The treasurer of the Vim and Vigour Sports and Social Club presented the following Receipts and Payments Account for the year ended 31 December 2004:

	£	£
Opening bank balance, 1 January 2004		2,400
Add Receipts		
Subscriptions re 2003	1,800	
re 2004	25,200	
Competition fees	3,150	
Proceeds from sale of sports equipment	2,100	
Sales of dance tickets	2,460	
		34,710
		37,110
Less Payments		
Refund of subscription (re 2003) overpaid	60	
Wages of sports staff	29,700	
Printing and advertising	2,250	
Repairs to sports equipment	1,500	
Competition prizes	1,800	
Dance expenses	1,350	
Sports equipment purchased	10,800	
Sundry expenses	2,460	
		(49,920)
Bank overdraft at 31 December 2004		(12,810)

At the club AGM, several members criticised the treasurer for failing to provide full financial information. As a result, an accountant was appointed to present an income and expenditure account and balance sheet to a special meeting of members.

The accountant compiled the following additional information

1 The assets and liabilities at the start and end of 2004 were:

	1 January	31 December
	£	£
Subscriptions due from members	1,800	1,560
Subscriptions received in advance	840	–
Stock of competition prizes	1,050	600
Value of photocopier (cost £6,000)	4,200	3,600
Sports equipment (depreciated value)	12,000	15,000
Sports equipment (cost)	45,000	25,800

2 Sports equipment with a net book value of £6,000 on 1 January 2004 was sold during the year. The equipment had been owned for exactly four years prior to its sale, and had been depreciated on the straight line basis with an estimated life of five years.

3 Subscription rates are being increased from 1 January 2005 to £120 p.a. compared with the existing level of £80 p.a.

a Prepare an income and expenditure account for the year ended 31 December 2004 and a balance sheet as at that date.

b Calculate the cash due to be received from subscriptions during 2005, on the assumptions that 20% of the existing membership resign during the year without paying their subscriptions and 40 new members are recruited. Assume that all members will have paid their subscriptions by the year-end.

163

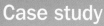

Case study

The treasurer of the Abracadabra Club does a vanishing trick

After a busy day, Marvin and Chiquita (see previous case studies) liked nothing better than to relax at the Abracadabra Club, where magicians meet to discuss the tricks of their trade over a drink. The honorary treasurer, Milton Bezzler, was due to present the club's financial statements for the year ended 31 December 2003 at the annual general meeting of the club, to be held on 1 January 2004. On the night before the AGM, the club's chairman received a postcard from Argentina with the following message:

I've vanished with the club's funds – how about that for a magic trick! Good-bye for ever, Milton

Chiquita was immediately asked by the club's committee to investigate how much Milton had stolen. She set to work, and found the following copy of the club's balance sheet at 31 December 2002:

	£	£
Fixed asset		
Computer (bought 1 January 2001), at net book value		1,000
Current assets		
Stock of drinks	200	
Debtors (100 Club subscriptions)	360	
Balance at bank:		
General account	2,099	
100 Club account	711	
	3,370	
Less **Current liabilities**		
Creditor (100 Club prizes owed)	(2,000)	
Net current assets		1,370
Total net assets		2,370
Accumulated fund		
Balance brought forward, 1 January 2002		3,652
Less Excess of expenditure over income for 2002		(1,282)
		2,370

Chiquita was able to prepare a summary of the club's bank statements for the year ended 31 December 2003 as follows. (Note that she had not had sufficient time to calculate the 100 Club receipts.)

Receipts	£
100 Club subscriptions	?
Dance ticket sales	1,267
Drinks sold at dance	265
Bank interest	120
Computer (sale proceeds)	700

Payments	£
100 Club prizes (re 2002)	2,000
100 Club prizes (re 2003)	2,000
Dance band's fees	866
New computer	1,000
Drinks purchased	165
Sundries	87

Notes:

1 The 100 Club is a money-raising venture, with the aim of recruiting 100 members who pay a subscription of £90 p.a. in return for the chance of winning a cash prize. A prize draw is held once a year. All except one of the subscriptions owing at 31 December 2002 was paid during the year, the unpaid subscription being regarded as a bad debt. The club recruited exactly 100 members during the year, 95 of whom had paid their subscriptions by the year-end. No other membership fees are payable by members of the Abracadabra Club.

2 There was a stock of drinks at the year-end of £175.

3 There was a creditor for drinks at the year-end, totalling £28.

4 Computers are depreciated at 20% p.a. on the straight line method, with a full year's depreciation charged in the year of purchase but none in the year of sale.

5 There were 'nil' balances in both bank accounts on 31 December 2003. Milton Bezzler had total authority to sign cheques. There were no cash transactions.

Required:

a Calculate how much Milton Bezzler appears to have stolen from the club.

b Prepare an income and expenditure account for the year ended 31 December 2003 in as much detail as possible from the above information, showing separately any profit or loss on drinks sales. Show the theft as an 'exceptional expense'.

c Prepare a balance sheet as at 31 December 2003.

d Explain one advantage and one disadvantage of presenting a simple receipts and payments account, rather than an income and expenditure account and balance sheet.

e How could clubs minimise the risk of a treasurer misappropriating funds?

(Answers in Appendix 3)

References

Financial summaries of the Astronomical Society of Edinburgh:

www.roe.ac.uk/asewww/publications/reports/2003

(Later years than 2003 may be available: when you access the page, scroll down until you reach the Financial Report.)

Can you find if the society bought any fixed assets during the year?

Income and expenditure account and balance sheet of the Ethiopiaid organisation (a limited company, but its financial statements follow the broad principles set out in this chapter): **www.ethiopiaid.org.uk** (click on 'Ethiopiaid Accounts').

See if you can find out how much income the organisation raised in the year.

> **Now look at this book's dedicated website at www.pearsoned.co.uk/black and work through the various additional exercises for this chapter.**

Chapter 9

Cash flow: past and future

Objectives   When you have read this chapter you will be able to:

➤ Understand the relative importance of cash and profit

➤ Prepare a simple cash flow statement based on past transactions

➤ Be aware of the relevant Financial Reporting Standard relating to cash flow statements

➤ Appreciate the necessity of forecasting future cash flows

➤ Understand the overall nature and purpose of business planning

9.1   Introduction

Cash is the lifeblood of a business. If it dwindles the business will die. But it is also a very difficult figure to fiddle.

This is how Professor Sir David Tweedie, chairman of the Accounting Standards Board, introduced the very first **Financial Reporting Standard**, FRS 1 *Cash Flow Statements*, in 1991. In our study of accounting so far, cash (by which we mean a business's cash in hand plus its bank balances, less any bank overdrafts) has perhaps taken a back seat when compared with profits: after all, accounting concepts require us to adjust cash for debtors, creditors, accruals, prepayments, unsold stock and provisions when preparing the profit and loss account. Even within the balance sheet, cash and bank balances are just two items appearing within the list of current assets, with no special prominence.

If cash really is the lifeblood of the business, it would make sense to give this asset a statement of its own, which is in fact what we do by preparing a **cash flow statement**, which summarises the cash inflows and outflows over the past financial period. In this chapter we also look at the crystal-ball-gazing aspect of accounting known as 'cash flow forecasting', where we attempt to anticipate the trend of future cash flows.

One of the many enigmas of accounting is that it is quite possible for profitable businesses to fail through poor cash management. After all, a creditor owed £20,000 is not going to be impressed by being told that, although the business made a profit of £100,000, the bank overdraft limit has been reached and no further cheques can be paid out.

The part of David Tweedie's comment referring to cash being 'a very difficult figure to fiddle' relates to the widely held (though inaccurate) perception that, whilst the existence (or non-existence) of cash and bank balances can be proved with certainty, 'profit' can be adjusted up or down ('fiddled') in accordance with a business's requirements, unrelated to the underlying financial transactions. The vast majority of information contained within the financial summaries is based on objective, verifiable data. However, there is scope for subjectivity as well, in such areas as the amount of depreciation to be charged, how stock should be valued, and whether a provision for doubtful debts is needed. The publication of accounting standards has narrowed considerably the areas of individuality available to accountants and their scope for 'creative accounting'. Remember, also, that many limited companies must appoint independent auditors who report on whether or not the accounts show a true and fair view of the business.

9.2 Cash versus profit

If a business has sufficient cash to draw upon to meet its liabilities as they fall due, it is said to have good **liquidity**. It can also be referred to as being **solvent**. This would also apply if it could quickly change assets into cash if the need arose ('cash equivalents'). These include investments such as shares which could be sold on a stock market, and bank deposit accounts where relatively short notice could be given to gain access to the money. Surprisingly enough, it is also possible for a business to be too liquid: if it has excessive cash then it is not reinvesting it. Rather than hoarding cash it should be buying new fixed assets, taking over other businesses or using the cash to fund research and development projects. In this way the business can expand and become more profitable. The ideal business is profitable and liquid, and in the next chapter we shall look at ways of analysing both these aspects of a company's performance.

Pause for thought

Can you ever have too much cash? Apparently, the combined wealth of the 200 richest men in the USA exceeds the total wealth of China, and the wealthiest, Bill Gates, had a fortune estimated at $59bn on 9 June 2004. Not all of it was in cash, though!

9.3 The cash flow statement

Just as there is a set way of presenting the profit and loss account and balance sheet, there is a format to follow for the **cash flow statement**. Although the statement is nothing more than a summary of cash and bank transactions over a financial period, the information is made more meaningful by grouping the transactions into key headings. These key headings are set out in the Financial Reporting Standard mentioned earlier (FRS 1), though at this stage in your studies it is sufficient to understand only a summarised version of the format.

FRS 1 in fact exempts small companies[1] from preparing a cash flow statement, though a separate Financial Reporting Standard for smaller enterprises issued in 1998 states that smaller businesses are 'encouraged, but not required, to provide a cash flow statement'.

All public limited companies have to present a cash flow statement as part of their published annual report, and it is regarded as a **primary statement** of equal importance to the profit and loss account and balance sheet. For example, Tesco plc's cash flow statement (in an abridged version) for 2002 (with 2001's figures given for comparison) was as follows:

Tesco plc
Cash flow statement for the year ended 27 February

	2002 £m	2001 £m
Net cash inflow from operating activities	2,038	1,937
Net interest paid	(177)	(161)
Tax	(378)	(272)
Net capital expenditure	(1,920)	(1,968)
Changes in financing	1,001	983
Dividends	(297)	(254)
Business acquisitions/disposals	(96)	(76)
Increase in cash for the period	171	189

Source: Abridged from *Tesco Plc Annual Report and Financial Statements 2002*. Courtesy of Tesco Stores Limited.

---

[1] Small, as defined by the Companies Act 1985.

The structure of the 2002 statement can be explained as follows:
Notes:

See note

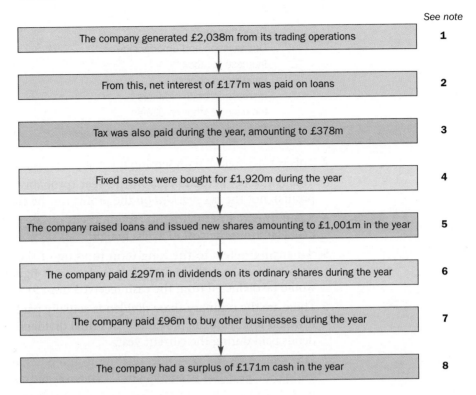

	See note
The company generated £2,038m from its trading operations	**1**
From this, net interest of £177m was paid on loans	**2**
Tax was also paid during the year, amounting to £378m	**3**
Fixed assets were bought for £1,920m during the year	**4**
The company raised loans and issued new shares amounting to £1,001m in the year	**5**
The company paid £297m in dividends on its ordinary shares during the year	**6**
The company paid £96m to buy other businesses during the year	**7**
The company had a surplus of £171m cash in the year	**8**

Notes

1 This is not the same as the profit for the year. To arrive at the figure, the profit has to be adjusted as follows:

(i) Add back any provisions deducted in arriving at the profit (particularly depreciation). This is because depreciation (and also profits or losses on the sale of fixed assets), whilst included in the profit and loss account, has no effect on cash flow.

(ii) Adjust for changing stock, debtors and creditors values, as follows:

Increase in cash flow requiring amounts to be added back to profit:

Change	Reason
Decrease in stock	Less cash tied up in stock
Decrease in debtors	More customers have paid their bills
Increase in creditors	We owe more (i.e. we have held on to our cash)

Decreases in cash flow requiring amounts to be deducted from profit:

Change	Reason
Increase in stock	More cash tied up in stock
Increase in debtors	Fewer customers have paid their bills
Decrease in creditors	We have paid more to our creditors

For Tesco in 2002, the 'net cash inflow from operating activities' figure was arrived at as follows:

	£m
Operating profit	1,322
Depreciation and amortisation	534
Increase in stock	(89)
Increase in debtors	(88)
Increase in trade creditors	292
Increase in other creditors	67
Net cash inflow from operating activities	2,038

2 This is a net figure, representing interest paid less any interest received.

3 This is the tax actually *paid* in the year (probably on the previous year's profits), not the tax *provided* on the profits for the current year.

4 Again, this is a net figure, so any proceeds of sale of fixed assets would be deducted from the cost of assets bought.

5 'Financing' refers to the long-term funding of the business from sources such as loans and share capital. It is also a net figure, so any loans repaid would be deducted from the cash received from loans and share issues.

6 These are the ordinary share dividends actually paid in the year. In practice it would represent the previous year's final dividend, plus any interim dividends paid during the current year.

7 This represents the cash flow relating to the purchase or sale of businesses during the year (for example, after a takeover bid). It is another net figure, so if it sold any businesses (for example, a subsidiary company) for cash this would be deducted.

8 The company finished the year with a surplus of £171m cash. Note how this compares with the year's reported operating profit of £1,322m.

Activity 9.1

The balance sheets of Copperfield plc as at 31 May 2004 and 31 May 2005 are as follows.

	2005 £000	2005 £000	2005 £000	2004 £000	2004 £000	2004 £000
Fixed assets (net book value)			54,000			47,000
Current assets:						
Stock		14,000			11,000	
Debtors		19,100			17,400	
		33,100			28,400	
Less						
Creditors due for payment within one year:						
Creditors	14,200			15,500		
Taxation	14,000			13,000		
Bank overdraft	19,600			10,900		
		(47,800)			(39,400)	
Net current liabilities			(14,700)			(11,000)
Total net assets			39,300			36,000

Capital and reserves

Ordinary shares of 5p each	21,000	10,000
Share premium account	7,500	17,500
Profit and loss account	10,800	8,500
	39,300	36,000

The summarised profit and loss accounts for the two years ended 31 May 2005 are as follows:

	2005	2004
	£000	£000
Gross profit	153,340	132,200
Less Interest paid	(10,000)	(10,000)
	143,340	122,200
Less Expenses	(105,640)	(94,900)
	37,700	27,300
Profit/(Loss) on sale of fixed assets	(1,400)	2,800
Profit before taxation	36,300	30,100
Less Taxation	(14,000)	(13,000)
Profit after tax	22,300	17,100
Less Dividends paid		(20,000)
(11,500)		
Retained earnings for the year	2,300	5,600
Retained earnings b/f	8,500	2,900
Retained earnings c/f	10,800	8,500

Notes:

1 A bonus issue was made during the year to 31 May 2005 by utilising £10,000 from the share premium account.

2 A summary of the company's fixed assets account in the general ledger for the year ended 31 May 2005 is shown below:

		£000			£000
1/6/04	Cost brought forward	87,000	31/5/05	To Disposals account	12,000
31/5/05	Additions	14,000	31/5/05	Cost carried forward	89,000
		101,000			101,000

The assets which were sold realised £2,400,000, which represented a loss on disposal of £1,400,000 when compared with their book value.

Produce a cash flow statement for the year ended 31 May 2005.

Answer

Step 1

Using the Tesco cash flow statement as our guide, we can start by calculating the net cash flow from operating activities. The major problem is that we are not given the depreciation total for the year, but have to calculate it. The clues we need are within the balance sheet and the fixed assets account given in the note. We can re-create the depreciation account, as follows:

Answer continued

Depreciation account

	£000		£000
Disposal of assets[a]	8,200	Balance b/f (87,000 – 47,000)	40,000
Balance c/f (89,000 – 54,000)	35,000	Depreciation for the year (balancing figure)	3,200
	43,200		43,200

[a] The assets were sold for £2.4m at a loss of £1.4m, so the net book value at the time of sale must have been £3.8m. If the cost of the assets sold (as shown in the fixed assets account) was £12m, the depreciation on the assets sold must have been £12m – £3.8m = £8.2m.

Step 2

Having calculated the depreciation for the year, we can proceed to calculate the net cash from operating activities. Because we show interest separately in the cash flow statement, we must start with the operating profit before interest:

	£000
Operating profit (36,300 + 10,000)	46,300
Depreciation (see Step 1)	3,200
Loss on sale of fixed assets	1,400
Increase in stock (14,000 – 11,000)	(3,000)
Increase in debtors (19,100 – 17,400)	(1,700)
Decrease in creditors (15,500 – 14,200)	(1,300)
Net cash inflow from operating activities	44,900

Step 3

We've done the hardest part, so we can now set out the cash flow statement as follows, starting with the net cash inflow from operating activities as calculated in Step 2:

Copperfield plc
Cash flow statement for the year ended 31 May 2005

	£000
Net cash inflow from operating activities	44,900
Interest paid[1]	(10,000)
Tax[2]	(13,000)
Net capital expenditure[3]	(11,600)
Changes in financing[4]	1,000
Dividends[5]	(20,000)
Business acquisitions/disposals	–
Decrease in cash for the period	(8,700)

Notes:
1 As there was no interest received, the word 'net' can be omitted.
2 The amount paid in the year (i.e. the previous year's provision).
3 This can be analysed as follows:

	£
Purchase of fixed assets	(14,000)
Receipts from sales of fixed assets	2,400

4 There was a bonus issue during the year. This is a *free* issue of shares so therefore does not involve a cash flow. The amount was £10,000 so the remaining part of the £11,000 difference between opening and closing share capital amounts must be a result of a new share issue.

5 This represents the dividends actually paid in the year.

Step 4

We can prove the closing figure in the cash flow statement by preparing a simple reconciliation of the opening and closing cash balances (the bank overdraft in this case):

	£000
Opening bank overdraft, 1 June 2004	10,900
Closing bank overdraft, 31 May 2005	19,600
Increase in overdraft (i.e. decrease in cash for the period)	(8,700)

9.4 Cash flow forecasts

Whereas cash flow statements are based on historic (past) events, a **cash flow forecast** is essentially a practical exercise where a business is looking ahead to assess not only future income and expenditure but also the level of funding required for a defined period. It is part of the budgeting process explained in Chapter 16.

Key areas to consider include:

- the period of the forecast (3, 6, 12 months, and so on)
- the degree of analysis required (weekly, monthly, quarterly, and so on)
- the timing of sales revenues
- the relative proportions of cash and credit sales
- potential changes in the level of overheads and the timing of their payment
- the effect of seasonal changes in income and expenditure.

The forecast is usually shown in a specific format, as in Figure 9.1.

There is no universally agreed way of presenting a cash flow forecast, but the advantage of the layout shown is that columns are provided for the business owner to insert not only the forecast results, but also the *actual* month's results when they are known. This provides an important means of financial control, as variances between forecast and actual can be investigated and appropriate action taken. No forecast is likely to be wholly accurate; it is the best estimate based on information available at the time of preparation. Some information may be wholly accurate, for example the amount of loan repayments due, or expenditure where the price has been agreed in advance. Other information, such as levels of sales income, might be based on a previous year's sales figures with adjustments made for inflation, relative decline or increase in trading, etc.

Figure 9.1
Cash flow forecast

Cash flow forecast from 1 January 2006 to 31 March 2006						
Period – Monthly	Jan-06	Jan-06	Feb-06	Feb-06	Mar-06	Mar-06
(£)	Forecast	Actual	Forecast	Actual	Forecast	Actual
Receipts						
Sales: cash	2,350		1,450		3,410	
Sales: debtors	1,620		1,200		2,330	
Capital injected	6,000		–		–	
Other receipts	–		–		1,000	
A: Total receipts	9,970		2,650		6,740	
Payments						
Purchases: cash	1,520		800		1,200	
Purchases: creditors	680		750		800	
Wages and salaries	2,210		2,210		2,420	
Rent, rates	300		300		320	
Light, heat, power	250		250		250	
Insurance	300		–		120	
Transport, packaging	140		60		250	
Maintenance	–		–		400	
Advertising	390		120		220	
Postage/stationery and telephone	220		200		220	
Professional fees	300		–		–	
Bank/finance charges and interest	350		300		400	
Drawings/fees	1,500		1,500		1,500	
Sundry expenses	400		400		400	
Loan repayments	500		500		500	
Capital expenditure	–		2,500		–	
B: Total payments	9,060		9,890		9,000	
C: Net cash flow (A – B)	910		(7,240)		(2,260)	
D: Opening bank balance	1,650		2,560		(4,680)	
E: Closing bank balance (D ± C)	2,560		(4,680)		(6,940)	
Note: Agreed overdraft facility	6,000		6,000		6,000	

Activity 9.2

Look carefully at the cash flow forecast in Figure 9.1, then answer the following questions:

1 What is the overall forecast change in the bank balance in the three months?
2 What action does the business need to take in March to avoid a major problem?
3 What forecast bank balance would start April's forecast?
4 Explain the meaning of 'capital injected' and 'capital expenditure'.

Answer

1 The balance is forecast to decline from £1,650 (positive balance) on 1 January to an overdraft of £6,940 at the end of March, an overall cash outflow of £8,590.
2 The overdraft limit is only £6,000 but this will be exceeded if the forecast proves accurate. The business must either renegotiate a higher overdraft facility, decrease expenditure or increase income.
3 An overdraft of £6,940.
4 Capital injected means that cash from the owner(s) is forecast to be paid in during January. Capital expenditure means that fixed assets are forecast to be purchased in February.

9.5 Cash flow forecasts and business planning

A cash flow forecast is often presented as part of a **business plan**. A business plan can have many different uses, one of which is to present a detailed appraisal of the business to a bank when applying for finance. However, it must not be seen as just a document to show the bank manager and then file away. A regularly updated business plan is an invaluable management tool, allowing performance to be monitored against targets ('forecast' compared with 'actual'), and provides direction for management and staff.

Business plans are usually written for one or more of the following reasons:

- To raise finance, by informing potential lenders or investors about the business.
- To identify the business's strengths and weaknesses.
- To identify opportunities for expansion and threats to the business's survival.
- To set realistic and achievable targets.
- To plan the future direction of the business.

The content of the business plan will vary depending upon what the business is aiming to achieve. Many business plans are highly complex documents, as the very survival of the business depends upon them. Every business plan should include the following as key components:

- Title page
- Contents page
- An executive summary (key points at a glance)
- Business background (brief history of the business, key personnel)
- Legal set-up – sole trader/partnership/limited company
- Summary of financial background of the business and its present financial state

- Short-/medium-/long-term plans for the business
- Mission statement ('why the business exists')
- Products and/or services
- Overview of each product or service
- Marketing strategies
- Organisation chart
- Forecast cash flows
- Forecast profit and loss account
- Forecast balance sheet
- Statement of how much funds are required, their intended purpose and their projected impact on the profitability of the business
- Potential rewards for investors.

Note that a forecast profit and loss account and balance sheet would be included in addition to the cash flow forecast. This will enable the reader of the plan to assess the anticipated profitability of the business (vital to a future investor) as well as its viability as shown by the change in its net asset position and liquidity as disclosed in the forecast balance sheet.

9.6 Summary

Key headings in a cash flow statement are:

Operating activities	Cash flowing from trading (start with net profit, then adjust it for depreciation, stock, debtors and creditors)
Interest	Cash flowing from paying and receiving interest during the period
Tax	Cash paid in respect of taxation in the period
Capital expenditure	Cash flow from buying and selling fixed assets during the period
Financing	Cash flow from selling shares or receiving or repaying loans during the period
Dividends	Cash paid for dividends in the period
Business acquisitions and disposals	Cash flow from buying or selling businesses in the period

9.7 Glossary

Business plan A document drawn up by a business for a number of different purposes, including planning, fund-raising and setting targets. A cash flow forecast is a key component of a business plan.

Cash flow The inflows and outflows of cash through a business over a particular period.

Cash flow forecast Predictions of cash inflows and outflows over a future period.

Cash flow statement	A summary of cash and bank transactions over a defined past period. When published it must be set out in a format prescribed by the relevant Financial Reporting Standard.
Financial Reporting Standards (FRSs)	Regulations which are expected to be followed by companies and accountants in order to comply with best practice.
Liquidity	The ability of a business to access enough cash (including bank balances) to pay debts as they fall due.
Primary statement	A financial summary of importance. Primary statements include the profit and loss account, the balance sheet and the cash flow statement.
Solvency	The ability of a business to pay its debts as they fall due. The opposite is *insolvency*.

? Self-check questions

1 Cash has been described as:
   a The lifebuoy of the business
   b The lifeboat of the business
   c The lifeline of the business
   d The lifeblood of the business

2 The definition of cash as used in cash flow statements includes:
   a Only cash balances
   b Only bank balances
   c Bank balances and bank overdrafts
   d Cash in hand plus bank balances less bank overdrafts

3 How can a profitable business fail?
   a Because it can't pay its bills
   b Because it has more current liabilities than current assets
   c Because it has a bank overdraft
   d Because it has too much cash

4 FRS 1 states that:
   a All companies must prepare a cash flow statement
   b All small companies must prepare a cash flow statement
   c All small companies must prepare a cash flow forecast
   d Small companies are exempt from preparing a cash flow statement

5 The heading in a cash flow statement 'Changes in financing' means:
   a The cash outflow due to loan interest payments being made
   b The cash flow from share and loan issues and repayments
   c Cash dividends paid to shareholders
   d The change in the level of bank balances in the period

6 If 'Taxation' is shown on the cash flow statement, it is likely to be:
   a The taxation paid this year on the current year's profit
   b The taxation payable next year on this year's profit
   c The taxation paid this year on last year's profit
   d The taxation provided on this year's profit

7   Depreciation is added back to profit when arriving at the cash flow from operating activities because:
   a Depreciation is only an estimated amount
   b Depreciation does not affect profit
   c Depreciation does not result in a flow of cash
   d Depreciation affects only the balance sheet, not the profit and loss account

8   If net profit before taxation and interest was £95,000, depreciation for the year was £17,000, stock has decreased during the year by £7,000, debtors have increased by £11,000 and creditors have decreased by £4,000, what is the overall cash flow from operating activities?
   a £104,000
   b £112,000
   c £98,000
   d £134,000

9   A business plan is often prepared:
   a To comply with accounting standards
   b To show customers where the head office is situated
   c To set targets for the business
   d To be filed away in a drawer

10 Which of the following are all primary statements?
   a The profit and loss account, balance sheet and cash flow statement
   b The profit and loss account, balance sheet and cash flow forecast
   c The profit and loss account, business plan and cash flow statement
   d The profit and loss account, balance sheet and financial reporting statement

   (Answers in Appendix 1)

Self-study questions

(Answers in Appendix 2)

Question 9.1   From the following information, calculate the missing figure in each column.

(£)	A	B	C	D
Net cash flow from operating activities	14,800	?	21,400	48,660
Net interest paid	(5,800)	(2,900)	(6,000)	(2,950)
Tax	(7,200)	(4,500)	(7,100)	(24,880)
Net capital expenditure	17,300	(2,970)	?	(6,520)
Changes in financing	800	(1,800)	14,680	(17,490)
Dividends	(9,820)	(4,200)	(3,300)	?
Increase/(Decrease) in cash for the period	?	6,200	11,750	(9,450)

Question 9.2   From the following information, calculate the cash flow from operating activities for each column. Put brackets around figures where appropriate.

(£)	A	B	C	D
Net profit before interest	36,620	29,937		20,060
Net loss before interest			22,660	
Depreciation	12,000	16,000	24,000	15,000
Increase in stock	9,650			14,850
Decrease in stock		5,840	5,622	
Increase in debtors			2,240	12,795
Decrease in debtors	7,980	6,722		
Increase in creditors	3,380		9,713	
Decrease in creditors		6,840		11,629
Cash flow from operating activities	?	?	?	?

Question 9.3 The balance sheets of Dombey plc as at 31 May 2004 and 31 May 2005 are as follows:

	31 May 2005		31 May 2004	
	£000	£000	£000	£000
Fixed assets (net book value)		43,000		32,000
Current assets:				
Stock	19,000		18,000	
Debtors	9,000		7,500	
Bank	–		2,800	
	28,000		28,300	
Less **Creditors due for**				
payment within one year:				
Creditors	6,100		9,900	
Taxation	5,000		4,000	
Bank overdraft	5,700		–	
	(16,800)		(13,900)	
Net current assets		11,200		14,400
Total net assets		54,200		46,400
Share capital and reserves				
Ordinary shares of 25p each		24,000		33,000
Share premium account		300		200
Retained earnings		29,900		13,200
		54,200		46,400

The summarised profit and loss accounts for the two years ended 31 May 2005 are as follows:

	2005	2004
	£000	£000
Gross profit	46,100	38,900
Less Expenses (including £1.2m interest)	(18,200)	(22,100)
	27,900	16,800
Less Loss on sale of fixed assets	(3,200)	–
Operating profit	24,700	16,800
Less Taxation	(5,000)	(4,000)
Operating profit after tax	19,700	12,800
Less Dividends paid	(3,000)	(2,000)
Retained profits	16,700	10,800
Retained profits b/f	13,200	2,400
Retained profits c/f	29,900	13,200

Notes:

1 A summary of the company's fixed assets account in the general ledger for the year ended 31 May 2005 is shown below:

		£000				£000
1 Jun 2004	Cost b/f	76,000	31 May 2005	To Disposals account		8,000
31 May 2005	Additions	22,000	31 May 2005	Cost c/f		90,000
		98,000				98,000

2 The assets which were sold realised £1,800,000, which represented a loss on disposal of £3,200,000 when compared with their book value.

Produce a cash flow statement for the year ended 31 May 2005, and reconcile the cash increase or decrease for the year as shown on the statement with the change in the bank balance shown in the balance sheets.

Question 9.4 The following information relates to The Marshes Gallery, which has been set up by Clara Pilbeam to help rural craftspeople to sell their products to the tourist trade. Clara is submitting a business plan to Midlays Bank plc. She has found what she thinks are ideal premises: a disused colliery building in South Wales. She has saved £4,000 as initial capital, which she would pay into the Gallery's bank account on 1 July 2006, which will be the effective starting date of the enterprise. Forecast information for the six months to 31 December 2006 is as follows:

- The landlord requires a deposit of £3,000, and rent of £1,000 per month, payable quarterly in arrears. The deposit will be paid on 1 July 2006, the first quarter's rent on 2 October 2006, the second quarter on 3 January 2007.
- Income will be generated from commissions on works of art sold through the gallery. The average commission taken by the gallery will be 40%, and sales of artworks are forecast as follows:

July	August	September	October	November	December
£8,000	£4,000	£7,000	£12,000	£18,000	£24,000

- All sales are for cash, and are banked immediately without deduction. Amounts due to artists are paid one month after the relevant sales are made.
- The Gallery will receive a one-off grant of £5,000 from the Welsh Tourist Board in August.
- The cost of redecorating the building will be £7,000, payable in two instalments: £4,000 in August, the balance in September.
- General overheads (including any bank interest payable) are expected to be £2,000 per month, payable one month in arrears.
- Wages to assistants will be £750 per month and are payable at the end of the month.
- Clara Pilbeam will draw £600 per month until December, when she will draw £900.
- Various items of equipment will be purchased for £3,000 in July, payable two months later. Depreciation for the six months will be £150.
- Initial advertising will cost £500, payable in August.

Prepare a cash flow forecast for The Marshes Gallery for the six months to 31 December 2006. Comment on the forecast, and state whether you think that the project appears feasible.

Case study

There's the profit, but where's the cash?

Machiq Limited (see previous case studies) was formed on 1 July 2003 and has been making increasing profits. By 30 June 2005 it reported the following summarised profit and loss accounts and balance sheets:

Machiq Limited
Profit and loss accounts for the year ended 30 June

	2005 £	2004 £
Gross profit	176,400	133,260
Less Expenses (includes interest of £1,800 p.a.)	(60,400)	(41,260)
Net profit for the year, before taxation	116,000	92,000
Less Provision for taxation	(26,950)	(18,400)
Net profit for the year, after taxation	89,050	73,600
Less Dividends	(32,000)	(31,500)
Retained profit for the year	57,050	42,100
Retained profit brought forward	42,100	–
Retained profit carried forward	99,150	42,100

Balance sheets as at 30 June

	2005 £	2005 £	2004 £	2004 £
Fixed assets (net book value)		165,980		74,040
Current assets:				
Stock	32,650		17,370	
Debtors	30,950		39,560	
Bank	–		6,240	
	63,600		63,170	
***Less* Creditors due for payment within one year:**				
Creditors	14,080		10,210	
Taxation	26,950		18,400	
Dividends approved but unpaid	32,000		31,500	
Bank overdraft	2,400		–	
	(75,430)		(60,110)	
Net current assets/(liabilities)		(11,830)		3,060
Total net assets		154,150		77,100
Capital and reserves				
Called-up share capital (5p shares)		24,000		14,000
Share premium account		31,000		21,000
Profit and loss account:				
Retained profit for the year		99,150		42,100
		154,150		77,100

The changes in the share capital and share premium account were due to a sale of shares to Trixie Richardson, who had recently left Kazam Limited after 10 years' service as chief accountant. Trixie was appointed managing director of Machiq Limited on 10 April 2005. During the year ended 30 June 2005, Machiq Limited bought two Braganza Rapido motor cars for £48,500 each for Marvin's and Chiquita's use. No assets were sold in the year. Trixie is concerned that, whilst the company seems to be profitable, its cash flow appears to be poor.

Required:

a Prepare a cash flow statement for the year ended 30 June 2005, and reconcile the cash increase or decrease for the year as shown on the statement with the change in the bank balance shown in the balance sheets.

b Do you agree with Trixie's opinion of the cash flow? What have been the key cash inflows and outflows in the year?

The three shareholders of Machiq Limited, Chiquita, Marvin and Trixie, decide to draw up a cash flow forecast for the six months ended 31 December 2005. They have an agreed bank overdraft limit of £6,000. They prepare the following predictions:

● *Income*. Sales will be £30,000 each month, except November which will be £40,000. Half the sales will be on credit, with debtors paying one month after the sale; the rest will be for cash. Debtors owing at 30 June 2005 will pay in July 2005.

● *Expenditure*. Purchases and all expenses other than wages and salaries will be a constant £35,000 per month, payable one month after purchase. Wages and salaries amounting to £6,000 per month will be paid at the end of the same month, but a bonus of an extra £8,000 will be paid in December. Creditors owing at 30 June 2005 will be paid in July. Assume that neither the taxation nor the proposed dividend will be paid during the period.

Required:

c Prepare the cash flow forecast for the six months ending 31 December 2005. Will Machiq Limited have to renegotiate its bank overdraft limit?

(Answers in Appendix 3)

References

Tesco plc's cash flow statement: **www.tesco.com/corporateinfo/**

A site that offers sample business plans: **www.bplans.com**

A web page which calculates Bill Gates' wealth on a daily basis:

philip.greenspun.com/WealthClock

> Now look at this book's dedicated website at **www.pearsoned.co.uk/black** and work through the various additional exercises for this chapter.

Chapter 10

Making sense of financial statements

Objectives

When you have read this chapter you will be able to:

➤ Understand the need for plc's to publish information

➤ Undertake preliminary research prior to analysing company accounts

➤ Appreciate the key components of an annual report, including the statement of total recognised gains and losses

➤ Distinguish between, and compute, a vertical and horizontal analysis of financial information and make a simple interpretation of the data revealed by the analysis

➤ Prepare ratios within five main groupings and analyse the data revealed

➤ Understand concerns regarding the validity of accounting information

10.1 Introduction

The published financial information of Tesco plc, as referred to in the previous chapter, comes in two versions:

● The Annual Review and Summary Financial Statement, intended for users who do not require fully comprehensive financial information but need only the highlights of the company's performance. The most recently published statement contained 37 pages. Summarised versions of the profit and loss account, balance sheet, cash flow statement and various other items of financial data appeared on six of these pages, the rest being devoted to general information about the company, with many full-colour photographs of stores, products, customers and employees

- The Annual Report and Financial Statements, which gives all the information required to be published by the Companies Act 1985, Accounting and Financial Reporting Standards and the Stock Exchange. This contained 40 pages, including not only the primary financial statements but also 16 pages of detailed notes to the accounts.

Tesco has approximately 285,000 shareholders (of whom 95,000 are also employees)[1] and the production of glossy, full-colour reports with tempting photographs of foodstuffs and smiling shop assistants is used partly as a public relations exercise to keep shareholders loyal and maintain confidence in the company. Smaller companies might have very few shareholders and so the annual accounts, whilst still containing the primary statements, will tend to be matter-of-fact documents without any frills. The Companies Act 1985 gives various exemptions to such companies, so even though information has to be published, it would not be nearly as comprehensive as that required of a plc.

Neither sole traders nor partnerships are required to publish accounts, and their financial summaries will normally be seen by only a handful of people: the owner or partners, the accountant who produced the accounts, the taxation authorities and possibly a bank manager. Any wider distribution is entirely at the discretion of the owner(s).

10.2 Data for analysis

The purpose of this chapter is to *make sense* of the information contained in the financial summaries: to analyse, interpret and come to a conclusion. To illustrate the analytical process, we shall use the financial statements of a fictitious company, Madison plc, for the years 2004 and 2005 as set out below.

Madison plc
(published) Profit and loss account for the years ended
31 December 2005 and 2004

	2005	2004
	£000	£000
Turnover	6,590	4,350
Less Cost of sales	(4,220)	(2,820)
Gross profit	2,370	1,530
Less Expenses:		
Administrative	(380)	(300)
Selling and distribution	(320)	(170)
Net profit before interest	1,670	1,060
Less Interest payable	(60)	(70)
Net profit before taxation	1,610	990
Less Taxation	(450)	(270)
Profit after taxation	1,160	720
Less Dividends	(360)	(120)
Retained earnings for the year	800	600
Retained earnings b/f	1,600	1,000
Retained earnings c/f	2,400	1,600

[1] Source: Tesco plc Annual Review and Summary Financial Statement 2004.

Madison plc
Balance sheets as at 31 December 2005 and 2004

	2005			2004		
	£000	£000	£000	£000	£000	£000
Fixed assets (net book value)			6,200			5,320
Current assets:						
Stock		2,200			680	
Debtors		550			500	
Bank balance		250			200	
		3,000			1,380	
Less Creditors due for payment within one year:						
Trade creditors	390			210		
Taxation	450			270		
Dividends approved but unpaid	360			120		
		(1,200)			(600)	
Net current assets			1,800			780
			8,000			6,100
Less Creditors due for payment after more than one year:						
Debentures			(1,000)			(1,500)
Total net assets			7,000			4,600
Capital and reserves						
Ordinary shares of £1 each			3,100			2,500
Share premium account			1,500			500
Profit and loss account			2,400			1,600
			7,000			4,600

Additional information:
Stock at 1 January 2004 = £640,000.
Stock market prices: end 2005 = 561p, end 2004 = 547p.
There were no 'cash' sales or purchases during either year.

Madison plc
Cash flow statement for the years ended 31 December 2005 and 2004

	2005	2004
	£000	£000
Net cash inflow from operating activities	665	810
Interest paid	(65)	(60)
Tax	(270)	(170)
Net capital expenditure	(1,260)	(320)
Changes in financing	1,100	–
Dividends	(120)	(90)
Business acquisitions/disposals	–	(160)
Increase in cash for the period	50	10

10.3 The first stage: preliminary research

There are many reasons for analysing financial statements, including the following:

- Investment – you may be an existing shareholder or considering investing in a business.
- Curiosity – you may have used a business's products or services and wish to find out more about what they do.
- Commercial reasons – you trade with the business or are considering trading with it.
- Lending decisions – banks and other financial institutions need to know if a business is capable of repaying loans or is in a sound position if loans are being requested.
- Self-interest – you may want to find out more about the company that employs you. For example, is it likely to continue trading and keep you as an employee?
- Business rivalry – how well or badly is a competitor doing compared with your business?
- Taxation – the taxation authorities may need to be satisfied that the accounts appear complete and trustworthy.
- Environmental factors – local communities and pressure groups may wish to find out more about local companies, including their employment and ecological attitudes.
- Economic analysis – business trends can be ascertained by analysing company results.

Source: *Daily Telegraph*, 28 October 1997. Courtesy of Alex Cartoon.

Those wishing to make the analysis may already know a great deal about the company, as shareholders, as workers or by virtue of publicly available information such as newspaper comment. The key background information which is needed prior to starting a detailed numerical analysis of the financial statements includes:

- Type of trade – what does the company do?
- Competitors – whom does it compete against? What share of the market does it have?
- Geographical spread – where does it sell its goods and services and which countries does it buy from?

- Management – who are the managers and how well qualified are they?
- Quality of products – how reliable are the products the company sells?

Much of this information can be gleaned from the 'non-financial' parts of the annual report, by accessing data via the Internet or in libraries, or even by visual inspection of products, stores, advertisements and so on. All this preliminary research is useful in placing the business in an appropriate context prior to making any detailed financial calculations.

The full annual reports of plc's will contain several sections in addition to the financial summaries, the key ones being as follows:

- *Operating and financial review*, which contains a commentary on the results of the period, a review of the group's needs and resources and an assessment of their shareholders' return on their investment in the company.
- *Directors' report*, which contains various items of statutory information such as the principal activities of the company, the names of the directors and auditors, a brief summary of the company's financial results and how many shares the directors own.
- *Auditors' report*, which is a statement from an independent qualified accountant (or firm of accountants) as to whether or not the accounts show a true and fair view of the state of the company's affairs and its profit or loss and cash flows.

Did you know?

International Accounting Standards (IASs) refer to this as a 'statement of recognised income and expenses'.

- **Statement of total recognised gains and losses**, which is a primary statement like the profit and loss account, balance sheet and cash flow statement. It summarises all the gains and losses which appear in the financial summaries. This means that it will show not only the profit for the period as revealed by the profit and loss account, but also profits shown only within the balance sheet such as revaluation gains on land and buildings credited to an asset revaluation reserve (see page 129).
- *Statement of accounting policies*, which sets out the principles adopted by the company when dealing with various items included within the summaries, such as how stocks are valued, what depreciation methods have been followed, and so on.
- *Notes to the financial statements*, which set out detailed explanations of figures contained within the financial statements to comply with the requirements of the Companies Acts, Accounting and Financial Reporting Standards and the Stock Exchange.

Having obtained a good general impression of the scope and nature of the business, the analyst should then read through the annual report, making a note of any unusual or interesting items such as changes in accounting policies and businesses acquired in the year. By looking at the 'bottom lines' of the three main financial summaries, an immediate impression can be gained of the business's progress in the year. For Madison plc, this shows:

Profit and loss account:	Retained profit for the year has increased from £600,000 to £800,000, with total retained earnings rising from £1.6m to £2.4m.
Balance sheet:	Total net assets/total capital employed has risen from £4.6m to £7m in the year.
Cash flow statement:	Cash has increased by £50,000, compared with an increase of only £10,000 in the previous year.

By all three measures the company appears to have performed well.

Activity 10.1

Obtain a copy of an annual report of a plc (see References at the end of the chapter) and identify the sections listed above. Read through the auditors' report to see if the accounts show a true and fair view, and try to find out how many shares the chief executive owns and how much he or she was paid as a director. Look at the bottom lines of the three main financial statements (use group figures where there is a choice). How do you think the company performed in the year?

Answer

Obviously the answer depends on which company's report you are looking at, but as an illustration, Tesco plc's 2004 annual report showed a true and fair view according to the auditors, PricewaterhouseCoopers. The company's chief executive, Sir Terry Leahy, owned 4.9 million shares and was paid a salary of £955,000 for the year. The company's financial summaries showed solid progress:

Profit and loss account:	Retained profit for the year increased from £503m to £584m.
Balance sheet:	Total net assets/total capital employed rose from £6,559m to £7,990m in the year.
Cash flow statement:	Cash increased by £282m compared with a decrease of £45m in the previous year.

Pause for thought

Tesco plc had 7.2bn shares in issue, so Sir Terry Leahy owned under 0.07% of the company, and his salary was 0.17% of the retained profits.

10.4 The second stage: horizontal and vertical analysis

Having gathered the background information, the next stage is to start the numerical analysis of the financial statements. Advanced mathematics is not required, but you should understand percentage and ratio calculations. Refresh your memory with the next activity.

Activity 10.2

Calculate the following:

(a) 6,815 as a percentage of 27,260.
(b) 3,720 as a percentage of 1,200.
(c) The increase from 3,120 to 11,232 as a percentage of the former figure.
(d) The decrease from 16,040 to 12,832 as a percentage of the former figure.
(e) The ratio of 5,541 compared with 18,470.
(f) The ratio of 46,000 compared with 11,500.

Answer

Calculation

(a) 25% $\dfrac{6,815}{27,260} \times 100 = 25\%$

(b) 310% $\dfrac{3,720}{1,200} \times 100 = 310\%$

(c) Increase of 260% $11,232 - 3,120 = 8,112$

$\dfrac{8,112}{3,120} \times 100 = 260\%$

(d) Decrease of 20% $16,040 - 12,832 = 3,208$

$\dfrac{3,208}{16,040} \times 100 = 20\%$

(e) 0.3:1 $\dfrac{5,541}{18,470} = 0.3$

(f) 4:1 $\dfrac{46,000}{11,500} = 4$

Horizontal and vertical analysis are simple means of comparing the relative size of individual components within the summaries. **Horizontal analysis** achieves this by calculating the percentage change from the preceding year to the current year, whereas **vertical analysis** expresses each profit and loss account item as a percentage of the sales total, each balance sheet item as a percentage of the total net assets, and cash flow statement items as a percentage of the net cash flow from operating activities.

Using the Madison plc statements, the analysis will be as follows (figures have been rounded to the nearest whole number):

Madison plc
(published) Profit and loss account for the years ended
31 December 2005 and 2004

	2005	2004	'Horizontal' analysis	'Vertical' analysis 2005	2004
	£000	£000	% change	%	%
Turnover	6,590	4,350	+ 51	100	100
Less Cost of sales	(4,220)	(2,820)	+ 50	(64)	(65)
Gross profit	2,370	1,530	+ 55	36	35
Less Expenses:					
Administrative	(380)	(300)	+ 27	(6)	(7)
Selling and distribution	(320)	(170)	+ 88	(5)	(4)
Net profit before interest	1,670	1,060	+ 58	25	24
Less Interest payable	(60)	(70)	− 14	(1)	(2)
Net profit before taxation	1,610	990	+ 63	24	23
Less Taxation	(450)	(270)	+ 67	(7)	(6)
Profit after taxation	1,160	720	+ 61	18	17
Less Dividends	(360)	(120)	+ 200	(5)	(3)
Retained earnings for the year	800	600	+ 33	12	14
Retained earnings b/f	1,600	1,000	+ 60		
Retained earnings c/f	2,400	1,600	+ 50		

Note that each percentage in the 'horizontal' column is calculated using the following formula:

$$\frac{2005 \text{ amount} - 2004 \text{ amount}}{2004 \text{ amount}} \times 100$$

The figures in the vertical columns are calculated as a percentage of the sales figure. The quickest way of doing this is to multiply each figure by the formula (entered as a constant on your calculator):

$$\frac{100}{\text{Sales figure}}$$

The balance sheet and cash flow statement can be analysed in a similar way:

Madison plc
Balance sheets as at 31 December 2005 and 2004

	2005	2004	'Horizontal' analysis	'Vertical' analysis 2005	2004
	£000	£000	% change	%	%
Fixed assets	6,200	5,320	+ 17	89	116
Current assets:					
Stock	2,200	680	+ 224	31	15
Debtors	550	500	+ 10	8	11
Bank balance	250	200	+ 25	4	4
	3,000	1,380	+ 117	43	30
Creditors due for payment within one year:					
Trade creditors	390	210	+ 86	6	5
Taxation	450	270	+ 67	6	6
Dividends approved but	360	120	+ 200	5	3
unpaid	(1,200)	(600)	+ 100	(17)	(13)
Net current assets	1,800	780	+ 131	26	17
	8,000	6,100	+ 31	114	133
Creditors due for payment after more than one year:					
Debentures	(1,000)	(1,500)	− 33	(14)	(33)
Total net assets	7,000	4,600	+ 52	100	100
Capital and reserves					
Ordinary shares of £1	3,100	2,500	+ 24	44	54
Share premium account	1,500	500	+ 200	21	11
Profit and loss account	2,400	1,600	+ 50	34	35
	7,000	4,600	+ 52	100	100

Note that each figure in the vertical analysis is expressed as a percentage of the balance sheet total.

Madison plc
Cash flow statement for the years ended 31 December 2005 and 2004

	2005	2004	'Horizontal' analysis	'Vertical' analysis 2005	2004
	£000	£000	% change	%	%
Net cash inflow from operating activities	665	810	– 18	100	100
Interest paid	(65)	(60)	+ 8	(10)	(7)
Tax	(270)	(170)	+ 59	(41)	(21)
Net capital expenditure	(1,260)	(320)	+ 294	(189)	(40)
Changes in financing	1,100	–	n/a	165	–
Dividends	(120)	(90)	+ 33	(18)	(11)
Business acquisitions/disposals	–	(160)	n/a	–	(20)
Increase in cash for the period	50	10	+ 400	8	1

Note that each figure in the vertical analysis is expressed as a percentage of the net cash flow from operating activities.

10.4.1 Interpreting the analysis

It is obvious that the company has expanded in 2005. The horizontal analysis shows within the profit and loss account how much the increase has been, and the noteworthy changes have been the size of dividends (increased by 200%), the seemingly disproportionate increase in selling and distribution expenses when compared with administration expenses (88% increase compared with 27%) and the reduction in interest (–14%) which has resulted from a part repayment of the debenture as disclosed by the balance sheet.

The vertical analysis reveals that the decline in administrative expenses as a percentage of sales (from 7% to 6%) has been offset by a similar increase in selling and distribution expenses. Other amounts have remained fairly constant, apart from the near doubling in dividend levels as a percentage of sales. Retained earnings as a percentage of sales have declined from 14% to 12% as a result of the increased dividends.

The balance sheet's horizontal analysis reveals the first worrying statistic about the company: the fact that stock levels have increased by 223% in the year, even though total net assets have increased by 'only' 52%. The 200% increase in the share premium account shows that the shares issued in the year were sold at an amount considerably in excess of their nominal value. The vertical analysis of the balance sheet again highlights the increasing amount of stock held by the company at the end of 2005 and the more generous dividend policy.

The horizontal analysis of the cash flow statement again shows some areas of concern. Net cash inflow from operating activities has declined by 18%, with massive increases in net capital expenditure (fixed asset purchases less sales). Overall there was a healthy 400% rise in the amount by which cash had increased. The vertical analysis for 2005 shows that the cash outflow on capital expenditure was almost matched by financing changes (new shares being issued less debentures repaid).

10.5 The third stage: ratio analysis

Having established the percentage movements between the two years, and assessed the relative strengths of the component parts of the financial statements, the next step is to calculate specific percentages and ratios to reveal further aspects of the business's performance. The following table represents the more common ones which are calculated, divided into five groups.

Group	Name of ratio	Formula
Profitability	ROCE (Return on capital employed)	$\dfrac{\text{Net profit before interest and tax}}{\text{Share capital} + \text{Reserves} + \text{Long-term loans}} \times 100$
	Gross margin (or Gross profit margin)	$\dfrac{\text{Gross profit}}{\text{Sales}} \times 100$
	Mark-up	$\dfrac{\text{Gross profit}}{\text{Cost of goods sold}} \times 100$
	Net margin (or Net profit margin)	$\dfrac{\text{Net profit before interest and tax}}{\text{Turnover}} \times 100$
Efficiency	Fixed assets turnover	$\dfrac{\text{Total sales}}{\text{Fixed assets at net book value}}$
	Stockturn	$\dfrac{\text{Average stock}}{\text{Cost of sales}} \times 365$
	Debtors' collection period	$\dfrac{\text{Trade debtors}}{\text{Credit sales}} \times 365$
	Creditors' payment period	$\dfrac{\text{Trade creditors}}{\text{Credit purchases}} \times 365$
Short-term solvency and liquidity	Current ratio (or Working capital ratio)	Current assets:Current liabilities
	Acid test (or Quick assets test)	(Current assets – Stock):Current liabilities
Long-term solvency and liquidity	Gearing	$\dfrac{\text{Preference shares (if any)} + \text{Long-term loans}}{\text{Share capital} + \text{Reserves} + \text{Long-term loans}} \times 100$ (note that there are other ways of calculating gearing: see page 199)
	Interest cover	$\dfrac{\text{Profit before interest}}{\text{Interest payable}}$
Investment ratios	eps (earnings per share)	$\dfrac{\text{Profit available for ordinary dividend}}{\text{Number of equity shares issued}}$
	p/e (price/earnings)	$\dfrac{\text{Market price}}{\text{Earnings per share}}$
	Dividend cover	$\dfrac{\text{Profit available to pay dividend}}{\text{Dividends paid and proposed}}$
	Dividend yield	$\dfrac{\text{Dividend per share}}{\text{Market price per share}} \times 100$

Using the data from Madison plc's financial summaries, the ratios are explained in sections 10.5.1–10.5.5.

10.5.1 Profitability ratios

	Madison plc	
Name of ratio	2005	2004
ROCE (Return on capital employed)	$\dfrac{1,670}{7,000 + 1,000} \times 100 = 20.87\%$	$\dfrac{1,060}{4,600 + 1,500} \times 100 = 17.38\%$
Gross margin (or Gross profit margin)	$\dfrac{2,370}{6,590} \times 100 = 35.96\%$	$\dfrac{1,530}{4,350} \times 100 = 35.17\%$
Mark-up	$\dfrac{2,370}{4,220} \times 100 = 56.16\%$	$\dfrac{1,530}{2,820} \times 100 = 54.26\%$
Net margin (or Net profit margin)	$\dfrac{1,670}{6,590} \times 100 = 25.34\%$	$\dfrac{1,060}{4,350} \times 100 = 24.37\%$

- *Return on capital employed* (ROCE) is a fundamental measure of business performance as it compares the profit before interest and tax with the total capital used to generate that profit. Notice that we have used year-end figures for capital rather than average figures for the year, though it is permissible to use the average. A viable business should generate a considerably higher return than that available by investing in a bank or other similar interest-bearing deposits. In the case of Madison plc, the return has increased marginally during the year, and is significantly higher than bank deposit rates. However, for a full assessment to be made (and this applies to all the ratios which we have calculated), we would also need to know comparative figures for other businesses operating in the same business sector. For example, if Madison plc was an engineering company and other engineering business were generating only 15% ROCE, we could assume that Madison was doing better than its competitors. If competitors were reporting ROCE of 27%, we might consider Madison plc to be underperforming. What is certain is that we cannot make any meaningful statement about *any* ratio without having some comparable figure (previous year, competitor's results, and so on) to use as a yardstick.

- **Gross margin** shows the proportion of sales revenue which resulted in a gross profit to the company. It is affected by various factors, including changing price levels and different products being sold ('sales mix'). The margin might be reduced by aggressive companies wanting to expand their share of the market, or increased if there is reduced competition. Inaccurate stock valuations or the theft of goods may also affect the ratio. In the case of Madison plc, there has been a slight upward movement in the year, resulting in £35.96 of gross profit out of every £100 sales (previous year: £35.17 per £100).

- *Mark-up* indicates the pricing policy of the business, as it shows the percentage addition to cost price to arrive at the selling price. In 2005, every £100 of goods bought by Madison plc was sold for £156.16 (previous year: £154.26).

Activity 10.3

The higher the gross margin, the higher will be the mark-up percentage. For example, a gross margin of 50% results in a mark-up of 100%, whilst a gross margin of 25% means a mark-up of 33.3%.

If a business has a gross margin of 20%, what would be the mark-up?

Answer

The mark-up is 25%.

(Sales = 100, cost of sales = 80, gross profit = 20, therefore mark-up is $\frac{20}{80} \times 100$.)

- *Net margin* shows the proportion of sales which resulted in a profit after all overheads (other than interest) had been deducted. In 2005, £25.34 out of every £100 sales resulted in net profit, an increase on the previous year's £24.37. Net profit can be improved by reducing overheads, but a balance has to be achieved between cutting expenses and maintaining business efficiency.

Activity 10.4

Calculate and comment upon the four profitability ratios for the large UK supermarket groups Tesco plc and Sainsbury plc, from the following information:

(£m)	Tesco plc		Sainsbury plc	
	2004	2003	2004	2003
Sales	17,158	16,452	16,433	14,500
Gross profit	1,308	1,235	1,317	1,183
Share capital and reserves	4,377	3,903	4,689	4,165
Long-term loans	1,230	812	804	949
Net profit	932	834	943	769

Answer

(%)	Tesco plc		Sainsbury plc	
Name of ratio	2004	2003	2004	2003
ROCE	16.62	17.69	17.17	15.04
Gross margin	7.62	7.51	8.01	8.16
Mark-up	8.25	8.12	8.71	8.88
Net margin	5.43	5.07	5.74	5.30

Comment: Tesco's ROCE slipped slightly in the year whereas Sainsbury's increased. However, Tesco's gross margin (and mark-up) increased whereas Sainsbury's declined, perhaps indicating that Tesco's prices were edging up towards those of Sainsbury, with Sainsbury cost-cutting to maintain its market share. Net margins for both companies improved in the year, with Sainsbury's higher than Tesco's in both years. Note how supermarket groups are under such intense competitive pressure that their gross margins are only slightly higher than their net margins.

10.5.2 Efficiency ratios

	Madison plc	
Name of ratio	2005	2004
Fixed assets turnover	$\dfrac{6{,}590}{6{,}200} = 1.06$ times	$\dfrac{4{,}350}{5{,}320} = 0.82$ times
Stockturn	$\dfrac{(2{,}200 + 680)/2}{4{,}220} \times 365 = 124.5$ days	$\dfrac{(680 + 640)/2}{2{,}820} \times 365 = 85.4$ days
Debtors' collection period	$\dfrac{550}{6{,}590} \times 365 = 30.5$ days	$\dfrac{500}{4{,}350} \times 365 = 42$ days
Creditors' payment period	$\dfrac{390}{5{,}760^a} \times 365 = 24.7$ days	$\dfrac{210}{2{,}860^b} \times 365 = 26.8$ days

[a] Purchases = Cost of sales + closing stock – opening stock (4,220 + 2,220 – 680).
[b] (2,820 + 680 – 640).

- *Fixed assets turnover* indicates that 2005 was a more efficient year than 2004 in that every £1 of fixed assets generated £1.06 of sales in 2005, but only 82p in the previous year.

- *Stockturn* shows the effect of the massively increased stock at the end of 2005 as it indicates that, on average, stock took 124.5 days to sell in 2005 but only 85.4 days in 2004. This is a significant increase and one which should cause concern to the company management. There may, however, be a rational explanation, such as a deliberate increase in the stock at the end of 2005 to coincide with a major sales campaign at the start of 2006.

- *Debtors' collection period* shows an improved time period for collecting outstanding debts, down from 42 days to just over 30 days. This could be because more resources have been applied to credit control, or prompt-payment discounts have been offered. Efficient businesses collect their debts quickly, as illustrated by Figure 10.1.

Pause for thought

The *European Business Survey* published by Grant Thornton in 2002 showed that the UK's average debtors' collection period was 41 days. The shortest settlement period in Europe was in Finland with an average of 26 days. The longest payment delays were in Greece at 83 days, and Italy at 78 days.

- *Creditors' payment period* shows that the company paid its creditors slightly faster in 2005 than in 2004. This may have resulted from being offered discounts for prompt payment. It is good practice not to pay creditors too quickly, as it is a form of interest-free credit to the business. However, great care must be taken not to alienate suppliers by delaying payment beyond a reasonable time.

Figure 10.1
Debt collection practice: good and bad

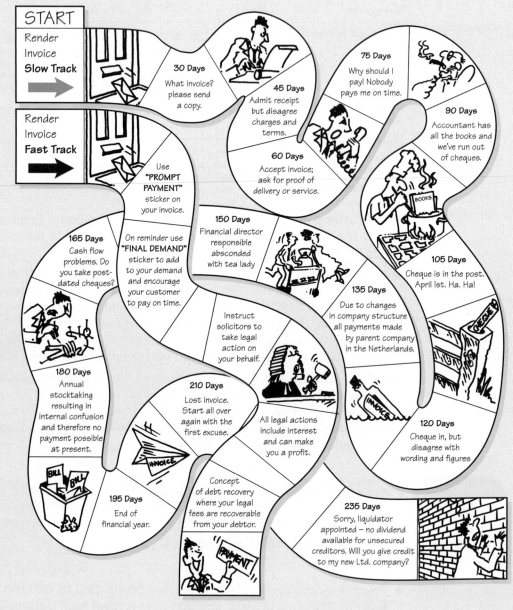

Source: Hyde Mahon Bridges Solicitors

Activity 10.5

Calculate and comment upon the four efficiency ratios for Tesco plc and Sainsbury plc, from the following information:

(£m)	Tesco plc		Sainsbury plc	
	2004	2003	2004	2003
Fixed assets	7,105	6,311	6,409	6,133
Stock (average)	625	567	793	743
Trade debtors	100	96	54	50
Trade creditors	1,100	972	1,084	902
Credit sales[a]	1,200	1,132	650	600
Total sales	17,158	16,452	16,433	14,500
Purchases	14,599	14,083	15,195	13,288
Cost of sales	15,850	15,217	15,095	13,289

[a]Estimated – the vast majority of the companies' sales are cash sales.

Answer

(%)	Tesco plc		Sainsbury plc	
Name of ratio	2004	2003	2004	2003
Fixed assets turnover	2.41 times	2.61 times	2.56 times	2.36 times
Stockturn	14.4 days	13.6 days	19.17 days	20.41 days
Debtors' collection	30.42 days	30.95 days	30.32 days	30.42 days
Creditors' payment	27.5 days	25.19 days	26.04 days	24.78 days

Comment: Sainsbury generated £2.56 of sales from every £1 of fixed assets (previous year £2.36) whereas Tesco declined from £2.61 to £2.41. One explanation could be that Tesco expanded by opening new supermarkets, with a time delay before sales were being generated from these new assets. Sainsbury increased the speed at which stock was sold (every 19.17 days compared with 20.41 days in the previous year), but it was no match for Tesco, which, despite a slow-down, still managed to sell its average stock every 14.4 days. Debtors' collection periods were fairly constant, but both companies took more interest-free credit off their suppliers.

10.5.3 Short-term solvency and liquidity ratios

	Madison plc	
Name of ratio	2005	2004
Current ratio (or Working capital ratio)	3,000:1,200 = 2.5:1	1,380:600 = 2.3:1
Acid test (or Quick assets test)	800[a]:1,200 = 0.67:1	700[b]:600 = 1.17:1

[a] (3,000 – 2,200)   [b] (1,380 – 680)

● The ideal **current ratio** (also known as the working capital ratio) is often quoted as somewhere between 1.5:1 and 2:1 (that is, between one and a half and twice as many current assets as current liabilities), but it depends upon the type of business, and many successful companies (notably those with a high proportion of cash sales) operate on current ratios of 1:1 or less.

The ratio gives a measure of the ability of a company to meet its current liabilities as they fall due, so, in theory at least, having more current assets than short-term creditors makes sense. In practice, efficient control of working capital will mean that:

● stock is kept to a minimum, otherwise too much stock may be held, resulting in high costs for storage and security, plus interest on overdrafts and loans used to pay for the stock

● debtors are encouraged to pay as soon as possible, otherwise inadequate control of debtors may result in uncollected debts

● 'surplus' cash or bank balances should be reinvested or returned to investors in the form of increased dividends

● trade creditors' payment periods might be lengthened to take advantage of interest-free credit periods.

If a company (particularly a young business) expands aggressively to gain market share, it might have to invest in fixed assets such as machinery and buildings, build up stock levels, and sell on extended credit terms, without having first built up sufficient working capital to enable it to service the finance charges on the amounts borrowed. For example, a business may get a lot of new orders beyond its existing capacity. After investing in new plant it may have no working capital left, and have to resort to heavy borrowing and reliance on extended credit terms from suppliers. If the creditors and lenders demand payment, the company may be forced to sell its fixed assets and go out of business. This is known as 'overtrading'. In most cases, the new orders bring in enough additional profit, cash flow and working capital to weather the storm.

Note that current ratios can be too high as well as too low. A company with a 6:1 ratio might have too much stock, poor credit control of debtors, or uninvested cash surpluses.

● The **acid test** is the crucial measure of whether a business seems able to meet its debts as they fall due. **Quick assets** are those which can be converted quickly into cash as the need arises, and it is normal to exclude stock and work-in-progress from the ratio. The ideal ratio is often quoted as 1:1 (£1 of quick assets to every £1 of current liabilities), but look at the supermarkets' calculations below to see how viable businesses can survive on much lower ratios. In the case of Madison plc, the exclusion of the high closing stock in 2005 results in a dramatic decline in the acid test ratio, which would be of concern to the company's directors.

Activity 10.6

Calculate and comment upon the two short-term solvency and liquidity ratios for Tesco plc and Sainsbury plc, from the following information:

(£m)	Tesco plc		Sainsbury plc	
	2004	2003	2004	2003
Current assets[a]	1,146	942	1,834	1,256
Stock (average)	625	567	793	743
Creditors[a] < 1 year	3,075	2,713	2,880	2,499

[a] Excluding Sainsbury's Bank.

Answer

(£m)	Tesco plc		Sainsbury plc	
	2004	*2003*	*2004*	*2003*
Current ratio	0.37:1	0.35:1	0.64:1	0.50:1
Acid test	0.17:1	0.14:1	0.36:1	0.21:1

Comment: It is apparent that neither company came anywhere near the 'ideal' ratios of 2:1 and 1:1. Put in simple terms, in the current year Tesco had only 17p of quickly realisable assets to meet each £1 of current liabilities. The massive cash inflows of the companies should ensure enough day-to-day liquidity to meet creditors as they fall due. However, there may come a point when any company is threatened with liquidation if it cannot ensure that suppliers are paid on time. Both companies have very poor acid test ratios, and would be looking to improve these in future years.

10.5.4 Long-term solvency and liquidity ratios

	Madison plc	
Name of ratio	2005	2004
Gearing	$\dfrac{1,000}{7,000 + 1,000} \times 100 = 12.5\%$	$\dfrac{1,500}{4,600 + 1,500} \times 100 = 24.6\%$
Interest cover	$\dfrac{1,670}{60} = 27.8$ times	$\dfrac{1,060}{70} = 15.14$ times

● **Gearing** reflects the relationship between a company's equity capital (ordinary shares and reserves) and its other forms of long-term funding (preference shares, debentures and so on). A company may exist solely on its equity (that is, have no gearing), but in order to expand it may have to issue preference shares carrying a fixed dividend rate, or borrow money on which interest must be paid. Management strategy may be to run a highly geared company, making use of a high proportion of borrowed funds to expand. This has its risks, as many companies have gone into liquidation due to borrowing money and then finding that insufficient profits are generated to repay the loans and interest. However, the rewards for ordinary shareholders can be much greater in a successful highly geared company than in its low-geared equivalent, as the increased profits, less the interest or fixed dividend payments, result in higher dividend payments. Figure 10.2 explains the advantages and disadvantages of different gearing levels.

Did you know?

Many companies deduct the value of cash and bank assets from their loan totals when calculating gearing, as presumably they could be used to repay debt if required by a lender.

There are a number of different ways to calculate gearing levels. In the example of Madison plc, the gearing percentage can never be greater than 100% as the loans are added to the divisor in the formula. Another way of calculating gearing would be to omit the loans from the divisor, in which case the gearing could be over 100% if borrowings were greater than the equity and reserves. (For Madison, the revised gearing calculation would become $(1,000/7,000) \times 100 = 14.3\%$ in 2005 and $(1,500/4,600) \times 100 = 32.6\%$ in 2004.) As long as the calculations are consistently made, either formula can be used. Madison's gearing has halved in 2005 as a result of the stronger balance sheet and the part repayment of the loan in the year.

Figure 10.2
Gearing levels

	Advantages		Disadvantages	
	Company	Shareholders	Company	Shareholders
High gearing	Prospect of high profit using borrowed money to expand	Prospect of high dividends	High interest burden	Risk of no dividends and company failure if profits can't cover high interest burden
Low gearing (or no gearing)	More profit available (as less interest), less risk of liquidation	Safety of dividends	Company reliant on internal funding, less scope to expand	Relatively low dividends, less scope for increases

● **Interest cover** indicates the relative safety of the interest payments by comparing the interest with the profit available to make the payments. Madison has nearly 28 times more profits than the interest payments, which appears very safe and will give assurance to lenders that there would have to be a very dramatic decline in profit before their interest payments were threatened.

Activity 10.7

Calculate and comment upon the two long-term solvency and liquidity ratios for Tesco plc and Sainsbury plc, from the following information:

(£m)	Tesco plc		Sainsbury plc	
	2004	2003	2004	2003
Profit before interest	932	834	943	769
Interest payable	90	74	55	78
Capital and reserves	4,377	3,903	4,689	4,165
Long-term debt	1,230	812	804	949

Answer

(£m)	Tesco plc		Sainsbury plc	
	2004	2003	2004	2003
Gearing	21.94%	17.22%	14.64%	18.56%
Interest cover	10.36 times	11.27 times	17.15 times	9.86 times

Comment: Tesco's gearing has increased and its interest cover has decreased in the year, the reverse of Sainsbury's position. In Activity 10.5 we saw how Tesco's fixed assets total had increased by nearly £800m, compared with an increase for Sainsbury's of only £276m. Tesco has been borrowing to expand, hence the increased gearing and poorer interest cover.

10.5.5 Investment ratios

	Madison plc		
Name of ratio	2005		2004
eps (earnings per share)	$\dfrac{\£1{,}160{,}000}{3{,}100{,}000 \text{ shares}} = 37.4\text{p}$		$\dfrac{\£720{,}000}{2{,}500{,}000 \text{ shares}} = 28.8\text{p}$
p/e (price/earnings)	$\dfrac{561\text{p}}{37.4\text{p}} = 15 \text{ times}$		$\dfrac{547\text{p}}{28.8\text{p}} = 19 \text{ times}$
Dividend cover	$\dfrac{1{,}160}{360} = 3.2 \text{ times}$		$\dfrac{720}{120} = 6 \text{ times}$
Dividend yield	$\dfrac{11.6\text{p}^{a}}{561\text{p}} \times 100 = 2.07\%$		$\dfrac{4.8\text{p}^{b}}{547\text{p}} \times 100 = 0.88\%$

[a] Dividends/No. of shares = £360,000/3,100,000.
[b] Dividends/No. of shares = £120,000/2,500,000.

- **Earnings per share (eps)** and the **price/earnings p/e) ratio** are important indicators of a company's performance. The eps is always shown at the foot of a plc's profit and loss account, its calculation being the subject of a Financial Reporting Standard.[2] The p/e ratio, where the market price per share is expressed as a multiple of the eps, is the clearest indication of how the stock market rates a particular company. The higher the multiple, the greater the expectation of future profits (**earnings**), with investors having pushed up the market price in anticipation. A low p/e ratio results from losses or poor profits, with a depressed share price. Although Madison's eps has increased (resulting from the 61% increase in after-tax profits but only a 24% increase in share capital), the stock market appears unimpressed as the p/e ratio has slumped from 19 times to 15 times in the year. If the stock market sentiment had remained as positive in 2005 as it had been in 2004, the share price would have been 711p (19 × 37.4p) instead of 561p.

- **Dividend cover** is similar to interest cover, in that it indicates the relative safety of the dividends for the year by comparing them with the profit available to make the payments. The increased dividends in 2005 have resulted in a halving of the cover, with available profit just over three times the dividend.

- **Dividend yield** measures the actual rate of return obtained by investing in an ordinary share at the current market price. Someone buying a Madison share at £5.61 would obtain a yield of 2.07%, which is a significant increase on that of the previous year.

Activity 10.8

Calculate and comment upon the four investment ratios for Tesco plc and Sainsbury plc, from the following information:

	Tesco plc		Sainsbury plc	
	2004	2003	2004	2003
Earnings (£m)	606	532	598	469
Dividends (£m)	277	255	294	264
No. of shares (million)	6,627	6,553	1,918	1,902
Market price (pence)	177	172	385	467

---

[2] FRS 22 *Earnings per Share.*

Answer

	Tesco plc		Sainsbury plc	
	2004	*2003*	*2004*	*2003*
eps (pence)	9.14	8.12	31.12	24.66
p/e (times)	19.37	21.18	12.37	18.94
Dividend cover (times)	2.19	2.09	2.03	1.78
Dividend yield (%)	2.36	2.26	3.98	2.97

Comment: The raw eps figures cannot be used for comparison between the companies as they have different numbers of shares in issue. However, the p/e ratio shows how Tesco is much more highly rated by the Stock Exchange than Sainsbury, with future profit expectations pushing up the share price. Dividend cover is broadly similar for the two companies, but the decline in Sainsbury's share price has increased the yield considerably in the current year.

10.6 The validity of the financial statements

In the analysis of company reports, it has been assumed that the information is accurate and reliable and provides a suitable basis for study. Whilst it is true that the published financial statements of a plc will be audited and so, with very rare exceptions, show a true and fair view according to an independent firm of qualified accountants, many objective observers have questioned the validity of financial statements for various reasons, including the following.

● Financial summaries are drawn up under the **historic cost convention**, whereby items are included at their purchase price at the time of acquisition, and *no account is taken of inflation* on the replacement price of assets such as stock or machinery. This problem is more acute when inflation rates are high, and attempts at introducing alternative inflation-adjusted accounting methods were tried in the 1970s and 1980s when UK inflation peaked at over 25% p.a. No method was felt reliable enough to replace the traditional historic cost convention, though it was considered acceptable to allow revaluations of certain assets (notably land and buildings) where market values had changed significantly when compared with book values. The use of asset revaluation reserves to record such changes was explained in Chapter 7.

● The rules and regulations of accounting allow flexibility, so that companies faced with the same accounting problem may come to differing solutions. This flexibility is seen by some as a strength of UK accounting procedures where the requirements of specific companies allow individual accounting treatments to be adopted where appropriate. An example is depreciation, where the judgement of the length of a time period over which assets should be depreciated is left to the discretion of the directors. In some countries, *governments* decree the time period for depreciating different types of asset. The issuing of Accounting and Financial Reporting Standards has greatly reduced the scope for creative accounting, but unscrupulous directors will always try and find a loophole.

● Information is based on past events, but it is argued that meaningful decisions can be taken only on the basis of forecasts of future performance. Unfortunately, the future is rather harder to verify than the past, so historical documents tend to be seen as a more reliable guide to future prospects than future predictions, however well researched. The ideal is perhaps a balance between the two, with a company's forecasts being published alongside the conventional historical information. However, companies are naturally reluctant to divulge information which may be of use to competitors, so the forecast information may be so vague and generalised as to be of little use to anybody.

10.7   Summary

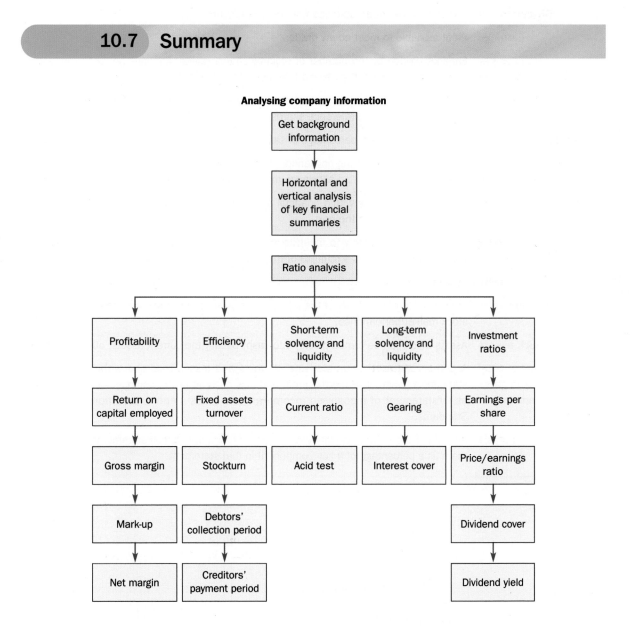

Analysing company information

10.8 Glossary

Acid test	The comparison between the 'quick' assets and the current liabilities (creditors due for payment within one year).
Current ratio	The comparison between current assets and current liabilities (creditors due for payment within one year).
Dividend cover	The ability of a company to meet its dividends, measured by expressing the profit available for dividends as a multiple of the dividends paid and proposed.
Dividend yield	The percentage return obtained from an investment.
Earnings	Profit available to meet equity dividends.
Earnings per share (eps)	Earnings divided by the number of ordinary shares issued. Earnings per share are always measured in pence in the UK and form part of the p/e ratio.
Gearing	The relationship between a company's equity capital (ordinary shares) and its other forms of long-term funding (preference shares, debentures and so on).
Gross (net) margin	Gross (net) profit as a percentage of sales.
Historic cost convention	The traditional accounting convention which values assets at their purchase price at the time of acquisition with no allowance made for subsequent inflation.
Horizontal analysis	Comparison of values within financial statements by calculation of percentage changes between one year and the next.
Interest cover	The ability of a company to meet its interest commitments, measured by expressing the profit before interest as a multiple of the interest paid and payable.
p/e ratio	See Price/earnings ratio.
Price/earnings ratio	Market price as a multiple of the latest earnings per share. Used as a relative measure of stock market performance.
Quick assets	Assets which can be turned quickly into cash. Usually the current assets, other than stock.
Statement of total recognised gains and losses	A primary statement summarising all gains and losses recorded within the financial statements, whether within the profit and loss account or the balance sheet. Referred to as a 'statement of recognised income and expenses' under International Accounting Standards.
Vertical analysis	Analysis of the relative weighting of components within financial statements by expressing them as a percentage of a key component in that statement.

? Self-check questions

1 Which of the following requires UK limited companies to publish financial information?
   a The Companies Act 1985
   b The Corporation Act 1992
   c European Union Directive 421B, 1994
   d The Partnership Act 1890

2 Which of the following, found within an annual report, is a primary statement?
   a Auditors' report
   b Operating and financial review
   c Statement of accounting policies
   d Statement of total recognised gains and losses

3 Horizontal analysis is:
   a The calculation of the relative weighting of components within a financial statement in a particular financial period
   b The comparison of the current year's figures with the previous year's figures
   c The comparison of one company's results with another company
   d The comparison of the profit and loss account with the balance sheet

4 ROCE means:
   a Return on current expenses
   b Reserves of capital equity
   c Return on capital employed
   d Ratio of capital employed

5 If total net assets are £45,600, current liabilities £12,700, stock £3,900 and fixed assets £29,000, what is the quick assets tatio?
   a 2:1
   b 2.3:1
   c 1.5:1
   d 1.75:1

6 Four companies have the following p/e ratios: A 17, B 24, C 12, D 8. Which of the following statements about the companies is incorrect?
   a B's share price must be twice that of C
   b A's share price is 17 times its earnings
   c D has the lowest share price relative to its earnings per share
   d B has the Stock Exchange's greatest expectations for future profit growth

7 A company starts its year with stock of £2m and ends with £3m. If it had an overall cost of sales of £12.5m, what was its stockturn in days?
   a 85 days
   b 1,825 days
   c 73 days
   d 7.3 days

8 Low gearing means:
   a A company depends largely on long-term loans
   b A company has few, if any, long-term loans
   c A company cannot pay a dividend
   d A company has high interest payments

9 An advantage to a company of high gearing is:
   a The company can rely on internal funding for expansion
   b High interest payments
   c Lower risk of liquidation
   d Prospect of high profits from using borrowed money for expansion

10 One of the criticisms of accounting information has been:
   a The information is always incorrect
   b Accountants never follow rules and regulations
   c Inflation is not normally reflected within the financial statements
   d Companies should report the future instead of the past

(Answers in Appendix 1)

? Self-study questions

(Answers in Appendix 2)

Question 10.1 Obtain an annual report of a trading company (see References at the end of this chapter). Produce a vertical and horizontal analysis of the company's profit and loss account, balance sheet and cash flow statement for the current and previous years, and identify the main areas of change disclosed by the analysis.

Question 10.2 The management of Ercall Limited pays particular attention to the ratios and percentages which they calculate from their annual accounts. For the year ended 31 December 2005, they have calculated the following figures, which they are comparing with those of another company, Roden Limited, shown alongside:

	Ercall Ltd	Roden Ltd
Gross profit margin	60%	5%
Net profit margin	20%	2%
Debtors' collection period	30 days	5 days
Current ratio	2:1	0.4:1
Gearing percentage	20%	70%

One of the two companies is a manufacturing company, the other is a food retailer, with an expanding number of stores.

a Which of the two companies is the food retailer? Give two reasons for your choice.
b Assuming that the total cost of sales of Ercall Ltd was £200,000 in 2005, the closing cash and bank balances were £11,004 and the average stock for 2005 was £40,000, calculate:
   (i) the total of Ercall Limited's debtors at 31 December 2005, assuming all sales were on credit terms
   (ii) the total of Ercall Limited's current liabilities at 31 December 2005.
c Assuming you were an ordinary shareholder of Roden Limited, what is the significance *to you* of the company's gearing percentage?

Question 10.3   The balance sheets of Rodington Ltd and Rowton Ltd at 31 May 2005 were as follows:

	Rodington £000	Rowton £000
Fixed assets	125	204
Current assets:		
Stock	85	120
Debtors	26	18
Bank balance	12	39
	123	177
Less **Creditors due for payment within one year**	(135)	(168)
Net Current Assets (Liabilities)	(12)	9
	113	213
Less **Creditors due for payment after more than one year**		
6% debentures	–	(100)
Total net assets	113	113
Capital and reserves		
Ordinary shares of £1	50	100
Reserves	63	13
	113	113

Notes:

1 The profits of Rodington Limited are expected to continue at £40,000 p.a. The profits of Rowton Limited have averaged £40,000 before debenture interest.

2 Balance sheets at 31 May 2004 for both companies showed broadly similar figures to those for 2005.

a From the balance sheets as at 31 May 2005, calculate the following ratios for both companies, and give a brief explanation of their significance:

(ii)   Gearing ratio

(ii)   Current ratio

(iii) Acid test ratio

(iv) Return on capital employed.

b Assume that you had been asked for advice by a cautious potential investor who has £20,000 available. Explain which of the two companies appears to represent the better choice of investment on the basis of the evidence provided.

c If the audit report on Rodington's accounts had stated that the business was not a going concern, how would that affect your views on the company, and in particular the advice given to the potential investor in (b) above?

Question 10.4   Uffington Limited was formed on 1 January 2005. The company's unpublished profit and loss account for 2005 and its balance sheet as at 31 December 2005 are as follows:

Uffington Limited
Profit and loss account for the year ended 31 December 2005

	£	£
Sales		670,000
Less Cost of goods sold		
Purchases	570,000	
Less Closing stock	(90,000)	480,000
Gross profit		190,000
Administration expenses	(117,350)	
Distribution expenses	(21,600)	(138,950)
Operating profit before interest		51,050
Interest payable		(5,600)
Profit for the year		45,450
Less Taxation		(5,450)
Profit after taxation		40,000
Less Dividend		(15,000)
Retained profit for the year		25,000

Balance sheet as at 31 December 2005

	Cost	Depreciation	Net
	£	£	£
Fixed assets:			
Freehold land	160,000	–	160,000
Fixtures	30,000	21,000	9,000
Motor vehicles	56,000	39,200	16,800
	246,000	60,200	185,800
Current assets:			
Stock		90,000	
Debtors		43,650	
Prepayments		600	
Bank		24,200	
		158,450	
Less **Creditors due for**			
payment within one year:			
Trade creditors	48,000		
Accruals	10,800		
Dividend approved but unpaid	15,000		
Taxation	5,450		
		(79,250)	
Net current assets			79,200
			265,000
Less **Creditors due for payment after more than one year:**			
7% debentures			(80,000)
Total net assets			185,000
Share capital and reserves			
Ordinary shares of £1 each			100,000
Share premium account			60,000
Reserves			25,000
			185,000

The company is about to embark on an expansion programme which will require at least £6m for the purchase of new businesses and to support investment in increased stock levels. The chairman of the company has called for an analysis of the 2005 figures before approaching possible sources of funding.

a Comment on the performance of Uffington Limited for the year ended 31 December 2005 and on its financial position at that date. Support your comments with eight relevant accounting ratios.

b Suggest, and comment on the suitability of, two alternative ways for the company to raise £6m.

> ## Case study

Esmeralda springs a surprise

On 3 July 2005, Marvin, the founder of Machiq Limited (see previous case studies), was sorting through the morning's correspondence. After reading one particular letter, he immediately summoned his fellow directors, Chiquita and Trixie, to an emergency meeting. He passed the letter round and awaited their comments. The letter read as follows:

Dear Marvin

I have not written to you since 30 June 2003, when I demanded compensation for the cruel way you sacked me and my family back in 2001. However, I realised that you would not pay me the £10m I demanded, so I devoted my energies to building a rival business. I rejoined my old employer, Kaboosh Limited, and worked so hard that I was appointed managing director. When my close friend and company chairman, Cardew Kaboosh, died two months ago, he left all his shares to me, so I now own 95% of the company. My company's performance has been so impressive that I now want to take over your company. I am enclosing a copy of the most recent profit and loss account and balance sheet of Kaboosh Limited for information.

Yours sincerely,
Esmeralda

After reading the letter, it was agreed that Trixie would analyse the financial summaries of Kaboosh Limited and compare them with those of Machiq Limited. She compiled the following summary:

Profit and loss accounts for the year ended 30 June 2005

	Machiq £	Kaboosh £
Sales	705,600	1,102,500
Less Cost of sales	(529,200)	(661,500)
Gross profit	176,400	441,000
Less Expenses	(58,600)	(175,000)
Net profit for the year before interest	117,800	266,000
Less Interest	(1,800)	(12,000)
Net profit for the year, before taxation	116,000	254,000
Less Provision for taxation	(26,950)	(47,000)
Net profit for the year, after taxation	89,050	207,000
Less Dividends	(32,000)	(55,000)
Retained profit for the year	57,050	152,000
Retained profit brought forward	42,100	645,000
Retained profit carried forward	99,150	797,000

Balance sheets as at 30 June 2005

	Machiq Limited		Kaboosh Limited	
	£	£	£	£
Fixed assets (net book value)		165,980		950,000
Current assets:				
Stock	32,650		251,300	
Debtors	30,950		142,500	
Bank	–		36,200	
	63,600		430,000	
Less Creditors due for payment				
within one year:				
Creditors	14,080		108,000	
Taxation	26,950		47,000	
Dividends approved but unpaid	32,000		55,000	
Bank overdraft	2,400		–	
	(75,430)		(210,000)	
Net current assets/(liabilities)		(11,830)		220,000
		154,150		1,170,000
Creditors due for payment				
after more than one year:				
6% debentures		–		(200,000)
Total net assets		154,150		970,000
Capital and reserves				
Called-up share capital (5p shares)		24,000		100,000
Share premium account		31,000		73,000
Profit and loss account:				
Retained profit for the year		99,150		797,000
		154,150		970,000

Additional information:

Stock figures represent average values.

Price/earnings ratios for companies in the manufacturing sector average 15 times earnings.
There were no cash sales or purchases during the year for either company.

Required:

a Analyse each company's results into the following five groups of ratios, and comment on the relative performance of each company:
(i) Profitability
(ii) Efficiency
(iii) Short-term solvency and liquidity
(iv) Long-term solvency and liquidity
(v) Investment ratios.

b Advise the directors of Machiq Limited as to whether they should agree to the company being taken over by Kaboosh Limited. State four additional items of information which they might need before they come to a final decision.

(Answers in Appendix 3)

References

To obtain annual reports (free of charge to UK addresses):
www.proshare.org/pi/reports.asp

Now look at this book's dedicated website at www.pearsoned.co.uk/black and
work through the various additional exercises for this chapter.

Chapter 11

Revision chapter (2)

Objectives When you have read this chapter you will be able to:

➤ Revise your knowledge of the first ten chapters

➤ Apply your knowledge to answer questions within a time-constrained examination

11.1 Introduction

This chapter consolidates the knowledge gained so far and is structured as follows:

● Practice examination paper 1: a one-hour examination paper consisting of 40 multiple-choice questions, covering the first ten chapters of the book.

● Practice examination paper 2: a two-hour examination paper consisting of five questions.

Solutions are provided in Appendix 4.

11.2 Practice examination paper 1

Time allowed ONE hour

This question paper contains FORTY multiple-choice questions. Read each question carefully and select ONE answer that you think is correct.

1 If a company is described as a 'going concern', it is:
   a About to close down
   b Not about to close down
   c A company people are concerned about
   d A rapidly expanding company

2 A company sells £150,000 of goods during the year, having been owed £12,000 by debtors at the start of the year and £18,000 at the end of the year. What sales figure will be shown in the profit and loss account for the year?
   a £150,000
   b £144,000
   c £156,000
   d £180,000

3 Which accounting concept overrides other concepts?
   a Prudence concept
   b Consistency concept
   c True and fair view concept
   d Accruals concept

4 An owner of a business had a capital balance of £85,000 at the end of the financial year. During the year, drawings of £14,000 had been made, and the business had made a net profit of £17,000. The owner paid in an inheritance of £40,000 into the business during the year. What was the opening capital balance?
   a £14,000
   b £156,000
   c £42,000
   d £122,000

5 In the accounting equation, assets plus expenses equals:
   a Liabilities + Capital + Income
   b Liabilities + Capital − Income
   c Liabilities − Capital + Income
   d Liabilities − Capital − Income

6 Why, if a business has money in the bank, does it appear as a debit balance in the business's ledger?
   a It is a mistake – it should be a credit balance
   b It is showing that the bank is a debtor of the business
   c As all the debits equal all the credits, there is no difference between a debit and credit balance
   d It shows that the business is in debt

7 A business pays a cheque for £4,100 for a van, of which £150 is for road tax. What would be the correct bookkeeping entries?
   a Dr Van £4,100, Cr Bank £4,100
   b Dr Bank £4,100, Cr Van £3,950 and Cr Motor expenses £150
   c Dr Motor expenses £4,100, Cr Bank £4,100
   d Dr Van £3,950 and Dr Motor expenses £150, Cr Bank £4,100

8 A cash float is:
   a A predetermined amount of petty cash which is paid out at regular intervals
   b Cash used only for buying fixed assets
   c A predetermined amount needed to meet petty cash expenditure, which is topped up at intervals
   d The amount of petty cash after all the petty cash expenditure has been deducted

9 A bank reconciliation statement is used for:
   a Ensuring that the business's own records of the bank account agree with the bank's records
   b Ensuring that the bank manager knows what cheques the business has been paying
   c Ensuring that the business does not exceed an agreed overdraft limit
   d Summarising all the business's banking transactions for the financial period

10 A financial period:
   a Is the same as a financial year
   b Is the same as the balance sheet date
   c Always ends on 31 December
   d Can be as long or as short as the business needs for a specific purpose

11 Stock is usually valued in a balance sheet at:
   a Selling price
   b Lower of cost and net realisable value
   c Lower of cost and gross realisable value
   d Lower of selling price and net realisable value

12 A business has a combined rent and rates account. During the year ended 31 December 2005, the business had an opening rent prepayment of £200 and an opening rates accrual of £300. During the year it paid £11,000 for rent and rates. At the end of the year, £900 had been prepaid for rates and there was an accrual of £600 for rent. What figure for rent and rates would appear in the profit and loss account?
   a £10,800
   b £10,600
   c £11,200
   d £11,400

13 A fixed asset which cost £60,000 has been owned for three years. It is depreciated at 40% p.a. on the reducing balance method. What value would be shown as its net book value at the end of the third year of ownership?
   a £21,600
   b £8,640
   c £12,960
   d nil

14 Which of the following would be prime (direct) costs of a furniture manufacturer?
   a Depreciation of woodworking machinery
   b Wood used to make furniture
   c Electricity used to heat the factory
   d The rent of the factory

15 In a manufacturing business, what is work-in-progress?
   a Partly completed goods
   b Goods in transit to a customer
   c Raw materials
   d Work about to start on manufacturing goods

16 Which one of the following summaries is an integral part of the double-entry bookkeeping system?
   a Cash flow statement
   b Balance sheet
   c Trial balance
   d Profit and loss account

17 A car which cost £14,000 is part-exchanged for a new car exactly 3 years after its purchase. Cars are depreciated on the straight line basis over 5 years, assuming a residual value of 10% of the purchase price. If the part-exchange value of the car was £4,000, what profit or loss would be recorded in the profit and loss account in the year of disposal?
   a £2,440 loss
   b £1,600 loss
   c £440 profit
   d £2,600 profit

18 Theoretical stock valuation methods such as FIFO would be used where:
   a Stock can be priced by looking at invoices
   b Stock is always sold in a set order, for example oldest stock is sold first
   c It is difficult or impossible to match stock with an invoiced price
   d Stock has not been counted at the end of the financial period

19 The debtors' balances included within the total of current assets on a balance sheet should be:
   a All the sales ledger balances
   b Only the good debts of the business
   c The sales ledger balances less any increase in a provision for doubtful debts
   d All the sales ledger balances except the bad debts

20 Which of the following is the 'odd one out'?
   a Provision for bad and doubtful debts
   b Provision for good debts
   c Provision for bad debts
   d Provision for doubtful debts

21 Why might a partnership charge interest on partners' drawings?
   a Because they want to increase the money taken out by partners
   b To deter partners from taking excessive amounts from the business
   c To ensure that all partners take an equal amount from the business
   d The Partnership Act 1890 states that they have to charge interest

22 A convertible loan stock is:
   a A loan issued by a company which can be converted into shares at a later date
   b Money borrowed to buy the managing director a convertible car
   c Raw materials lent to the business which are to be converted into a finished product
   d A loan issued by a company which can be converted into a different currency at a later date

23 A liability found in a limited company's balance sheet but not a sole trader's balance sheet is:
   a Corporation tax
   b Creditors
   c Accruals
   d Overdraft

24 A holder of a preference share has the following advantages over an ordinary shareholder:
   a A dividend which will increase if profits increase
   b A greater number of votes for each share held
   c Preferential prices if buying the company's products
   d Priority over ordinary shareholders for payment of dividends and also capital repayment if the company fails

25 A bonus issue by a company has the following effect:
    a Existing shareholders are given more shares
    b Existing shareholders are given the right to buy more shares
    c Non-shareholders are invited to buy shares in the company
    d Directors receive a salary bonus

26 A share premium is:
    a The amount shareholders pay for a share
    b The increase in value in a share after it is sold
    c The difference between the stock market price of a share and the nominal value of that share
    d The difference between the price at which a company sells a share and the nominal value of that share

27 A 'statement of affairs' is broadly comparable to a:
    a Cash flow statement
    b Trial balance
    c Balance sheet
    d Profit and loss account

28 A business does not keep full accounting records, but you find that its opening debtors were £2,500 and its closing debtors were £6,000. Cash and cheques received from customers in the period totalled £49,300, bad debts suffered totalled £120, and £400 discount was allowed to customers for prompt payment. What is the total sales for the period?
    a £53,320
    b £52,720
    c £46,320
    d £52,800

29 Which of the following pairs *both* result in a positive cash flow?
    a Decrease in stock and decrease in creditors
    b Increase in stock and increase in creditors
    c Increase in creditors and increase in debtors
    d Decrease in stock and decrease in debtors

30 If a company shows sales £60,000 and gross profit £12,000, which of the following calculations are correct?
    a Mark-up 20%, gross margin 25%
    b Mark-up 400%, gross margin 5%
    c Mark-up 33%, gross margin 50%
    d Mark-up 25%, gross margin 20%

31 Which one of the following statements is always true?
    a The directors of a company own the company
    b The auditors of a company produce the financial statements
    c The company's reserves are represented by bank balances
    d The shareholders of a company own the company

32 If a company has much more borrowed capital than equity capital, which of the following statements is always true?
    a If interest rates rise, the company will have to close
    b The company will expand faster than a company with no borrowings
    c The company is said to be highly geared
    d The company is said to be low geared

33 If the directors of a plc need to raise money for the company, which of the following would not achieve that effect?

   a A bonus issue of shares

   b A rights issue of shares

   c A new issue of shares to the general public

   d Issuing a debenture

34 A company has net current assets of £20,000, including stock valued at £22,000. The total of current assets is £60,000 and the current ratio is 1.5:1. What is the acid test ratio?

   a 2:1

   b 0.95:1

   c 0.5:1

   d 2.7:1

35 A limited company with a share capital of 500,000 ordinary shares of £1 each makes a rights issue on a '3 for 2' basis at £3 each. What effect will this have on the balance sheet after all the rights have been paid for by shareholders?

   a Share capital + £1,750,000, share premium +£1,750,000

   b Share capital +£1,000,000, share premium +£750,000

   c Share capital +£750,000, share premium +£1,500,000

   d Share capital +£1,500,000, share premium no change

36 What does a sole trader's 'unlimited liability' mean?

   a The owner may lose his or her personal assets if the business fails

   b The owner is not insured against the risks of running the business

   c There is no limit to how much creditors can demand to be paid

   d The sole trader is operating as a limited company

37 A limited company has a very high gearing level. If interest rates increase, but no other changes take place, which one of the following statements is certain?

   a The company will cease trading

   b The company's borrowings will increase

   c The company's gross profit will decrease

   d The company's net profit will decrease

38 If a company has a net margin of 20%, which of the following statements is certain about that company?

   a The company's fixed assets exceed its current assets

   b The company can pay all its bills

   c The company is making a profit

   d The company's current assets exceed its current liabilities

39 If a company's p/e ratio this year is 17, whereas last year it was 11, which of the following statements is certain?

   a The company has made more profit this year

   b The company's share price is higher this year than last year

   c The stock market regards the company as a greater risk this year than last year

   d The share price this year is a greater multiple of the reported earnings per share than it was last year

40 If a company's shares are stated to have a dividend cover of 5 times, which of the following statements is certain about that company?

   a The share price is five times its dividend

   b The dividend is five times the profits per share after tax

   c The dividend is five times the profits per share before tax

   d The share price is five times the dividend per share

| 11.3 | **Practice examination paper 2** |

Time allowed TWO hours.

Answer one of the two questions in Section A and all three questions in Section B. All questions carry equal marks.

Section A. Answer either question 1 or question 2

Question 1 The trial balance of Aubrey Locke, a sole trader, at 31 May 2005 is as follows:

	Dr	Cr
	£	£
Bank	3,840	
Cash	120	
Forklift truck: cost	20,000	
Forklift truck: depreciation to 31 May 2004		4,500
Motor cars: cost	18,000	
Motor cars: depreciation to 31 May 2004		6,000
Sales		375,000
Purchases	195,000	
Opening stock at 1 June 2004	62,000	
Rent	20,000	
Sales returns	420	
Electricity	8,000	
Debtors	16,200	
Creditors		14,600
Discount received		180
Wages and salaries	37,000	
Provision for doubtful debts at 1 June 2004		2,640
Bad debts written off	520	
General office expenses	18,000	
Owner's drawings	18,500	
Capital at 1 June 2004		14,680
	417,600	417,600

Notes:
1 Closing stock is £50,000.
2 Electricity of £2,000 is to be accrued at the year-end.
3 Rent of £4,000 has been prepaid at the year-end.
4 Depreciation on the forklift is calculated over 4 years on the straight line method, assuming a residual value of £2,000.
5 Depreciation on the cars is calculated at 40% on the reducing balance method.
6 The provision for doubtful debts is to be decreased by £400.

a Prepare a profit and loss account for the year ended 31 May 2005 and a balance sheet as at that date.
b If Aubrey Locke had been operating his business as a limited company, there are likely to be additional items of information you would expect to see when compared with the financial statements of a sole trader.
  (i) List three additional items you would expect to find in a company's profit and loss account.
  (ii) List three additional items you would expect to find in a company's balance sheet.

Question 2 Wilma Tonbridge started a business on 1 January 2004, with her own capital of £10,000 and an interest-free long-term loan of £20,000 from a friend. Her business retails Tonies, which are luxury fluffy toys sold at £80 each. Wilma, who has little knowledge of accounting, produced the following statement of her business's financial situation at the end of her first year's trading:

Balance account

	£	£
Cash received from selling 2,000 Tonies		160,000
Less Cash paid:		
Wages	56,000	
Purchases	127,200	
Rent and rates	16,000	
Office expenses	9,600	
Loan repayment	4,000	
		(212,800)
Loss		(52,800)

Wilma sent the statement to her bank manager, who immediately told Wilma to find an accountant to produce a set of financial statements drawn up according to Generally Accepted Accounting Principles. Wilma instructs you to prepare these statements.

You confirm that the amounts shown in Wilma's statements agree with details shown in the business's bank statements, but you find the following additional information:

1 A further 600 Tonies were sold in 2004, but not paid for during the year.
2 Wilma estimates that 5% of debtors are doubtful.
3 £7,000 is owed for purchases received in the year.
4 Wilma's starting capital and the loan were used to buy computers and office furniture and fittings with an estimated life of 5 years and an anticipated residual value of £5,000.
5 Wages of £1,600 and office expenses of £800 were accrued at the end of the year.
6 Stock at the end of the year was valued at £9,200.
7 The rent and rates covered the period from 1 January 2004 to 31 March 2005.
8 The wages figure included £32,000 taken by Wilma for her own personal use.

Did you know?

If your course does not require detailed bookkeeping knowledge, you can omit part b of this question.

a Prepare a profit and loss account for the year ended 31 December 2004 and a balance sheet as at that date.
b Show, in as much detail as possible from the above information, the ledger accounts for Wages and also for Rent and rates. Close off the two accounts and bring down balances at 1 January 2005.

Section B. Answer all three questions in this section

Question 3 A company has just appointed a non-accountant as its new chairman. He makes the following comment to the managing director, who is a qualified accountant:

> I am under constant pressure from the shareholders, who always demand increased dividends from ever greater profits. You follow the prudence concept, which to my mind results in the lowest possible profits!

a Explain the meaning of the prudence concept.
b Name and briefly explain three fundamental accounting concepts, other than the prudence concept.
c Analyse three relevant factors which either support or contradict the chairman's comments.

Question 4 The management of Eastbourne Ltd has calculated the following statistics from its results for the year ended 31 December 2005. Equivalent average figures from a relevant trade association are also given.

	Eastbourne Ltd	Trade average
Gross profit margin	50%	40%
Net profit margin	10%	8%
Return on capital employed	16%	12%
Acid test	1:1	1.5:1
Gearing	80%	30%

a Explain the significance of, and the basis of calculation for, each of the five statistics listed above.

b Explain why, if you were informed that Eastbourne Ltd's current ratio was 6:1, compared with a trade average of 2:1, this might not indicate a satisfactory situation.

Question 5 The owner or owners of a small enterprise can choose between various forms of business organisation, including sole trading and limited company status.

a Explain the advantages and disadvantages of sole trading and limited company status in connection with the following areas:

(i) Liability for debts

(ii) Ability to raise capital

(iii) Legal formality.

b A business is having a number of problems with customers who either cannot or will not pay their debts. For the year ended 31 December 2005, these include:

(i) Customer A, who has died penniless, owing £800.

(ii) Customer B, who refuses to pay a debt of £600, despite many reminders. It is believed that B has the means to pay.

(iii) Customer C, who in July and August 2005 had paid eight amounts of £10 per week towards a total debt of £300.

There is also:

(iv) Customer D, who was a bad debtor three years ago for £500, but has come into money and has paid off his debt.

The business had total debtors, before any adjustments for the above, totalling £45,000. It had a provision for doubtful debts of £1,400 on 1 January 2005.

Show relevant extracts from the business's profit and loss account for the year ended 31 December 2005 and balance sheet as at that date relating to debtors after making all adjustments required by the above information.

References

Some general websites useful for seeing an overall view of the accountants' role in industry and commerce:

Accounting web: **www.accountingweb.co.uk**

Accountancy Age: **www.accountancyage.com**

Institute of Chartered Accountants in England and Wales: **www.icaew.co.uk**

Rutgers: **accounting.rutgers.edu**

Now look at this book's dedicated website at **www.pearsoned.co.uk/black** and work through the various additional exercises for this chapter.

Chapter 12

An introduction to management accounting

Objectives

When you have read this chapter you will be able to:

➤ Define management accounting and cost accounting

➤ Understand the classification of costs

➤ Analyse costs by function, type, behaviour and time

12.1 Introduction

Did you know?

One clear distinction between fincial accounting and management accounting is in the field of auditing, where CIMA members are not recognised by the Companies Act as qualified to act as the statutory 'external' auditor of a limited company.

The majority of the information contained in the preceding chapters of this book has been concerned with *financial accounting*, which is the branch of accounting which records, summarises and interprets financial transactions to satisfy the information needs of the various user groups such as investors, lenders, creditors and employees. It is sometimes referred to as meeting the *external* accounting needs of the organisation. Another major branch of accounting is **management accounting**, which is sometimes referred to as meeting the *internal* accounting needs of the organisation, as it is designed to help managers with decision making and planning. As such, it often involves estimates and forecasts, and is not subject to the same regulatory framework (including Financial Reporting Standards and Companies Acts) as financial accounting. The distinction is not always clear-cut (for example, is ratio analysis the province of a management accountant or a financial accountant?) though there is a separate UK professional organisation (CIMA) which promotes the interests of management accountants.

12.2 A definition of management accounting

The Chartered Institute of Management Accountants (CIMA) has defined management accounting as:

An integral part of management concerned with identifying, presenting and interpreting information used for:

- *formulating strategy*
- *planning and controlling activities*
- *decision taking*
- *optimising the use of resources*
- *disclosure to shareholders and others external to the entity*
- *disclosure to employees*
- *safeguarding assets*

The above involves participation in management to ensure that there is effective:

- *formulation of plans to meet objectives (strategic planning)*
- *formulation of short term operation plans (budget/profit planning)*
- *acquisition and use of finance (financial management) and recording of transactions (financial accounting and cost accounting)*
- *communication of financial and operational information*
- *corrective action to bring plans and results into line (financial control)*
- *reviewing and reporting on systems and operations (internal audit, management audit)*[1]

The CIMA definition is deliberately all-embracing, and there are some obvious infringements on what financial accountants might see as their territory. It reinforces the notion that there are overlaps between financial and management accounting, particularly in the recording, interpreting and communicating aspects. There is also a vital sub-branch of management accounting, called **cost accounting**, which is defined by CIMA as:

the establishment of budgets, standard costs and actual costs of operations, processes, activities or products; and the analysis of variances, profitability or social use of funds.

As management accounting (and cost accounting) is not subject to a regulatory framework, the way in which information is prepared is entirely at the discretion of the users of the information. A fundamental area to explore is the level and nature of costs such as raw materials, overheads and labour. Although these are summarised by financial accountants when preparing profit and loss accounts, a more detailed analysis can be of benefit to managers.

12.3 The classification of costs

One of the key aspects of management accounting is the analysis of the organisation's costs as part of the process of identifying, presenting and

---

[1] CIMA (2000) *Management Accounting: Official Terminology*. London: CIMA.

interpreting information referred to earlier. When we looked at summaries produced by the financial accountant (particularly the profit and loss account), the main criterion for cost analysis was whether the revenue expense related to the cost of goods sold (in which case it was deducted in arriving at the *gross profit*) or to a general overhead expense, in which case it was deducted from the gross profit in arriving at the *net profit*. However, for the management accountant, a much more detailed analysis of costs is required. There are several methods of classifying costs, each method looking at costs from a different perspective. For example, costs could be classified by:

● Function
● Type
● Behaviour
● Time.

Each of these needs to be understood before we can proceed to a consideration of the major cost analysis techniques referred to in the next chapter.

Activity 12.1

Which of the following would be considered valid reasons for analysing costs?

1 To keep costs down
2 To plan ahead
3 To establish appropriate selling prices
4 To compare with competitors' costs
5 To maximise profitability.

Answer

All of the above, except that in (4) you can only make a detailed comparison with competitors' costs by having access to that company's financial data, which is unrealistic. However, published financial information in an annual or interim report contains some cost information (see Chapter 7).

12.3.1 Analysis by function

Costs can be grouped according to the functional department which incurs them, such as production, sales, distribution and administration. Each of these would have one or more **cost centres**. Generally, a cost centre is a location, person or item of equipment – or a group of these – in relation to which costs may be ascertained and used for control purposes. Some costs, such as rent and rates, cannot be traced to one cost centre directly. These costs are gathered to an overall cost centre and are then arbitrarily apportioned to the other cost centres. For this reason they are sometimes known as **service centres** (see Figure 12.1).

Figure 12.1
Allocation of costs to functional departments

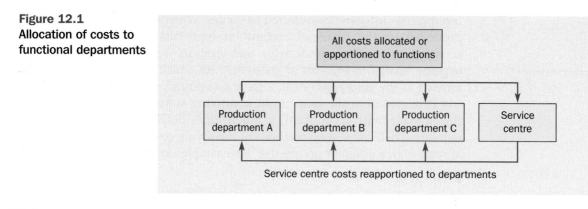

12.3.2 Analysis by type

We have already briefly looked at direct and indirect costs in Chapter 4, but it is useful to consider their definition:

- **Direct costs** are those costs which can be readily identified with the item or service being produced, such as the raw materials and labour specific to the task. They are also known as *prime costs*. An example would be the cloth used in making a dress and the machinist's time to cut and sew it.
- **Indirect costs**, also known as *overhead costs*, are all those costs incurred in the organisation which cannot be objectively identified with a specific item or service. An example would be the cost of an advertising campaign to promote a new range of clothing.

The costs which comprise *total production* cost are related to the number of items which are produced: the greater the volume of production, the greater we would expect the total production cost to be. If a firm trebled its output, it is likely that both direct and indirect costs would be affected. If a firm enjoys economies of scale then costs may increase by less than the percentage change in production. If a firm suffers diseconomies of scale, costs may increase by more than the percentage change in production. Costs which relate to production in this way are sometimes called **product costs**.

Activity 12.2

Which of the formulae (a)–(d) below relate to the following?

- Total production cost
- Prime cost
- Total cost
- Total overhead cost?

a Direct materials + Direct labour + Direct expenses
b Indirect material + Indirect labour + Indirect expenses
c Total production cost + Selling and administration overhead
d Prime cost + Production overhead

Answer

a Prime cost
b Total overhead cost
c Total cost
d Total production cost

12.3.3 Analysis by behaviour

Over time or over a specific range of production, some costs tend to be unaffected by the level of output, whereas others will change as output changes. In fact, overheads can be divided into three classifications, as follows:

● **Fixed overheads**, which accrue with the passage of time, and which, within certain limits of output and turnover, tend to be unaffected by fluctuations in the level of activity. Examples are rent, rates, insurance and management salaries. Figure 12.2 shows the behaviour of fixed costs over a period.

Figure 12.2
The behaviour of fixed costs over a period

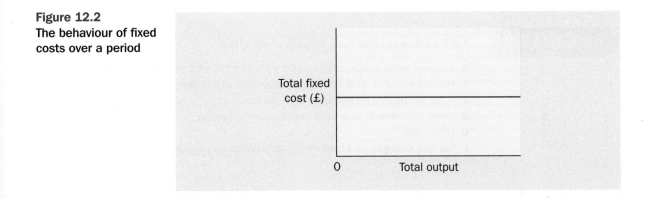

● **Variable overheads**, such as raw materials and packaging, which do fluctuate with the level of activity. Figure 12.3 shows the behaviour of variable costs over a period.

Figure 12.3
The behaviour of variable costs over a period

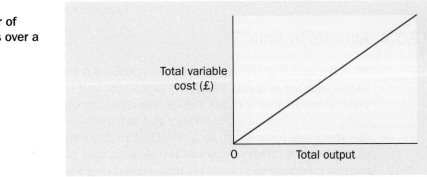

● **Semi-fixed** (or semi-variable or 'mixed') **overheads**, which contain both fixed and variable elements and which in consequence are only partly affected by changes in the levels of activity. For example, telephone charges would be part fixed rental and part based on usage. In cost analysis, such costs must be divided (however arbitrarily) between their fixed and variable elements. Figure 12.4 shows the behaviour of semi-fixed costs over a period.

Figure 12.4
The behaviour of semi-fixed costs over a period

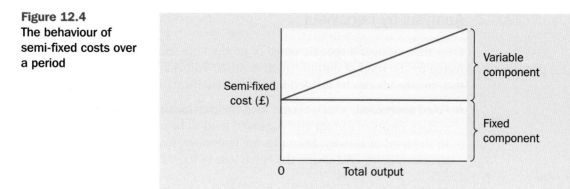

Activity 12.3

Are the following costs fixed, variable or semi-fixed?

a Metered water supply, part paid by a fixed rental, part by usage
b Royalties paid to an author, as a percentage of the sale price of books
c A flat fee paid to an author to write an article
d Sales commission as a percentage of sales revenue
e Office rent
f Car hire charges, part fixed rental, part based on mileage

Answer

a Semi-fixed cost
b Variable cost
c Fixed cost
d Variable cost
e Fixed cost
f Semi-fixed cost

12.3.4 Analysis by time

We have seen that the costs which comprise total production cost are related to the number of items which are produced, and that costs which relate to production in this way are sometimes called *product costs*. However, some costs, such as rent, rates, insurance and management salaries, will be fixed in the short run (usually up to a year) but in the long run might change (for example, as a factory expands production into larger premises, rent will increase). Because such costs are time-related they are sometimes referred to as **period costs**.

Activity 12.4

Which of the following costs would be fixed in the short run?

a Royalties paid to a photographer for using an image in a book
b Depreciation (straight line method)
c Insurance premium
d Directors' salaries
e Wages paid to hourly-paid construction workers

Answer | (b), (c) and (d) would tend to be fixed but (a) and (e) would increase with the number of books produced or the amount of work done, respectively.

12.4 Summary

Cost classified by:	Type of cost	
	Direct	*Indirect*
Function	Allocated to production departments	Allocated or apportioned to production departments and service centre, then service centre reapportioned to production departments
Type	Direct costs, readily identified with item being produced	Indirect costs (overheads) not readily identified with item being produced
Behaviour	Variable – they fluctuate with the level of activity	Most indirect cost is fixed, but some (e.g. sales commission, power for machinery) will be variable
Time	Change in the short run	Tend to be fixed in the short run but may change in the long run (period costs)

12.5 Glossary

Cost accounting The establishment of budgets, standard costs and actual costs of operations, processes, activities or products; and the analysis of variances, profitability or social use of funds.

Cost centre A location, person or item of equipment – or a group of these – in relation to which costs may be ascertained and used for control purposes.

Direct costs Costs which can be readily identified with the particular units or type of product, such as raw materials and manufacturing wages.

Fixed overheads Costs which remain constant, regardless of the level of production. For example, factory insurance might remain constant whether production is high or low.

Indirect costs Expenses which cannot be directly associated with the items being produced, such as supervisors' wages, the factory canteen, and rent and rates.

Management accounting The internal accounting needs of an organisation, involving planning, forecasting and budgeting for decision-making purposes.

Period costs Costs, such as rent, rates, insurance and management salaries, which tend to be fixed in the short run (usually up to a year) but in the long run might change.

Product costs Costs incurred in the manufacturing process.

Semi-fixed overheads Costs where part is variable and part is fixed. For example, a service contract for vans may consist of a fixed annual charge plus a variable charge based on mileage. Also known as semi-variable or mixed overheads.

Service centre Some costs, such as rent and rates, cannot be traced to one cost centre directly. These costs are gathered to a service centre and are then arbitrarily apportioned to the other cost centres.

Variable overheads Costs which change with the level of production. For example, a nail factory uses more iron if more nails are produced.

? Self-check questions

1 Which of the following is *not* considered to be part of the role of the management accountant?
   a Formulating strategy for management
   b Optimising a firm's resources
   c Acting as an auditor on behalf of shareholders in a limited company
   d Reviewing a firm's financial systems for management

2 Which one of the following would be considered a direct cost of a car factory?
   a The cost of a marketing campaign
   b Power used by welding robots
   c Wages paid to production line workers
   d The salary paid to the managing director

3 Which of the following would not be considered a valid reason for analysing cost data?
   a To help evade taxation
   b To maximise profitability
   c To set selling prices
   d To help efficiency

4 Direct costs are also referred to as:
   a Prime costs
   b Variable costs
   c Fixed costs
   d Semi-fixed costs

5 Indirect costs are also referred to as:
   a Semi-fixed costs
   b Prime costs
   c Overhead costs
   d Fixed costs

6 The classification of costs according to whether they are direct or indirect is referred to as analysis by:
   a Function
   b Behaviour
   c Time
   d Type

7 The formula 'total production cost + selling and administration overhead' refers to:
   a Total manufacturing cost
   b Total cost
   c Prime cost
   d Factory indirect cost

8 Which of the following is another term for 'semi-fixed cost'?
   a Semi-direct cost
   b Semi-variable cost
   c Semi-indirect cost
   d Semi-prime cost

9 A fashion company pays a designer a royalty of 5% on the selling price of every dress based on her design. Such a cost would be classified as a:
   a Semi-variable cost
   b Fixed cost
   c Semi-fixed cost
   d Variable cost

10 Which one of the following would be considered a *period cost*?
   a A cost which is fixed in the short term but in the long run may change
   b A cost which does not tend to change over time
   c A cost which changes with the level of production
   d A cost which is incurred for one period only

(Answers in Appendix 1)

? Self-study questions

(Answers in Appendix 2)

Question 12.1 From the following data for Cosysnooze, a company that makes duvets, calculate the following:
   a Total fixed costs
   b Total variable costs
   c Fixed cost per duvet
   d Variable cost per duvet
   e Total cost per duvet.

   (Production: 3,481 units)

	£	% variable
Raw materials	1,505	100
Direct labour	1,161	100
Direct expenses	2,838	100
Indirect material	3,560	5
Indirect labour	3,378	7
Indirect expenses	1,544	6
Selling overhead	2,481	20
Administration overhead	2,745	5

Question 12.2 Referring to the information in Question 12.1, what do you think would be a reasonable selling price for one duvet? If Cosysnooze aims to achieve a net profit margin of 10%, what price would it charge for each duvet?

> Case study

The great disappearing profits trick

When Trixie started to analyse the financial information of Machiq Limited (see previous case studies) following Esmeralda's takeover bid, she realised that although the company as a whole appeared profitable, no one had looked at the financial information from a management accountant's viewpoint. In particular, there had been no attempt to consider the nature of the costs incurred and how they may have affected the relative profitability of the two main divisions of the business: Performing and Retailing. After some research, Trixie produced the following analysis:

Machiq Limited: year ended 30 June 2005

	£	Notes
Sales	705,600	30% Performing, 70% Retailing
Cost of sales	(529,200)	80% of costs are variable, divided 10% Performing, 90% Retailing
Gross profit	176,400	
Expenses	(58,600)	Overall 60% fixed, 40% variable, with 35% of the total relating to Performing, the rest to Retailing
Net profit for the year, before taxation	117,800	

Required:

Redraw the analysis to show the relevant net profit or net loss for each division.

(Answers in Appendix 3)

References

The official website of the Chartered Institute of Management Accountants: **www.cimaglobal.com**

The Duncan Williamson website contains much helpful information: **www.duncanwil.co.uk/classcost.htm**

> Now look at this book's dedicated website at **www.pearsoned.co.uk/black** and work through the various additional exercises for this chapter.

Chapter 13

Absorption costing and marginal costing

Objectives

When you have read this chapter you will be able to:

➤ Understand the principles of absorption costing

➤ Understand what is meant by the absorption of costs and explain the difference between the allocation and the apportionment of costs

➤ Understand the costing method known as activity-based costing (ABC)

➤ Understand the principles of marginal costing and the role of the contribution

➤ Contrast absorption and marginal costing

13.1 Introduction

In the previous chapter we saw how costs could be analysed in various ways, such as by function, type, behaviour and time. For a business to operate efficiently, there must be a systematic method (or methods) in place to show the impact of costs on profits and to ensure that costs are reflected in an appropriate manner when evaluating the firm's output. This chapter looks at the two key methods: absorption costing and marginal costing. Absorption costing charges a share of *all* overheads to products, whereas marginal costing splits costs between variable and fixed and analyses the *contribution* which is made by products towards meeting the fixed costs of the organisation.

13.2 Absorption costing

Absorption costing is also called 'total costing', as it requires all costs to be 'absorbed' by the firm's output in order to establish a 'full cost' per item. This enables a selling price to be set which not only covers cost but also ensures a satisfactory profit. The allocation of costs must be as fair and reasonable as possible, and this is achieved by the four-stage process described below.

13.2.1 Stage 1: Allocation of costs to cost centres

Businesses are usually divided into various functions, including production, sales, distribution and administration. Each of these would have one or more *cost centres*. Overheads which relate solely to one specific cost centre will be allocated to that centre. Some costs, such as advertising, might be related to several cost centres, in which case they are gathered to an overall cost centre (referred to as a 'service centre') which is then apportioned in a logical way to the other cost centres. Figure 13.1 illustrates this process.

Figure 13.1
Allocation of costs to cost centres

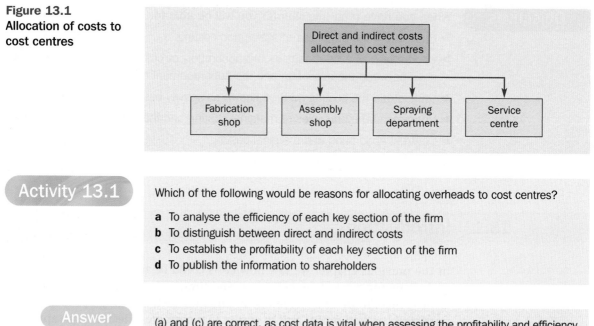

Activity 13.1

Which of the following would be reasons for allocating overheads to cost centres?

a To analyse the efficiency of each key section of the firm
b To distinguish between direct and indirect costs
c To establish the profitability of each key section of the firm
d To publish the information to shareholders

Answer

(a) and (c) are correct, as cost data is vital when assessing the profitability and efficiency of the firm; (b) is not a *reason* for allocating costs, although it is relevant when making the allocation; (d) is incorrect, as detailed cost data is not prepared for shareholders.

13.2.2 Stage 2: Apportionment of overheads

Because some overheads apply to the business as a whole and not specifically to one cost centre (for example, an insurance premium for all buildings, including factories and offices), these general overheads must be apportioned on an appropriate basis to cost centres. Some of these costs (relating to nonspecific areas such as administration or general distribution) may be apportioned to service centres. Figure 13.2 illustrates this process.

**Figure 13.2
Apportionment of
general overheads**

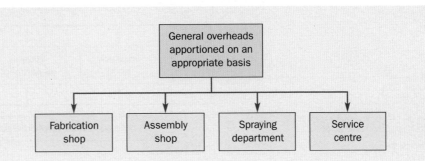

Look at the following costs and then choose what you think would be the most suitable basis of apportionment.

Costs:
a Rent
b Depreciation of computers
c Insurance
d Heating
e Personnel
f Power

Bases of apportionment:
1 Machine-hours used
2 Number of employees within each cost centre
3 Floor area of each cost centre
4 Volume of buildings occupied by cost centre
5 Value of assets within each cost centre
6 Value of computers within each cost centre

a 3, b 6, c 5, d 4, e 2, f 1

13.2.3 Stage 3: Reapportionment of overheads

As all overheads must eventually be absorbed into the production output, the service centre overheads must be reapportioned to the product cost centres, again using a reasonable basis: for example, warehousing overheads could be apportioned to products depending on the volume of each product stored, or maintenance overheads according to time spent in attending breakdowns in each production area. At the end of this process, *all* overheads will have been allocated to production. Figure 13.3 illustrates this process.

Figure 13.3
Reapportionment of service overheads

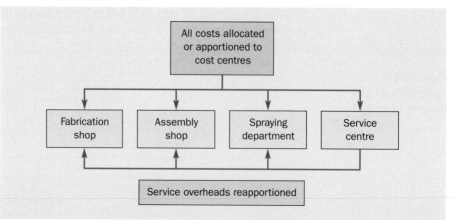

Activity 13.3

A company with three different product lines, X, Y and Z, selling for £6, £5 and £4 each respectively, incurs a £9,000 advertising cost to get the company's name publicised. Unit sales of the products are in the proportions X 25%, Y 35% and Z 40%, and annual turnover is £242,500, split X £75,000, Y £87,500 and Z £80,000. Which of the following ratios would be a reasonable basis for reapportionment?

a 6:5:4
b 25:35:40
c 75:87.5:80

Answer

The correct answer is (c), as this recognises both the unit costs and the number of units sold. The sales price, (a), is not relevant to the overall advertising cost, and the percentages of units sold, (b), do not take into account the relevant sales revenue per item.

13.2.4 Stage 4: Absorption of production centre costs into products

Finally, the cost centre overheads are charged to ('absorbed by') the individual cost units being produced by the cost centre.

A cost unit could be a tub of ice cream, an hour of an architect's time, a barrel of beer. In fact there are as many different cost units as there are types of business. You need to ask yourself 'what is being sold?' to determine the appropriate cost unit.

Overheads are absorbed on the basis of an *overhead absorption rate* (OAR), which is established by dividing the total overhead by the most appropriate *activity level* (for example, total chargeable hours, total units of production, total machine-hours, total labour-hours). The item chosen as the activity level will be that which is most reliable and relevant to the specific business: for example, for a car repairer it might be on the basis of the rate per labour-hour charged to the customer, whereas for a pet food manufacturer it might be the rate per tonne of food produced.

The total cost per cost unit can then be found by adding together the direct materials cost, the direct labour cost and the overheads absorbed according to the OAR.

For example, if the OAR is £5 per machine-hour (that is, one machine working for one hour), a cost unit which takes 6 machine-hours will absorb £5 × £6 = £30 overheads. If selling prices are determined at 80% above total cost, and assuming that *direct* costs are £10 per cost unit, the selling price would be 180% × (£10 + £30) = £72. Figure 13.4 illustrates this process.

Figure 13.4
Costs allocated or apportioned to production cost centres

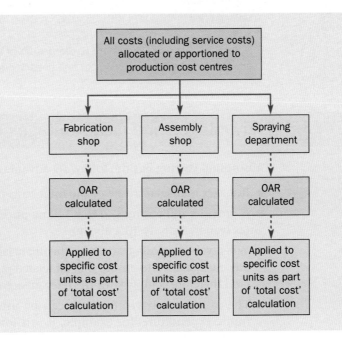

Activity 13.4

A company produces 2,000 units of Yogies and 800 units of Zeldas each month. Direct materials cost £2 per unit for Yogies and £4 per unit for Zeldas. One hour of direct labour charged at £16 per hour is needed to produce one unit of each product. The total overheads for the company are £8,400 per month.

If a mark-up of 40% on costs is required, what selling prices should be charged per unit for Yogies and Zeldas, assuming that the overhead absorption rate is based on the rate per unit? Show a cost statement explaining how you arrive at your figures.

Answer

The selling prices are: Yogies £29.40 per unit, Zeldas £32.20 per unit.

Workings

$$\text{Overhead absorption rate (OAR)} = \frac{\text{Total overheads}}{\text{Total units}}$$

$$= \frac{£8,400}{2,800} = £3 \text{ per unit}$$

Cost statement:

	Yogies	Zeldas	Total
Units	2,000	800	2,800
Direct materials (£2 per Yogie, £4 per Zelda)	4,000	3,200	7,200
Direct labour (£16 per unit)	32,000	12,800	44,800
Prime costs	36,000	16,000	52,000
Overheads (£3 per unit – see above)	6,000	2,400	8,400
Total cost	42,000	18,400	60,400
Total cost per unit	£21.00	£23.00	
Mark-up (40%)	£8.40	£9.20	
Selling price	**£29.40**	**£32.20**	

Note: What we have seen here is the benefit of using absorption (total) costing to arrive at a realistic selling price per unit of each product.

13.3 Advantages and disadvantages of absorption costing

Absorption costing has the following advantages:

● It makes managers aware of the total costs incurred within cost centres.

● It provides full costings so that selling prices can be established by mark-up (as seen in Activity 13.4 above).

● When valuing closing stocks for the financial accounts, absorption cost methods must be used to ensure that all related production overheads are included (and therefore comply with the relevant accounting standard, SSAP 9).

● The overhead absorption rate can be used when producing budgets of future expenditure: for example, if it is forecast that 10,000 direct-labour-hours are expected to be chargeable next year, and the OAR is £20 per direct-labour-hour, budgeted overheads would be £200,000.

However, absorption costing has the following disadvantages:

- Apportionment of overheads is often made on an arbitrary basis, so total costs may in fact be unrelated to reality.
- Unrealistic total costs would lead to unrealistic setting of selling prices where 'mark-up on cost' is used.
- The intention is that the OAR will lead to the absorption of all costs into cost units. In practice, because it is usually based on *estimates* of costs and activity, there is likely to be either an underabsorption (leading to losses as not all costs will be charged to customers) or overabsorption of overheads (leading to inflated prices and reduced sales).
- It ignores the important distinction between variable, fixed and semi-fixed costs (see 'marginal costing' below).

Activity 13.5

Acme Shirts Limited has produced the following analysis of its product range:

Shirt range

	Formal £000	Sports £000	Casual £000	Total £000
Sales (A)	340	200	300	840
Direct materials	60	50	70	180
Direct labour	40	50	48	138
Variable overheads	80	60	40	180
Other factory costs (apportioned)	60	70	68	198
Total factory cost (B)	(240)	(230)	(226)	(696)
Gross profit/ (loss) (A) − (B)	100	(30)	74	144
Non-production overheads (assume all fixed)				(80)
Net profit				64

The managing director has reviewed the information and believes that the Sports shirt range should be discontinued since it appears to be making a loss. Do you agree with this course of action, and what would be its effect if implemented?

Answer

The allocation of all costs to products has resulted in a gross loss of £30,000 on the Sports shirt range, so it would appear that, by closing the division, the business's net profit would increase from £64,000 to £94,000. However, this ignores the fact that some of the factory costs apportioned to the Sports division will remain, even if the division is closed. This aspect is explored in Activity 13.8 below, so we will defer a decision until that activity is completed.

13.4 Activity-based costing (ABC)

Many companies have traditionally used direct labour rates (either 'cost' or 'hours') as the basis for their overhead absorption rates. However, with the move from labour-intensive methods of production to computer-based and robotic forms of manufacture, more relevant and up-to-date forms of costing techniques have evolved. **Activity-based costing (ABC)** moves away from using, for example, the number of labour-hours involved in making a product as the basis for overhead absorption and instead seeks to relate costs to the *activities* which generate, or drive, the costs. These 'cost drivers' could be the key stages in the manufacturing and distribution process, such as:

● Setting up machines prior to manufacture

● Machine usage during manufacture

● Quality control tests

● Order handling.

Each cost driver would then be used as the basis for overhead absorption.

The next two activities contrast overhead absorption based, firstly, on traditional absorption costing techniques and, secondly, on activity-based costing.

Activity 13.6

Lexicon Ltd manufactures two products, Gribbs and Huttles. Gribbs require 1 direct-labour-hour and Huttles require 2 direct-labour-hours in a single production cost centre. Three overhead generating activities have been identified: setting up, quality testing and order handling. The following data is available:

Overhead costs:	
Setting-up costs	£60,000
Quality testing costs	£50,000
Order handling	£30,000
	£140,000

	Total	Gribbs	Huttles
Number of units	11,000	4,000	7,000
Number of direct-labour-hours	18,000	4,000	14,000
Number of set-ups	20	8	12
Number of quality tests	50	20	30
Orders	40	15	25

Calculate the overhead cost of one Gribb and one Huttle, using traditional absorption costing techniques.

Answer

Using direct labour rate as the basis for absorption,

$$\frac{\text{Overhead cost}}{\text{Direct-labour-hours}} = \frac{£140,000}{18,000} = £7.78 \text{ per labour-hour}$$

Therefore, overhead cost per unit using absorption costing is:

$$1 \text{ Gribb} = 1 \text{ hour} \times £7.78 = £7.78$$

$$1 \text{ Huttle} = 2 \text{ hours} \times £7.78 = £15.56$$

Activity 13.7

Using the same data for Lexicon Ltd (see Activity 13.6), calculate the product cost for Gribbs and Huttles using the activity-based costing technique.

Answer

Overhead activity	Cost	Cost driver	Cost per cost driver
Setting up	£60,000	20 set-ups	£3,000 per set-up
Quality testing	£50,000	50 tests	£1,000 per test
Order handling	£30,000	40 orders	£750 per order

Cost attribution to products according to activity:

	Gribbs	Huttles	Total
Setting up	8 × £3,000 = 24,000	12 × £3,000 = 36,000	60,000
Quality testing	20 × £1,000 = 20,000	30 × £1,000 = 30,000	50,000
Order handling	15 × £750 = 11,250	25 × £750 = 18,750	30,000
	55,250	84,750	140,000

Therefore overhead cost per unit is:

1 Gribb (55,250/4,000 units) = £13.81

1 Huttle (84,750/7,000 units) = £12.11

13.5 Absorption costing and activity-based costing compared

In the two activities involving Gribbs and Huttles, per unit overheads under traditional absorption costing techniques would have been Gribbs £7.78 and Huttles £15.56. Therefore, under this method, total overheads would be absorbed as follows:

Gribbs	4,000 × £7.78 =	£31,120	
Huttles	7,000 × £15.56 =	£108,920	
Total		£140,040	(£140,000 rounded)

Under activity-based costing, however, they would have been Gribbs £13.81 and Huttles £12.11. Therefore, under this method, total overheads would be absorbed as follows:

Gribbs	4,000 × £13.81 =	£55,240	
Huttles	7,000 × £12.11 =	£84,770	
Total		£140,010	(£140,000 rounded)

These are very different per unit figures, so which ones are more reliable?

Both methods charge out *all* the overheads to products, it is just the relative *proportions* between the products which alter. Which looks more reasonable? Although Huttles take 3.5 times as many direct-labour-hours as Gribbs, they have only 1.5 times the number of set-ups and quality tests and 1.7 times the number of orders. Using the direct labour rate seems to skew the costing unfairly towards Huttles when in terms of cost-driving activities, Huttles are far less demanding. Activity-based costing appears to be the method that is more realistic.

13.6 Marginal costing

Marginal costing is an alternative method of costing to absorption costing and is based on the view that, in the short run, fixed costs do not alter and they have to be borne regardless of the level of production or sales in that period. The variable costs which can be accurately allocated are termed **marginal costs**.

In marginal costing, the calculation of the **contribution** is of vital importance. The contribution is the difference between the variable (marginal) cost and the selling price:

$$S - V = C$$

where S = sales price, V = variable (marginal) cost and C = contribution. In other words, every time a product is sold, a contribution is made towards meeting the fixed costs of the business. Once the fixed costs have been met, each contribution represents a profit:

$$\text{Total C} - \text{Total F} = \text{Total P}$$

where C = contribution, F = fixed costs and P = profit, if C > F. If C < F, the business has made a loss.

Under this method, *fixed costs are not allocated or apportioned to individual cost units*. Note that the term 'contribution' is *not* the same as 'profit'. A firm makes a profit only when its total contribution exceeds its fixed costs, as explained in Figure 13.5.

**Figure 13.5
Contribution, fixed costs and profit**

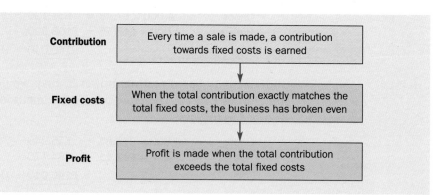

The best way to understand marginal costing is to work through an example.

Example 13.1

A ready-mixed concrete company has two divisions, trade (T) and domestic (D). T division delivers to professional builders whereas D division deals with the amateur DIY market. Total overheads for the company for November are £100,000, which have been divided (on absorption cost principles) between the two divisions in the ratio T 65% and D 35%.
Other relevant information is:

	T	D
Variable cost per load	£20	£15
Selling price per load	£60	£80
Loads sold in November	2,000	400
Fixed costs (total) £54,000		

Using absorption cost principles, T's profit is £55,000 (sales 2,000 × £60 = £120,000 less £65,000 costs) whereas D makes a loss of £3,000 (sales 400 × £80 = £32,000 less £35,000 costs). The total profit is £52,000 (£55,000 profit – £3,000 loss).

To apply marginal cost principles, we can calculate the contribution made from each load in each division:

Sales – Variable costs = Contribution

so T division's contribution is £40 (£60 – £20) and D division's contribution is £65 (£80 – £15).

Finally, we can calculate the total contribution being made by each division towards meeting the fixed costs, and the total profit being earned by the company. T division's total contribution is £80,000 (2,000 loads × £40) and D division's is £26,000 (400 loads × £65), making a total contribution of £106,000.

Total profit = Total contribution – Fixed costs

so the profit is:

£106,000 – £54,000 = £52,000

which is the same total profit as shown under absorption cost principles.

The managing director of the company has seen D division's loss (£3,000) under absorption cost principles and wants to shut the division down. What would be the effect on total profit if this happened?

If the division were closed, *D's contribution of £26,000 would disappear*, leaving all the fixed costs to be borne by T division. Remember that total contribution less total fixed costs = profit, so the revised profit after shutting D division would be £80,000 – £54,000 = £26,000, exactly half what it is with D division in operation.

Activity 13.8

Look back at the Acme Shirts Limited problem in Activity 13.5. What conclusion can be drawn regarding the Sports Shirt division if marginal costing techniques are used?

Answer

If the results for the period were redrawn using marginal costing techniques, the Sports Shirt division is shown as making a *positive* contribution of £40,000 towards meeting the fixed costs of the whole business, as shown below:

| | | Shirt range | | |
| | Formal | Sports | Casual | Total |
	£000	£000	£000	£000
Sales (A)	340	200	300	840
Less Variable costs:				
Direct materials	60	50	70	180
Direct labour	40	50	48	138
Other variable overheads	80	60	40	180
Total variable costs (B)	(180)	(160)	(158)	(498)
Contribution (C) (= A – B)	160	40	142	342

Less Fixed costs			
Other factory costs	(198)		
Non-production overheads	(80)		
Total fixed costs (D)			(278)
Net profit (C – D)			64

The conclusion must be that the Sports Shirt division should *not be closed*. If it were decided to close that division, net profit would reduce by £40,000 to only £24,000.

13.7 Using the contribution for 'what-if' calculations

Now that we know how to calculate the contribution, it is time to realise what a useful bit of management information it is. For example, what if the concrete company's managing director (see Example 13.1) was looking at December's forecasts? Cost data was unchanged from November, but he wants answers to the following questions:

● How many loads need to be delivered to make a specified profit?

● How many loads need to be delivered to break even (the **break-even point** is where contribution exactly meets fixed costs)?

● What would be the effect on profits or losses if T division's load delivery increased by a specific percentage, but D division's declined?

All these questions can be answered by using the contribution figure.

Let's see how these calculations work. Remember from Example 13.1 that relevant figures for the two divisions in November were:

	T	D
Loads delivered	2,000	400
Contribution per load (£)	40	65
Total contribution in October (£)	80,000	26,000
Total fixed costs £54,000		
Total profit £52,000		

Specified profit calculations

Assuming demand from D division is static, how many loads have to be delivered from T division to generate an extra £10,000 profit?

Each T load gives a contribution of £40, so it would need a further 250 loads (250 × £40 = £10,000) to generate an extra £10,000 profit.

How many to break even?

If D's loads remain at their November level, how many loads need to be delivered by T division to break even overall?

D's contribution in November was £26,000 towards total fixed costs of £54,000. To break even, T's contribution must exactly equal the remaining £28,000, so 700 (£28,000/£40 contribution per load) loads must be delivered by T division to break even.

Effect on profits of changing activity levels

What would be the effect on company profits if T's deliveries were 20% higher than in November, but D's deliveries were 40% lower?

November's deliveries were: T 2,000; D 400, so December's would be: T 2,400 and D 240. Contribution would then be: T 2,400 × £40 = £96,000; D 240 × £65 = £15,600.

Total contribution = £111,600 − £54,000 fixed costs = £57,600 profit (£5,600 higher than November).

13.8 Absorption costing and marginal costing compared

Figure 13.6 summarises the key differences between absorption and marginal costing techniques.

Figure 13.6
Absorption costing and marginal costing compared

	Absorption costing	Marginal costing
Advantages	Indicates total costs of products and services (useful where pricing is on a 'cost plus' basis)	'Contribution per unit' useful for management purposes, including break-even analysis (see Chapter 15)
	Identifies profitability of different products and services	No arbitrary apportionment of costs
	Fits in well with financial accounting summaries showing gross and net profit, and for stock valuation	Identification of product units making a positive contribution is a better guide than an arbitrary overall profit calculation
Disadvantages	Potentially misleading guide to profitability of product units and could lead to closure of units making a positive contribution to meeting fixed costs	Might be difficult to determine variable/fixed costs: many costs are semi-fixed
	Arbitrary allocation of fixed costs to product units in many cases	Does not accord with financial accounting split of gross/net profit

13.9 Summary

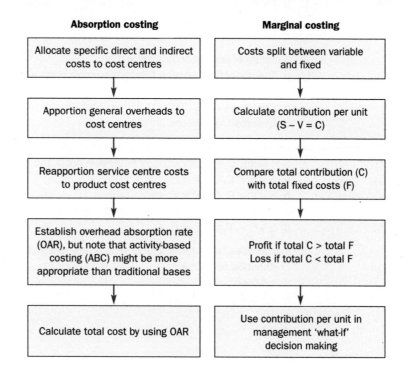

Absorption costing	Marginal costing
Allocate specific direct and indirect costs to cost centres	Costs split between variable and fixed
Apportion general overheads to cost centres	Calculate contribution per unit (S − V = C)
Reapportion service centre costs to product cost centres	Compare total contribution (C) with total fixed costs (F)
Establish overhead absorption rate (OAR), but note that activity-based costing (ABC) might be more appropriate than traditional bases	Profit if total C > total F Loss if total C < total F
Calculate total cost by using OAR	Use contribution per unit in management 'what-if' decision making

13.10 Glossary

Absorption costing A management accounting technique where costs are allocated or apportioned to various product lines to establish the profitability or overall cost of each product.

Activity-based costing (ABC) A method of cost apportionment which seeks to relate costs to the activities which generate or 'drive' the costs.

Break-even point The point at which a business's revenue exactly meets its cost.

Contribution The difference between sales revenue and variable costs. It can be calculated either on a per unit basis (for 'what-if' calculations) or in total (to assess overall profitability).

Marginal cost The extra cost that would result from producing one extra unit.

Marginal costing A management accounting technique where costs are divided between variable and fixed, and a contribution is established by deducting the variable costs from the sales revenue.

? Self-check questions
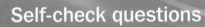

1 In a company manufacturing paint, which of the following would not be a direct cost?
   a The cost of paint tins
   b The cost of dyes to colour the paint
   c The cost of advertising the paint
   d The cost of chemicals used to make the paint

2 Another name for direct costs is:
   a Prime costs
   b Fixed costs
   c Absorbed costs
   d Overhead costs

3 A feature of absorption costing is that:
   a The distinction between fixed and variable costs is ignored
   b A contribution is established
   c Only direct costs of production are considered
   d Loss-making divisions are closed

4 Which of the following equations best represents marginal costing, where F = fixed costs, S = sales, C = contribution, V = variable costs and P = profit?
   a $S - F = C, C - V = P$
   b $S - V = C, C - P = F$
   c $S - V = C, C - F = P$
   d $S - C = V, V - F = P$

5 If total sales revenue for 1,000 units is £5,000 and total variable costs are £3,000, the contribution per unit is:
   a £3,000
   b £2,000
   c £5
   d £2

6 If the variable costs per unit are £6, and 500 units have been sold for £5,000, the total contribution is:
   a £4,000
   b £2,000
   c £3,000
   d £8,000

7 If total fixed costs are £12,000, the selling price per unit is £12 and the variable costs per unit are £8, the break-even point is:
   a 12,000 units
   b 3,000 units
   c 1,500 units
   d 4,500 units

8 If the break-even point is 6,000 units and the contribution per unit is £6, total fixed costs must be:
   a £2,000
   b £18,000
   c £12,000
   d £36,000

9 If fixed costs are £32,000, maximum sales are £100,000 and variable costs are £60,000 at this level, the turnover required to break even is:
   a £80,000
   b £53,334
   c £19,200
   d £32,000

10 If fixed costs are £160,000 and the contribution per unit is £2, the number of units to be sold to achieve a profit of £60,000 is:
   a 80,000
   b 50,000
   c 110,000
   d 440,000

(Answers in Appendix 1)

? Self-study questions

(Answers in Appendix 2)

Question 13.1 Abalone operates three production departments and one service department. It estimated monthly overheads for the company at £72,600, divided as follows:

	Production departments			Service department
	A	B	C	D
	£	£	£	£
Indirect labour (£)	20,000	16,000	8,000	7,000
Other indirect labour (£)	10,000	6,000	3,000	2,600
	30,000	22,000	11,000	9,600

D's expenses are to be apportioned between the production departments in the ratio: A 40%, B 40%, C 20%.

Apportion D's overheads to the production departments.

Question 13.2 Boadle Limited makes five different products: Alphas, Betas, Gammas, Deltas and Epsilons. Costs per unit are: direct costs £22, £18, £35, £30 and £43 respectively, Variable overheads: £11, £9, £16, £15 and £19 respectively. Fixed expenses for a month are estimated at £8,200, which has been allocated to each unit produced as: Alphas £17, Betas £13, Gammas £19, Deltas £15 and Epsilons £18. The company adds 20% on to the total cost of each product by way of profit.

a Calculate the price per unit of each product, based upon absorption (total cost) pricing.

b Advise the company as to which products it should produce, if selling prices are restricted to: Alphas £59, Betas £25, Gammas £80, Deltas £44 and Epsilons £92.

c If maximum output per product is 100 units, calculate the profit or loss for the company as a whole if it:

(i) Produced the entire range of products

(ii) Produced only the products you recommended in (b) above. (Assume that unused capacity cannot be used for other products).

Question 13.3 Complete the white boxes in the following table. Assume that A – E are separate businesses.

	A	B	C	D	E
Sales in units			4,000	6,000	15,000
Sales (£)	40,000	60,000	48,000	90,000	
Variable costs (£)	10,000		32,000	54,000	30,000
Contribution (£)	30,000	10,000	16,000		75,000
Contribution per unit (£)	6	0.5		6	
Fixed costs (£)	14,400		7,000		50,000
Profit/(loss) (£)		(5,000)		12,000	
Break-even point (units)	2,400	30,000		4,000	
Profit/(loss) if 3,000 units sold					

Question 13.4 Rumpole Ltd is proposing an expansion of their product range by manufacturing a new product. It is proposed that the new product will sell for £15 per item and will have a market between 10,000 and 15,000 items per year. An analysis of the costs at these levels of production is:

Units:	10,000	15,000
	£	£
Materials	40,000	60,000
Labour	70,000	95,000
Overheads	50,000	55,000

a Calculate the variable cost per unit and the total fixed cost.

b Calculate how many units of the product must be manufactured to:

● break even

● earn a profit of £13,000.

c Calculate how much profit or loss would be made if only 7,000 units were manufactured and sold.

> Case study

Who is Mrs Eadale?

The directors of Machiq Limited (see previous case studies) decided to reject Esmeralda's takeover bid and instead devoted their talents to developing new products. Trixie, the managing director, had been sent an e-mail containing a recipe for a vanishing potion and decided to investigate the possibility of setting up a separate division to produce and promote it. The creator of the recipe, who had signed herself 'Mrs Eadale', said that the potion was totally harmless and caused only temporary invisibility. She also insisted that, as an absolute condition of her allowing Machiq Limited to use the recipe free of charge, the directors must test the potion on themselves before selling it to the general public.

Chiquita, the finance director, produced the following information:

Maximum production and sales p.a. (bottles)	15,000
	£
Selling price per bottle	14
Ingredients per bottle	3
Cost of bottle and label	1
Direct labour cost per bottle	2
Rent, rates and other fixed costs relating to bottling division	20,000
Portion of company's general overheads allocated to bottling division	130,000

Required:

a Using the absorption costing technique, would the new division be viable? Show your calculations.

b What recommendation might have been made if marginal costing had been used to evaluate the proposed new division? Show your calculations.

c Using marginal costing techniques, calculate:
  (i)   the break-even point (in bottles),
  (ii) the number of bottles which would have to be sold to earn £16,000 profit for the bottling division,
  (iii) how much profit or loss would be made if only 4,000 bottles were sold.

(Answers in Appendix 3)

A footnote:

Marvin, Chiquita and Trixie set up the bottling division. They sent an invitation to Esmeralda to join them at a celebration champagne 'test the potion' party to show there were no hard feelings after her failed takeover bid. Esmeralda replied saying that she would be very pleased to watch the three directors vanish and looked forward to toasting their health in champagne beforehand. Unfortunately, a waiter hired for the occasion inadvertently poured the potion into the champagne glasses, and the guests, after raising their glasses to the toast of 'Mrs Eadale', drank the 'champagne' and promptly disappeared without trace.

References   A (very) critical appraisal of activity-based costing: **users.aol.com/caspari/l118.htm**

Now look at this book's dedicated website at www.pearsoned.co.uk/black and work through the various additional exercises for this chapter.

Chapter 14

Product costing

Objectives When you have read this chapter you will be able to:

➤ Distinguish between specific order costing and operation costing

➤ Apply specific costing techniques to job, batch, contract, process and service costing

14.1 Introduction

Product costing is the technique of establishing the cost of a finished item or items by combining direct costs with relevant allocated and apportioned indirect costs. The methods used will vary depending upon the custom and practice of specific industries and also the methods of production employed. In particular it is usual to classify product costing into two main groups, specific order costing and operation costing:

● *Specific order costing* is applicable where the work consists of jobs or batches of production, and separate large-scale contracts.

● *Operation costing* is relevant where a product or service results from a sequence of continuous or repetitive operations or processes.

Whichever approach is adopted to ascertain costs, the basic principles of determining costs (as outlined in Chapter 12) will apply. It is only the method of collecting and presenting cost data which differs.

14.2 Specific order costing

14.2.1 Job costing

Job costing is used where work is undertaken to a customer's specific requirements. Often a quote is given before work commences, and this can subsequently be compared with the actual costs to establish whether the work was done too cheaply and to improve future job costing. It is likely that no two jobs will be exactly the same and the job might be completed relatively quickly. Contrast a 'job' with a 'long-term contract', which normally spans at least two financial accounting periods and is of a significantly greater value than a 'job'.

Activity 14.1

Some of the following would be considered 'jobs', whereas others would be considered 'long-term contracts'. Decide which is which.

a A routine car service at a garage
b A builder agreeing to construct 8,000 houses for a property developer
c A plumber who installs a water heater
d An oil rig being constructed by a shipyard
e An illustrator commissioned to provide a drawing for a book cover
f A website design company whose 20 employees will be producing a comprehensive website for an online bank over the next two years

Answer

Only (a), (c) and (e) will be regarded as 'jobs' – the rest are substantial long-term contracts.

14.2.2 Quotations and job cost sheets

Each order will be given a unique reference number and all costs relating to that job will be allocated or apportioned to that number. A job cost sheet is prepared which summarises all relevant costs of a specific job. Before a customer places an order, they may ask for a quotation (estimate of cost). For example, Digitalis Ltd has been asked to quote for the design of a website by e-veg Ltd, an online greengrocer. Digitalis, which gives the reference number EV6325 to the job, estimates that special software costing £1,000 will have to be purchased for this project and that two designers will work on the website at 30 hours per week for three weeks at a rate of £40 per hour. Overheads are recovered by the direct-labour-hour method at £30 per hour. A mark-up of 40% is added to arrive at the fee payable by the customer. This is the quotation for the project:

Job No. EV6325

e-veg Ltd Quotation for website construction

Item	Estimate
Direct materials	1,000
Direct labour: (2 × 30) × 3 × £40 per hour	7,200
Overheads: 180 direct-labour-hours @ £30 per hour	5,400
Total costs	13,600
Add mark-up 40%	5,440
Price chargeable to customer	19,040

After a quotation has been given to the customer, the customer will either accept or reject it or haggle for better terms. Once the job is completed, the 'actual' costs can be compared. Assume that Digitalis Ltd has completed the design of e-veg Ltd's website. The special software cost £1,400 and the two designers worked only 26 hours per week for two weeks, but were paid at a rate of £60 per hour. Other details were as per the quotation. Here is the job cost sheet for the project (the 'variance' column is simply the difference between estimated and actual figures):

Job No. EV6325

e-veg Ltd Job cost sheet

Item	Estimate	Actual	Variance
Direct materials	1,000	1,400	+400
Direct labour: (actual 104 × £60)	7,200	6,240	−960
Overheads: (actual 104 × £30)	5,400	3,120	−2,280
Total costs	13,600	10,760	−2,840
Add mark-up	5,440	8,280	+2,840
Price chargeable to customer	19,040	19,040	−

Due (apparently) to efficient working, Digitalis Ltd earned £2,840 more profit than originally estimated.

14.2.3 Batch costing

Where similar or identical items are manufactured in batches, **batch costing** is used. This follows the same procedure as job costing, but the price of one unit is found by dividing the total costs of the batch by the number of units produced.

Activity 14.2

Moby Ltd manufactures mobile phone fascias in batches of 50,000. During March, Batch no. 711 was poorly finished, resulting in only 44,000 fascias being completed. The remainder were scrapped. Costs were as follows:

Raw materials	£900
Direct labour	£1,200
Overhead recovery	£660

What was the cost per fascia in Batch no. 711?

Answer	Total costs (900 + 1,200 + 660) = £2,760, divided by 44,000 = 6.3p cost per fascia.

14.2.4 Contract costing

Contracts are distinguished from jobs for costing purposes, as they are of significant value and usually span more than one accounting period. Specifically, an accounting standard (SSAP 9 *Stocks and Long-term Contracts*) gives a definition of a long-term contract and provides rules for determining how to treat such contracts in the financial accounting summaries. For *management accounting* purposes, costs are allocated and apportioned to contracts in much the same way as for jobs. However, the complexity and scale of many contracts will require comprehensive cost recording systems, with 'contract accounts' being maintained to record such aspects as:

- Cost of materials sent to the site, less any materials returned from the site
- Labour (direct and indirect relating to the contract)
- Value of plant and machinery used on the site
- On-site costs such as security, lighting, power
- Charges by subcontractors related to the contract
- Head office costs apportioned to the contract.

With many contracts, the customer makes progress payments based on the proportion of the contract completed, as certified by an architect or surveyor. The contract may allow for 'retention money' to be withheld by the customer (for example, 10% of each stage payment) as a guarantee against poor workmanship and so on.

Profit or losses on contracts

The accounting standard relating to long-term contracts allows companies to recognise a profit (known as an 'attributable' profit) before the contract's completion. Otherwise, companies engaged in very long contracts would show 'nil' profits for several years and then have a 'bonanza' profit in the year of completion. This distortion goes against the accruals (matching) concept studied in earlier chapters and would result in potential investors being reluctant to invest in companies where dividends might not be paid for many years. The downside is that, because of the prudence concept, the standard requires that if a *loss* is forecast on the contract (a 'foreseeable' loss), the *whole* loss (that is, not just the part relating to a specific accounting period) should be recognised as soon as it is foreseen.

14.3 Operation costing

14.3.1 Process costing

In specific order costing, each job, batch or contract is costed separately. Where products are produced in a single process, or where the product of one process becomes the material of a second process, a different costing system is needed since products can no longer be identified individually. Under **process costing**, the firm is divided into departments which tend to be limited to one process or operation. Accounts are kept for each process, with materials, labour, expenses and overheads being debited to the process and scrap (materials with some recovery value) being credited (see Figure 14.1). These methods tend to be used by such industries as chemicals, distillation, steel-making and food processing.

Figure 14.1
Process costing

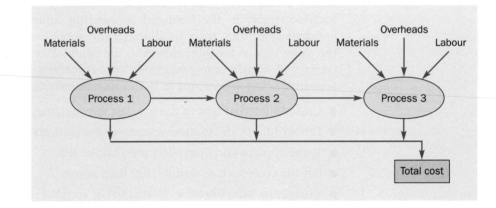

In most processes there is a degree of wastage, but this loss might be either 'normal' or 'abnormal':

● **Normal loss** is where waste is inherent in the production process, and is seen as a legitimate expense to be borne by 'good' production.

● **Abnormal loss** is in excess of normal wastage and may be caused by inefficient working or poor materials. This is written off to the profit and loss account. Occasionally, abnormal *gains* might be recorded where very favourable conditions have given rise to greater production than would have been expected. Such gains would be recorded separately and credited to the profit and loss account.

Activity 14.3

Squaretree Ltd's Choc-o-crunch production line has three processes: baking, chocolate covering and wrapping. In June, 500,000 Choc-o-crunches were produced. Details of each process's costs for that month are as follows:

	Baking £	Chocolate covering £	Wrapping £
Direct materials	20,000	16,000	8,000
Direct labour	4,500	5,180	1,600
Production overhead	2,500	2,620	2,600
Abnormal loss	–	3,000	–

Calculate the cost of one Choc-o-crunch.

Answer

Cost summary:

	Baking £	Chocolate covering £	Wrapping £
Brought forward from previous process	n/a	27,000	47,800
Direct materials	20,000	16,000	8,000
Direct labour	4,500	5,180	1,600
Production overhead	2,500	2,620	2,600
Total costs	27,000	50,800	60,000
Abnormal loss	–	(3,000)	–
Carried forward to next process	27,000	47,800	n/a
Cost of finished goods			60,000

$$\text{Cost of one Choc-o-crunch} = \frac{£60,000}{500,000} = 12p$$

14.3.2 Service costing

The costing of specific services such as hospitals or universities is different from costing production departments, mainly in the way cost data is collected and how costs are then allocated to cost units.

With services, cost units may be composites such as a 'patient-day' in a hospital or a 'passenger-mile' in a transport company, whereas universities might use 'full-time equivalent students'. There is no general rule – it depends on what is of most use to the organisation. Whatever cost unit is decided upon, the calculation of unit cost is similar to the calculation used in a production department:

$$\text{Cost per service unit} = \frac{\text{Total costs for the period}}{\text{Number of service units supplied in the period}}$$

Activity 14.4

A hospital has incurred costs of £3,600,000 during July and 8,000 patient-beds have been occupied during the month. What is the cost per patient bed?

Answer

$$\frac{£3,600,000}{8,000} = £450$$

Activity 14.5

Match the service industries on the left to the most appropriate service cost unit on the right:

a	Hotel	**1**	Dog-days
b	Airline	**2**	Meals served
c	Caterer	**3**	Rooms occupied
d	Laundry	**4**	Garments processed
e	Boarding kennel	**5**	Passenger-miles

Answer *a* 3, **b** 5, **c** 2, **d** 4, **e** 1

14.4 Summary

	Specific order costing			Operation costing	
	Job costing	*Batch costing*	*Contract costing*	*Process costing*	*Service costing*
Applies to:	Work done to a customer's specific requirements, but see 'contract' definition	Similar or identical items manufactured in batches	Work of significant value usually spanning more than one financial accounting period	One or more processes continually producing items	Service industries
Examples:	Car repair, landscaping a garden	Cakes in a small bakery, pottery items	Bridge construction, building a school	Confectionery, medicine	Universities, hospitals
Specific features:	Job cost sheet prepared with all relevant costs, possibly as a quotation for a customer	As job costing, but the price per unit is found by dividing total batch costs by the number of units produced	Contract accounts kept for each contract. Progress payments depend on work certified. SSAP 9 is relevant. Profits can be taken before contract completed, but foreseeable losses must also be recognised	Cost of one process added to those of subsequent processes until total cost found. Unit cost found by dividing total cost by production of a specific period. Losses might be normal or abnormal	Total cost is found by the usual methods, but the cost unit might be a composite such as patient-day or full-time equivalent student

14.5 Glossary

Abnormal loss   A loss of materials in excess of normal wastage, possibly caused by inefficient working or poor materials. The loss is not passed on to customers but is absorbed by the company.

Batch costing   A specific order costing system where similar or identical items are manufactured in batches.

Contract costing   A specific order costing system for contracts of significant value and usually spanning more than one accounting period.

Job costing   A specific order costing system used where work is undertaken to a customer's specific requirements.

Normal loss   A loss of materials where waste is inherent in the production process, and is seen as a legitimate expense to be borne by 'good' production.

Process costing An operation costing system used where products are produced in a single process, or where the product of one process becomes the material of a second process.

Product costing The technique of establishing the cost of a finished item or items by combining direct costs with relevant allocated and apportioned indirect costs.

Service costing An operation costing system used for the costing of specific services such as hospitals or universities.

? Self-check questions

1 Which one of the following would be classified as a long-term contract for costing purposes?
a An electrician rewiring a domestic house
b A printer producing 5,000 copies of an accountancy textbook
c A road bridge being constructed between two islands 10 km apart
d A carpenter constructing a garden bench to a specific design

2 A quotation is:
a An estimate of cost given as a price guide to a customer
b A record of the order placed by a customer
c The final price of a job
d The labour cost of a job, without any material costs included

3 A company gives a quotation for a job which requires 100 kg of materials @ £14 per kg, 50 direct-labour-hours @ £40 per hour and overheads recovered on the basis of direct-labour-hours at £25 per hour. A mark-up of 50% is added. What is the price chargeable to the customer?
a £2,375
b £4,750
c £9,500
d £6,975

4 Using the information in question 3 above, and assuming the customer accepts the quotation, what profit would be earned if the actual job takes twice as many materials, the same number of direct labour hours but only 80% of the labour costs, and the quoted price cannot be renegotiated?
a £7,125
b £1,325
c £2,800
d £2,375

5 Mojo Ltd manufactures pond pumps in batches of 400. During April, Batch no. 145 had a slight manufacturing fault, resulting in only 390 pumps being completed. The remainder were scrapped. Costs were: raw materials £2,000, labour and overheads £3,000. What was the cost per pump?
a £12.82
b £12.50
c £500
d £10

6 In a long-term building contract, retention money is:
a The overall value of the contract
b A progress payment made by the customer as the contract progresses
c Money withheld by the builder as a guarantee against future problems
d Money withheld by the customer as a guarantee against future problems

7 In a long-term contract, profit earned on the contract prior to its completion is:
a Included as an 'attributable profit' when calculating the company's overall profit or loss for the year
b Included only when the contract is completed
c Estimated at the commencement of the contract and then included in company profits at an even rate over the life of the contract
d Included only when all payments under the contract have been made

8 In process costing, wastage caused by inefficient working or poor materials is usually known as:
a Normal gain
b Normal loss
c Abnormal loss
d Abnormal gain

9 Which of the following businesses would be most likely to use 'tonne-kilometres' as an appropriate cost unit?
a A food processing factory
b A road haulage company
c A university
d A publishing company

10 Which of the following businesses would be most likely to use 'full-time equivalent students' as an appropriate cost unit?
a A farmer
b An abattoir
c A university
d A chemical production company

(Answers in Appendix 1)

Self-study questions

(Answers in Appendix 2)

Question 14.1 a What is meant by 'specific order costing'?
b In what ways does specific order costing differ from process costing?

Question 14.2 Barney plc manufactures deluxe cat baskets in batches of 300. During April, Batch no. 567 took 20 hours to machine. Sixty cat baskets failed to pass an inspection, but of these, 40 were thought to be rectifiable. The remaining 20 were scrapped, and the scrap value was credited to the cost of the batch as a whole. Rectification work took nine hours. Costs were as follows:

Batch No. 567	£
Raw materials per cat basket	1.60
Scrap value per cat basket	0.86
Machinists' hourly rate	4.20
Machine-hour overhead	3.60
Setting up of machine – normal machining	21.00
Setting up of machine – rectification	18.00

Calculate:

a The cost of a full batch, in total and per unit, if all units pass inspection.

b The actual cost of Batch no. 567, in total and per unit, after crediting the recovery value of the scrapped items, and including the rectification costs.

c The loss incurred because of defective work.

> ## Case study

The antidote to the potion

The detective investigating the mysterious disappearance of the directors of Machiq Limited (see previous case studies) was searching the home of Esmeralda, the chief suspect in the case. He opened a drawer and extracted a notepad with the word 'Antidote' written on the front cover. He turned the page, and read as follows:

The antidote to the vanishing potion can be manufactured in 1,000 bottle batches as follows:

Firstly, the mixing process: Combine 10 kg of Wart Powder with 5 kg of Elbow Grease. One person to mix by hand for 10 hours and then transfer to the liquidising process. There the three liquidising workers will each spend 4 hours adding 14 kg of Snod Grass whilst supervising the liquidising procedure. Three-quarters of the mixture will evaporate in the liquidising process as a normal loss.

Finally, the antidote must be bottled. This process will take 2 persons 5 hours each.

Ingredients can all be obtained from Stoob the Chemist at the following prices: Wart Powder £80 per kg, Elbow Grease £60 per kg and Snod Grass £40 per kg. The mixing operative is paid £4.50 per hour, liquidising workers are each paid £4.75 per hour and the bottling operative is paid £5.00 per hour. Bottles cost £1 each. Other overheads would be mixing £590, liquidising £420, bottling £380.

Required:

Calculate the cost of manufacturing one bottle of antidote.

(Answer in Appendix 3)

References Here's how a US lecturer has explained the topic:
http://basrv.mgt.ncu.edu.tw/teacher_1/1

> Now look at this book's dedicated website at **www.pearsoned.co.uk/black** and work through the various additional exercises for this chapter.

Chapter 15

Break-even and cost–volume–profit analysis

When you have read this chapter you will be able to:

➤ Prepare and interpret a break-even chart

➤ Prepare and interpret a profit/volume chart

15.1 Introduction

This chapter explores ways of using the information generated from cost behaviour analysis in visual ways. We learn to produce charts which enable management to see at a glance such information as the profit or loss at any specific trading level, the break-even point, the activity needed to reach a target profit, and so on.

15.2 Break-even charts

In Chapter 12 we looked at cost behaviour. Try Activity 15.1 to see how much you remember.

Activity 15.1

Here are two charts which show varying cost behaviour. Each has costs and revenue on the vertical axis and output on the horizontal axis. Which graph shows:

a Fixed costs

b Variable costs?

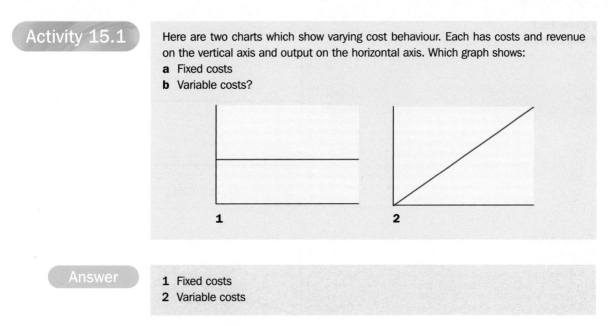

1   2

Answer

1 Fixed costs
2 Variable costs

15.2.1 A combination of graphs

The **break-even chart** is in fact a combination of three graphs:

● Fixed costs

● Total costs (that is, fixed *and* variable costs at each level of activity)

● Sales revenue.

Remember that any semi-fixed costs have to be split between fixed and variable when analysing cost data.

The break-even chart will, amongst other things, indicate approximate profit or loss at different levels of activity: it is based on a mixture of known and forecast information, and so gives a general idea of likely performance rather than an absolutely accurate picture.

Let's look at an example. Berwick plc, which makes one product, has forecast the following data:

Output level (units)	1,000	2,000	3,000	4,000	5,000
Sales (£)	1,200	2,400	3,600	4,800	6,000
Variable costs (£)	400	800	1,200	1,600	2,000
Fixed costs (£)	2,000	2,000	2,000	2,000	2,000

If we were producing separate graphs which plot fixed costs, total costs and revenue, they would look like Figures 15.1 to 15.3.

Figure 15.1
Fixed costs

Figure 15.2
Total costs

Figure 15.3
Total sales revenue

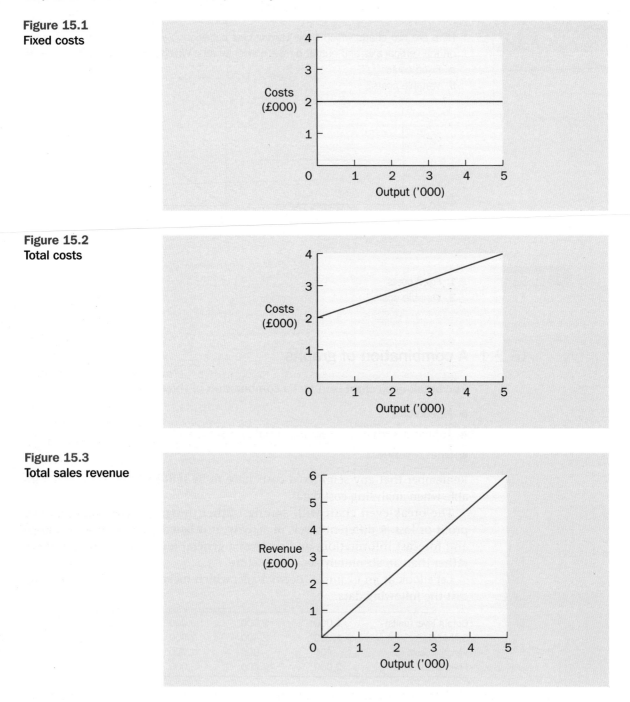

The break-even chart combines all three graphs, as shown in Figure 15.4:

Figure 15.4
Break-even chart

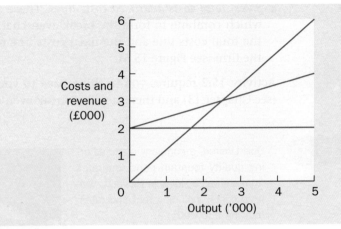

15.2.2 Interpreting the chart

The various elements of the break-even chart are as follows:

- *Break-even point.* This is where the sales line meets the total costs line, in other words, where sales revenue exactly matches total costs and neither a profit nor a loss is made. We can determine the level of sales in units needed to break even by taking a line from the break-even point down to the x-axis. (You could also refer back to Chapter 13 to remind yourself of the formulae that can be used to calculate break-even using the contribution per unit).

- *Profit/loss areas.* Losses are incurred until the break-even point is reached. After this, profit begins to be made. The profit becomes greater as more sales are made. Managers can see at a glance the likely profit or loss at any level of activity.

- *Margin of safety.* This is the distance between the break-even point and the budgeted maximum sales activity. Sales can fall short of expectations by up to (but not exceeding) the margin of safety and the firm will still make a profit.

Figure 15.5
Break-even chart

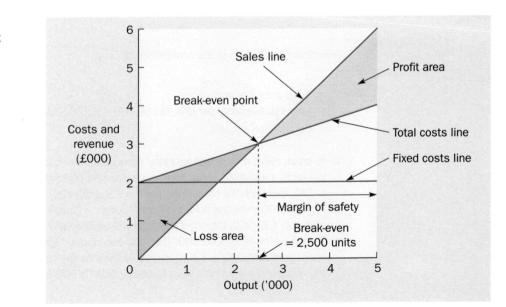

- *Sales, total costs and fixed costs lines.* These are the three separate graphs which combine to form the break-even chart. Note that the area between the total costs line and the fixed costs line represents the *variable* costs of the firm (see Figure 15.5).

Activity 15.2 requires you to think back to your studies of marginal costing (see Chapter 13) and then prepare a break-even chart.

Activity 15.2

Quill Limited, a company manufacturing quality fountain pens, operates from a small building in Newport, with fixed costs, including rent and rates, totalling £30,000 p.a.

During 2004 it expects to produce 4,000 pens, to retail at £50 each. Total costs (including fixed costs) at this level of production would be £150,000.

a Calculate the number of pens the company must sell in order to break even (that is, make neither a profit nor a loss).

b Calculate the company's likely profit or loss if it manages to sell only 3,200 pens.

c How many pens would it have to sell to make a profit of £40,000?

d The company is considering an additional special order from a local company, Global Gherkins plc, for 6,000 pens engraved with that company's logo. It is prepared to pay only £35 for each pen. The cost of engraving each pen is estimated at £2. No additional machinery or buildings would be needed to fulfil the order. Should Quill Limited accept the order?

e Show the information (without the special order from Global Gherkins plc) in the form of a break-even chart. Read off the profit or loss at a sales level of 1,000 pens.

Answer

Preliminary calculation of the contribution per unit:

	£
Sales price per unit	50
Less Variable costs per unit, (£150,000 – £30,000)/4,000	30
Contribution per unit	20

a To break even, it must sell as many pens as are needed for the total contribution to exactly equal fixed costs. Fixed costs are £30,000 and the contribution per unit is £20, therefore the break-even point is £30,000/£20 = **1,500 pens.**

b If only 3,200 pens are sold, total contribution = 3,200 × £20 = £64,000. Fixed costs are £30,000, therefore the profit will be £64,000 – £30,000 = **£34,000.**

c To make a profit of £40,000, the total contribution (profit + fixed costs) would need to be £40,000 + £30,000 = £70,000. As the contribution per unit is £20, the number of pens which need to be sold is £70,000/£20 = **3,500.**

d The decision whether or not to accept the additional special order is based on whether the order will make a positive contribution. The contribution per unit will be as follows:

	£
Sales price per unit	35
Less Variable costs per unit (£30 + £2)	32
Contribution per unit	3

As the order is for 6,000 pens, the additional positive contribution will be 6,000 × £3 = £18,000, therefore **Quill Limited should accept the order.**

e Break-even chart

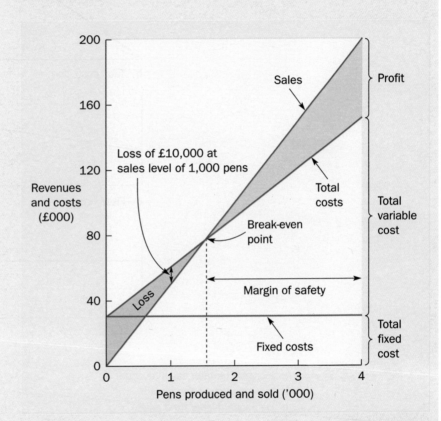

Note: The *margin of safety* indicates the number of units between the break-even point (1,500 pens) and the maximum output (4,000 pens). This informs management how much leeway they have if costs rise and the break-even point starts to 'travel' to the right along the total cost line. Obviously, if the break-even point is reached only on or after the 4,000-pen output line, no profit will be made unless the management take action to reduce costs, increase output or increase the selling price.

15.2.3 Changes in costs and revenue

Clearly, if costs and revenue change, the position of the lines will change, as will the break-even point and the profit/loss areas.

Activity 15.3

In each of the charts below, a change in the position of the lines is indicated. Assuming no other changes, state the effect the movement would have on profits.

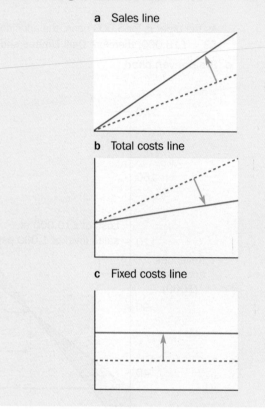

a Sales line

b Total costs line

c Fixed costs line

Answer

a Increase (greater sales revenue)
b Increase (lower total costs)
c Decrease (higher fixed costs)

15.2.4 Limitations of break-even charts

Although break-even charts have the advantage of providing a visual picture of a firm's predicted performance, they do have limitations, including the following:

● They are useful only in the short run where the assumptions hold true.

● The split between fixed and variable costs may not be clear-cut.

● Fixed costs may in fact change over time, so the line may need to rise in steps; for example, further factory space may have to be rented if sales output doubles.

- In reality, the sales line may not be linear, as discounts may be given to encourage higher sales.
- Variable costs may fall per unit, with higher production due to efficiency savings, bulk purchasing discounts and so on.

15.3 Profit/volume chart

A **profit/volume chart** (p/v chart) is a simplified version of the break-even chart, showing only the likely profit or loss at any given level of sales volume. It looks rather different because the horizontal axis splits the vertical axis into 'profit' and 'loss' sections, as shown in Figure 15.6 (using data from Berwick plc used earlier):

Figure 15.6
Profit/volume chart axes

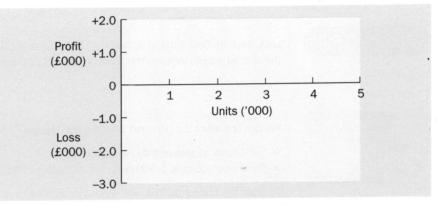

Only one line is plotted, which represents the profit or loss at each level of sales. The distance between this line and the horizontal axis represents either the total loss (below the line) or total profit (above the line). The point where the lines cross is the break-even point. To draw the line, any two coordinates can be plotted, for example:

- The fixed costs at zero activity
- The break-even point
- Total costs at maximum activity.

The chart would then appear as shown in Figure 15.7.

Figure 15.7
Profit/volume chart

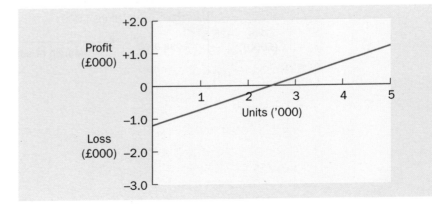

The various elements of a profit/volume chart are shown in Figure 15.8.

**Figure 15.8
Elements of a
profit/volume chart**

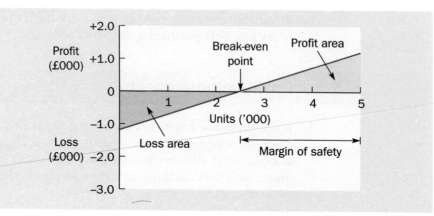

Activity 15.4

Look back at Quill Limited in Activity 15.2. Construct a profit/volume chart (without the special order). Indicate the profit or loss if 3,000 pens are sold.

Answer

We can construct the p/v chart with two coordinates:

● Fixed costs at zero activity are £30,000
● Break-even point is 1,500 pens (as calculated in Activity 15.2).

To draw the horizontal axis, we know that maximum activity is 4,000 pens. For the vertical axis, maximum loss if zero activity = fixed costs of £30,000, and maximum profit at maximum activity would be total contribution less fixed costs [(4,000 × £20) − £30,000] = £50,000. The chart is shown below.

Profit/volume chart

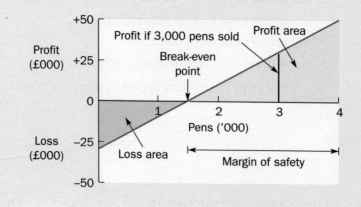

15.4 Summary

	Break-even charts	Profit/volume charts
y-axis (vertical)	Costs and revenue	Profits/losses
x-axis (horizontal)	Output	Output
Lines plotted	Sales, total costs, fixed costs	Profit/loss at all activity levels
Information available	Break-even point, costs and revenue at all activity levels, margin of safety, profit/loss areas	Break-even point, margin of safety, profit/loss areas
Advantages	More information than profit/volume chart	Simplicity – how much profit or loss at a specific activity level?
Disadvantages	Oversimplified information may lead to poor decisions	Limited information compared with break-even chart

15.5 Glossary

Break-even chart   A graphical representation of the profits, losses, sales revenues and costs at any level of activity.

Profit/volume chart   A graphical representation of profit or loss at any level of activity.

? Self-check questions

1   Which of the following cannot be seen on a break-even chart?
   a   Unsold stock
   b   Fixed costs
   c   Variable costs
   d   Sales revenue

2   A break-even chart shows maximum unit sales at 300 at £500 each, maximum profit of £60,000, a break-even point of 100 units and a loss of £30,000 if no units are sold. What is the total of fixed costs?
   a   £150,000
   b   £90,000
   c   £30,000
   d   £60,000

3   Using the information given in question 2, what is the margin of safety?
   a   600 units
   b   100 units
   c   300 units
   d   200 units

4 Using the information given in question 2, what profit or loss would be earned if 150 units are sold?

  a £75,000 profit

  b £15,000 profit

  c £30,000 profit

  d £15,000 loss

5 Which one of the following is *not* a limitation of a break-even chart?

  a Fixed costs may change over time, due, for example, to the need to rent additional premises as production increases

  b The split between fixed and variable costs may not be clear-cut

  c They are only useful in the short run when assumptions hold true

  d The break-even point cannot be indicated on it

6 In a profit/volume chart, which one of the following is *not* a coordinate which could be plotted?

  a Fixed costs at zero activity

  b The break-even point

  c Profit at maximum activity

  d Variable costs at maximum activity

7 A company has maximum sales activity of 4,000 units, each with a contribution of £8. Its profit/volume chart shows a break-even point of 1,500 units and a maximum profit of £20,000. What are the total fixed costs of the company?

  a £12,000

  b £32,000

  c £20,000

  d £52,000

8 Using the information in question 7 above, how much profit would be made if 3,000 units are sold?

  a £24,000

  b £12,000

  c £15,000

  d £20,000

9 Using the information in question 7 above, what is the margin of safety for the company?

  a 4,000 units

  b 1,500 units

  c 2,500 units

  d 5,500 units

10 If the contribution per unit increases, the break-even point on a profit/volume chart will:

  a Move to the right

  b Be unchanged

  c Move to the left

  d Move downwards

(Answers in Appendix 1)

(Answers in Appendix 2)

Question 15.1   Indicate the following information on the proforma break-even chart below.

- The break-even point
- The 'loss' area
- The margin of safety
- Fixed costs
- Variable costs
- Sales
- The 'profit' area

Question 15.2   From the following information produce a break-even chart for Basil Limited:

Maximum sales and production (units)	10,000
Fixed costs (£)	18,000
Sales price per unit (£)	6
Variable cost per unit (£)	1.50

From the chart, answer the following questions:

a What is the break-even point in units?
b How much profit or loss is made if 6,000 units are sold?
c What is the margin of safety in units?
d How many units must be sold for Basil Ltd to make a profit of £4,500?

Question 15.3   From the following information, prepare a profit/volume chart, and indicate the profit or loss if 6,000 units are sold:

Maximum sales	10,000 units
Fixed costs	£60,000
Contribution per unit	£15

Case study

Chiquita's chart

Chiquita, the finance director of Machiq Limited (see previous case studies), had, prior to her mysterious disappearance, produced a break-even chart for the new product the company was considering making. The information she used was as follows:

Selling price per bottle of vanishing potion	£15
Variable costs per bottle	£6
Fixed costs relating to the bottling division	£20,000

Maximum production was set at 15,000 bottles.

Required:

a Prepare a break-even chart based on the above information.

b Indicate on the chart the break-even point and the areas of profit and loss.

c Indicate on the chart the profit or loss if 12,000 bottles were sold.

(Answers in Appendix 3)

References   Here's a Canadian lecturer's way of explaining the subject:
www.acad.humberc.on.ca/~martinov/CHAPTER5.html#Intro

Now look at this book's dedicated website at **www.pearsoned.co.uk/black** and work through the various additional exercises for this chapter.

Chapter 16

Budgeting

Objectives When you have read this chapter you will be able to:

➤ Understand the uses and benefits of budgeting

➤ Understand the meaning and significance of limiting factors

➤ Appreciate the different types of budgets and their use in the planning process

16.1 Introduction

You are getting near to the end of this accounting book. You have been working hard and you need a break. An advert in a travel agency tells you that you could fly to the Seychelles next week for a seven-day holiday for only £699. You phone to book the tickets and give your credit card details. The phone goes on hold and you are listening to Vivaldi for what seems like half an hour. Then the travel agent comes back on the line to say that you haven't got enough credit available to book the tickets, and politely ends the call. You know that you are up to your bank overdraft limit, and are in debt to friends and family and cannot ask them for any further loans. Dreams of the Seychelles are replaced by the harsh reality that you can just scrape together the cost of a daytrip to Brighton or Blackpool. If only you had budgeted . . . Businesses need to budget as well – we have already looked at one aspect of this, the cash flow forecast (see Chapter 9), and in this chapter we look at the entire budgeting process.

16.2 Reasons for budgeting

Good management involves reviewing not only past and current performance but also the evaluation of what might happen to the business in the future. Think about various types of changes which might have an impact on the future of a business.

Activity 16.1

Which of the following events would be likely to have a significant impact on the future development of a business?

a Introduction of new technology to speed up manufacture

b Introduction of new products

c Increased competition in the sector

d Changes in consumer buying patterns

Answer

All of the above.

16.3 Long- and short-term planning

Organisations will tend to have two types of plan: long-term and short-term:

● **Long-term plans** (covering at least 5 years) set out the strategic objectives of the firm. They consider the general growth of the market, competition in the period, anticipated profit levels, strategic acquisitions and general economic factors such as trends in interest rates.

● **Short-term plans** (usually covering the next 12 months) detail the financial and organisational objectives compatible with the achievement of the long-term plan. This will be drawn up in far greater detail than the long-term plan and is referred to as **'the budget'**.

Let's consider a detailed definition of a budget:

A budget is a quantitative statement, for a defined period of time, prepared and agreed in advance, showing planned revenues, costs, assets, liabilities and cash flows.[1]

The budget is a plan for action and can be used to control and plan the organisation's activities. It can be used to delegate responsibility to departments and allow senior management to concentrate on investigating major deviations from the plan. This is called 'management by exception' and enables managers to concentrate on those aspects of the business which have not performed as planned (having performed either better or worse). At the end of the budget period, the plan is evaluated and divisional performance appraised against the agreed objectives and targets.

---

[1] CIMA (2000) *Official Terminology*. London: CIMA.

It should be understood that a firm may have many different plans in force at the same time, for example:

- Plans to improve the quality of the product or service
- Plans to improve employee relations
- Plans to increase market share
- Plans to maximise the benefits of research and development

and so on.

The nature of each plan will largely depend on the subject matter – plans relating to product design will be in technical rather than monetary terms; plans to improve employee welfare will be in the language of human relations. The financial budget will be in monetary terms, and this is what we concentrate on in this chapter.

16.4 Limiting factors

For all businesses, **limiting factors** will cause constraints in many areas, such as the availability of raw materials or the capacity of machinery. Where there is more than one constraint, the **key factor** is the most important limiting factor at any one time, and is the one which management needs to resolve before tackling the next one to emerge.

Activity 16.2

Match the limiting factors on the left to the related business activity on the right:

a	Shortage of skilled researchers	1	Exporting
b	Lack of overseas representatives	2	Product development
c	Worn-out machinery	3	Increasing production

Answer

a 2, b 1, c 3

16.5 The budget process

In small businesses, the budgeting process may be very informal, with the owner having a rough idea of where the business is going and then negotiating an annual overdraft limit with the bank manager to avoid a situation where cheques might be returned unpaid.

For larger firms, the budgeting process is much more formal and will involve many employees, only a handful of whom might be accountants. Figure 16.1 shows a flowchart of a typical budgeting process in a large company.

Figure 16.1
Typical budgeting process in a large company

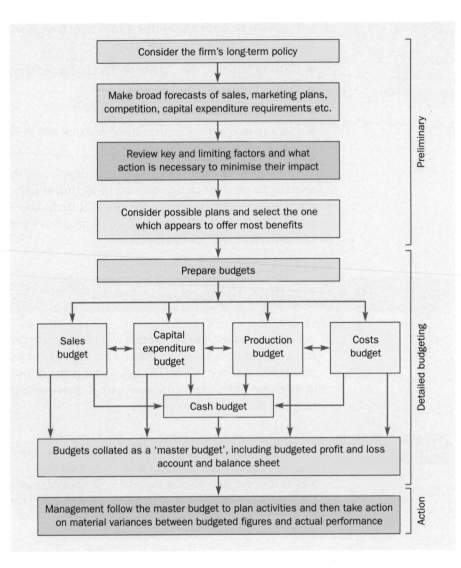

16.6   Preparing a budget

If sales are the limiting factor then budgets will be prepared by working from the sales budget. If the firm can estimate how many units of each product it can sell month by month then it can work back from this figure to estimate production and stock levels. If more is produced than can be sold, stocks will increase, but if sales exceed production, stock declines. Once the monthly production is estimated, further estimations can be made of plant requirements, materials, labour and overheads.

If productive capacity is the limiting factor, the sales budget will be determined by output, as will the materials and labour budgets.

Activity 16.3

Preparing a sales budget

Kumquat plc has four products: Limbards, Mintons, Nestrals and Obloids. Sales (the limiting factor) in January are expected to total 8,000 units, in the ratio 5:4:3:2 respectively. Sales in each month from February to April are expected to grow at 5% per month for each product, except Mintons which will grow by only 3% per month.

Set out in tabular form the forecast sales in units for each product in each of the four months, January to April. Work to the nearest whole number.

Answer

Sales budget

	January (units)	February (units)	March (units)	April (units)
Limbards	2,857	3,000	3,150	3,308
Mintons	2,286	2,355	2,426	2,499
Nestrals	1,714	1,800	1,890	1,985
Obloids	1,143	1,200	1,260	1,323
	8,000	8,355	8,726	9,115

Workings:

	January (units)	February (units)	March (units)	April (units)
Limbards	(5/14 × 8,000) 2,857	(Jan +5%) 3,000	(Feb +5%) 3,150	(Mar +5%) 3,308
Mintons	(4/14 × 8,000) 2,286	(Jan +3%) 2,355	(Feb +3%) 2,426	(Mar +3%) 2,499
Nestrals	(3/14 × 8,000) 1,714	(Jan +5%) 1,800	(Feb +5%) 1,890	(Mar +5%) 1,985
Obloids	(2/14 × 8,000) 1,143	(Jan +5%) 1,200	(Feb +5%) 1,260	(Mar +5%) 1,323
	8,000	8,355	8,726	9,115

Activity 16.4

Preparing a materials purchases budget

Kumquat plc (see Activity 16.3) uses two basic raw materials – Dructose and Zitamint – to make its products. Ingredients are mixed in the following quantities to make one unit of each product:

	Dructose kg	Zitamint kg
Limbards	2	2
Mintons	2	1
Nestrals	3	1
Obloids	1	1

Sales in January are forecast as follows:

	Units
Limbards	2,857
Mintons	2,286
Nestrals	1,714
Obloids	1,143

▶

Activity 16.4
continued

Opening stocks of each raw material at 1 January are Dructose 5,000 kg, Zitamint 4,000 kg. Losses by evaporation in a month are equivalent to 10% of opening stock levels. Each kilogram of Dructose costs £6 and each kilogram of Zitamint costs £4.

Show a materials purchase budget for January only, on the assumption that opening and closing stock levels are to be identical, and that there were no opening stocks of completed units at 1 January.

Answer

Materials purchases budget

January	Sales/Materials	Dructose	Sales/Materials	Zitamint
Limbards	2,857 × 2	5,714	2,857 × 2	5,714
Mintons	2,286 × 2	4,572	2,286 × 1	2,286
Nestrals	1,714 × 3	5,142	1,714 × 1	1,714
Obloids	1,143 × 1	1,143	1,143 × 1	1,143
Total (kg)		16,571		10,857
Opening Stock	5,000		4,000	
Less evaporation (10%)	(500)	4,500	(400)	3,600
		12,071		7,257
Closing stock level (same as opening stock)		5,000		4,000
Materials to be purchased (kg)		17,071		11,257
Total materials cost (£)	@ £6	102,426	@ £4	45,028

16.7 The cash budget

We saw in Chapter 9 how important cash flow statements are when analysing a firm's performance. These are based on past activity, usually summarising inflows and outflows of the previous accounting year. In the same chapter we saw how cash flow forecasts are prepared. Look back at page 173 to remind yourself. These forecasts become part of the budgeting documentation and are vital for the planning process, in particular to:

● Ensure that sufficient cash is available when needed

● Reveal any expected cash shortage so that a loan, overdraft or other funding can be negotiated in good time

● Identify areas where payments can be delayed or inflows brought in earlier (for example, by offering cash discounts) to help cash flow

● Reveal cash surpluses which can be invested or utilised within the firm.

Activity 16.5

Preparing information for a cash budget

Kumquat plc (see Activities 16.3 and 16.4) allows its customers to pay in the month following sale, but pays its own creditors two months after purchase. Relevant details for January are as follows:

	January	Sales price per unit
		£
Forecast sales	_units_	
Limbards	2,857	36
Mintons	2,286	24
Nestrals	1,714	40
Obloids	1,143	15
Forecast purchases	£	
Dructose	102,426	
Zitamint	45,028	

What data relating to cash receipts or payments will appear in Kumquat plc's cash budget related to the above information?

Answer

Cash receipts from debtors will appear in February's cash budget (that is, one month after the sale is made), as follows:

Limbards	2,857 × 36 =	102,852
Mintons	2,286 × 24 =	54,864
Nestrals	1,714 × 40 =	68,560
Obloids	1,143 × 15 =	17,145
Total		243,421

Cash payments to creditors totalling £147,454 (102,426 + 45,028) will appear in March's cash budget (that is, two months after the purchase is made).

16.8 Master budgets

When all the individual budgets have been completed, a **master budget** can be prepared. This is a compilation of the agreed subsidiary budgets (sales, production, and so on) but also includes a set of forecast 'final' accounts (profit and loss account, balance sheet and cash flow statement) prepared for the full budget period. Usual accounting adjustments (accruals, prepayments, depreciation and so forth) are applied in the preparation of the profit and loss account and balance sheet, but of course it is all based on future _forecast information_ rather than _actual historic data_. The master budget, as its name implies, acts as the guiding framework for the firm's future development.

16.9 Summary

The key features of the budgeting process are:

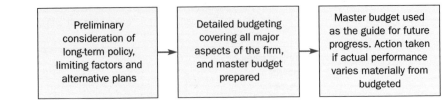

Preliminary consideration of long-term policy, limiting factors and alternative plans	Detailed budgeting covering all major aspects of the firm, and master budget prepared	Master budget used as the guide for future progress. Action taken if actual performance varies materially from budgeted

16.10 Glossary

Budget A quantitative statement, for a defined period of time, prepared and agreed in advance, showing planned revenues, costs, assets, liabilities and cash flows.

Key factor The most pressing limiting factor at any one time.

Limiting factor Constraints on the growth of the firm.

Long-term plans Strategic objectives of the firm over at least the next 5 years.

Master budget A compilation of the agreed subsidiary budgets (sales, production and so on) including a set of forecast 'final' accounts (profit and loss account, balance sheet and cash flow statement) prepared for the full budget period.

Short-term plans Financial and organisational objectives over the next 12 months compatible with the long-term plan.

? Self-check questions

1 A plan is considered to be long-term if it covers a period of at least:
   a 5 years
   b 10 years
   c 2 years
   d 20 years

2 A short-term plan is likely to cover the next:
   a 2 weeks
   b 6 months
   c 12 months
   d 1 month

3 Management by exception refers to:
   a Management absences from work
   b The investigation of major deviations from forecasts
   c Exceptional management skills
   d The preparation of the master budget

4 Which one of the following will be written mainly in financial terms?
   a Plans for the product design
   b Workforce requirements
   c Planned changes to the way products will be marketed
   d Bank borrowing requirements

5 Which one of the following would not be regarded as a limiting factor for a firm?
   a The lack of ability of the managing director
   b An unexpected order from an established customer
   c A shortage of raw materials
   d Insufficient power supplies to run machinery

6 A master budget is:
   a Last year's budget to be used as the basis for this year's
   b This year's actual results to be compared with the forecast results
   c Only the cash budget, as that is the most important budget
   d A compilation of the agreed subsidiary budgets and forecast profit and loss account and balance sheet

7 Ali plc has three products: K, L and M. Sales (the limiting factor) in January are expected to total 5,000 units, in the ratio 5:4:1 respectively. Sales in each month from February to March are expected to grow at 10% per month for each product. What will be the sales of product L in March?
   a 2,420
   b 2,400
   c 6,050
   d 6,620

8 Using the information in question 7 above, if actual sales for product K in March are 2,904, what is the percentage variance from the forecast sales for that month?
   a −4%
   b +20
   c +6
   d −25%

9 A company is preparing a cash flow forecast. In January it forecasts its net cash inflow as £90,000, but in February it forecasts a net cash outflow of £75,000. If it starts on 1 January with a bank overdraft of £50,000, what will be its forecast bank balance on 28 February?
   a £115,000 (overdrawn) bank balance
   b £35,000 (positive) bank balance
   c £35,000 (overdrawn) bank balance
   d £115,000 (positive) bank balance

10 A company is producing its forecast profit and loss account. Which one of the following will not be taken into account when producing the information?
   a Accruals
   b Prepayments
   c Cash flow
   d Depreciation

(Answers in Appendix 1)

? Self-study questions

(Answers in Appendix 2)

Question 16.1 A manufacturing company makes a single product. The sales forecast for September is 11,800 units. Each unit uses 10 kg of material A and 6 kg of material B. Material A costs £6.50 per kg and B costs £9 per kg.

The anticipated stock levels at the beginning and end of September are:

	1 September	30 September
Finished products	2,800 units	3,600 units
Unused material A	700 kg	500 kg
Unused material B	400 kg	900 kg

Produce the following budget figures for the month of September:
a Production of finished units
b Materials usage of A and B in kg
c Materials purchases of A and B in kg and £.

Question 16.2 When preparing a budget, an organisation must first consider its limiting factors and key factor. Explain what you understand by the terms 'limiting factor' and 'key factor' and identify three constraints that could be a limiting factor in an organisation.

Question 16.3 Talbot plc manufactures car alarms, and its trading results for the year ended 31 October 2005 are as follows:

	£000	£000
Sales (800,000 alarms)		7,200
Costs:		
Materials: direct, variable	1,600	
Labour: direct, variable	960	
Labour: indirect, fixed	280	
Other production overheads: variable	400	
Other production overheads: fixed	640	
Selling overheads: variable	480	
Selling overheads: fixed	360	
Distribution overheads: variable	280	
Distribution overheads: fixed	120	
Administration overheads: fixed	600	
		(5,720)
Net profit for the year		1,480

Talbot Ltd is planning next year's activity and its forecasts for the year ended 31 October 2006 are as follows:

1 A reduction in selling price per car alarm to £8 per alarm is expected to increase sales volume by 50%.
2 Materials costs per unit will remain unchanged, but 5% quantity discount will be obtained.
3 Hourly direct wage rates will increase by 10%, but labour efficiency will be unchanged.
4 Variable selling overheads will increase in total in line with the increase in sales revenue.

5 Variable production and distribution overheads will increase in line with the 50% increase in sales volume.
6 All fixed costs will increase by 25%.

    a Prepare a budgeted profit statement for the year to 31 October 2006 showing total sales and marginal costs for the year and also contribution and net profit per unit.

    b Calculate the break-even point for the two years and explain why the break-even point has changed. Comment on the margin of safety in both years.

    c Calculate the sales volume required (using the new selling price) to achieve the same profit in 2006 as in 2005.

    d A director comments that 'with these figures, all we have to do to work out our budgeted profit is to multiply the net profit per unit by the units we want to sell'. Why is this statement incorrect?

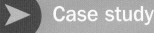

Case study

Reappearance, followed by glowing and floating . . .

The directors of Machiq Limited (see previous case studies) staged a miraculous reappearance after vanishing at a product test organised by their arch business rival, Esmeralda (a.k.a. Mrs Eadale). Antidote had been sprayed liberally around the company's headquarters, and this had had the desired effect of neutralising the vanishing potion. Esmeralda also returned and, as an act of repentance, decided immediately to give up the business world and devote herself to charitable work.

Realising that the business had (almost literally) been left floating in thin air, the three directors, Marvin, Chiquita and Trixie, decided to plan ahead. In particular, they wanted to consider reopening a manufacturing division to make two products: Glow Gel and Floating Juice, both to be sold in 1-kg tubs.

They decided to produce a budget for the year ending 30 June 2006 relating to these two products. The following information is available:

- Both products use the same raw materials, Luminos and Schlepp. One kilo of Glow Gel uses 6 litres of Luminos and 8 litres of Schlepp. One kilo of Floating Juice uses 10 litres of Luminos and 4 litres of Schlepp.
- Forecast sales are 16,000 kg of Glow Gel and 12,000 kg of Floating Juice.
- The company plans to hold stocks of 1,200 kg of Glow Gel and 800 kg of Floating Juice on 30 June 2006, and at the same date forecasts stocks of raw materials as 15,200 litres of Luminos and 9,200 litres of Schlepp.
- Due to environmental factors beyond the company's control, it is forecast that there will be losses of items in store as follows:

Glow Gel	100 kg
Floating Juice	200 kg
Luminos	1,000 litres
Schlepp	400 litres

- The cost price of one litre of Luminos is £4, and one litre of Schlepp costs £2.50.

Required:
Prepare a materials purchase budget for the two products for the year to 30 June 2006.

(Answer in Appendix 3)

References

Free business planning software is sometimes available to students. Ask at your local bank's enquiries desk.

For details of shareware packages for budgeting and business planning: **planmagic.com**

> **Now look at this book's dedicated website at www.pearsoned.co.uk/black and work through the various additional exercises for this chapter.**

Chapter 17

Investment appraisal

Objectives   When you have read this chapter you will be able to:

➤ Understand the term 'investment appraisal'

➤ Understand the meaning of the 'time value of money'

➤ Evaluate alternative projects using a variety of investment appraisal techniques, including net present value, internal rate of return and payback methods

➤ Appreciate the advantages and disadvantages of each method

17.1   Introduction

Businesses often have to make choices between different projects in which to invest. Many of these are for the long term, and represent significant strategic decisions. They might result in the future success or failure of the company. At their simplest, choices of investment may be made on subjective criteria. For example, if a company's car fleet manager knows how many cars are needed within a specific price range, the decision will probably be taken on the basis of the different build quality, specification and fuel consumptions of various car models. Once investment decisions become more complex, various techniques would be needed to assess them. What if the car fleet manager is faced with a bewildering choice of payment methods over differing time periods?

When deciding whether to commit finances to a long-term investment, the firm's management must consider the following:

● How costs, revenues and interest rates are likely to change over time.

● How technology is likely to develop.

● What risks the firm is prepared to take.

● What are the alternative opportunities for investment.

It is wrong to assume that a company will always choose to invest in the cheapest option available to it. For example, cheaper machinery may be of poorer quality and may demand greater maintenance than more expensive equivalents. The process of evaluating capital projects and of estimating costs and revenues associated with them is known as **investment appraisal**.

17.2   Present values and future values

One of the basic concepts of investment appraisal is that of the *time value of money*, which, in simple terms, tells us that money received at a future date is worth less than the same amount of money received today. Conversely, money received today is worth more than the same amount of money receivable at a future date. The key reason for this is that money received today can be invested to accumulate interest, so that, for example, if £100 is invested for a year at 10% compound interest per annum, it will have grown to £110 at the end of the first year [£100 + (10% × £100)], £121 at the end of the second year [£110 + (10% × £110)] and so on.

17.2.1 From present values to future values

When considering investment appraisal techniques, the initial £100 investment (from the previous example) would be referred to as a **present value**, whereas the amounts as increased by interest (£110 and £121) are referred to as **future values**. This change is shown diagrammatically in Figure 17.1.

**Figure 17.1
From present value to future value**

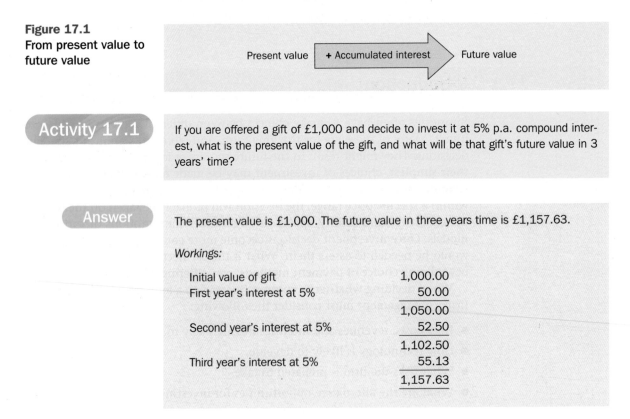

Present value | + Accumulated interest | Future value

Activity 17.1

If you are offered a gift of £1,000 and decide to invest it at 5% p.a. compound interest, what is the present value of the gift, and what will be that gift's future value in 3 years' time?

Answer

The present value is £1,000. The future value in three years time is £1,157.63.

Workings:

Initial value of gift	1,000.00
First year's interest at 5%	50.00
	1,050.00
Second year's interest at 5%	52.50
	1,102.50
Third year's interest at 5%	55.13
	1,157.63

17.2.2 From future values to present values

We have seen how a present value of £100 invested at an interest rate of 10% p.a. has a future value of £110 in one year's time and £121 in two years' time. With this information, we can also say that if interest rates are 10% p.a., an investor can regard £110 receivable in one year's time as being equivalent to £100 now, or £121 receivable in two years' time as being equivalent to £100 now. This process of converting a future money value into a present value equivalent is referred to as **discounting**. It is shown diagrammatically in Figure 17.2.

Figure 17.2
From future value to present value

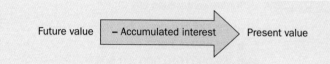

To convert future values into present values, individual calculations could be made of accumulated interest which could then be deducted from the 'future' amounts. However, this could be very complicated when dealing with many different interest rates over many different periods. To simplify the process, tables can be used that provide **discount factors**. These are decimals which, when applied to future values, convert them into present values. A discount factor table is shown in Figure 17.3.

Figure 17.3
Discount factors at various interest rates and at the end of various time periods

Years	Interest rates						
	4%	5%	6%	7%	8%	9%	10%
1	0.961	0.952	0.943	0.935	0.926	0.917	0.909
2	0.925	0.907	0.890	0.873	0.857	0.842	0.826
3	0.889	0.864	0.840	0.816	0.794	0.772	0.751
4	0.855	0.823	0.792	0.763	0.735	0.708	0.683
5	0.822	0.784	0.747	0.713	0.681	0.650	0.621
6	0.790	0.746	0.705	0.666	0.630	0.596	0.564
7	0.760	0.711	0.665	0.623	0.583	0.547	0.513
8	0.731	0.677	0.627	0.582	0.540	0.502	0.467
9	0.703	0.645	0.592	0.544	0.500	0.460	0.424
10	0.676	0.614	0.588	0.508	0.463	0.422	0.386
11	0.650	0.585	0.527	0.475	0.429	0.388	0.350
12	0.625	0.557	0.497	0.444	0.397	0.356	0.319
13	0.601	0.530	0.469	0.415	0.368	0.326	0.290
14	0.577	0.505	0.442	0.388	0.340	0.299	0.263
15	0.555	0.481	0.417	0.362	0.315	0.275	0.239

Activity 17.2

Using the discount factor table, convert the following future values into present values:

a £5,000 receivable in 11 years' time (8% interest rate)
b £3,000 receivable in 4 years' time (5% interest rate)
c £10,000 receivable in 1 year's time (10% interest rate)
d £1,000 receivable in 2 years' time (7% interest rate)

Answer

The present values are:

a £2,145 (£5,000 × 0.429)
b £2,469 (£3,000 × 0.823)
c £9,090 (£10,000 × 0.909)
d £873 (£1,000 × 0.873)

Note that, in all cases, the present value is a lower amount than the future value, and the greater the interest rate and the longer the time period, the smaller the present value will be.

17.3 Investment appraisal using discounting techniques

17.3.1 Discounted cash flow (DCF)

When a firm has a choice of projects in which to invest, a thorough evaluation would include not only the initial cost of each alternative but also the future cash flows that they will generate over their lives. For example, assume a company has a choice between two machines, A and B, each costing £10,000. Each machine has an estimated life of 3 years with no scrap value. Machine A is expected to generate yearly earnings of £100, £200 and £1,000, whereas machine B has estimated yearly earnings of £600, £500 and £100. If the machines are to be compared in terms of their earning power, it is not sufficient simply to add the total earnings (A = £1,300, B = £1,200), since we know that money received in the future is worth less than the same amount of money received now. In order to find each machine's comparative value, the income flow must be converted into *present value* terms, a process known as 'discounting the cash flow'. Using the discount factor table in Figure 17.3, and assuming an interest rate of 8%, the **discounted cash flow (DCF)** calculations can be set out as follows:

Year	Machine A		Machine B	
	Future value × Discount factor	Present value	Future value × Discount factor	Present value
1	£100 × 0.926	92.60	£600 × 0.926	555.60
2	£200 × 0.857	171.40	£500 × 0.857	428.50
3	£1,000 × 0.794	794.00	£100 × 0.794	79.40
Discounted cash inflow		1058.00		1063.50

Did you know?

If managers are comparing projects with different degrees of risk, they might apply a higher discount rate to the riskier project as a way of making a more balanced assessment.

According to the calculations, machine B has a higher discounted cash inflow than machine A. Remember that the forecast undiscounted future cash flows for machine A were £100 higher than for machine B.

Another use for the DCF investment appraisal method arises when a firm is comparing future cash *outflows*. For example, there might be a choice of financing the purchase of two identical lorries, C and D. Lorry C can be bought with an initial deposit of £20,000 followed by two annual payments of £15,000 (total £50,000). Lorry D can be purchased over a slightly longer period, with an initial deposit of £5,000 followed by four annual payments of £12,000 (total £53,000). Interest rates are 6% p.a. Using the discounted cash flow table (Figure 17.3), we can evaluate the two purchase methods, as follows:

Year	Lorry C		Lorry D	
	Future value × *Discount factor*	*Present value*	*Future value ×* *Discount factor*	*Present value*
0	n/a	20,000	n/a	5,000
1	£15,000 × 0.943	14,145	£12,000 × 0.943	11,316
2	£15,000 × 0.890	13,350	£12,000 × 0.890	10,680
3			£12,000 × 0.840	10,080
4			£12,000 × 0.792	9,504
Discounted cash outflow		47,495		46,580

Lorry D shows the *lowest* discounted cash outflow, so it appears that this lorry's method of financing is preferable to that of lorry C. Note that the initial deposits required at the start of the financing period are already 'present' values that do not require discounting. The term 'year 0' is used when describing cash flows that occur at the start of the time period.

Activity 17.3

Using the discounted cash flow table, evaluate two identical projects, E and F, each of which require the payment of an initial deposit of £10,000. Project E is financed by three equal annual instalments of £30,000; project F is financed by two equal annual instalments of £45,000. Assume a 5% p.a. interest rate.

Answer

Year	Project E		Project F	
	Future value × *Discount factor*	*Present value*	*Future value ×* *Discount factor*	*Present value*
0	n/a	10,000	n/a	10,000
1	£30,000 × 0.952	28,560	£45,000 × 0.952	42,840
2	£30,000 × 0.907	27,210	£45,000 × 0.907	40,815
3	£30,000 × 0.864	25,920		
Discounted cash outflow		91,690		93,655

As project E has the lower discounted cash outflow, this would appear to be preferable to project F.

17.3.2 **Net present value (NPV)**

In addition to using the DCF investment appraisal technique to evaluate projects that have *either* cash inflows or cash outflows, there are many situations where there is a mixture of inflows and outflows that have to be considered. For example, a firm might be considering a new project (G) that requires an initial payment of £100,000, followed by a further payment one year later of £50,000. The project is forecast to generate three annual cash inflows of £60,000 each, and at the end of the project (end of year 3) assets related to the project are expected to be sold for £30,000. Assume a 9% p.a. interest rate. To evaluate this project we use the DCF technique seen earlier to convert future cash outflows to present values, but we also factor in the present values of the cash inflows to arrive at the **net present value (NPV)**, as follows (cash outflows are shown in brackets):

Year	Future value × Discount factor	Present value
0	n/a	(100,000)
1	£50,000 × 0.917	(45,850)
	£60,000 × 0.917	55,020
2	£60,000 × 0.842	50,520
3	£60,000 × 0.772	46,320
	£30,000 × 0.772	23,160
NPV		+29,170

The project is recording a *positive* NPV of £29,170 (discounted cash inflows exceed discounted cash outflows). When assessing an investment project, the general rule is that projects with a positive NPV are acceptable, those with negative NPVs are not. Projects with higher NPVs are preferable to those with lower NPVs.

Pause for thought

A quick way of calculating the discounted value where the same future values are receivable (or payable) each year for several years is to add together the individual discount factors for each year and then multiply the 'annual' monetary amount by that one factor. For example, in project G above, we made three separate calculations to establish the present value of £60,000 received each year for three years (£55,020 + £50,520 + £46,320 = £151,860). We would have reached the same result if we had added the three factors (0.917 + 0.842 + 0.772 = 2.531) and multiplied the result by £60,000 (£60,000 × 2.531 = £151,860). Some discount factor tables also show the **cumulative discount factors** for this purpose, for example, the 9% discount factors would be shown as:

Year	Factor	Cumulative factor
1	0.917	0.917
2	0.842	1.759
3	0.772	2.531
:		
:		

Activity 17.4

A firm has the choice of three machines, H, I or J, but it can afford only one. Interest rates are 10% p.a. Machine H costs £10,000; machine I costs £13,000; machine J costs £15,000. Forecast cash inflows are as follows (£):

Year	H	I	J
1	3,000	4,000	5,500
2	4,000	6,000	6,500
3	5,000	7,000	8,200

Calculate the NPV of each machine using the discount factor table (Figure 17.3).

Answer

The NPVs of the three machines can be calculated as follows:

Year	Discount factor	Machine H		Machine I		Machine J	
		Cash flow	Present value	Cash flow	Present value	Cash flow	Present value
0	n/a	(10,000)	(10,000)	(13,000)	(13,000)	(15,000)	(15,000)
1	0.909	3,000	2,727	4,000	3,636	5,500	5,000
2	0.826	4,000	3,304	6,000	4,956	6,500	5,369
3	0.751	5,000	3,755	7,000	5,257	8,200	6,158
NPV			−214		+849		+1,527

Machine H has a negative NPV, so this would be unacceptable. Both of the other machines have a positive NPV, and since machine J's NPV is greater than that of machine I, machine J would be chosen.

17.3.3 Internal rate of return (IRR)

When we found the net present value for machines H, I and J in the previous activity, we used an interest rate – known as the **discount rate** – of 10%. Machine H's NPV was negative but machines I and J's were positive. Another method of comparing alternative projects is to establish the *specific* discount rate that, if applied to the cash flows relating to that project, would reduce the NPV to zero. We call the rate of discount that makes NPV = 0 the **internal rate of return (IRR)**. The IRRs of different projects can easily be compared against each other (the highest being preferred), and also against the firm's average interest rates payable on borrowed capital (the **cost of capital**). Projects that would earn a lower IRR than the cost of capital would be rejected in favour of those that earned an IRR in excess of the cost of capital.

The IRR is found by discounting the net cash flows at different rates – by trial and error – until the NPV is zero (or near to zero).

Activity 17.5

Project K costs £10,000 and has expected net annual cash flows of £3,000 at the end of year 1, £4,000 at the end of year 2 and £4,300 at the end of year 3. By a process of trial and error using interest rates of 5%, 6% and 7%, establish the internal rate of return for the project.

Answer

The IRR is 6%, as shown in the following table:

Year	Net cash flows £	Discount factors (5%)	Present values £	Discount factors (6%)	Present values £	Discount factors (7%)	Present values £
0	(10,000)	n/a	(10,000)	n/a	(10,000)	n/a	(10,000)
1	3,000	0.952	2,856	0.943	2,829	0.935	2,805
2	4,000	0.907	3,628	0.890	3,560	0.873	3,492
3	4,300	0.864	3,715	0.840	3,612	0.816	3,509
NPV			+199		+1		−194

As the NPV at 6% is (almost) zero, this is the IRR for the project.

17.4 Investment appraisal using non-discounting techniques

Methods of investment appraisal that consider the time value of money rely heavily upon the following estimates:

- The life of the project
- The rate of interest which will be appropriate throughout its life
- The level of net cash flows.

Each of these estimates demands an ability to forecast; and the further into the future one goes, the greater is the risk of the forecasts being wrong. Because of this, and the complexities of discounting techniques, many firms still use methods that ignore time values. These are called *non-discounting methods*, and the most common of these is called the 'payback period' method.

17.4.1 Payback period

The **payback period** approach ignores interest rates and time values altogether, and looks solely at how *long* the investment takes to pay for itself (the 'payback period'). Although unsophisticated, it is useful were there is uncertainty about the forecasts – perhaps economic circumstances are unclear – as the investment decision is taken simply on the basis of which project is fastest at repaying its initial investment. Any cash flows occurring after the **payback** is achieved are ignored.

Activity 17.6

A firm has a choice of three projects, L, M and N. Each costs £15,000, and forecast cash flows are as follows:

Year	L	M	N
	£	£	£
0	(15,000)	(15,000)	(15,000)
1	3,000	4,000	2,000
2	4,000	5,000	4,000
3	5,000	6,000	9,000
4	6,000	6,000	7,000
5	10,000	6,000	7,000
6	16,000	6,000	7,000

Calculate each project's payback period. On the basis of this appraisal technique, which project would be recommended?

Answer

The payback periods of each project are as follows:

Project L = 3½ years [3,000 + 4,000 +5,000 + (½ × 6,000) = £15,000]
Project M = 3 years (4,000 + 5,000 + 6,000 = £15,000)
Project N = 3 years (2,000 + 4,000 + 9,000 = £15,000)

It would appear that M and N would be equally preferred. However, if one looks closely at project N, it is seen that over half of the payback earnings (£9,000) arise in the third year – the *discounting* methods of investment appraisal have told us that the value of money declines the further into the future it is received. Also, looking beyond the payback period, we can see that project N goes on to earn a further £21,000 in the final three years, whereas project M earns only £18,000. The payback method completely ignores earnings that occur after the payback period. Project L, which was originally rejected, is projected to earn £31,000 after the payback period of 3½ years – perhaps project L should have been chosen after all?

17.4.2 Accounting rate of return (ARR)

The **accounting rate of return (ARR)** technique establishes the percentage annual return generated by a project over its life. It compares the non-discounted *profit* flows with the capital to be invested in the project. 'Profit' for this purpose is usually defined as net profit before interest and taxation. For example, a project costing £250,000 that generates net profits before interest and taxation of £500,000 over a 10-year period would have an accounting rate of return of 20% p.a., based on the following formula:

$$\text{ARR} = \frac{\text{Average annual net profit before taxation and interest}}{\text{Capital employed}} \times 100\%$$

$$\frac{(\pounds500,000/10)}{\pounds250,000} \times 100\% = 20\% \text{ p.a.}$$

This method provides a percentage that can be compared with the percentage rates of return of other potential projects and also the percentage cost of capital. Like the payback method, it ignores the time value of money, and the relative proportions of profit received earlier or later in the project's life are not taken into consideration. A project earning the bulk of its profits in the first few years would normally be preferable to another where most profits are earned near the end of the project's life.

Activity 17.7

Calculate the ARR of a project that requires an initial capital investment of £4m and is estimated to return net profits before interest and taxation totalling £1.6m over a 5-year period.

Answer

The ARR is 8%, calculated as follows:

$$\frac{\text{Average annual net profit before taxation and interest}}{\text{Capital employed}} \times 100\%$$

$$\frac{(\text{£1.6m}/5)}{\text{£4m}} \times 100\% = 8\% \text{ p.a.}$$

17.5 Summary

Discounting methods		Advantages	Disadvantages
Discounted cash flow (DCF)	Converts future cash flows into present values by using discount factors	Considers the time value of money. Looks at the whole life of projects	Discount rate chosen might be unrealistic. Need to use discount tables. Future cash flows might be difficult to predict with any accuracy
Net present value (NPV)	Converts both cash inflows and outflows relating to a specific project into present values, the end result being a 'net' present value	As DCF, but takes both cash inflows and outflows into consideration	As DCF
Internal rate of return (IRR)	Establishes the discount rate that, if applied to the cash flows relating to a specific project, would reduce the NPV to zero. This enables competing projects to be compared in terms of the percentage return they would earn after discounting	As DCF, but evaluation can be achieved on the basis of comparative percentage returns	As DCF
Non-discounting methods			
Payback	Evaluates competing projects solely by reference to the speed with which the initial investment is repaid	Simple to use and understand. Useful as an additional appraisal method where forecasts are particularly uncertain	Ignores time value of money. Ignores cash flows after pay-back period is reached
Accounting rate of return (ARR)	The percentage return per annum generated by a project over its lifetime	Simple to use and understand. Uses *profit* as the basis for the calculation rather than cash flows, which ties in with other accounting ratios	Ignores time value of money and when profit is earned

17.6 Glossary

Accounting rate of return The percentage annual return generated by a project over its life, calculated by comparing the non-discounted profit flows with the capital to be invested in the project.

ARR See Accounting rate of return.

Cost of capital See Discount rate.

Cumulative discount factor Combined discount factors used to facilitate the calculation of present values when the same sum is to be received or paid over several successive periods.

DCF See Discounted cash flow.

Discount factor The decimal used to convert a future value into a present value.

Discount rate The rate of interest used in the discounting process, sometimes referred to as the *cost of capital*.

Discounted cash flow Future cash flows converted to present values by the use of discount factors.

Discounting The process of converting future values into present values.

Future value The present value plus accumulated compound interest up to the time when the cash flow occurs.

Internal rate of return The discount rate which results in a zero net present value. It is used to compare alternative projects (that with the highest IRR is chosen) and/or to evaluate a project's rate of return with the firm's cost of capital.

Investment appraisal The process of comparing two or more potential investment projects to establish which is more favourable to the firm.

IRR See Internal rate of return.

Net present value The difference between a project's discounted cash outflows and inflows.

NPV See Net present value.

Payback The point when a project's cash flows match the cost of the project.

Payback period The time taken for a project to repay its original investment, using non-discounted cash flows.

Present value A cash flow occurring at the commencement of a project, or a 'future' value less the accumulated interest occurring between the commencement of a project and the time in the future when the cash flow occurs.

1 What is the future value in exactly 3 years' time of an investment of £1,000 received today and invested at 5% compound interest?
   a £1,215.50
   b £1,157.63
   c £1,150
   d £1,102.50

2 A two-year project is being evaluated using a discount rate of 7% p.a. It is expected to have a cash inflow of £40,000 at the end of its first year and £60,000 at the end of its second year. What is the present value of the future cash flows if the discount factors are: year 1 0.935 and year 2 0.873?
   a £100,000
   b £89,780
   c £91,020
   d £72,320

3 If two projects have different levels of risk, what can managers do to make their investment appraisal more realistic?
   a Apply a lower discount rate to the riskier project
   b Not consider the riskier project
   c Apply a higher discount rate to the riskier project
   d Ignore any cash inflows occurring after the first 3 years

4 Under which one of the following circumstances could a cumulative discount factor be used?
   a Where the same future values are receivable or payable each year for several years
   b Where different future values are receivable or payable each year for several years
   c Where the payback period method of investment appraisal is being used
   d Where the accounting rate of return method of investment appraisal is being used

5 Which one of the following could be considered as a benefit of using the payback period method of investment appraisal?
   a Both present and future values are being considered
   b The time value of money is considered
   c All cash flows arising on the project are brought into the calculation
   d It is simple to calculate

6 As a result of using various investment appraisal techniques, a firm has established that machine A has a payback period of 4 years, machine B has a negative internal rate of return of 6%, machine C has a net present value of £50,000 and machine D has an accounting rate of return of 8% p.a. Based on this information alone, which one of the machines would appear to be the least favoured investment?
   a Machine A
   b Machine B
   c Machine C
   d Machine D

7 Which one of the following methods of investment appraisal requires a trial-and-error approach for its calculation?
   a Internal rate of return
   b Payback period
   c Accounting rate of return
   d Net present value

8 A company is evaluating two alternative projects, X and Y, each of which will cost £50,000. Project X is expected to generate £20,000 p.a. for 3 years and project Y is expected to generate £15,000 p.a. for 4 years. At the end of each project, assets will be sold for £10,000 relating to project X and £15,000 relating to project Y. The discount rate is 5% and relevant discount factors are: year 1 0.952, year 2 0.907, year 3 0.864 and year 4 0.823. What is the net present value of each project?
   a Project X £4,460, project Y £3,190
   b Project X £20,000, project Y £25,000
   c Project X £13,100, project Y £15,535
   d Project X £63,100, project Y £65,535

9 Using the information contained in question 8, what is the payback period for each project?
   a Project X 3 years, project Y 4 years
   b Project X 2 years, project Y $2\frac{1}{3}$ years
   c Project X $2\frac{1}{2}$ years, project Y $3\frac{1}{3}$ years
   d Project X $1\frac{1}{2}$ years, project Y $2\frac{1}{3}$ years

10 Which one of the following is an acceptable definition of the internal rate of return?
   a The annualised profits as a percentage of the amount invested
   b The discounted cash flows as a percentage of the amount invested
   c The time it takes to repay the initial investment
   d The discount rate that results in a zero net present value for a project

(Answers in Appendix 1)

? Self-study questions

(Answers in Appendix 2)

Question 17.1 A project (A) costs £3,000 today and is expected to generate a cash flow of £10,000 in a year's time, whereas an alternative project (B) costing £4,000 today is forecast to generate £12,000 in 2 years' time. Calculate the net present value of each project, and state which project appears to be preferable.

Use a 10% p.a. discount rate. Relevant discount factors are:

Year 1	0.909
Year 2	0.826

Question 17.2 Using the net present value method of investment appraisal, contrast two projects, C and D. Project C will cost £10,000 and will generate £9,000 p.a. for 3 years. Project D will cost £12,000 but will generate £7,000 p.a. for 4 years. The discount rate is 6% p.a. Relevant discount factors are:

	Factor	Cumulative factor
Year 1	0.943	0.943
Year 2	0.890	1.833
Year 3	0.840	2.673
Year 4	0.792	3.465

Question 17.3 Two projects, G and H, cost £20,000 and £30,000 respectively. Project G is estimated to produce annual cash flows of £4,000 for 10 years whereas project H is estimated to produce annual cash flows of £5,000 for 8 years.

Which project would be chosen, using the payback method?

Question 17.4 Using a range of discount rates between 5% and 8% p.a., establish by trial and error the internal rate of return of the following project:

Year 0	Cash outflow	£20,000
Year 1	Cash inflow	£6,700
Year 2	Cash inflow	£8,600
Year 3	Cash inflow	£8,100

Relevant discount factors are:

Year	Discount rate			
	5%	6%	7%	8%
1	0.952	0.943	0.935	0.926
2	0.907	0.890	0.873	0.857
3	0.864	0.840	0.816	0.794

Question 17.5 A private hospital needs to equip an operating theatre by installing new medical equipment. The equipment costs £700,000 to buy outright, and is expected to require continuing maintenance costs of £30,000 p.a. for 5 years. At the end of 5 years it is expected to have a scrap value of about £100,000. With the benefits deriving from the new equipment, the hospital can expect to generate about £300,000 p.a. for the first three years, falling to an additional £200,000 p.a. for the remaining two years.

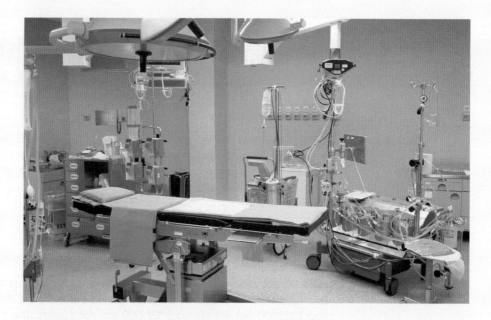

An alternative is to lease slightly more advanced equipment, which would require an initial deposit of £400,000, followed by 5 annual end-of-year payments of £120,000 each. The lessor will maintain the equipment and will reclaim the equipment at the end of year 5. Income is expected to increase by £300,000 p.a. over the entire five-year period.

Assume that the cost of capital is 8% p.a.

Discount factors at 8% p.a. are:

Year	Discount factor	Cumulative factor
1	0.926	0.926
2	0.857	1.783
3	0.794	2.577
4	0.735	3.312
5	0.681	3.993

Should the hospital buy or lease, and what additional information might be needed before a final decision is taken?

Case study

Machiq Limited's bid for world domination

Marvin and Chiquita (see previous case studies) had seen their business, Machiq Limited, change considerably over the years to a point where its brand name was recognised throughout the country. However, the two directors were very ambitious and believed that there was a worldwide market for the company's products if only they could achieve global brand awareness. To this aim, they decided to investigate the cost of launching their own television channel (Machiq TV) to broadcast advertisements for Machiq Limited's products 24 hours a day, 7 days a week to the northern hemisphere. Alternatively, they intended to consider a joint venture with Kaboosh Limited to launch a satellite (Matrix 1) that would enable the whole world to receive advertisements for both company's products.

Available data is as follows:

Machiq TV:
Initial set-up costs: £250m
Annual running costs: £100m
Estimated life of project: 5 years
Value of assets released at the end of the project: £40m
Increased sales as a result of advertising products: £60m in the first year, growing cumulatively by 50% each year for the following four years.

Matrix 1 satellite:
Initial set-up costs: £700m
Annual running costs: £50m
Value of assets released at the end of the project: £10m
(Note: all the above to be shared 50/50 with Kaboosh Limited)

Estimated life of the project: 6 years

Increased sales for Machiq Limited as a result of advertising products globally: £80m in the first year, growing cumulatively by 20% each year for the following five years.

Funding for both projects would be at a cost of capital of 6%.

Relevant discount factors at 6% p.a. are:

Year		Cumulative
1	0.943	0.943
2	0.890	1.833
3	0.840	2.673
4	0.792	3.465
5	0.747	4.212
6	0.705	4.917

Required:

Using the net present value method of investment appraisal, critically evaluate the two proposals.

(Answer in Appendix 3)

References   Websites relating to investment appraisal

Bized: www.bized.ac.uk/timeweb/reference/using_experiments.htm

Duncan Williamson: www.duncanwil.co.uk/invapp.html

Now look at this book's dedicated website at www.pearsoned.co.uk/black and work through the various additional exercises for this chapter.

Chapter 18

Revision chapter (3)

Objective When you have completed this chapter you will be able to:

➤ Relax, knowing that you have worked hard enough to get a very good result in your accountancy course!

18.1 Introduction

This chapter consolidates the knowledge gained on the management accounting topics contained in Chapters 12–17 by providing an examination paper consisting of four questions. Solutions are provided in Appendix 4.

18.2 Practice examination paper 3

Time allowed THREE hours.
Answer all four questions. All questions carry equal marks.

Question 1
Spectacular plc is a company that manufactures computer equipment. It has three production departments and a service department, and has produced the following budgeted cost of production for the year ended 31 March 2005:

		£	£
Production cost	Direct materials	240,000	
	Carriage inwards	10,000	
	Direct wages	200,000	
			450,000
Indirect wages	Department P	8,000	
	Department Q	12,000	
	Department R	18,300	
	General service department	6,700	
			45,000

Other costs	Consumable stores	32,000	
	Rent	21,000	
	Light and heat	14,000	
	Power	36,000	
	Depreciation (20% × cost)	80,000	
	Insurance: machinery	2,000	
			185,000
			680,000

The following data relates to the physical and performance aspects of the company:

Department	Area m²	Cost of plant £	Stores requisitions	Power consumption kW	Direct-labour-hours	Direct labour cost	Machine-hours
P	15,000	140,000	180	80	100,000	50,000	70,000
Q	22,500	180,000	120	100	80,000	60,000	90,000
R	20,000	10,000	100	5	220,000	90,000	10,000
Service	12,500	70,000	–	15	–	–	–

The general service department is apportioned to the production departments on the basis of direct labour cost.

a Prepare an overhead analysis for the departments, showing clearly the basis of apportioning costs to departments.

b Prepare a computation of hourly cost rates (direct-labour-hours or machine-hours) of overhead absorption for each production department.

c Critically assess the two overhead absorption rates calculated in (b) above.

Question 2

Fripple Limited manufactures coats. The company's management is preparing a budget for the next financial year and has prepared the following information:

	£
Selling price per coat	100
Materials per coat	25
Direct labour per coat	30
Overheads: variable per coat	5
Fixed overheads (total) £240,000 p.a.	

The company is planning to manufacture 16,000 coats in the next year.

a Calculate by formula, showing your workings:
  (i) The maximum profit if all coats are sold
  (ii) The break-even point (number of coats)
  (iii) The margin of safety (number of coats)
  (iv) The profit or loss if 11,000 coats are manufactured and sold.

b Prepare a cost/volume chart showing all the information calculated in (a) above.

c A supermarket chain has approached Fripple Limited with a view to placing a special order for 5,000 coats bearing a prominent advertisement, but is only prepared to pay £70 per coat. The additional cost of embroidering the advertisement would be £6 per coat. This order would be within the capacity of the company and fixed costs would remain unchanged. Should Fripple Limited accept the order?

Question 3

Humbug Ltd manufactures artificial Christmas trees in batches of 600. During October, Batch no. 701 was manufactured at the rate of 12 per hour. Ninety of the trees failed quality tests, but of these, 50 were thought to be rectifiable. The remaining 40 were scrapped, and the scrap value was credited to the cost of the batch as a whole. Rectification work took 6 hours. Costs were as follows:

Batch No 701	£
Raw materials per tree	2.40
Scrap value per tree	0.75
Machinists' hourly rate	4.80
Machine-hour overhead	5.30
Setting up of machine: normal machining	15.00
Setting up of machine: rectification	10.00

a Calculate the cost of a full batch, in total and per unit, if all units pass inspection.

b Calculate the actual cost of Batch no. 701, in total and per unit, after crediting the recovery value of the scrapped trees, and including the rectification costs.

c Calculate the loss incurred because of defective work.

Question 4

Appraise plc is considering manufacturing and developing a new product requiring a £2m investment. The following are estimates of costs and revenues for the first five years of the product's life:

1 Forecast sales:

Year	Quantities sold units	Selling price £ per unit
1	5,000	250
2	15,000	230
3	22,000	200
4	15,000	200
5	5,000	200

2 New machinery will be bought at the start of the project at a cost of £2m. It is expected to have a resale value of £150,000 at the end of 5 years.

3 Labour costs will be £40 per unit in year 1, rising by £2 per unit in each succeeding year.

4 Materials costs will be £80 per unit for the first two years of production, rising by 10% in year 3, and by a further £6 in each of years 4 and 5.

5 Other costs will be £25 per unit. These are forecast to remain unchanged over the life of the project.

6 The cost of capital to the company is 6% p.a.

Relevant discount factors are:

Year	Discount factor
1	0.943
2	0.890
3	0.840
4	0.792
5	0.747

    a Evaluate the project by calculating the:
      (i) Net present value
      (ii) Payback period.
    b Advise the company whether it should proceed with the new product.
    c The capital for the project will be raised either by a rights issue to existing ordinary shareholders, or by the issue of 6% debentures. Explain the effect of each alternative upon the company's profitability and gearing.

References

Now that you have completed this book, you might be thinking of a career in accountancy. These are the website addresses of the main accountancy bodies in the UK.

Institute of Chartered Accountants in England and Wales: **www.icaew.co.uk**

The Association of Chartered Certified Accountants: **www.acca.org.uk**

Institute of Chartered Accountants in Scotland: **www.icas.org.uk**

Chartered Institute of Management Accountants: **www.cimaglobal.com**

Association of Accounting Technicians: **www.accountingtechnician.co.uk**

> Now look at this book's dedicated website at **www.pearsoned.co.uk/black** and work through the various additional exercises for this chapter.

Appendix 1

Answers to self-check questions

Chapter	Question									
1	1d	2a	3c	4b	5a	6b	7c	8c	9d	10a
2	1c	2d	3a	4c	5b	6c	7d	8a	9c	10b
3	1b	2b	3c	4c	5c	6d	7a	8a	9c	10d
4	1c	2b	3a	4d	5a	6c	7b	8c	9d	10a
5	1c	2a	3d	4b	5a	6d	7b	8c	9a	10c
6	1a	2c	3b	4d	5a	6a	7c	8b	9d	10b
	11a	12b	13d	14a	15c	16b	17b	18c	19a	20a
	21c	22c	23d	24a	25b	26b	27c	28c	29a	30b
	31c	32a	33a	34d	35b					
7	1c	2d	3d	4a	5b	6b	7a	8c	9c	10d
8	1c	2a	3a	4c	5d	6a	7c	8d	9b	10b
9	1d	2d	3a	4d	5b	6c	7c	8a	9c	10a
10	1a	2d	3b	4c	5a	6a	7c	8b	9d	10c
12	1c	2c	3a	4a	5c	6d	7b	8b	9d	10a
13	1c	2a	3a	4c	5d	6b	7b	8d	9a	10c
14	1c	2a	3d	4b	5a	6d	7a	8c	9b	10c
15	1a	2c	3d	4b	5d	6d	7a	8b	9c	10c
16	1a	2c	3b	4d	5b	6d	7a	8a	9c	10c
17	1b	2b	3c	4d	5d	6b	7a	8c	9c	10d

Answers to self-study questions

Chapter 1

Question 1.1

	Assets £	Liabilities £	Capital £
1	25,630	14,256	11,374
2	39,156	23,658	15,498
3	619,557	352,491	267,066
4	69,810	54,947	14,863
5	57,058	21,596	35,462
6	36,520	12,010	24,510
7	151,632	65,342	86,290
8	114,785	17,853	96,932
9	212,589	65,769	146,820
10	265,108	63,527	201,581
Totals	1,591,845	691,449	900,396

Note that Assets less Liabilities = Capital.

Question 1.2 **a** 'Going concern' is a key accounting concept, which assumes that the business can continue to trade for the foreseeable future. If it did not apply then that would indicate that the business had a very uncertain future, with a real possibility of failure.

b *Accruals concept*. When calculating the profit or loss of an organisation, all income and related expenditure for a specified period should be included, not simply money paid or received.

Consistency concept. Accounting procedures used should be the same as those applied previously for similar items. This allows comparability of financial summaries over time.

Prudence concept. Accountants should be cautious in the valuation of assets or the measurement of profit. The *lowest* reasonable estimate of an asset's value should be taken, whilst a forecast loss would be included but not a forecast profit.

c The overriding concept is that of 'true and fair view', which refers to the need for the financial statements to show truth and fairness, even if it means abandoning one or more of the fundamental accounting concepts.

Question 1.3 The most recent figures at the time of this publication are given below. The balance sheet information is from the 'group' figures, not 'company' figures. You may have been able to access more recent figures.

(£m)	Tesco		J. Sainsbury	
	2004	2003	2004	2003
(from the balance sheets)				
Total net assets (i.e. fixed and current assets, less liabilities)	5,566	5,014	4,909	4,804
(from the profit and loss account)				
Total sales ('turnover') for the year	23,653	20,988	17,162	17,244
Operating profit before taxation	1,322	1,166	571	437

a Overall value for the latest year shows that Tesco has a greater balance sheet value than Sainsbury (13.4% higher).
b Tesco's sales were higher than Sainsbury's by 37.8%.
c Tesco's profit was higher than Sainsbury's, by 131.5%, and when profit is compared with the value of each company, Tesco's profit was 23.75% whereas Sainsbury recorded only 11.6%. This is known as the 'return on capital employed' – see Chapter 10.
d The total net assets of Tesco have grown by 11% and those of Sainsbury by only 2.2% between the two years, so both companies have been expanding – Tesco at a much faster rate. Tesco's sales increased by 12.7% in the year, but Sainsbury's sales declined marginally, showing that Sainsbury was struggling to maintain its share of the market. Tesco's profit increased by 13.4%, but Sainsbury's showed a significant increase of 30.7%. A more detailed analysis of both companies is given in Chapter 10.

Chapter 2

Question 2.1

Sales account

	£		£
12 Dec Cash repaid to customer	65	17 Dec Cash received	84,000
31 Dec Balance c/d	209,535	22 Dec Sales day book	125,600
	209,600		209,600
		1 Jan Balance b/d	209,535

Bank charges account

	£		£
12 Oct Charges	112	13 Dec Refund due to bank error	26
12 Nov Charges	145	31 Dec Balance c/d	231
	257		257
1 Jan Balance b/d	231		

Question 2.2

	Assets £	Expenses £	Liabilities £	Capital £	Income £
1 The business pays a cheque of £100 for phone charges	− £100 (Bank)	+ £100 (Phone charges)			
2 The business pays a creditor £250	− £250 (Bank)		− £250 (Creditor)		
3 The owner takes out £100 in cash from the business	− £100 (Cash)			− £100 (Drawings)	
4 Goods are sold to a debtor for £900	+ £900 (Debtors)				+ £900 (Sales)
5 Petrol is bought on credit for £60		+ £60 (Petrol)	+ £60 (Creditor)		
Summary (overall change)	+ £450	+ £160	− £190	− £100	+ £900

Note that Assets + Expenses = Liabilities + Capital + Income.

Question 2.3

	Assets £	Expenses £	Liabilities £	Capital £	Income £
1 The owner pays in £6,000 to start the business's bank account	+ £6,000 (Bank)			+ £6,000 (Capital)	
2 The business pays wages of £200 by cheque	− £200 (Bank)	+ £200 (Wages)			
3 Goods are bought for £400 on credit from Goff Limited		+ £400 (Purchases)	+ £400 (Creditor)		
4 Goods are sold on credit to Plod plc for £510	+ £510 (Debtor)				+ £510 (Sales)
5 A computer is bought for £600 with a cheque	+ £600 (Fixed Asset) − £600 (Bank)				
6 Stationery is bought for £50 with a cheque	− £50 (Bank)	+ £50 (Stationery)			
Summary (overall change)	+ £6,260	+ £650	+ £400	+ £6,000	+ £510

Note that Assets + Expenses = Liabilities + Capital + Income.

Question 2.4

Rachel Roberts' business

Bank

		£			£
1 Oct	Capital	9,000	1 Oct	Purchases	4,000
2 Oct	Sales	600	3 Oct	Advertising	30
5 Oct	Sales	700		Printing	45
		10,300	4 Oct	Rent	100
			6 Oct	Drawings	400
			7 Oct	Sales returns	40
					4,615
			7 Oct	Balance c/d	5,685
		10,300			10,300
8 Oct	Balance b/d	5,685			

Cash

		£			£
1 Oct	Capital	100	1 Oct	Stationery	60
2 Oct	Sales	280	6 Oct	Wages	260
5 Oct	Sales	130			320
			7 Oct	Balance c/d	190
		510			510
8 Oct	Balance b/d	190			

Capital

		£			£
			1 Oct	Bank	9,000
				Cash	100
					9,100

Purchases

		£		£
1 Oct	Bank	4,000		

Stationery

		£		£
1 Oct	Cash	60		

Sales

	£			£
		2 Oct	Bank	600
			Cash	280
		5 Oct	Bank	700
			Cash	130
				1,710

Advertising

		£		£
3 Oct	Bank	30		

Printing

		£		£
3 Oct	Bank	45		

Rent

		£		£
4 Oct	Bank	100		

Wages

		£		£
6 Oct	Cash	260		

Drawings

		£		£
6 Oct	Bank	400		

Sales returns

		£		£
7 Oct	Bank	40		

Rachel Roberts

Trial balance as at 7 October

	Dr	Cr
	£	£
Bank	5,685	
Cash	190	
Capital		9,100
Purchases	4,000	
Stationery	60	
Sales		1,710
Advertising	30	
Printing	45	
Rent	100	
Wages	260	
Drawings	400	
Sales returns	40	
	10,810	10,810

Question 2.5

Casper Peabody's Business

Purchases Day Book

		£
1 May	C. Moss	630
	J. Carter	419
	A. McKeane	330
3 May	A. Iqbal	560
	A. McKeane	210
		2,149

Sales Day Book

		£
2 May	K. Palfreyman	199
	L. Patel	870
		1,069

Purchase Returns Day Book

		£
4 May	J. Carter	80
7 May	A. Iqbal	40
		120

Sales Returns Day Book

		£
5 May	L. Patel	62

Purchases Ledger

C. Moss

		£			£
			1 May	Invoice	630

J. Carter

		£			£
4 May	Returns	80	1 May	Invoice	419
6 May	Bank	339			
		419			419

A. McKeane

		£			£
			1 May	Invoice	330
			3 May	Invoice	210
					540

A. Iqbal

		£			£
7 May	Returns	40	3 May	Invoice	560

Sales Ledger

K. Palfreyman

		£		
2 May	Invoice	199		

L. Patel

		£			£
2 May	Invoice	870	5 May	Returns	62
			6 May	Bank	808
		870			870

General Ledger

Bank

		£			£
6 May	L. Patel	808	6 May	J. Carter	339

Sales

		£			£
			7 May	Sales day book	1,069

Purchases

		£		
7 May	Purchases day book	2,149		

Purchase returns

		£			£
			7 May	Purchase returns day book	120

Sales returns

		£		
7 May	Sales returns day book	62		

Question 2.6   **Lara Kelly: Petty Cash Book**

£/p			£/p
200.00	14 Oct	Transfer from Cash Book	
		Travel expenses	25.56
	15 Oct	Window cleaning	14.29
	16 Oct	Train fares	18.45
	17 Oct	Dog kennel	40.00
		Dog food	19.00
	18 Oct	Postage	2.65
	19 Oct	Loan to Hiram Decker	10.00
	20 Oct	Window cleaning	23.85
		Total expenditure for the week	153.80
		Balance c/d	46.20
200.00			200.00
46.20	21 Oct	Balance b/d	
153.80		Transfer from Cash Book	
200.00			

Question 2.7 **Paul Pascoe's journal**

			Dr £	Cr £
a	Debit	Andrew Young's sales ledger account	400	
	Credit	Andrew Cheung's sales ledger account		400
	– Correction of misposting to A. Young's account			
b	Debit	Stationery	80	
	Credit	Bank		80
	– Correction of reversed entries (£40 to cancel incorrect entry, plus £40 for correct entry = £80)			
c	Debit	Purchases	200	
	Credit	Dingle Dynamics' purchase ledger account		200
	– Correction of omitted entry			

Chapter 3

Question 3.1 **a** Controls are needed not only to ensure the accuracy and completeness of the data recorded within the bookkeeping system and financial summaries, but also to safeguard the business assets. Controls can help to minimise fraud by means of adequate supervision of tasks and a suitable allocation of duties. No one member of staff should have total responsibility for a financial function without the need for the work to be supervised or checked by others. Examples of controls include:

- Bank reconciliation statements
- Sales and purchase ledger control accounts
- The imprest system of petty cash
- The trial balance.

b

Sales ledger control account

	£		£
Opening debtors	86,250	Opening credit balances	370
Total sales invoices	610,200	Sales returns	3,200
		Cheques received	577,800
		Closing debtors	
		(balancing figure)	115,080
	696,450		696,450

Purchases ledger control account

	£		£
Purchases returns	770	Opening creditors	92,100
Cheques paid	472,450	Total purchase invoices	463,750
Closing creditors	82,630		
(balancing figure)			
	555,850		555,850

Question 3.2 **a** The accruals concept ensures that all relevant income and expenditure appears in the profit and loss account, not just the cash paid and received. Adjustments for accruals and prepayments, opening and closing stock and provisions for depreciation are all examples of how the income for a period has to be matched with the relevant expenditure for the same period.

b

Polly Harris's Books

General Ledger

Stock

		£			£
1/5/04	Opening stock b/f	50,000	30/4/05	P & L account	50,000
30/4/05	P & L account	60,000	30/4/05	Closing stock c/d	60,000
		110,000			110,000
1/5/05	Opening stock b/d	60,000			

Telephone

		£			£
30/4/05	Bank	4,000	30/4/05	P & L account	4,900
	Accrual c/d	900			
		4,900			4,900
			1/5/05	Accrual b/d	900

Rent

		£			£
1/5/04	Bank	15,000	30/4/05	P & L account	30,000
1/11/04	Bank	22,500	30/4/05	Prepaid c/d	7,500
		37,500			37,500
1/5/05	Prepaid b/d	7,500			

Question 3.3 **a** The official definition of depreciation contained within Financial Reporting Standard (FRS) 15 *Tangible Fixed Assets* is:

The measure of the cost or revalued amount of the economic benefits of the tangible fixed asset that have been consumed during the period. Consumption includes the wearing out, using up or other reduction in the useful economic life of a tangible fixed asset whether arising from use, effluxion of time or obsolescence through either changes in technology or demand for the goods and services produced by the asset.

Depreciation is relevant to the fundamental accounting concepts in the following ways:

- *Accruals concept*. Depreciation ensures that a reasonable estimate of the loss in value of the fixed asset is matched to the accounting periods in which the loss is incurred.
- *Prudence concept*. It would be unrealistic to ignore the decline in value of fixed assets over time, and depreciation is the means by which such loss is recognised within the financial statements.
- *Consistency concept*. Once the accounting policy for depreciation is adopted, it should be applied consistently to all similar assets, unless the application of this concept results in a breach of the overriding 'true and fair view' concept.
- *Going concern concept*. It is always assumed that the business is a going concern unless it is stated otherwise, so it is reasonable to assume that fixed assets will be depreciated over their useful economic life based on the estimates made at the time of acquisition. If a business is not considered as a going concern, assets should be written down to a realistic value, possibly based on a 'forced sale' (i.e. the value which would be realised if the business was forced to sell them by creditors).

b

Machinery

		£			£
1/1/04	Cost	65,000	31/12/04	Balance c/d	65,000
1/1/05	Balance b/d	65,000	31/12/05	Balance c/d	65,000
1/1/06	Balance b/d	65,000	31/12/06	Balance c/d	65,000
1/1/07	Balance b/d	65,000			

Computers

		£			£
1/1/04	Cost	20,000	31/12/04	Balance c/d	20,000
1/1/05	Balance b/d	20,000	31/12/05	Balance c/d	20,000
1/1/06	Balance b/d	20,000	31/12/06	Balance c/d	20,000
1/1/07	Balance b/d	20,000			

Motor cars

		£			£
1/1/05	Cost	45,000	31/12/05	Balance c/d	45,000
1/1/06	Balance b/d	45,000	31/12/06	Balance c/d	45,000
1/1/07	Balance b/d	45,000			

Provision for depreciation on machinery

		£				£
31/12/04	Balance c/d	12,000	31/12/04	P & L account		12,000
31/12/05	Balance c/d	24,000	1/1/05	Balance b/d		12,000
			31/12/05	P & L account		12,000
		24,000				24,000
			1/1/06	Balance b/d		24,000
31/12/06	Balance c/d	36,000	31/12/06	P & L account		12,000
		36,000				36,000
			1/1/07	Balance b/d		36,000

Provision for depreciation on computers

		£				£
31/12/04	Balance c/d	5,000	31/12/04	P & L account		5,000
31/12/05	Balance c/d	10,000	1/1/05	Balance b/d		5,000
			31/12/05	P & L account		5,000
		10,000				10,000
			1/1/06	Balance b/d		10,000
31/12/06	Balance c/d	15,000	31/12/06	P & L account		5,000
		15,000				15,000
			1/1/07	Balance b/d		15,000

Provision for depreciation on motor cars

		£				£
31/12/05	Balance c/d	18,000	31/12/05	P & L account		18,000
			1/1/06	Balance b/d		18,000
31/12/06	Balance c/d	28,800	31/12/06	P & L account		10,800
		28,800				28,800
			1/1/07	Balance b/d		28,800

c

Profit and loss account for the year ended 31 December 2006 (extract)

Expenses include:

	£
Depreciation on machinery	12,000
Depreciation on computers	5,000
Depreciation on motor cars	10,800

Balance sheet as at 31 December 2006 (extract)

	Cost	Accumulated depreciation	Net book value
	£	£	£
Fixed assets			
Machinery	65,000	36,000	29,000
Computers	20,000	15,000	5,000
Motor cars	45,000	28,800	16,200
	130,000	79,800	50,200

Question 3.4

Louise Jones
Profit and loss account for the year ended 30 November 2005

	£	£
Sales		75,972
Less Cost of goods sold		
Opening stock at 1 December 2004	7,224	
Add Purchases	49,600	
	56,824	
Less Closing stock at 30 November 2005	(12,400)	
		(44,424)
Gross profit		31,548
Less Expenses		
Wages	11,590	
Accountancy	350	
Advertising	285	
Bank charges	74	
Depreciation: fixtures and fittings	800	
Depreciation: motor van	1,600	
Light and heat	1,030	
Motor expenses	518	
Postage and printing	390	
Rent and rates	2,900	
Repairs	810	
Telephone and insurance	619	
		(20,966)
Net profit		10,582

Louise Jones
Balance sheet as at 30 November 2005

	Cost	Accumulated depreciation	Net book value
	£	£	£
Fixed assets			
Fixtures and fittings	11,400	4,200	7,200
Motor van	8,900	4,800	4,100
	20,300	9,000	11,300
Current assets			
Stock		12,400	
Debtors		7,384	
Prepayments		200	
Bank		3,600	
Cash		120	
		23,704	
***Less* Current liabilities**			
Creditors	8,140		
Accruals	130		
		(8,270)	
Net current assets			15,434
Total net assets			26,734

Capital

Opening balance, 1 December 2004	23,652	
Add Net profit	10,582	
	34,234	
Less Drawings	(7,500)	
Closing balance at 30 November 2005		26,734

Chapter 4

Question 4.1   **Amber: Profit and loss account for the year ended 30 April 2005**

	£	£
Raw materials		
Opening stock at 1 May 2004	8,320	
Add Purchases of raw materials	52,450	
	60,770	
Less Closing stock at 30 April 2005	(9,641)	
Cost of raw materials		51,129
Other direct costs:		
Production labour		47,653
Prime cost of production		98,782
Indirect factory costs:		
Factory expenses	89,322	
Depreciation of factory	6,000	
		95,322
		194,104
Add Opening work-in-progress	35,620	
Less Closing work-in-progress	(32,040)	
		3,580
Total factory production cost c/d		197,684
Sales		253,620
Less Cost of goods sold		
Opening stock at 1 May 2004	12,634	
Add Total factory production cost b/d	197,684	
	210,318	
Less Closing stock at 30 April 2005	(13,671)	
		(196,647)
Gross profit		56,973
Add Discount received		114
		57,087
Less **Expenses**		
Office expenses	34,600	
Discount allowed	840	
Depreciation	3,600	
		(39,040)
Net profit		18,047

Blue: Profit and loss account for the year ended 31 May 2005

	£	£	£
Sales		184,162	
Less Sales returns		(580)	
			183,582
Less Cost of goods sold			
Opening stock at 1 June 2004		12,700	
Add Purchases	65,210		
Carriage inwards	360		
	65,570		
Less Purchases returns	(2,600)		
		62,970	
		75,670	
Less Closing stock at 31 May 2005		(10,700)	
			(64,970)
Gross profit			118,612
Add Discount received			120
			118,732
Less Expenses			
General office expenses		54,923	
Carriage outwards		240	
Depreciation: office		2,300	
Discount allowed		320	
			(57,783)
Net profit			60,949

Cerise: Profit and loss account for the year ended 30 June 2005

	£	£
Fees from clients		85,400
Less Expenses		
General office expenses	21,500	
Discount allowed	160	
Depreciation: office	1,600	
		(23,260)
Net profit		62,140

Question 4.2

Wesley Timpson
Profit and loss account for the year ended 30 November 2005

	£	£	£
Sales		245,610	
Less Sales returns		(2,350)	
			243,260
Less Cost of goods sold			
Opening stock at 1 December 2004		15,684	
Add Purchases	124,100		
Carriage inwards	6,200		
	130,300		
Less Purchases returns c/f	(2,910)		

Less Purchases returns	b/f	(2,910)		
		127,390		
		143,074		
Less Closing stock at 30 November 2005		(16,822)		
			(126,252)	
Gross profit			117,008	
Add Discount received		640		
Bank interest received		140		
			780	
			117,788	
Less **Expenses**				
Wages and salaries		47,231		
Carriage outwards		900		
Depreciation: office furniture		2,500		
computers		900		
motor cars		4,500		
Postage and stationery		2,710		
Sundry office expenses		3,571		
Telephone		1,499		
Light and heat		5,230		
Discount allowed		533		
			(69,574)	
Net profit			48,214	

Question 4.3

Betta Buys

Profit and loss account for the year ended 28 February 2006

	£	£	£
Sales			425,000
Less **Cost of goods sold**			
Opening stock at 1 March 2005		90,000	
Add Purchases		204,000	
		294,000	
Less Closing stock at 28 February 2006		(70,000)	
			(224,000)
Gross profit			201,000
Less **Expenses**			
Wages and salaries		62,000	
Rent		12,000	
Electricity		5,000	
Depreciation: shop fittings		5,200	
Depreciation: car		2,880	
			(87,080)
Net profit			113,920

Betta Buys
Balance sheet as at 28 February 2006

	Cost	Accumulated depreciation	Net book value
	£	£	£
Fixed assets			
Shop fittings	30,000	15,600	14,400
Motor car	12,000	7,680	4,320
	42,000	23,280	18,720
Current assets			
Stock		70,000	
Debtors		35,200	
Prepayments		3,000	
Bank		960	
Cash		250	
		109,410	
Less Current liabilities			
Creditors	27,600		
Accruals	1,000		
		(28,600)	
Net current assets			80,810
Total net assets			99,530
Capital			
Opening balance, 1 March 2005		10,610	
Add Net profit		113,920	
		124,530	
Less Drawings		(25,000)	
Closing balance at 28 February 2006			99,530

Question 4.4

Helen Thorne
Profit and loss account for the year ended 31 May 2005

	£	£
Sales	324,650	
Less Sales returns	(1,250)	
		323,400
Less Cost of goods sold		
Opening stock at 1 June 2004	34,500	
Add Purchases	168,220	
	202,720	
Less Closing stock at 1 May 2005	(27,880)	
		(174,840)
Gross profit		148,560
Add Discount received		690
		149,250
Less expenses		
Assistants' wages	33,100	
Insurance	5,900	
Telephone and e-mail	5,400	
Light and heat	6,230	

Security guards' wages	12,800
Repairs to premises	3,970
Amortisation of leasehold premises	3,000
Depreciation of safe	2,880
Depreciation of shop fittings	3,400
Rent and rates	17,000
Discount allowed	1,520
Website charges	905
Publicity and advertising	9,740
Sundry expenses	3,940
	(109,785)
Net profit	39,465

Helen Thorne
Balance sheet as at 31 May 2005

	Cost £	Accumulated depreciation £	Net book value £
Fixed assets			
Leasehold premises	60,000	21,000	39,000
Safe	12,000	7,680	4,320
Shop fittings	34,000	13,600	20,400
	106,000	42,280	63,720
Current assets			
Stock		27,880	
Debtors		3,400	
Prepayments		525	
Cash		520	
		32,325	
Less **Current liabilities**			
Creditors	19,670		
Accruals	600		
Bank overdraft	2,380		
		(22,650)	
Net current assets			9,675
Total net assets			73,395
Capital			
Opening balance, 1 June 2004		58,630	
Add Net profit		39,465	
		98,095	
Less Drawings		(24,700)	
Closing balance at 31 May 2005			73,395

Chapter 5

Question 5.1

Profit and loss account for the year ended 31 December 2005 (extract)

	£
Expenses include:	
Provision for depreciation on vessels	240,000
Loss on disposal of vessels	152,500

Balance sheet as at 31 December 2005 (extract)

	Cost	Accumulated depreciation	Net book value
	£	£	£
Vessels	1,600,000	645,000	955,000

Note:

Vessels	£
Cost at 1 January 2005	1,950,000
Add Additions in year	700,000
	2,650,000
Less Disposals at cost	(1,050,000)
Cost at 31 December 2005	1,600,000

Depreciation at 1 January 2005	1,102,500
Add Provision for the year	240,000
	1,342,500
Less Depreciation on disposals	(697,500)
Depreciation as at 31 December 2005	645,000
Net book value as at 31 December 2005	955,000
Net book value as at 1 January 2005	847,500

Workings (figures in £000):

			Vessel		
	Invisible	Submersible	Outrageous	Implausible	Total
Depreciation p.a.	$\dfrac{£450 \times 75\%}{5}$ = 67.5	$\dfrac{£600 \times 75\%}{5}$ = 90	$\dfrac{£900 \times 75\%}{5}$ = 135	$\dfrac{£700 \times 75\%}{5}$ = 105	
Depreciation to 1/1/05	67.5 × 5 = 337.5	90 × 4 = 360	135 × 3 = 405	(none)	1,102.5
Depreciation for 2005	(none)	(none)	135	105	240
Net book value at disposal	450 – 337.5 = 112.5	600 – 360 = 240	n/a	n/a	
'Proceeds' of disposal	nil	200	n/a	n/a	
Loss on disposal	112.5	40	n/a	n/a	152.5

Question 5.2 **a** (i) *FIFO method*:

	Purchase price			
	70p	*90p*	*£1.10*	*1.30*
Years ended 30 September:				
2001 Purchases	120,000			
Sales (FIFO)	(100,000)			
Subtotal	20,000			
2002 Purchases		120,000		
Sales (FIFO)	(20,000)	(80,000)		
Subtotal	—	40,000		
2003 Purchases			120,000	
Sales (FIFO)		(40,000)	(100,000)	
Subtotal		—	20,000	
2004 Purchases				120,000
Sales (FIFO)			(20,000)	(80,000)
Subtotal			—	40,000

Value of stock under the FIFO method = 40,000 × £1.30 = £52,000.

(ii) *LIFO method*:

	Purchase price			
	70p	*90p*	*£1.10*	*1.30*
Years ended 30 September:				
2001 Purchases	120,000			
Sales (LIFO)	(100,000)			
Subtotal	20,000			
2002 Purchases		120,000		
Sales (LIFO)	–	(100,000)		
Subtotal	20,000	20,000		
2003 Purchases			120,000	
Sales (LIFO)	–	(20,000)	(120,000)	
Subtotal	20,000	–	–	
2004 Purchases				120,000
Sales (LIFO)	–	–	–	(100,000)
Subtotal	20,000	–	–	20,000

Value of stock under the LIFO method = (20,000 × 70p) + (20,000 × £1.30) = £40,000.

(iii) *AVCO method:*

	Mats in stock	Price	Value (£)	Average
Purchases, year ended 30/9/01	120,000	70p	84,000	
Sales, year ended 30/9/01	(100,000)	70p	(70,000)	
Subtotal at 30/9/01	20,000		14,000	
Purchases, year ended 30/9/02	120,000	90p	108,000	
Subtotal	140,000		122,000	
Average (£122,000/140,000)				87.14p
Sales, year ended 30/9/02	(100,000)	87.14p	(87,140)	
Subtotal at 30/9/02	40,000		34,860	
Purchases, year ended 30/9/03	120,000	£1.10	132,000	
Subtotal	160,000		166,860	
Average (£166,860/160,000)				£1.043
Sales, year ended 30/9/03	(140,000)	£1.043	(146,020)	
Subtotal at 30/9/03	20,000		20,840	
Purchases, year ended 30/9/04	120,000	£1.30	156,000	
Subtotal	140,000		176,840	
Average (£176,840/140,000)				£1.263
Sales, year ended 30/9/04	(100,000)	£1.263	(126,300)	
Closing stock	**40,000**	**£1.263**	**50,540**	

Value of stock (allowing for rounding adjustments) under the AVCO method = **£50,540.**

b In the UK, FIFO is preferred to LIFO because:
- the Inland Revenue does not accept profit figures based on LIFO stock valuations
- SSAP 9, the accounting standard relating to stock valuations, does not consider the method acceptable, as LIFO results in unrealistically high cost of sales figures
- the stock valuation tends to be outdated (as in the above example, where stock at 30 September 2004 is partly based on values current at 30 September 2001).

Question 5.3 **a** This is the application of the prudence concept to stock valuation in order to ensure that asset values are not overstated. Cost represents all those costs incurred in the normal course of business in bringing the product to its present location and condition. Net realisable value is the estimated proceeds from the sale of items of stock less all further costs to completion and less all costs to be incurred in marketing, selling and distributing directly related to the items in question.

b Orange Lace
Cost £9,000
Net realisable value £2,000 – £500 = £1,500
Therefore valued at the lower figure, £1,500.

Injured Turtles
Cost £16,000
Net realisable value £4,000 – (2,750 + 2,650) = £1,400 loss
Therefore it would be omitted from the stock calculation (stock written down to zero) as the stock would be thrown away rather than be exported at a loss.

Question 5.4 **a** Bad debts occur when a customer has bought goods or services and does not pay for them. The company selling the goods or services has given up trying to recover the debt, and accepts that it has lost money on the transaction.

Doubtful debts occur when there is an element of doubt as to whether a customer will pay for goods or services, but it has not reached the stage where the company is prepared to write off the debt as bad.

b

Bickley Brothers
Profit and loss account for the year ended 31 May 2003

	£	£
Expenses include:		
Bad debts written off		2,400
Increase in provision for doubtful debts		500

Balance sheet as at 31 May 2003

	£	£
Current assets include:		
Debtors	11,125	
Less Provision for doubtful debts	(3,500)	
		7,625

Bickley Brothers
Profit and loss account for the year ended 31 May 2004

	£	£
Added to gross profit:		
Decrease in provision for doubtful debts		300
Expenses include:		
Bad debts written off		600

Balance sheet as at 31 May 2004

	£	£
Current assets include:		
Debtors	17,030	
Less Provision for doubtful debts	(3,200)	
		13,830

c When Lord Fitztightly's debt was written off as bad in the year ended May 2003, the customer's account in the sales ledger would have been closed. In the following year, the receipt of the amount owing is taken as additional income straight to the profit and loss account – described as 'bad debt recovered' (Dr bank account Cr profit and loss account). There are no relevant entries in the balance sheet.

Chapter 6

Question 6.1

Felicity Frankton
Profit and loss account for the year ended 30 September 2005

	£	£	£
Sales			105,800
Less Cost of goods sold			
Opening stock at 1 October 2004		16,520	
Add Purchases	32,410		
Add Carriage in	320		
		32,730	
		49,250	
Less Closing stock at 30 September 2005		(14,560)	
			(34,690)
Gross profit			71,110
Less Expenses			
Wages and salaries		18,500	
Bad debts		500	
Carriage outwards		430	
Discount allowed		340	
Light and heat		2,200	
Provision for doubtful debts (1,210 − 800)		410	
Rent and rates (3,200 + 600)		3,800	
Sundry office expenses (10,200 − 200)		10,000	
Loss on sale of car[1]		400	
Depreciation on car[2]		4,200	
Depreciation on computer[3]		722	
			(41,502)
Net profit			29,608

Notes:
1 (7,900 − 6,000) − 1,500.
2 60% × [(16,500 − 7,900) − (7,600 − 6,000)].
3 3,610/5.

Felicity Frankton
Balance sheet as at 30 September 2005

Fixed assets	Cost	Accumulated depreciation	Net book value
	£	£	£
Computers	3,610	2,572	1,038
Motor cars	8,600	5,800	2,800
	12,210	8,372	3,838
Current assets			
Stock		14,560	
Debtors	24,200		
Less Provision for doubtful debts	(1,210)		
		22,990	

Prepayments		200
Bank		1,260
		39,010
Less Current liabilities		
Creditors	13,600	
Accruals	600	
		(14,200)
Net current assets		24,810
Total net assets		28,648
Capital		
Opening balance, 1 October 2004		15,940
Add Net profit		29,608
		45,548
Less Drawings		(16,900)
Closing balance at 30 September 2005		28,648

Question 6.2

Patrick Cooper
Profit and loss account for the year ended 31 December 2004

	£	£	£
Sales (289,512 – 100)			289,412
Less Cost of goods sold			
Opening stock at 1 January 2004		5,620	
Add Purchases		132,950	
		138,570	
Less Closing stock at 31 December 2004		(4,900)	
			(133,670)
Gross profit			155,742
Less expenses			
Wages and salaries		39,540	
Bad debts written off		250	
Discount allowed		200	
Bank interest		950	
Administration expenses (55,500 – 150)		55,350	
Increase in provision for doubtful debts		250	
Selling expenses (37,790 + 300)		38,090	
Depreciation on equipment[1]		2,680	
Loss on sale of equipment[2]		140	
			(137,450)
Net profit			18,292

Notes:

1 $20\% \times (14{,}000 - 600)$.

2 Cost – Depreciation to date of sale = $600 - (60\% \times 600) = 240$.
Loss = $240 - 100$ proceeds = 140.

Patrick Cooper
Balance sheet as at 31 December 2004

	Cost	Accumulated depreciation	Net book value
Fixed assets	£	£	£
Equipment	13,400	4,670	8,730
Current assets			
Stock		4,900	
Debtors	6,300		
Less Provision for doubtful debts	(550)		
		5,750	
Prepayments		150	
Cash		140	
		10,940	
Less **Current liabilities**			
Creditors	5,210		
Accruals	300		
Bank overdraft	1,600		
		(7,110)	
Net current assets			3,830
Total net assets			12,560
Capital			
Opening balance, 1 January 2004		16,268	
Add Net profit		18,292	
		34,560	
Less Drawings		(22,000)	
Closing balance at 31 December 2004			12,560

Chapter 7

Question 7.1 A partnership is not a collection of sole traders, as the partners run the business in the knowledge that they will be *sharing* the risks and rewards. Although sole trading suits many people, it can be helpful to be able to draw on the expertise of others. Sharing of problems and the ability to discuss business possibilities is also a very positive aspect of a partnership. It is very difficult to expand a business with only one owner, and bringing in partners can draw in finance which is otherwise unavailable.

Question 7.2

Disraeli and Gladstone
Profit and loss account (appropriation section)
for the year ended 31 December 2004

	£	£
Net profit for the year		40,000
Less Salary to Disraeli		(9,000)
		31,000
Less Interest on capital		
Disraeli (5% × £20,000)	1,000	
Gladstone (5% × £15,000)	750	
	c/f	(1,750)

		b/f	(1,750)
			29,250
Disraeli: share of profit ($\frac{2}{3} \times$ £29,250)		19,500	
Gladstone: share of profit ($\frac{1}{3} \times$ £29,250)		9,750	
			29,250

Disraeli and Gladstone
Balance sheet as at 31 December 2004

	£	£
(Assets less liabilities)		43,000
Disraeli's capital account		
Opening balance, 1 January 2004	20,000	
Add Salary	9,000	
Interest on capital	1,000	
Share of profit	19,500	
	49,500	
Less Drawings	(18,000)	
Closing balance, 31 December 2004		31,500
Gladstone's capital account		
Opening balance, 1 January 2004	15,000	
Add Interest on capital	750	
Share of profit	9,750	
	25,500	
Less Drawings	(14,000)	
Closing balance, 31 December 2004		11,500
		43,000

Question 7.3 **a** Problems:
- Partners may be incompetent, and there may be personality clashes.
- Partners have unlimited liability for the debts of the partnership.

b There is a grain of truth in the quotation, but it must be recognised that trading as a limited company requires compliance with a much stronger regulatory framework than applies to a partnership. This is to protect the interest of creditors who, though warned of the limited liability of the owners by the inclusion of 'Ltd' or 'plc' in the business's name, are still entitled to the assurance that the business is run properly and in accordance with the law by the directors.

c See pages 126–7 for the advantages and disadvantages of limited liability status.

Question 7.4 Although there have been many well-publicised cases of unscrupulous directors defrauding shareholders and creditors, the vast majority of limited liability companies are run on perfectly legal lines, providing returns to shareholders, salaries to employees and trade with suppliers nationally and internationally. Limited liability status has obvious attractions to entrepreneurs as they can take business risks without the burden of placing their personal assets in jeopardy. However, their own investments in the company have no special safeguard, and will be lost if the business fails. Company law and financial reporting standards exist to try to protect shareholders and creditors from crooked businesspeople, but it could be argued that there have been swindlers and confidence tricksters in existence for thousands of years, before limited liability status was ever thought of.

Question 7.5

Morse Ltd

Profit and loss account for the year ended 31 December 2004

	£	£
Sales		462,600
Less Cost of goods sold		
Opening stock at 1 January 2004	14,900	
Add Purchases	140,800	
	155,700	
Less Closing stock at 31 December 2004	(17,650)	
		(138,050)
Gross profit		324,550
Add Decrease in provision for doubtful debts		600
		325,150
Less Expenses		
Directors' remuneration	59,200	
Salesforce wages	65,230	
Office salaries	34,900	
Advertising and website charges (15,300 – 160)	15,140	
Interest	2,502	
Carriage out	632	
Bad debts	750	
Depreciation on delivery vehicles		
[30% × (143,600 – 27,800)]	34,740	
Office expenses (33,897 + 800)	34,697	
		(247,791)
Net profit for the year, before taxation		77,359
Less Provision for taxation		(24,000)
Net profit for the year, after taxation		53,359
Less Dividends:		
Final		(5,000)
Retained profit for the year		48,359

Morse Ltd

Balance sheet as at 31 December 2004

	Cost	Accumulated depreciation	Net book value
Fixed assets	£	£	£
Delivery vehicles	143,600	62,540	81,060
Current assets			
Stock		17,650	
Trade debtors	64,100		
Less Provision for doubtful debts	(1,000)		
		63,100	
Prepayments		160	
Bank		11,500	
		92,410	
Less Creditors due for payment within one year			
Trade creditors	32,711		
Accruals	800		

Taxation	24,000	
Dividend (agreed but unpaid)	5,000	
		(62,511)
Net current assets		29,899
		110,959
Less **Creditors due for payment after more than one year**		
Debenture (repayable 2012)		(10,000)
Total net assets		100,959
Capital and reserves		
Called-up share capital (50p shares)		25,000
Share premium account		15,000
Profit and loss account:		
Balance at 1 January 2004	12,600	
Retained profit for the year	48,359	
		60,959
		100,959

Question 7.6

a Reserves do not equal cash. The total of reserves, when added to the nominal value of the share capital, equal the *total net assets* (i.e. all the assets less all the liabilities) of the company.

b A revenue reserve (e.g. the profit and loss account) has been built up from profits accumulated as a result of the trading operations of the business reflected in the profit and loss account. Such reserves are referred to as being *distributable* – they are available for dividend payments.

A capital reserve (e.g. share premium account, asset revaluation reserve) represents share capital (nominal value plus any premium) paid into the company by shareholders, plus any *unrealised gains* recorded as a result of revaluing assets. Capital reserves are *undistributable* – they are not available for the payment of dividends.

c A share premium is the difference between the price paid to a company for shares and the nominal value of those shares. In the example, the company must have sold its shares at £1.75 each (called-up share capital £100,000 plus share premium account £75,000 = £175,000, divided by 100,000 shares).

d An asset revaluation reserve is created to record an increase in the valuation of a fixed asset (usually land and buildings). If several years have elapsed since the purchase of the land (or its last revaluation), the value as recorded in the balance sheet may be unrealistically low, and distort the overall net asset values shown. The other balance sheet item affected is the fixed asset being revalued.

e A bonus issue could be made, which in effect returns reserves (capital or revenue) without cash payments being made. The bonus issue is a free issue of shares to shareholders, pro rata to their existing shareholdings.

f The rights issue would be for 150,000 shares (100,000 × 3/2). 150,000 shares at £2.40 each = £360,000 of which £150,000 is the nominal value (added to 'called-up share capital') and £210,000 is share premium (added to 'share premium account').

Chapter 8

Question 8.1 a

Delia Trelawney – 'Soul Trading'
Profit and loss account for the year ended 31 May 2005

	£	£
Sales (see Working 1)		39,220
Less Cost of goods sold		
Opening stock (balancing figure)	5,625	
Purchases (see Working 2)	15,069	
	20,694	
Less Closing stock	(3,045)	
		(17,649)
Gross profit (55% × £39,220)		21,571
Less **Expenses**		
Wages	6,000	
Advertising	520	
Rent and rates	1,500	
Telephone and electricity (203 + 871 – 140)	934	
Sundry expenses	603	
Loss on sale of van	480	
Depreciation of shop fittings (see Working 3)	3,082	
		(13,119)
Net profit		8,452

Delia Trelawney – 'Soul Trading'
Balance sheet as at 31 May 2005

	£	£	£
Fixed assets			
Shop fittings at cost brought forward		7,900	
Additions in the year		6,402	
		14,302	
Depreciation to 1 June 2004 (see Working 3)	4,029		
Depreciation for the year (see Working 3)	3,082		
		(7,111)	
			7,191
Current assets			
Stock		3,045	
Bank		6,340	
		9,385	
Less **Current liabilities**			
Trade creditors	6,320		
Accruals	203		
		(6,523)	
Net current assets			2,862
Total net assets			10,053
Capital			
Opening balance (see Working 4)		8,991	

Add Net profit		8,452
		17,443
Less Drawings (6,670 + 720)		(7,390)
		10,053

Working 1:

Cash banked	35,500
Less Sale of van	(3,000)
	32,500
Add Used for holiday and wages	6,720
	39,220

Working 2:

Purchases control

	£		£
Cheques paid	10,854	Creditors b/f	2,105
Creditors c/f	6,320	Purchases (=)	15,069
	17,174		17,174

Working 3:

Depreciation of shop fittings

	Owned at 31 May 2004	Bought in to 31 May 2005	Total
	£	£	£
Cost	7,900	6,402	14,302
2002/3 Depreciation	(2,370)	—	(2,370)
	5,530		
2003/4 Depreciation	(1,659)	—	(1,659)
	3,871		
2004/5 Depreciation	(1,161)	(1,921)	(3,082)
	2,710	4,481	7,191

Depreciation to 1 June 2004 = 2,370 + 1,659 = 4,029.

Working 4:

Opening balance sheet at 1 June 2004

	£	£	£
Fixed assets: Van			3,480
Shop fittings (see Working 3)			3,871
			7,351
Current assets			
Stock		5,625	
Less Current liabilities			
Creditors	2,105		
Accrual	140		
Bank overdraft	1,740	(3,985)	
			1,640
			8,991
Capital			8,991

b Ways of keeping better control over creditors' invoices include:

- Maintain a creditors' ledger.
- File invoices systematically and have a set period for payment.
- Check invoices against statements received.
- Keep a purchases day book.
- Stamp invoices paid when cheques are sent.
- Don't pay individual invoices; pay only monthly statements from creditor.

Question 8.2

Tilly Snowdon

Profit and loss account for the year ended 31 December 2004

	£	£
Sales (see Working 1)		97,650
Less Cost of goods sold		
Opening stock	16,800	
Purchases (see Working 2)	67,100	
	83,900	
Less Closing stock	(23,700)	
		(60,200)
Gross profit		37,450
Less **Expenses**		
Wages	9,070	
Rent and rates	4,600	
Light and heat	3,900	
Van running expenses	1,400	
Adverts (840 − 140 + 120)	820	
Insurance (560 + 80 − 120)	520	
Bad debts	100	
Depreciation: van (see Working 3)	1,500	
Depreciation: fittings (see Working 4)	1,215	
Loss on sale of van (see Working 3)	400	
Sundries	2,800	
		(26,325)
Net profit		11,125

Tilly Snowdon

Balance sheet as at 31 December 2004

	£	£	£
Fixed assets			
Van: at cost		6,000	
Less Depreciation		(1,500)	
			4,500
Fittings: cost b/f		1,500	
Additions in year		3,000	
		4,500	
Depreciation b/f	450		
Provision for year	1,215		
		(1,665)	
			2,835
		c/f	7,335

		b/f	7,335

Current assets

Stock at cost		23,700
Debtors		750
Prepayments		120
		24,570

Less Current liabilities

Creditors	3,300		
Accruals	120		
Bank overdraft	6,670		
		(10,090)	

Net current assets		14,480
Total net assets		21,815

Capital

Opening balance (see Working 5)		21,190
Net profit		11,125
		32,315
Less Drawings		(10,500)
		21,815

Working 1:
Sales

	£		£
Debtors b/f	600	Cash[a]	97,400
Sales =	97,650	Written off	100
		Debtors c/f	750
	98,250		98,250

[a] Cash banked 86,900, plus drawings 10,500 = 97,400.

Working 2:
Purchases

	£		£
Cheques	66,200	Creditors b/f	2,400
Creditors c/f	3,300	Purchases =	67,100
	69,500		69,500

Working 3:

Van Account (at net book value)

	£		£
b/f	2,400	Proceeds (contra)	2,000
Cost	4,000	P & L depreciation (on new van)	1,500
Trade-in (contra)	2,000	P & L loss on sale	400
		c/f	4,500
	8,400		8,400

Note: 'Contra' means that both debit and credit entries cancel each other within the same ledger account.

Working 4:

Depreciation on fittings = [(1,500 + 3,000) − 450] × 30% = 1,215.

Working 5:

Opening capital

	£	£
Van (2,400 less depreciation 450)		1,950
Fittings		1,500
Stocks		16,800
Debtors		600
Prepayments		80
Bank		2,800
		23,730
Less Creditors	2,400	
Accruals	140	
		(2,540)
		21,190

Question 8.3

Razmatazz Sports and Social Club

Income and Expenditure Account for the year ended 31 December 2004

	£	£
Income		
Subscriptions (see Working 1)		14,160
Less **Expenditure**		
Wages	8,450	
Loss on dances (2,060 − 1,778)	282	
Competitions [(850 + 2,200 − 450) − 2,590]	10	
Depreciation on van (25% × £6,300)	1,575	
Depreciation on computer	200	
Depreciation on sports equipment	800	
Loss on sale of van (see Working 2)	1,250	
Printing and advertising	2,070	
Repairs	800	
Motor expenses	1,200	
Sundry expenses	1,180	
		(17,817)
Surplus of expenditure over income		(3,657)

Razmatazz Sports and Social Club

Balance sheet as at 31 December 2004

	Cost	Accumulated depreciation	Net book value
Fixed assets	£	£	£
Van	6,300	1,575	4,725
Computer	2,000	600	1,400
Sports equipment	8,000	2,600	5,400
	16,300	4,775	11,525

Current assets

Stock of prizes		450	
Debtors: subscriptions		1,620	
		2,070	

***Less* Current liabilities**

Creditors: prepaid subscriptions	720		
Bank overdraft	2,722		
		(3,442)	
Net current liabilities			(1,372)
Total net assets			10,153

Accumulated fund

Opening balance (see Working 3)		13,810	
Less Surplus of expenditure over income		(3,657)	
			10,153

Working 1:

Subscriptions

	£		£
Owing b/f	1,440	Cash re 2003	620
Income and Expenditure a/c	14,160	Cash re 2004	14,080
Prepaid c/f	720	Owing c/f	1,620
	16,320		16,320

Working 2:

Sale of van

	£		£
Cost	4,000	Depreciation[a]	1,750
		Bank	1,000
		Loss on sale (I & E a/c)	1,250
	4,000		4,000

[a] 1st year: 25% × £4000 = £1,000, plus (2nd year) 25% × (£4,000 − £1,000) = £750.

Working 3:
Opening accumulated fund balance

	£
Van (cost £4,000 less depreciation £1,750)	2,250
Computer	1,600
Sports equipment	6,200
Prizes	850
Debtors: subscriptions owing	1,440
Bank	1,470
	13,810

Question 8.4 a

Vim and Vigour Sports and Social Club
Income and expenditure account for the year ended 31 December 2004

	£	£
Income		
Subscriptions (see Working 1)		27,540
Competitions: fees	3,150	
prizes	(2,250)	
		900
Dance: ticket sales	2,460	
expenses	(1,350)	
		1,110
		29,550
Less **Expenditure**		
Wages	29,700	
Depreciation on photocopier	600	
Depreciation on sports equipment	1,800	
Loss on sale of equipment	3,900	
Printing and advertising	2,250	
Repairs	1,500	
Sundry expenses	2,460	
		(42,210)
Surplus of Expenditure over Income		(12,660)

Vim and Vigour Sports and Social Club
Balance sheet as at 31 December 2004

	Cost	Accumulated depreciation	Net book value
Fixed assets	£	£	£
Photocopier	6,000	2,400	3,600
Sports equipment	25,800	10,800	15,000
	31,800	13,200	18,600
Current assets			
Stock of prizes		600	
Debtors: subscriptions		1,560	
		2,160	
Less **Current liabilities**			
Bank overdraft		(12,810)	
Net current liabilities			(10,650)
Total net assets			7,950
Accumulated fund			
Opening balance (see Working 2)		20,610	
Less Surplus of expenditure over income		(12,660)	
			7,950

Working 1:

Subscriptions

	£		£
Owing b/f	1,800	Prepaid b/f	840
Refund	60	Cash re 2003	1,800
Income and Expenditure a/c	27,540	Cash re 2004	25,200
		Owing c/f	1,560
	29,400		29,400

Working 2:

	£
Accumulated fund as at 1 January 2004	
Photocopier	4,200
Sports equipment	12,000
Prizes	1,050
Debtors: subscriptions owing	1,800
Bank	2,400
	21,450
Less Subscriptions in advance	(840)
	20,610

b

	Members	£
No. of members in 2004 (£27,600[a]/£80)	345	
Less Members resigning (20% × 345)	(69)	
	276	
New members	40	
	316	
Cash due in 2005:		
316 members × £120		37,920
Add Cash due in 2005 re 2004		1,560
Total cash due		39,480

[a] (840 + 25,200 + 1,560).

Chapter 9

Question 9.1 A: £10,080
B: £22,570
C: £(7,930)
D: £(6,270)

Question 9.2

(£)	A	B	C	D
Net profit before interest	36,620	29,937		20,060
Net loss before interest			(22,660)	
Depreciation	12,000	16,000	24,000	15,000
Increase in stock	(9,650)			(14,850)
Decrease in stock		5,840	5,622	
Increase in debtors			(2,240)	(12,795)
Decrease in debtors	7,980	6,722		
Increase in creditors	3,380		9,713	
Decrease in creditors		(6,840)		(11,629)
Cash flow from operating activities	50,330	51,659	14,435	(4,214)

Question 9.3

Dombey plc
Cash flow statement for the year ended 31 May 2005

	£000
Net cash inflow from operating activities (see Note 1)	28,800
Interest paid	(1,200)
Tax	(4,000)
Net capital expenditure (22,000 – 1,800)	(20,200)
Changes in financing	(8,900)
Dividends	(3,000)
Business acquisitions/disposals	–
Decrease in cash for the year (see Note 2)	(8,500)

Note 1:
Reconciliation of operating profit to net cash inflow from operating activities

	£000
Operating profit before interest (24,700 + 1,200)	25,900
Depreciation charges (see Working)	6,000
Loss on sale of tangible fixed assets	3,200
Increase in stock	(1,000)
Increase in debtors	(1,500)
Decrease in creditors	(3,800)
	28,800

Note 2:
Analysis of changes in cash during the year	£000
Balance at 1 June 2004	2,800
Decrease in cash for the year	(8,500)
Balance at 31 May 2005	(5,700)

Working:

Disposals account

	£000		£000
Cost	8,000	Proceeds	1,800
		Depreciation[a]	3,000
		P & L	3,200
	8,000		8,000

Depreciation account

	£000		£000
Disposals (see Depreciation a/c)	3,000	Balance b/f (76,000 − 32,000)	44,000
Balance c/f (90,000 − 43,000)	47,000	P & L[a]	6,000
	50,000		50,000

[a] Balancing figures.

Question 9.4 The forecast (see Figure A2.1 on p. 341) appears to show a healthy business, with the closing bank balance reaching £17,700 by the end of the year. However, payments in January 2007 are forecast to reach £19,400 (rent, general overheads and the 60% of December's sales due to artists). No overdraft limit has been agreed, so Clara would have to convince the bank that her business can survive into the following year. She would need a temporary overdraft for September (£750) and at least £1,700 in January (£19,400 − £17,700). The worrying aspect of the business is that it may be seasonal, so the overdraft might have to rise sharply in the first quarter of 2007.

Chapter 10

Question 10.1 There is no set answer to this question.

Question 10.2 **a** Roden Limited is likely to be the food retailer, for the following reasons.
- Food retailing produces a small gross profit margin, but the fast turnover ensures that profit is earned much faster than in a manufacturing business.
- Very few retail food sales are made on credit terms, so the year-end debtors' figure will be very low. Due to the fast stock turnover, creditors' totals might be twice as much as stock, giving rise to the negative current (working capital) ratio for Roden Limited of 0.4:1.

b (i) *Debtors*:
Ercall Limited's sales can be calculated as £200,000 × 100/40 (because the gross margin of 60% means that cost of sales must be 40% of the sales figure). If the debtors' collection period is 30 days, then the debtors' total is 30/365 of the sales figure: (30/365) × £500,000 = £41,096.

Figure A2.1

Clara Pilbeam: The Marshes Gallery cash flow forecast from 1 July 2006 to 31 December 2006

Clara Pilbeam: The Marshes Gallery cash flow forecast from 1 July 2006 to 31 December 2006						
Period – Monthly	July	August	September	October	November	December
(£)						
Receipts						
Sales: cash	8,000	4,000	7,000	12,000	18,000	24,000
Capital injected	4,000	–	–	–	–	–
Other receipts: grant	–	5,000	–	–	–	–
A: Total Receipts	12,000	9,000	7,000	12,000	18,000	24,000
Payments						
Due to artists	–	4,800	2,400	4,200	7,200	10,800
Wages	750	750	750	750	750	750
Deposit to landlord	3,000	–	–	3,000	–	–
Rent	–	–	3,000	–	–	–
Redecorating premises	–	4,000	3,000	–	–	–
General overheads	–	2,000	2,000	2,000	2,000	2,000
Clara's drawings	600	600	600	600	600	900
Equipment	–	–	3,000	–	–	–
Advertising	–	500	–	–	–	–
B: Total payments	4,350	12,650	11,750	10,550	10,550	14,450
C: Net cash flow (A – B)	7,650	(3,650)	(4,750)	1,450	7,450	9,550
D: Opening bank balance	–	7,650	4,000	(750)	700	8,150
E: Closing bank balance (D ± C)	7,650	4,000	(750)	700	8,150	17,700
Note: Agreed Overdraft Facility	(none)	(none)	(none)	(none)	(none)	(none)

Note: Depreciation does not appear in the forecast, as it is a 'non-cash' expense.

(ii) *Creditors*:

The current ratio (current assets : current liabilities) is 2:1. Current assets for Ercall Limited are:

	£
Stock	40,000
Debtors (as calculated above)	41,096
Bank and cash	11,004
	92,100

Therefore current liabilities are $1/2 \times £92,100 = £46,050$.

c Roden Limited is highly geared, which indicates that the company has significant borrowings. As an ordinary shareholder, you would need to be satisfied that the company can repay the interest due on such loans and that the return generated by the borrowed capital is greater than the cost of financing it. Highly geared companies carry more risk than low-geared companies, but can produce higher returns if the company and its profits expand as a result of the borrowings.

Question 10.3 **a**

		Rodington	Rowton	Comments
(i)	Gearing	Nil	$\dfrac{100}{100 + 113} = 47\%$	Gearing for Rowton is a high 47%, whereas Rodington has no fixed return borrowings
(ii)	Current ratio	123:135 = 0.9:1	177:168 = 1.05:1	Both companies have low working capital ratios, Rodington worse than Rowton
(iii)	Acid test	38:135 = 0.28:1	57:168 = 0.34:1	Both companies are exposed to liquidity ratio problems if creditors start demanding payment
(iv)	ROCE	$\dfrac{40,000}{113,000} = 35.4\%$	$\dfrac{40,000}{113,000 + 100,000} = 18.8\%$	Rodington has almost twice the ROCE of Rowton. Are they in comparable business sectors?

b Rowton is more vulnerable due to high gearing and lower ROCE. Both companies show poor working capital/acid test ratios, but this may be a feature of their type of trade (for example, supermarkets).

If Rodington would be prepared to issue a debenture secured on its assets, then the investor might be better off with Rodington, though again the lack of liquidity would be worrying. Neither seems suitable for a cautious investor.

c If the going concern concept was not applicable, then Rodington would be heading for receivership, with asset values (almost certainly) being downgraded, and provisions being made for the likely costs of liquidation.

The advice to the potential investor in that situation would be to steer well clear of the company.

Question 10.4 **a** Any eight of the following ratios:

From P & L account:

Mark-up	190/480 × 100	39.6%
Gross profit margin	190/670 × 100	28.4%
Net profit margin	51,050/670,000 × 100	7.6%
ROCE	51,050/265,000 × 100	19.3%
Earnings per share	40,000/100,000	40p
Interest cover	51,050/5,600	9.1 times
Dividend cover	40,000/15,000	2.7 times

From balance sheet:

Asset turnover	670,000/185,800 × 100	360.6%
Current ratio	158,450/79,250	2:1
Acid test	68,450/79,250	0.86:1
Gearing	80,000/(185,000 + 80,000) × 100	30.2%
Stockturn	90,000/480,000 × 365	68.4 days
Debtors' collection	43,650/670,000 × 365	23.8 days
Creditors' payment	48,000/570,000 × 365	30.7 days

Comment: One year's figures should never be taken by themselves as a measure of a company's performance, as other figures are needed for comparison, for example, those of previous years or competitors. With this major proviso, we can see that the company had a 'textbook' current ratio, a seemingly strong ROCE (when compared with what we know of prevailing interest rates), a good safety level for interest payments (profit available being 9.1 times the interest) and realistic debtors' and creditors' collection ratios. Gearing is on the high side, but as we have seen, the interest is covered strongly.

b £6m is a significant amount for a company which made only £40,000 profit after taxation. However, possibilities for raising capital include:
- A rights issue (but it is a new company, so would shareholders put in so much more capital so quickly?)
- Loans (but existing debentures could be secured on assets, so it is unlikely that there would be enough security available for more loans).

Note that, as a private limited company, it could not sell its shares to the general public.

Chapter 12

Question 12.1 **a** Total fixed costs £12,568.
b Total variable costs £6,644.
c Fixed cost per duvet £3.61.
d Variable cost per duvet £1.91.
e Total cost per duvet £5.52.

Workings:

	£	% variable	% variable	£ variable	£ fixed
Raw materials	1,505	100	0	1,505	0
Direct labour	1,161	100	0	1,161	0
Direct expenses	2,838	100	0	2,838	0
Indirect material	3,560	5	95	178	3,382
Indirect labour	3,378	7	93	236	3,142
Indirect expenses	1,544	6	94	93	1,451
Selling overhead	2,481	20	80	496	1,985
Administration overhead	2,745	5	95	137	2,608
Total	19,212			6,644	12,568
Cost per duvet (3,481 produced)				1.91	3.61

Question 12.2 The company must charge a price in excess of the total cost of £5.52 in order to make a profit.

If the company hopes to make a net profit margin of 10%, it would charge:

$$£5.52 \times \frac{100}{(100 - 10)} = £6.13 \text{ per duvet}$$

Chapter 13

Question 13.1

	Production departments			Service department
	A £	B £	C £	D £
Indirect labour	20,000	16,000	8,000	7,000
Other indirect labour	10,000	6,000	3,000	2,600
	30,000	22,000	11,000	9,600
Department D's expenses	3,840	3,840	1,920	(9,600)
Total	33,840	25,840	12,920	

Question 13.2

	Alphas	Betas	Gammas	Deltas	Episilons
Direct costs	22	18	35	30	43
Variable costs	11	9	16	15	19
Marginal costs	33	27	51	45	62
Fixed costs	17	13	19	15	18
Total costs	50	40	70	60	80
Profit mark-up 20%	10	8	14	12	16
Full cost prices (answer a)	**60**	**48**	**84**	**72**	**96**
Selling prices	59	25	80	44	92

	Alphas	Betas	Gammas	Deltas	Episilons	Total
Recommend company should produce (i.e. where selling prices are greater than total cost (**answer b**)	Yes	No	Yes	No	Yes	
Sales of all products (selling prices × 100)	5,900	2,500	8,000	4,400	9,200	30,000
Variable costs (100 × marginal costs)	3,300	2,700	5,100	4,500	6,200	(21,800)
Fixed costs (total)						(8,200)
Profit (**answer c(i)**)						**Nil**
If only 'recommended' products were manufactured:						
Sales	5,900		8,000		9,200	23,100
Variable costs	3,300		5,100		6,200	(14,600)
Fixed costs (total)						(8,200)
Profit (**answer c(ii)**)						**300**

Question 13.3

	A	B	C	D	E
Sales in units	5,000	20,000	4,000	6,000	15,000
Sales (£)	40,000	60,000	48,000	90,000	105,000
Variable costs (£)	10,000	50,000	32,000	54,000	30,000
Contribution (£)	30,000	10,000	16,000	36,000	75,000
Contribution per unit (£)	6	0.5	4	6	5
Fixed costs (£)	14,400	15,000	7,000	24,000	50,000
Profit/(loss) (£)	15,600	(5,000)	9,000	12,000	25,000
Break-even point (units)	2,400	30,000	1,750	4,000	10,000
Profit/(loss) if 3,000 units sold	3,600	(13,500)	5,000	(6,000)	(35,000)

Question 13.4 a

	10,000 units	15,000 units	Change +5,000 units
	£	£	£
Total costs	160,000	210,000	+ 50,000

Therefore variable costs = £50,000/5,000 units = £10 per unit

Variable costs @ £10 per unit: 100,000 for 10,000 units; 150,000 for 15,000 units

Answer: fixed costs = **£60,000**

b Break-even = Fixed costs/contribution per unit
Contribution per unit = Selling price (£15) – Variable cost (see (a) above) (£10) = £5
Therefore the break-even point = £60,000/£5 = 12,000 units.
To earn a profit of £13,000, total contribution must be:
Fixed costs £60,000 + Profit £13,000 = £73,000
As contribution per unit is £5, they must sell 73,000/5 = **14,600 units.**

c If only 7,000 units were manufactured and sold, the total contribution would be 7,000 × £5 = £35,000, which is £25,000 less than the fixed costs of £60,000. Therefore a **loss of £25,000** is made.

Chapter 14

Question 14.1 **a** Specific order costing is the basic costing method applicable where the work consists of separate contracts, jobs or batches, each of which is authorised by a special order or contract.

b Process costing is the basic costing method where goods or services result from a sequence of continuous or repetitive operations or processes to which costs are charged before being averaged over the units produced during the period. Since individual units of output are not easily identified (unlike specific order costing), the process itself therefore becomes the cost centre rather than the unit of output. The costs are collected for each process and averaged over the output of that process for the period.

Question 14.2 **a**

	Cost	
	Unit	Total
	£	£
Raw materials (1.60 × 300)	1.60	480
Wages (£4.20 × 20 hours)	0.28	84
Overheads (20 × £3.60)	0.24	72
Setting-up costs	0.07	21
Cost of full batch	2.19	657

b

	£	£
Cost of full batch		657.00
Add Rectification costs		
Wages (9 hours × £4.20)	37.80	
Overheads (9 hours × £3.60)	32.40	
Setting-up costs	18.00	
		88.20
		745.20
Less Income from scrapped components 20 × £0.86		(17.20)
Total cost of 280 cat baskets		728.00
Cost of batch per unit £728/280		2.60

c

	£
280 units should have cost 280 × £2.19 (see (a) above)	613.20
Actual cost (see (b) above)	728.00
Loss	114.80

Chapter 15

Question 15.1 Break-even chart

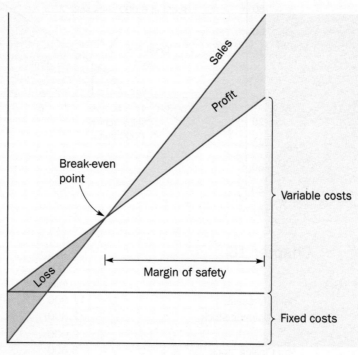

Question 15.2 Break-even chart for Basil Limited

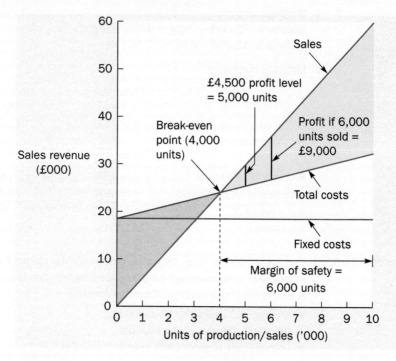

The answers to the four questions are as follows:

a 4,000 units

b £9,000

c 6,000 units

d 5,000 units

Question 15.3 Profit/volume chart

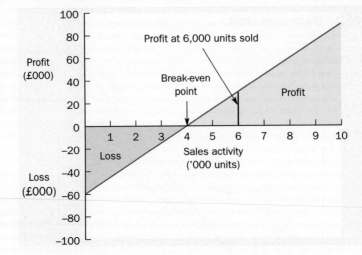

Chapter 16

Question 16.1 a

	Units
Sales forecast:	11,800
Less Opening stock	(2,800)
	9,000
Add Closing stock	3,600
Production required	12,600

b Materials usage:
Material A: 12,600 × 10 kg = 126,000 kg
Material B: 12,600 × 6 kg = 75,600 kg

c Materials purchases:

	Material A kg	Material B kg
Usage (see (b) above)	126,000	75,600
Less Opening stock	(700)	(400)
	125,300	75,200
Add Closing stock	500	900
Materials to be purchased	125,800	76,100
Value per kg (£)	6.50	9.00
Total value	£817,700	£684,900

Question 16.2 Limiting factors are areas within the business which restrict the growth of that business. At any one time, there will be a key factor which needs to be addressed before the business can make progress. Examples include:

● Shortage of adequately trained workers
● Unreliable supplies of raw materials
● Unavailability of spare parts to repair machinery.

Question 16.3 **a**   **Budgeted profit statement for the year ended 31 October 2006**

	£000	£000
Sales (1,200,000 alarms × £8)		9,600
Less **Marginal costs:**		
Materials: direct, variable [1.2m × (£2 − 5%)]	2,280	
Labour: direct, variable [1.2m × (£1.20 + 10%)]	1,584	
Other production overheads: variable (1.2m × 50p)	600	
Selling overheads: variable 1.2m × (60p + 33%)	960	
Distribution overheads: variable 1.2m × 35p	420	
		(5,844)
Contribution (per unit: 3,756,000/1.2m = £3.13)		3,756
Less **Fixed costs:**		
Labour: indirect, fixed (280,000 + 25%)	350	
Other production overheads: fixed (640,000 + 25%)	800	
Selling overheads: fixed (360,000 + 25%)	450	
Distribution overheads: fixed (120,000 + 25%)	150	
Administration overheads: fixed (600,000 + 25%)	750	
		(2,500)
Net profit for the year (per unit: 1,256,000/1.2m = £1.05)		1,256

b Break-even points for the year ended 31 October 2005:

	£
Sales	£7,200,000
Less Variable costs (total)	£3,720,000
Contribution	£3,480,000

Per unit: £3,480,000/800,000 = £4.35
Total fixed costs = £5,720,000 − £3,720,000 = £2m
Break-even point = £2m/£4.35 = 459,770 units

Break-even point for the year ended 31 October 2006:
Fixed costs/contribution per unit (see (a) above): £2.5m/£3.13 = **798,722 units**
Contribution per unit is forecast to fall from £4.35 to £3.13, and fixed cost increase by £500,000, so more units have to be sold to break even.

The margin of safety (maximum planned production less break-even point) for the two years is:

Year ended 31 October 2005:   800,000 − 459,770 = 340,230 units
Year ended 31 October 2006: 1,200,000 − 798,722 = 401,278 units

A large margin of safety indicates that the company can reduce production substantially if it has to, without incurring losses. A short margin of safety indicates that a large reduction in output may cause the firm to make losses.

c To make £1,480,000 profit in 2006, the total contribution must be the required profit plus the fixed costs £2,500,000 = £3,980,000. Each unit is forecast to contribute £3.13 in that year, so (£3,980,000/£3.13) = 1,271,565 units to be sold.

d The comment ignores the fact that variable costs change with production whereas fixed costs tend not to. Net profit does not increase uniformly with sales output. Firstly, the *contribution* (sales less variable costs) must meet the fixed costs of the business, and only then is profit made.

Chapter 17

Question 17.1

Year	Future value × Discount factor	Project A	Future value × Discount factor	Project B
0	n/a	(3,000)	n/a	(4,000)
1	0.909 × £10,000	9,090	–	
2			0.826 × £12,000	9,912
NPV		6,090		5,912

Project A has a higher net present value, so would be chosen, on this basis, in preference to project B.

Question 17.2

Year	Future value × Discount factor	Project C	Future value × Discount factor	Project D
0	n/a	(10,000)	n/a	(12,000)
1–3	£9,000 × 2.673	24,057		–
1–4			£7,000 × 3.465	24,255
NPV		14,057		12,255

Project C has a higher net present value, so would be chosen, on this basis, in preference to project D. Note that the calculations have been made simpler by using the cumulative discount factors. This is only possible where the same amounts are receivable (or payable) over a number of years.

Question 17.3 Project G pays back its initial investment in 5 years (£4,000 × 5 = £20,000), whereas project H pays back its initial investment in 6 years (£5,000 × 6 = £30,000). Project G has a shorter payback period, so would be chosen, on this basis, in preference to project H. Note that cash flows arising after the payback period has been reached are ignored, as is the time value of the money.

Question 17.4

Year	Net cash flows £	5% Discount factors	5% Present values £	6% Discount factors	6% Present values £	7% Discount factors	7% Present values £	8% Discount factors	8% Present values £
0	(20,000)	n/a	(20,000)	n/a	(20,000)	n/a	(20,000)		(20,000)
1	6,700	0.952	6,378	0.943	6,318	0.935	6,265	0.926	6,204
2	8,600	0.907	7,800	0.890	7,654	0.873	7,508	0.857	7,370
3	8,100	0.864	6,998	0.840	6,804	0.816	6,609	0.794	6,431
NPV			1,176		776		382		5

As the 8% discount rate reduces the NPV to (near) zero, that is the internal rate of return for the project.

Question 17.5

Buy the equipment:

Year		Future value × Discount factor	Present value
0	Cost	n/a	(700,000)
1–5	Maintenance	£30,000 × 3.993	(119,790)
5	Scrap value	£100,000 × 0.681	68,100
1–3	Income	£300,000 × 2.577	773,100
4	Income	£200,000 × 0.735	147,000
5	Income	£200,000 × 0.681	136,200
NPV (positive)			304,610

Lease the equipment:

Year		Future value × Discount factor	Present value
0	Deposit	n/a	(400,000)
1–5	Lease payments	£120,000 × 3.993	(479,160)
	Income	£300,000 × 3.993	1,197,900
NPV (positive)			£318,740

Buying the equipment outright appears to be the cheaper option by just over £14,000. However, it should be borne in mind that buying the equipment requires an immediate payment of £700,000 compared with a deposit to the lessor of only £400,000. If there is uncertainty surrounding the potential income generation, then leasing might have its advantages, as payback is reached in just over two years (income of £600,000 in two years nearly matches the lease payments of £640,000 in the same period). Total payments in the first two years when buying the equipment (including maintenance) are £760,000, but income in that period is only £600,000.

Other considerations would be the relative quality of the equipment (note that the leased equipment is slightly more advanced than that purchased outright), its relative reliability, and the status of both the lessor and the supplier of the equipment. The latter point is particularly important as the hospital will require continuing maintenance for the five-year period, either paid for annually in the case of the equipment being purchased outright, or as part of the leasing package.

Chapter 1 – Marvin makes a career choice

a

	£
Income in week ending 7 July:	
Fee for Conjuring Show appearance	750
Less Travel expenses	(20)
Profit	730

b

	£	£
Fixed assets		
Costume		3,000
Magic book		2,000
Cards		400
		5,400
Current assets		
Bank account	750	
Less **Current liability**		
Creditor (Kazam Limited)	(400)	
		350
		5,750

Because of the accounting equation (A – L = C), Marvin's capital at 7 July was £5,750.

Proof:
Marvin paid for the costume, the book and the travel expenses out of his own private resources (£3,000 + £2,000 + £20 = £5,020), and the business made a profit during the week of £730 which increased the value of his capital to £5,750.

Chapter 2 – Marvin buys rabbits!

a, b, c

Cash book

		Cash £	Bank £			Cash £	Bank £
7 Jul	Fee		750	10 Jul	Travel	15	
10 Jul	Fee	100		11 Jul	Cleaning		18
12 Jul	Fee		120	12 Jul	Travel	9	
		100	870	14 Jul	Utd Rabbit		240
				14 Jul	Kazam Ltd		400
						24	658
				14 Jul	Balance c/d	76	212
		100	870			100	870
15 Jul	Balance b/d	76	212				

General Ledger

Capital

	£		£
14 Jul Balance c/d	5,020	1 Jul Costume	3,000
		2 Jul Magic Book	2,000
		7 Jul Travel	
			20
	5,020		5,020
		15 Jul Balance b/d	5,020

Costume

	£		£
1 Jul Capital	3,000	14 Jul Balance c/d	3,000
15 Jul Balance b/d	3,000		

Magic Book

	£		£
2 Jul Capital	2,000	14 Jul Balance c/d	2,000
15 Jul Balance b/d	2,000		

Playing Cards

	£		£
3 Jul Kazam Limited	400	14 Jul Balance c/d	400
15 Jul Balance b/d	400		

Fees

	£		£
14 Jul Balance c/d	1,220	7 Jul Bank	750
		10 Jul Cash	100
		12 Jul Bank	120
		13 Jul Mr & Mrs Peter	250
	1,220		1,220
		Jul 15 Balance b/d	1,220

Travel expenses

	£		£
7 Jul Capital	20	14 Jul Balance c/d	44
10 Jul Cash	15		
12 Jul Cash	9		
	44		44
15 Jul Balance b/d	44		

Rabbits (an expense)

		£			£
8 Jul	United Rabbit Corp'n	240	14 Jul	Balance c/d	240
15 Jul	Balance b/d	240			

Rabbit food

		£			£
8 Jul	Amalgamated Carrots	250	14 Jul	Balance c/d	250
15 Jul	Balance b/d	250			

Cleaning

		£			£
11 Jul	Bank	18	Jul 14	Balance c/d	18
15 Jul	Balance b/d	18			

Purchase returns

		£			£
14 Jul	Balance c/d	60	14 Jul	Amalgamated Carrots	60
			15 Jul	Balance b/d	60

Purchase Ledger

Kazam Limited

		£			£
14 Jul	Bank	400	3 Jul	Playing cards	400

United Rabbit Corporation

		£			£
14 Jul	Bank	240	8 Jul	Rabbits	240

Amalgamated Carrots plc

		£			£
14 Jul	Purchase returns	60	8 Jul	Rabbit food	250
14 Jul	Balance c/d	190			
		250			250
			15 Jul	Balance b/d	190

Sales Ledger

Mr & Mrs Peter

		£			£
13 Jul	Fees	250	14 Jul	Balance c/d	250
15 Jul	Balance b/d	250			

d

Marvin the Magician
Trial balance as at 14 July

	Dr £	Cr £
Cash	76	
Bank	212	
Capital		5,020
Costume	3,000	
Magic book	2,000	
Playing cards	400	
Fees		1,220
Travel expenses	44	
Rabbits (an expense)	240	
Rabbit food	250	
Cleaning	18	
Purchase returns		60
Amalgamated Carrots plc (creditor)		190
Mr & Mrs Peter (debtor)	250	
	6,490	6,490

Chapter 3 – Esmeralda appears, then disappears

Marvin the Magician
Profit and loss account for the six months ended 31 December 2000

	£	£
Sales of novelties (2500 + 350)		2,850
Less Cost of sales		
Opening stock at 1 July 2000	–	
Add Purchases	1,700	
	1,700	
Less Closing stock at 31 December 2000	(80)	
		(1,620)
Gross profit on sales of novelties		1,230
Add Appearance fees as entertainer		18,320
		19,550
Less Expenses		
Wages (1200 + 100)	1,300	
Travel (2600 – 50)	2,550	
Rabbit expenses	430	
Cleaning	140	
Depreciation – magician's equipment	540	
Depreciation – disappearing lady apparatus	400	
		(5,360)
Net profit		14,190

Balance sheet as at 31 December 2000

	£	£	£
Fixed assets			
Magician's equipment, at cost (3,000 + 2,000 + 400)		5,400	
Less Depreciation (20% for half-year)		(540)	
			4,860
Disappearing lady apparatus		2,000	
Less Depreciation (40% for half-year)		(400)	
			1,600
			6,460
Current assets			
Stock		80	
Debtors		350	
Prepayment – travel		50	
Bank		120	
Cash		560	
		1,160	
***Less* Current liabilities**			
Creditors (Kaboosh Ltd, 1,700 – 1,500)	200		
Accrual – wages	100		
		(300)	
Net current assets			860
Total net assets			7,320
Capital			
Opening balance (as per case study in Chapter 2)		5,020	
Add Net profit		14,190	
		19,210	
Less Drawings		(11,890)	
Closing balance at 31 December 2000			7,320

Chapter 4 – Marvin makes magic

**Manufacturing, trading and profit and loss account
for the year ended 30 June 2001**

	£	£
Raw materials		
Purchases of raw materials		
(note: no opening stock)	15,621	
Less Closing stock at 30 June 2001	(6,320)	
Cost of raw materials		9,301
Other direct costs:		
Production labour		5,820
Prime cost of production		15,121
Indirect costs:		
Rent and rates	3,600	
Light and heat	2,500	
Other workshop expenses	4,100	
Depreciation of workshop machinery	500	
		10,700
Total production cost c/d		25,821

Sales			45,821
Less Cost of goods sold			
Purchases (note: no opening stock)		3,400	
Total production cost b/d		25,821	
		29,221	
Less Closing stock at 30 June 2001		(2,400)	
			(26,821)
Gross profit			19,000
Add Appearance fees as entertainer			34,500
			53,500
Less Expenses			
Assistant's wages		12,400	
Travel		5,510	
Rabbit expenses		430	
Cleaning		280	
Depreciation – magician's equipment		1,080	
Depreciation – disappearing lady apparatus		800	
			(20,500)
Net profit			33,000

Balance sheet as at 30 June 2001

	£	£	£
Fixed assets			
Magician's equipment, at cost		5,400	
Less Depreciation		(1,080)	
			4,320
Disappearing lady apparatus		2,000	
Less Depreciation (40%)		(800)	
			1,200
Workshop machinery		3,600	
Less Depreciation		(500)	
			3,100
			8,620
Current assets			
Stock (6,320 + 2,400)		8,720	
Debtors (Mrs Featherskew)		200	
Prepayment – rent and rates		600	
Bank		660	
Cash		40	
		10,220	
Less Current liabilities			
Creditors (Kaboosh Ltd)	240		
Accruals (£200 + £100)	300		
		(540)	
Net current assets			9,680
Total net assets			18,300
Capital			
Opening balance (as per case study in Chapter 2)		5,020	
Add Net profit		33,000	
		38,020	
Less Drawings		(19,720)	
Closing balance at 30 June 2001			18,300

Chapter 5 – Esmeralda doesn't disappear, so Chiquita appears

a

	£
Cost of the equipment	2,000
Depreciation to 30 June 2001	800
One month's depreciation to disposal date:	
$\frac{1}{12} \times [40\% \, (2,000 - 800)]$	40
Total depreciation to date of disposal	(840)
Net book value at date of disposal (2,000 – 840)	1,160
Proceeds	1,000
Loss on disposal	160

b The £200 bad debt will be written off to profit and loss account, thus reducing net profit. Debtors (current assets) also decrease by this amount.

Doubtful debts do not affect the sales ledger as the account is kept alive as long as there is a glimmer of hope of payment. However, to abide by the prudence concept, profits are set aside from the profit and loss account to ensure that all the doubtful debts are covered by the provision. The total provision is then deducted from the total debtors (after any bad debts have been deleted). The effect on profits depends on whether the provision is being created, increased or decreased:

- Created: the full amount of the provision comes out of profit.
- Increased: only the extra amount needed comes out of profit.
- Decreased: the surplus provision is added back to increase the profit.

Chapter 6 – Marvin's second birthday

Profit and loss account for the year ended 30 June 2002

	£	£
Sales		35,900
Less Cost of goods sold		
Opening stock at 1 July 2001	2,400	
Add Purchases	15,600	
	18,000	
Less Closing stock at 30 June 2002	(2,500)	
		(15,500)
Gross profit		20,400
Add Appearance fees as entertainer		45,200
		65,600
Less Expenses		
Assistant's wages	24,600	
Travel (£6,220 – prepaid £450)	5,770	
Bad debt	200	
Increase in provision for doubtful debts (5% × £2,600)	130	
Cleaning	1,570	
Depreciation – magician's equipment	1,300	
Depreciation – 'saw the lady in half' prop [(£3,000 – £600)/4]	600	
Loss on disposal of disappearing lady apparatus	160	
		(34,330)
Net profit		31,270

Balance sheet as at 30 June 2002

	£	£	£
Fixed assets			
Magician's equipment, at cost		7,700	
Less Depreciation (1,080 + 1,300)		(2,380)	
			5,320
'Saw the lady in half' prop		3,000	
Less Depreciation		(600)	
			2,400
			7,720
Current assets			
Stock		2,500	
Debtors	2,600		
Less Provision for doubtful debts	(130)		
		2,470	
Prepayment – travel		450	
Bank		5,160	
		10,580	
***Less* Current liabilities**			
Creditors	480		
Accruals	250		
		(730)	
Net current assets			9,850
Total net assets			17,570
Capital			
Opening balance, 1 July 2001		18,300	
Add Net profit		31,270	
		49,570	
Less Drawings		(32,000)	
Closing balance at 30 June 2002			17,570

Chapter 7 – Marvin and Chiquita make Machiq, but Esmeralda makes trouble

a
Machiq & Co.
Profit and loss account (appropriation section)
for the year ended 30 June 2003

	£	£
Net profit for the year		58,800
Appropriated as follows:		
Marvin: share of profit (60% × £58,800)	35,280	
Chiquita: share of profit (40% × £58,800)	23,520	
		58,800

Machiq & Co.
Balance sheet as at 30 June 2003 (extract)

	£	£
(Total net assets)		35,000
Marvin's Capital Account		
Opening balance, 1 July 2002	17,570	
Add Share of profit	35,280	
	52,850	
Less Drawings	(32,850)	
Closing balance, 30 June 2003		20,000
Chiquita's Capital Account		
Opening balance, 1 July 2002	10,000	
Add Share of profit	23,520	
	33,520	
Less Drawings	(18,520)	
Closing balance, 30 June 2003		15,000
		35,000

b   **Machiq Limited**
Profit and loss account for the year ended 30 June 2004 (extract)

	£
Net profit for the year, before taxation	92,000
Less Provision for taxation (20% × £92,000)	(18,400)
Net profit for the year, after taxation	73,600
Less Dividend (£2.25 × 14,000 shares)	(31,500)
Retained profit for the year	42,100

Machiq Limited
Balance sheet as at 30 June 2004 (extract)

	£
Capital and reserves	
Called-up share capital (£1 shares)[1]	14,000
Share premium account[2]	21,000
Profit and loss account:	
Retained profit for the year	42,100
	77,100

Notes:

1 The balances transferred from Machiq & Co. (see above) were Marvin £20,000, Chiquita £15,000 (ratio 4:3), so the share capital of £14,000 is allocated as follows: Marvin (4/7) = 8,000 shares, Chiquita (3/7) = 6,000 shares.

2 The partners' balances totalled £35,000, so the share premium must be £35,000 less the nominal value of £14,000 = £21,000.

Chapter 8 – The treasurer of the Abracadabra Club does a vanishing trick

a Workings to establish 100 Club receipts:

Subscriptions account (number of members in brackets)

		£				£
1/1/03	Opening debtors (4)	360	31/12/03 Bank: subs re 2002 (3)			270
31/12/03	Income and		Bad debt written			
	expenditure		off to I&E			
	account (100)	9,000	account		(1)	90
			Bank: subs re			
			2003	(95)		8,550
			Closing debtors	(5)		450
		9,360				9,360

Bank summary:

	£	£
Opening balances (2,099 + 711)		2,810
Add Subscriptions (see workings above) (270 + 8,550)	8,820	
Other receipts as listed	2,352	
		11,172
		13,982
Less Payments as listed		(6,118)
Closing balance at bank should have been		7,864

Therefore, as the bank balances were nil, **£7,864** is the amount missing.

b

The Abracadabra Club
Income and expenditure account for the year ended 31 December 2003

	£	£
Income		
Membership subscriptions (see workings)	9,000	
Profit on sale of drinks[1]	47	
Profit on dances[2]	401	
Bank interest	120	
		9,568
Less **Expenditure**		
100 Club prizes	2,000	
Bad debt written off	90	
Loss on sale of computer (1,000 − 700)	300	
Depreciation on computer (20% × £1,000)	200	
Sundries	87	
Exceptional expenditure: theft of cash	7,864	
		(10,541)
Surplus of expenditure over income		(973)

Notes:

1 Profit on sale of drinks:

Sales		265
Less Cost of sales		
Opening stock	200	
Purchases (165 + 28)	193	
	393	
Less Closing stock	(175)	
		(218)
Profit		47

2 Profit on dances:

Ticket sales	1,267
Less Band fees	(866)
Profit	401

c

The Abracadabra Club
Balance sheet as at 31 December 2003

	£	£	£
Fixed assets			
Computer		1,000	
Less Depreciation		(200)	
			800
Current assets			
Bar stock		175	
Subscriptions owing		450	
Bank		–	
		625	
Less **Current liabilities**			
Creditors – drinks		(28)	
Net current assets			597
Total net assets			1,397
Accumulated fund			
Opening balance, 1 January 2003		2,370	
Less Surplus of expenditure over income		(973)	
Closing balance, 31 December 2003			1,397

d One advantage and one disadvantage of presenting a simple receipts and payments account, rather than an income and expenditure account and balance sheet, are as follows.
- *Advantage.* Requires no knowledge of accounting principles, just the ability to summarise cash and bank information.
- *Disadvantage.* Does not disclose the club's surplus or deficit for the financial period, or its assets and liabilities at the end of that period.

e Clubs could minimise the risk of a treasurer misappropriating funds by the following means:
- Ensuring that more than one person is required to sign cheques.
- Requiring an external audit of the club's finances.
- Seeking references before appointing the treasurer.
- Always ensuring that more than one person is present when cash receipts are being counted.
- Requiring regular reports of the financial position from the treasurer.
- Asking the bank to send duplicate bank statements to another club official at regular intervals.

Chapter 9 – There's the profit, but where's the cash?

a
Machiq Limited
Cash flow statement for the year ended 30 June 2005

	£
Net cash inflow from operating activities[1]	120,060
Interest paid	(1,800)
Tax	(18,400)
Capital expenditure	(97,000)
Changes in financing	20,000
Dividends	(31,500)
Decrease in cash for the period	(8,640)

Reconciliation of cash balances at start and end of the period:	
Opening bank balance, 1 July 2004	6,240
Closing bank overdraft, 30 June 2005	(2,400)
Decrease in cash for the period	(8,640)

Note:

		£
1	Operating profit (116,000 + 1,800)	117,800
	Depreciation (see Working 1)	5,060
	Increase in stock (32,650 – 17,370)	(15,280)
	Decrease in debtors (39,560 – 30,950)	8,610
	Increase in creditors (14,080 – 10,210)	3,870
	Net cash inflow from operating activities	120,060

Working 1:

Fixed Assets (at net book value)

	£		£
Balance b/f	74,040	P & L account (depreciation for the year)[a]	5,060
Additions (2 cars)	97,000	Balance c/f	165,980
	171,040		171,040

[a] There were no disposals during the year, so the balance on this account must be the depreciation charged for the year.

b The cash flow statement clearly shows the main cause of the decrease in cash for the year: the purchase of the two luxury cars for Marvin and Chiquita. If more modest vehicles costing, say, £15,000 each had been purchased, there would have been a positive cash flow of nearly £60,000. If Trixie can curb the extravagance of her fellow shareholders then the company can both be profitable and have strong liquidity.

c

Cash flow forecast from 1 July 2005 to 31 December 2005
Period – Monthly

£	Jul	Aug	Sept	Oct	Nov	Dec
Receipts						
Sales – cash	15,000	15,000	15,000	15,000	20,000	15,000
Sales – debtors	30,950	15,000	15,000	15,000	15,000	20,000
A: Total receipts	45,950	30,000	30,000	30,000	35,000	35,000
Payments						
Purchases and office expenses – creditors	14,080	35,000	35,000	35,000	35,000	35,000
Wages and salaries	6,000	6,000	6,000	6,000	6,000	14,000
B: Total payments	20,080	41,000	41,000	41,000	41,000	49,000
C: Net cash flow (A – B)	25,870	(11,000)	(11,000)	(11,000)	(6,000)	(14,000)
D: Opening bank balance	(2,400)	23,470	12,470	1,470	(9,530)	(15,530)
E: Closing bank balance (D ± C)	23,470	12,470	1,470	(9,530)	(15,530)	(29,530)
Note: Agreed overdraft facility	6,000	6,000	6,000	6,000	6,000	6,000

The company will have to renegotiate its bank overdraft facility during October, or alternatively it will have either to increase its forecast sales income or to reduce its expenditure.

Chapter 10 – Esmeralda springs a surprise

a Ratio analysis:

Group	Name of ratio	Machiq Limited	Kaboosh Limited
(i) Profitability	ROCE (Return on capital employed)	76.4%	22.7%
	Gross margin (or Gross profit margin)	25%	40%
	Mark-up	33.3%	66.7%
	Net margin (or Net profit margin)	16.7%	24.1%
(ii) Efficiency	Fixed assets turnover	4.25 times	1.16 times
	Stockturn	22.5 days	138.7 days
	Debtors' collection period	16 days	47.2 days
	Creditors' payment period	9.7 days	59.6 days
(iii) Short-term solvency and liquidity	Current ratio (or Working capital ratio)	0.84:1	2.05:1
	Acid test (or Quick assets test)	0.41:1	0.85:1
(iv) Long-term solvency and liquidity	Gearing	nil	17.1%
	Interest cover	65 times	22 times
(v) Investment ratios	eps (earnings per share	18.6p	10.35p
	p/e (price/earnings)	(assume) 15	(assume) 15
	Dividend cover	2.78 times	3.76 times
	Dividend yield	2.4%	1.77%

Comments:

(i) Profitability:

We are comparing just one year's results for each company, so we must be cautious in drawing conclusions, as trends may show an improvement or decline when compared with previous years. With this proviso, Machiq Limited's ROCE is impressively high compared with Kaboosh's, indicating that Machiq is operating profitably from a relatively low capital base. It could also mean that Kaboosh has been investing in new fixed assets, and expects profitability to increase significantly as a result.

Kaboosh's margins are higher than Machiq's. If we assume that the companies are selling the same type of goods, then Machiq could seemingly raise its prices without affecting sales. Another interpretation is that Kaboosh is controlling its costs and buying prices much more efficiently than Machiq.

(ii) Efficiency:

In terms of efficiency, in all respects Machiq is performing better than Kaboosh. Fixed assets are producing over three times as much sales, stock is sold every 22.5 days (compared with a lengthy 138.7 days) and debts are being collected three times as quickly. The only surprise is that creditors are paid so quickly – it would be more efficient to take advantage of interest-free credit and pay creditors after approximately 30 days. Kaboosh's stockturn is very worrying – why has it let stock build up to such an extent? Is part of the stock unsaleable and perhaps overvalued?

(iii) Short-term solvency and liquidity:

Kaboosh has a 'textbook' current ratio, though the acid test could be slightly stronger. Machiq's ratios are very low, and the acid test shows only 41p of quickly realisable assets for every £1 of current liabilities. Machiq's management should reassess the dividend levels to improve the current and acid test ratios.

(iv) Long-term solvency and liquidity:

Machiq has no long-term borrowings (it is assumed that the interest shown in the profit and loss account is overdraft interest), so the gearing is zero. Kaboosh is low-geared at 17.1%. Neither company has any problems over safety of interest payments, with cover of 65 and 22 times respectively.

(v) Investment ratios:

Neither company would have a stock market price (not being listed plc's), so the p/e ratio may not be a realistic comparison. However, the dividend yield has been calculated on the basis of a share price 15 times the eps. Both companies have reasonable safety of dividend, though Machiq's generous dividend policy results in a higher yield than that of Kaboosh.

b Purely on the basis of the ratio comparison with Machiq Limited, the key concerns within Kaboosh Limited's financial statements are:

- Low return on capital employed
- Poor working capital control, especially stock.

Within Machiq Limited's statements, the key concerns are:

- Lower profit margins
- Poor liquidity.

The poor liquidity, if uncorrected, could prove fatal to Machiq Limited, so the directors need to address this problem urgently. Once they can overcome this, they may feel that they do not need to sell out to Kaboosh Limited, especially in view of Machiq's massively higher return on capital employed. Before a decision can be taken, the following further information is needed:

- How much is Kaboosh Limited offering for the shares in Machiq Limited?
- What steps is Kaboosh Limited taking to overcome its poor working capital control?
- What plans does Kaboosh Limited have for improving its return on capital employed?
- What roles will the three directors of Machiq Limited have in the new company, and are they acceptable? What salaries would they be paid?

Chapter 12 – The great disappearing profits trick

				Total		Performing division		Retailing division
	£	£	£	£	£	£
Sales				705,600		211,680		493,920
Less Cost of sales:		
Variable (80%)	423,360				42,336		381,024
Fixed (20%)	105,840				10,584		95,256
		(529,200)			(52,920)		(476,280)
Gross profit				176,400		158,760		17,640
Less expenses:		
Variable (40%)	23,440				8,204		15,236
Fixed (60%)	35,160				12,306		22,854
		(58,600)			(20,510)		(38,090)
Net profit (net loss)				117,800		138,250		(20,450)

Summary:

The Performing division appears to have made a net profit of £138,250 but the Retailing division appears to have made a net loss of £20,450.

Chapter 13 – Who is Mrs Eadale?

a Using absorption costing principles, the bottling division would 'absorb' all the relevant costs, as follows:

	£	£
Forecast sales revenue (15,000 × £14)		210,000
Direct costs (15,000 × £6)	90,000	
Fixed costs of bottling division	20,000	
		(110,000)
Gross profit		100,000
Company costs absorbed by division		(130,000)
Net loss		(30,000)

b Using marginal costing techniques, the information would be redrawn as follows:

	£
Forecast sales revenue (15,000 × £14)	210,000
Less Variable costs (15,000 × £6)	(90,000)
Contribution	120,000
Less Fixed costs of division	(20,000)
Profit of division	100,000

On this basis it can be seen that the bottling division would make a positive contribution of £120,000 to meeting the general costs of the business as a whole.

c The answers to the questions are as follows:

(i) The contribution per bottle is £14 – £6 = £8, so to meet the fixed costs of £20,000 (that is, the break-even point), **2,500 bottles** must be sold (£20,000/£8).

(ii) To earn £16,000 profit for the division, total contribution would need to be £36,000 (P + F = C). At a contribution of £8 per bottle, **4,500 bottles** would need to be sold.

(iii) If 4,000 bottles were sold, total contribution would be £32,000. After deducting fixed costs of £20,000, profit would be **£12,000**.

Postscript:
Did you notice that 'Mrs Eadale' is an anagram of the name 'Esmeralda'?

Chapter 14 – The antidote to the potion

	Mixing £	Liquidising £	Bottling £
Brought forward from previous process	n/a	1,735	2,772
Materials:			
Wart Powder 10 kg @ £80	800	–	–
Elbow Grease 5 kg @ £60	300	–	–
Snod Grass 14 kg @ £40	–	560	–
Bottles (1,000 × £1)	–	–	1,000
Labour:			
Mixing 10 hours × £4.50	45	–	–
Liquidising 3 × (4 hours × £4.75)	–	57	–
Bottling 2 × (5 hours × £5)	–	–	50
Other overheads	590	420	380
Total costs	1,735	2,772	4,202
Carried forward to next process	1,735	2,772	–
Cost of finished production			4,202
Cost per bottle			**£4.20**

Note: The normal loss caused by evaporation is a cost to be borne by the remaining production.

Chapter 15 – Chiquita's chart

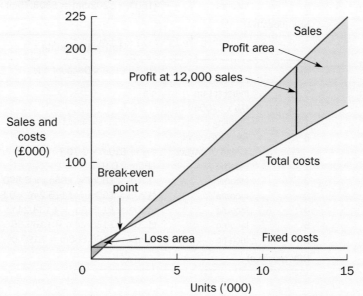

Chapter 16 – Reappearance, followed by glowing and floating …

	Glow Gel	Floating Juice
	kg	kg
Sales	16,000	12,000
Provision for losses	100	200
Closing stock	1,200	800
Production budget	17,300	13,000

	Luminos litres	Schlepp litres
Materials needed to produce:		
17,300 kg of Glow Gel	103,800	138,400
13,000 kg of Floating Juice	130,000	52,000
Usage budget	233,800	190,400
Provision for losses	1,000	400
	234,800	190,800
Closing stock	15,200	9,200
Materials purchase budget (A)	250,000	200,000
Cost per litre (B)	£4	£2.50
(A) × (B)	£1m	£0.5m
Total cost of materials		**£1.5m**

Chapter 17 – Machiq Limited's bid for world domination

Machiq TV

Year		Future value × Discount rate	Present value £
0	Cost	n/a	(250,000,000)
1–5	Running costs	£100m × 4.212	(421,200,000)
5	Assets released	£40m × 0.747	29,880,000
1	Income	£60m × 0.943	56,580,000
2	Income	(150% × £60m = £90m) × 0.890	80,100,000
3	Income	(150% × £90m = £135m) × 0.840	113,400,000
4	Income	(150% × £135m = £202.5m) × 0.792	160,380,000
5	Income	(150% × £202.5m = £303.75m) × 0.747	226,901,250
NPV (negative)			**(3,958,750)**

Matrix 1 satellite

Year		Future value × Discount rate	Present value £
0	Initial set-up (1/2 x £700m)	n/a	(350,000,000)
1–6	Running costs	(1/2 ×) £50m × 4.917	(122,925,000)
6	Assets released at end of project	(1/2 ×) £10m × 0.705	3,525,000
1	Income	£80m × 0.943	75,440,000
2	Income	(120% × £80m = £96m) × 0.890	85,440,000
3	Income	(120% × £96m = £115.2m) × 0.840	96,768,000
4	Income	(120% × £115.2m = £138.24m) × 0.792	109,486,080
5	Income	(120% × £138.24m = £165.888m) × 0.747	123,918,336
6	Income	(120% × £165.888m = £199.066m) × 0.705	140,341,530
NPV (positive)			**161,993,946**

Answers to practice examination papers 1, 2 and 3

Paper 1 (multiple choice)

1	b	11	b	21	b	31	d
2	a	12	b	22	a	32	c
3	c	13	c	23	a	33	a
4	c	14	b	24	d	34	b
5	a	15	a	25	a	35	c
6	b	16	d	26	d	36	a
7	d	17	a	27	c	37	d
8	c	18	c	28	a	38	c
9	a	19	b	29	d	39	d
10	d	20	b	30	d	40	b

Paper 2

Question 1 a

Aubrey Locke
Profit and loss account for the year ended 31 May 2005

	£	£
Sales	375,000	
Less Sales returns	(420)	
		374,580
Less **Cost of goods sold**		
Opening stock at 1 June 2004	62,000	
Add Purchases	195,000	
	257,000	
Less Closing stock at 31 May 2005	(50,000)	
		(207,000)
Gross profit		167,580
Add Decrease in provision for doubtful debts	400	
Discount received	180	
		580
		168,160
Less **Expenses**		
Wages and salaries	37,000	
Rent	16,000	
Electricity	10,000	
Bad debts written off	520	
General office expenses	18,000	

Depreciation on forklift truck		
[(20,000–2,000)/4]	4,500	
Depreciation on cars		
[40% × (18,000 – 6,000)]	4,800	
		(90,820)
Net profit		77,340

Aubrey Locke
Balance sheet as at 31 May 2005

	Cost	Accumulated depreciation	Net book value
Fixed assets	£	£	£
Forklift truck	20,000	9,000	11,000
Motor cars	18,000	10,800	7,200
	38,000	19,800	18,200
Current assets			
Stock		50,000	
Debtors	16,200		
Less Provision for doubtful debts	(2,240)		
		13,960	
Prepayments		4,000	
Bank		3,840	
Cash		120	
		71,920	
***Less* Current liabilities**			
Creditors	14,600		
Accruals	2,000		
		(16,600)	
Net current assets			55,320
Total net assets			73,520
Capital			
Opening balance at 1 June 2004		14,680	
Add Net profit		77,340	
		92,020	
Less Drawings		(18,500)	
Closing balance at 31 May 2005			73,520

b A limited company's profit and loss account contains:
- Directors' salaries
- Corporation tax
- Dividends.

A limited company's balance sheet contains:
- Additional creditors (taxation and dividends agreed but unpaid)
- Share capital
- Reserves.

Question 2 a

Wilma Tonbridge
Profit and loss account for the year ended 31 December 2004

	£	£
Sales		208,000
Less Cost of goods sold		
Add Purchases	134,200	
Less Closing stock at 31 December 2004	(9,200)	
		(125,000)
Gross profit		83,000
Less Expenses		
Wages and salaries	25,600	
Rent and rates	12,800	
Provision for doubtful debts	2,400	
Office expenses	10,400	
Depreciation on computers, etc.	5,000	
		(56,200)
Net profit		26,800

Wilma Tonbridge
Balance sheet as at 31 December 2004

	Cost	Accumulated depreciation	Net book value
Fixed assets	£	£	£
Computers, etc.	30,000	5,000	25,000
Current assets			
Stock		9,200	
Debtors	48,000		
Less Provision for doubtful debts	(2,400)		
		45,600	
Prepayments		3,200	
		58,000	
Less Current liabilities			
Creditors	7,000		
Accruals	2,400		
Bank overdraft	52,800		
		(62,200)	
Net current liabilities			(4,200)
			20,800
Less Long-term loan			(16,000)
Total net assets			4,800
Capital			
Opening balance at 1 January 2004		10,000	
Add Net profit		26,800	
		36,800	
Less Drawings		(32,000)	
Closing balance at 31 December 2004			4,800

b

Wages account

		£			£
31/12/04	Bank	56,000	31/12/04	Transfer to Drawings	32,000
31/12/04	Accrual c/d	1,600	31/12/04	Profit and loss account	25,600
		57,600			57,600
			1/1/05	Accrual b/d	1,600

Rent and rates account

		£			£
31/12/04	Bank	16,000	31/12/04	Profit and loss account	12,800
			31/12/04	Prepaid c/d	3,200
		16,000			16,000
1/1/05	Prepaid b/d	3,200			

Question 3 **a** Prudence, also known as conservatism, is the concept whereby revenue and profits are not anticipated but are recognised by inclusion in the profit and loss account only when realised in the form of either cash or other assets, the ultimate cash realisation of which can be assessed with reasonable certainty. Provision is made for all known liabilities (expenses and losses), whether the amount of these is known with certainty or is a best estimate in the light of the information available.

b ● Going concern concept
  ● Accruals concept
  ● Consistency concept.

(See Chapter 1 for definitions)

c Factors include (any three):
  ● The need not to overstate profits or assets
  ● The need not to understate losses or liabilities
  ● It is up to the management to resist shareholders' demands if they are against the interests of the company
  ● The need for accountants to follow existing statute and accounting standards in producing published information.

Question 4 **a**

Gross profit margin	(GP/Sales) × 100	Eastbourne Ltd's margin is higher than average. Possible reasons include lack of competition, better buying policies, errors in stock counts
Net profit margin	(NP/Sales) × 100	Eastbourne Ltd's margin is higher than average. Possible reasons include greater control of expenses, more automation (lower wage costs)
ROCE	PBIT[a]/Capital employed (total net assets + loans) × 100	Eastbourne Ltd's margin is higher than average. Possible reasons include greater efficiency overall, less competition
Acid test	Ratio of (current assets – stock): Current liabilities	Eastbourne Ltd's margin is lower than average. Possible reasons include better use of interest-free credit from trade creditors, fewer credit sales than average
Gearing	Fixed % borrowing/ Capital employed or Fixed % borrowing/ Capital employed + Fixed % borrowing	Eastbourne Ltd's margin is much higher than average. Possible reasons include past expansion financed by borrowings, or borrowing in anticipation of future expansion

[a] Profit before interest and taxation.

b A current ratio of 6:1 might indicate too much stock being carried, poor control of debtors, or surplus bank balances not being reinvested into fixed assets.

Question 5 **a** (i) Liability for debts:
Sole trader: unlimited liability for debts of business.
Limited company: shareholders' liability limited to the value of the share capital invested or agreed to be invested in the company.

(ii) Ability to raise capital:
Sole trader: restricted to loans from family, friends and banks.
Limited company: private limited company cannot issue invitation to general public to invest, but ownership is split into shares, so investment becomes more attractive to friends, family and other acquaintances who then become part-owners rather than creditors.

Public limited companies can sell their shares to the general public and have the potential to raise much more than any other type of business organisation.

(iii) Legal formality:
A sole trader is the most informal form of business organisations, with no specific rules and regulations to follow, other than the general ones of informing government authorities if taxable profits are made or if VAT registration is needed.

Limited companies are subject to the Companies Acts, which require the companies to submit accounts, file an annual report and hold an annual general meeting, among other things. Public limited companies may also have to follow Stock Exchange regulations.

b **Profit and loss account for the year ended 31 December 2005 (extract)**

Income includes:

Bad debt recovered (Customer D)	500
Decrease in provision for doubtful debts	
(Customers B & C doubtful at year-end)	
[b/f 1,400 – c/f (600+220)]	580

Expenses include:

Bad debt written off (Customer A)	800

Balance sheet as at 31 December 2005 (extract)

Debtors (Customer A written off)	
(£45,000 – £800)	44,200
Less Provision for doubtful debts	(820)
	43,380

Paper 3

Question 1 **a** Spectacular plc: Overhead analysis sheet

Overhead	Basis of apportionment	P	Q	R	Service
Indirect wages	(Actual)	8,000	12,000	18,300	6,700
Consumable stores	Requisitions	14,400	9,600	8,000	–
Rent	Area	4,500	6,750	6,000	3,750
Light and heat	Area	3,000	4,500	4,000	2,500
Power	kW	14,400	18,000	900	2,700
Depreciation	20% × cost	28,000	36,000	2,000	14,000
Insurance: machinery	Cost of plant	700	900	50	350
		73,000	87,750	39,250	30,000
Service	Direct labour cost	7,500	9,000	13,500	(30,000)
		80,500	96,750	52,750	–

b Computation of hourly rates of overhead absorption

Basis	P	Q	R
Direct-labour-hours	$\dfrac{80,500}{100,000} = £0.805$	$\dfrac{96,750}{80,000} = £1.209$	$\dfrac{52,750}{220,000} = £0.24$
Machine-hours	$\dfrac{80,500}{70,000} = £1.15$	$\dfrac{96,750}{90,000} = £1.075$	$\dfrac{52,750}{10,000} = £5.275$

c Labour-hour rates are applicable if work is labour intensive. They relate to time, and overcome fluctuating wage rates and different grades of worker. A disadvantage could be the time and cost of maintaining labour records. Machine-hour rates are applicable where work is capital intensive. They also relate to time and can be analysed by individual machine or group of machines. A disadvantage could be the reliability of the data and the time and cost of collecting it.

Question 2   **a**   (i)   Contribution = £100 − (£25 + £30 + £5) = £40, so maximum profit is:

Total contribution	16,000 × £40 =	£640,000
Less Fixed costs		(£240,000)
Maximum profit		**£400,000**

(ii)   Break-even point = Fixed costs/contribution per coat:
£240,000/£40 = **6,000 coats**

(iii)   Margin of safety = Maximum production less break-even point
16,000 − 6,000 = **10,000 coats**

(iv)   If 11,000 coats are sold, contribution = 11,000 × £40 = £440,000. Fixed costs
are £240,000, so profit = £440,000 − £240,000 = **£200,000**.
(Alternative calculation: 11,000 coats = 5,000 more than the break-even point;
5,000 × £40 contribution = £200,000).

b

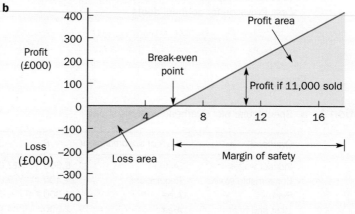

c   The contribution from the special order will be £70 − (25 + 30 +5 + 6) = £4. Total additional contribution = 5,000 × £4 = £20,000 with no additional fixed costs, so the order
should be accepted, provided that it does not cause disruption to existing production.

Question 3   **a**

	Cost	
	Unit	*Total*
	£	£
Raw materials (2.40 × 600)	2.400	1,440
Wages (£4.80 × 50 hours)	0.400	240
Overheads (50 hours × £5.30)	0.442	265
Setting-up costs	0.025	15
Cost of full batch	3.267	1,960

b

Cost of full batch		1,960.00
Add Rectification costs		
Wages (6 hours × £4.80)	28.80	
Overheads (6 hours × £5.30)	31.80	
Set-up costs	10.00	
		70.60
		2,030.60
Less Income from scrapped trees 40 × £0.75		(30.00)
Total cost of 560 trees		2,000.60
Cost of batch per unit £2,000.60/560		3.57

c

560 units should have cost 560 × £3.267 (see (a) above)		1,829.52
Actual cost (see (b) above)		2,000.60
Loss		171.08

Question 4 **a** (i) Net present value is (positive) £1,027,000 (workings below).

(ii) The payback period is reached after 2¼ years. The net cash flows (undiscounted) as shown in the workings table below are: year 1 £525,000, year 2 £1,245,000, total £1,770,000. The additional £230,000 needed to match the £2m investment is reached roughly one-quarter of the way through year 3's net cash flow of £946,000.

b The project is forecast to generate a positive NPV, and the payback is reached after less than half of the project's total anticipated life. On each of these criteria, it would appear that the project is worth proceeding with. One point to query is whether it is realistic for 'other costs' to remain at £25 per unit over the project's life.

c A rights issue to existing ordinary shareholders gives them the opportunity to make a further investment in the company's equity capital. Their return is in the form of dividends, which are at the directors' discretion and are dependent upon profits being made. As such, any ordinary dividends are an *appropriation* of profits, not an expense against profits. Issuing more ordinary shares has the effect of reducing the company's gearing level.

If the company decides to issue debentures, it is committing itself to paying interest over the life of the loan, which is an expense that reduces profit. The debentures are usually secured against company assets so that if the company is unable to pay the interest or the loan itself, the lenders can sell all or part of the secured assets to obtain the money. Issuing more debentures has the effect of increasing the company's gearing level.

The decision as to which alternative to choose depends on a number of factors, including the company's existing borrowing levels and the length of time for which it needs the additional capital (the debenture could be repaid but the equity capital is usually permanent).

Workings:

Year	Units	Labour	Materials	O'heads	Total cost	Sales	Net cash flow	Discount factor	PV
		£000	£000	£000	£000	£000	£000		£000
0					(2,000)		(2,000)	n/a	(2,000)
1	5,000	200	400	125	(725)	1,250	525	0.943	495
2	15,000	630	1,200	375	(2,205)	3,450	1,245	0.890	1,108
3	22,000	968	1,936	550	(3,454)	4,400	946	0.840	795
4	15,000	690	1,410	375	(2,475)	3,000	525	0.792	416
5	5,000	240	500	125	(865)	1,000	135	0.747	101
							150	0.747	112
NPV									1,027

Index